THE *BOUNTY* FROM THE BEACH

CROSS-CULTURAL AND CROSS-DISCIPLINARY ESSAYS

THE *BOUNTY* FROM THE BEACH
CROSS-CULTURAL AND CROSS-DISCIPLINARY ESSAYS

EDITED BY SYLVIE LARGEAUD-ORTEGA

PRESS

PACIFIC SERIES

Published by ANU Press
The Australian National University
Acton ACT 2601, Australia
Email: anupress@anu.edu.au

Available to download for free at press.anu.edu.au

ISBN (print): 9781760462444
ISBN (online): 9781760462451

WorldCat (print): 1057900911
WorldCat (online): 1057900648

DOI: 10.22459/BB.10.2018

This title is published under a Creative Commons Attribution-NonCommercial-NoDerivatives 4.0 International (CC BY-NC-ND 4.0).

The full licence terms are available at
creativecommons.org/licenses/by-nc-nd/4.0/legalcode

Cover design and layout by ANU Press. Cover image: Sylvie Largeaud-Ortega, *The* Bounty *from the Beach*, 2018, watercolour.

This edition © 2018 ANU Press

Contents

Acknowledgements vii

List of Illustrations ix

Introduction 1
Sylvie Largeaud-Ortega

1. Contextualising the *Bounty* in Pacific Maritime Culture 21
   Jean-Claude Teriierooiterai

2. Pitcairn before the Mutineers: Revisiting the Isolation
   of a Polynesian Island 67
   Guillaume Molle and Aymeric Hermann

3. Reading the Bodies of the *Bounty* Mutineers 95
   Rachael Utting

4. Nordhoff and Hall's *Mutiny on the Bounty*: A Piece
   of Colonial Historical Fiction 125
   Sylvie Largeaud-Ortega

5. A Ship is Burning: Jack London's 'The Seed of McCoy'
   (*Tales of the Pacific*, 1911), or Sailing Away from Pitcairn 153
   Jean-Pierre Naugrette

6. Brando on the *Bounty* 173
   Roslyn Jolly and Simon Petch

7. *Bounty* Relics: Trading in the Legacy of Myth and Mutiny 207
   Adrian Young

Bibliography 235

Acknowledgements

I would like to thank the 2013–14 second-year undergraduate students in Anglophone Pacific Island Studies at the University of French Polynesia (UPF): their enthusiastic contributions to the first *Bounty* International Festival in Papeete, their keen interest in Pacific history, literature and culture, and their overwhelming kindness first inspired me with this project. I am also very grateful to the 2015–16 students for heartily taking up the torch at the second *Bounty* International Festival.

This class was supported by the staff of the UPF Library, whom I also wish to thank. I am particularly grateful to UPF librarians Willy Saint-Albin, Rufin Yune and Vincent Deyris for having *Bounty*-related books and articles speedily shipped to Tahiti from around the world.

I am sincerely thankful to the UPF Traditional and Contemporary Societies in Oceania Research team department (EA4241 EASTCO) for their generous financial support, which has allowed the manuscript to be copyedited.

My heartfelt thanks to Meredith Wilson, Justine Molony and Emily Hazlewood for their exhaustive reviewing and copyediting.

Each of this volume's contributions has been meticulously peer-reviewed by at least two scholars. My very warm thanks to Robert Louis Abrahamson, Stephen Curley, John Gascoigne, Roslyn Jolly, Anaïs Maurer, Tillman Nechtman, Sandhya Patel, Nancy Saint Clair, Bruno Saura, Philip Steer and Jacques Vernaudon for their generous expertise. My thanks also go to my colleague Chris Ballard, who generously shared his vast scholarship on Pacific Island studies.

I am extremely grateful to Herb Ford, who runs the Pitcairn Island Study Center at Pacific Union College, for his in-depth reviewing of the complete manuscript, and his enriching and encouraging comments. I would also like to thank the anonymous reviewers of this volume for their thorough analysis and enlightening suggestions.

I express my gratitude to Emmanuel Descleves, Frank Jacob, Véronique Larcade, Joshua Nash, Rebecca Nesvet and Nancy Saint Clair, who started contributing to this project but had to stop along the way – their insights were always illuminating. My very warm thanks to all this volume's co-authors: Roslyn Jolly and Simon Petch, Guillaume Molle and Aymeric Hermann, Jean-Pierre Naugrette, Jean-Claude Teriierooiterai, Rachael Utting and Adrian Young. It has been a real pleasure working with them all along. Some contributors have kindly assisted me in the editing process: Nancy Saint Clair with her sensitive readings, Adrian Young with his information on *Bounty* experts, and above all Roslyn Jolly with her impeccable scholarship and outstanding reviews.

Finally, *māuruuru* most of all to Pascal Ortega, and Anaïs and Jules Maurer, who have been subjected to prolonged exposure to *Bounty*-related topics. I cannot thank them enough for their loving support. Pascal has provided ever challenging intellectual debates; Anaïs, eye-opening discussions on postcolonial and Pacific Island studies; and Jules, healthy outdoor breaks – each according to their own expertise. Without the three of them, this volume would not have been what it is.

List of Illustrations

Figure 1.1. Geographic origin of the breadfruit and related species. The shaded areas correspond to the lands that emerged during the last glaciation about 10,000 years ago. 38

Figure 1.2. In this painting, modern double canoes built on the model of the old double canoes, are visible in the foreground while, in the background, like ghosts of the past, the silhouette of the old double canoes is evident. 41

Figure 2.1. Location of Pitcairn Islands in relation to the Gambier Islands. 68

Figure 2.2. Location of archaeological sites on Pitcairn. 76

Figure 2.3. Typical stone adze blades and a tiki from Pitcairn 78

Figure 2.4. Patterns of interaction involving Pitcairn and the Gambier islands 87

Figure 3.1. Detail from William Hodges, *A View taken in the bay of Oaite Peha [Vaitepiha] Otaheite [Tahiti] ('Tahiti Revisited')*, 1776 106

Figure 3.2. Tahitian Gorget (*taumi*). Crescent-shaped breast ornament decorated with feathers, hair and shark's teeth 110

Figure 3.3. George Cruikshank, *A Point of Honor*. 112

Figure 3.4. The triskelion emblem, on a Manx coin dating from 1733 115

Introduction

Sylvie Largeaud-Ortega
University of French Polynesia

In recent decades, global attention has converged on the Pacific Region as a geopolitical strategic nexus. The vast inner expanse of Oceania was once considered 'the hole in the doughnut',[1] as Tongan writer Epeli Hauʻofa ironically puts it, where nuclear tests were carried out virtually unimpeded. In the typical destruction–preservation logic of post-contact history, this region is now viewed as a unique ecological treasure-trove and the site of major climate change challenges. Given the historical and environmental stakes, a selection of cross-disciplinary essays that take the *Bounty* as their point of departure aims to offer readers an enriched understanding of the history and culture of the Polynesian Triangle – a vast region of Oceania made up of over 1,000 islands spanning from Hawaiʻi in the north, to Rapa Nui/Easter Island in the east and Aotearoa/New Zealand in the south-west. It seeks to provide nuanced perspectives on how the region and its people have been represented across a range of media, including literature, material culture and film. In a collective effort to think this world in its complexity, this volume aims to reorient the *Bounty* focus away from the West,[2] where most *Bounty* narratives and studies have emerged, to the Pacific, where most of the original events unfolded. It delves into the history and culture of the Polynesian Islands touched by the *Bounty* events and it embraces them within a wider fold of their relation to the West. Engaging with 'culturally patterned way

---

1   Epeli Hauʻofa, 'The Ocean in Us', *The Contemporary Pacific*, vol 10, no 2, 1998, p 397.
2   Throughout the book, the West is meant as the 'geographically imprecise but widely accepted cultural and ideological divide between rich and poor, colonizer and colonized, metropolitan and post-colonial' (Rod Edmond, *Representing the South Pacific: Colonial Discourse from Cook to Gauguin*, Cambridge, Cambridge University Press, 1997, p 16).

or ways of experiencing and understanding history',[3] it examines Pacific Island histories and historicities and their representations in literature, films and culture. Far from abiding by narratives of the 'vanishing native', it celebrates Oceanic vitality.

This volume therefore launches on a discursive journey across the Pacific Ocean, exploring those Polynesian Islands impacted by the *Bounty*, and navigating the reverberations of the *Bounty* events in the West and their backwash to the Polynesian Islands, from the late 18th century to the present time. It also largely shifts focus from famous *Bounty* figures, such as Sir Joseph Banks, Captain William Bligh and Fletcher Christian, who come to contemporary readers almost as dramatic actors having been reimagined in print, cinema and mythology for over two centuries. Instead, it pays more attention to the 'little people on both sides of the beach' as documented by historian Greg Dening:

> I wanted to write the history of people whom the world would esteem as 'little'. I wanted to write history from below. Not of kings and queens. Not of heroes. Not of writers of constitutions, saviours of nations. 'Little people'. Those on whom the forces of the world press most hardly. I wanted to celebrate their humanity, their freedoms, their creativity, the ways they crossed the boundaries around their lives, the way they crossed their beaches.[4]

Dening's phrasing may seem to carry a whiff of condescension; yet it is well known to Pacific scholars that his 'little people on both sides of the beach' are as important as Gayatri Chakravorty Spivak's 'subalterns'.[5] His expression best fits our purpose: to investigate the *Bounty* heritage from the standpoint of the beach. The beach is a metaphor for culture contact and conflict in the Pacific Islands. It is this liminal place that transforms Islanders and voyagers, islands and ships, each time it is crossed. Referring to the *Bounty*, we will analyse the way newcomers – however 'little' they may look – create new islands, and how these changes may occasionally impact the world. This volume's 'little people' do stand 'on both sides of

---

3   Emiko Ohnuki-Tierny, 'Introduction: The Historicization of Anthropology', in *Culture through Time: Anthropological Approaches*, Emiko Ohnuki-Tierny (ed), Stanford, Stanford University Press, 1990, p 4; cited in Chris Ballard, 'Oceanic Historicities', *The Contemporary Pacific*, vol 26, no 1, 2014, p 102.
4   Greg Dening, 'Writing, Rewriting the Beach: An Essay', in Alun Munslow & Robert A Rosenstone (eds), *Experiments in Rethinking History*, New York & London, Routledge, 2004, pp 30–55, 54.
5   Gayatri Chakravorty Spivak, 'Can the Subaltern Speak?', in Patrick William & Laura Chrisman (eds), *Colonial Discourse and Post-Colonial Theory: A Reader*, Hennel Hempstead, Harvester Wheatsheaf, 1993.

the beach': they are Polynesian or European or, as beaches are crossed and remade, no longer one without the other, but bound together in processes of change.[6] Among these people are *Bounty* sailors, beachcombers,[7] Pitcairners and indigenous Pacific Islanders of the past and the present. Our collection also examines the works of some renowned Western writers and actors who, turning mutineers after their own fashion and in their own times, themselves crossed the beach and attempted to illuminate the 'little people' involved in the *Bounty* narratives. These prominent writers and actors put in the spotlight characters who were disregarded on account of race, class or geographical distance from the dominant centres of power. These people are 'little' only because they have been silenced. Theirs is 'the silence of those who for one reason or another had no voice, or whose voice was never their own but always someone else's'.[8] Inspired by Dening's empowering voice, our purpose is to fill that silence.

'Smallness is a state of mind', Epeli Hau'ofa famously stated. These essays accordingly balance the smallness of *Bounty*-related events against the vastness of Hau'ofa's 'sea of islands'.[9] They investigate how generations have been fascinated by a relatively anecdotal mutiny while overlooking its capacious Oceanic frame and holding the Pacific Islands as a mere backdrop to the event. The time seems ripe for a cross-cultural and cross-disciplinary scholarly volume to ponder the part these islands may actually have been playing in relation to the *Bounty*, and to the world.

---

6   Greg Dening, *Islands and Beaches: Discourse on a Silent Land, Marquesas 1774–1880*, Melbourne, Melbourne University Press, 1980.
7   'Beachcombing [is] the act of repudiating western civilisation by jumping ship, crossing the beach and attempting to join an island culture' (Edmond, 1997, p 17).
8   Dening, 1980, p 32.
9   Epeli Hau'ofa, 'Our Sea of Islands', in *We Are the Ocean: Selected Works*, Honolulu, University of Hawai'i Press, 2008, p 31.

Bounty history in a nutshell

The seeds of the *Bounty* mission were sown in Tahiti in the middle of the Pacific Ocean.[10] During James Cook's first exploration of the Pacific in 1769, botanist Joseph Banks enjoyed a three-month stay in early contact Tahiti.[11] The episode was best remembered in Britain for Banks' boisterous appreciation of local *vahine*,[12] but Banks had a connoisseur's eye for native plants, too, and he had noticed the multiple virtues of '*uru*, or Tahitian breadfruit. The large fruit needed hardly any care, its 30 or so varieties could be harvested from large robust trees over a good part of the year, it had strong nutritional value and it could be fermented into *māhi*, which kept for months. Back in Britain, Sir Joseph Banks became president of the Royal Society and botanical advisor to King George (known as *Kini Iore* to Tahitians). He suggested transplanting breadfruit saplings to the British West Indies in order to secure cheap food for British plantation owners' slaves. The plan, however, was delayed until Britain had fought (and lost) the American War of Independence. By that time, the British West Indies were no longer supplied by the former 13 colonies, and hurricanes had devastated the West Indian island plantations where thousands of slaves were starving to death. The breadfruit mission was finally agreed upon. Banks had a small coastal trader refitted into a cutter and renamed *Bounty*. He recommended William Bligh, an officer who, like him, was a Tahitian old-timer: as sailing master, Bligh had spent three months in Tahiti in 1777 during Cook's third voyage and had meticulously charted the Pacific. On 23 December 1787, HMAV *Bounty* sailed for the South Pacific under the command of Lieutenant Bligh.

---

10   For 'a succinct, even-handed account' of the *Bounty* events (Edmond, 1997, p 274, n 6), see OHK Spate's *Paradise Found and Lost* (London, Routledge, 1988). This Introduction's *Bounty* narrative has been inspired by the following texts, Greg Dening, *Mr Bligh's Bad Language: Passion, Power and the Theatre on the Bounty* (Cambridge, Cambridge University Press, 1992); Caroline Alexander, *The Bounty: The True Story of the Mutiny on the Bounty* (London, Harper Perennial, 2003); Anne Salmond, *Bligh. William Bligh in the South Seas* (Auckland, Penguin Viking, 2011); Vanessa Smith & Nicholas Thomas (eds), *Mutiny and Aftermath: James Morrison's Account of the Mutiny on the Bounty and the Island of Tahiti* (Honolulu, University of Hawai'i Press, 2013); and Robert W Kirk, *Paradise Past: The Transformation of the South Pacific, 1520–1920* (Jefferson, North Carolina, McFarland, 2012).
11   For discussion of the 'discovery' of Tahiti by Europeans, see Anne Salmond, *Aphrodite's Island: The European Discovery of Tahiti* (Berkeley & Los Angeles, University of California Press, 2009).
12   *Vahine*: Tahitian for 'woman'.

INTRODUCTION

When Tahitians sighted the ship on 26 October 1788, they may have thought her arrival untimely. They were well into *Matari'i-i-raro* or *tau o'e*, the season of scarcity, and visitors meant an unplanned strain on their resources.[13] They nevertheless showered the Europeans with massive gifts of food and warmly welcomed former and new acquaintances. They probably relished the compensating prospect of garnering iron tools and, with some luck, British guns and ammunitions that might help tip balances in local warfare. Little did they suspect that the *Bounty* visitors intended to collect over a thousand breadfruit plants, for which they would need to spend over five months in Tahiti.

The *Bounty*'s arrival was also untimely for the British. The Admiralty had postponed the ship's departure from Britain for so long that, reaching Cape Horn at the start of austral winter, the small vessel had been unable to round it due to extreme weather conditions. After many failed attempts, she had turned the long way around Africa. By the time the *Bounty* finally anchored in Tahiti, full breadfruit season was over and Bligh had no option but to remain there much longer than any Western ship before. Durable connections were thus allowed to develop between Tahitians and their European visitors. Both sides got to know each other's cultures better and often adopted them. At the end of their prolonged sojourn, the *Bounty* men had gained not only plants, but also a keen taste for Tahitian hospitality and a correspondingly sharp resentment of ship discipline. As for several Tahitians, they had developed an ever stronger appetite for iron and firearms and an increased familiarity with British ways of life, which impacted their daily lives. They had also contracted several diseases, many of them fatal.[14]

The *Bounty* eventually left Tahiti for the West Indies on 4 April 1789, loaded with a massive cargo of breadfruit. The existing tensions between Bligh and Fletcher Christian, his acting master, soon became acrimonious. A mere three weeks later, near the Friendly Islands (today's Tonga), tensions reached a climax when, in front of all, Bligh stingingly accused Christian of stealing coconuts. Mutiny broke out the following morning, on 28 April 1789: it was a rash affair, a matter of a few hours, under the leadership of Christian and a handful of men who seized the arms chest

---

13   Tahitians had already given provisions to the *Lady Penrhyn*, a British convict ship that had left Tahiti only three months before the *Bounty* arrived.
14   Diseases that were innocuous to Europeans could prove fatal to non-immune island populations. For a thorough study of encounters between Tahitians and the *Bounty*, see Vanessa Smith's *Intimate Strangers: Friendship, Exchange and Pacific Encounters* (Cambridge, Cambridge University Press, 2010).

and the ship. Bligh and 18 loyalists were ordered on board the *Bounty*'s launch. Twenty-five men remained on the *Bounty*, some against their will. The *Bounty*'s mission had been disrupted and most of the breadfruit was thrown overboard into the Pacific Ocean.

The reasons for the mutiny have been the subject of extensive conjecture and are only briefly discussed here. The most obvious reason, and the one favoured by both Bligh and popular *Bounty* mythology, is that the mutineers pined for Tahiti. If Tahitian allurement is indeed to account for the mutiny, then much of the onus may be on the Admiralty and Banks: the *Bounty* lingered in Tahiti as a result of their shoddy planning.[15] The Admiralty and Banks erred in their management not only of time, but also of living space, for the *Bounty* proved far too small for such a long journey. Being less than 27.5 metres long, she was not rated a Navy ship, on which account Bligh was not made Captain, but Lieutenant – a less imposing rank to his crew. Banks had had the commander's great cabin converted into a nursery for plants, which further dented the symbols of Bligh's authority. Allotted a small pantry for a cabin, Bligh virtually shared his living quarters with master's mates and midshipmen, which made it all the harder for him to engender respect. The absence of other commissioned officers on board led to Christian's appointment as acting master. Neither was Bligh afforded with marines to ensure his security and impose his orders.

In this context, Bligh resorted to food rationing as a method of discipline, for which he was deemed niggardly. His propensity to verbally abuse his men was also a source of dissent. In his eponymous study of Bligh's bad language, Greg Dening highlights his 'offensive', 'abusive and intemperate' expostulations.[16] In sharp contrast with *Bounty* mythology, however, Bligh did not resort to physical violence. He was, on the contrary, an inordinately nonviolent commander and a lighter flogger than most. 'On his two voyages to the Pacific in the *Bounty* and the *Providence* he

---

15   See William Bligh's reports, A Narrative of the Mutiny, Letters 1782–1805 (Safe 1/40 and Family Correspondence, Safe 1/45, The National Archives, London); Minutes of the Proceedings of a Court-Martial on Lieutenant William Bligh and certain members of his crew, to investigate the cause of the loss of HMS *Bounty* on charges formulated by Captain William Bligh (PRO Adm 1/5328, part 2, published in Owen Rutter (ed), *The Voyage of the Bounty's Launch as related in William Bligh's Despatch to the Admiralty and the Journal of John Fryer* (London, Golden Cockerel Press, 1934)); and William Bligh, *Mutiny on Board HMS Bounty*, Pete Goss (foreword) (London, Adlard Coles Nautical, 2014). See also Rolf Du Rietz, *Peter Heywood's Tahitian Vocabulary and the Narrative by James Morrison: Some Notes on their Origin and History* (Banksia 3, Uppsala, Sweden, Dahlia Books, 1986).
16   Dening, 1992, pp 55–59.

flogged fewer of his crew, actually and proportionately, than any other captain who came into the Pacific in the eighteenth century.'[17] Bligh was much less of a flogger than Captain Cook whose name, in contrast, remains untarnished. Tahitians could also have testified that, unlike Cook, Bligh did not take Tahitian hostages to retrieve fugitives,[18] nor did he have any Islanders' ears cut off to chastise thieves.

Once separated from the *Bounty*, the severely overloaded and under-provisioned launch reached Timor under Bligh's command, losing only one man to Tongan attackers. The 48-day passage of 3,618 nautical miles,[19] in an open boat on rations suited to five days, has gone down in the annals of European maritime history as a masterful achievement, and Bligh was liberally acclaimed upon his return to Britain.[20]

As to the mutineers on the *Bounty*, they now had to hide from the Royal Navy to escape hanging for their crime. Under Christian's command, they sailed to Tubua'i in the Austral archipelago, then back to Tahiti where they picked up Tahitian partners and livestock in order to settle back on Tubua'i where, Christian presumed, they should be sufficiently distant from the usual courses followed by European ships. As may be presumed, Tahitians were astounded to see the *Bounty* reappear on 6 June 1789 without Bligh and with a reduced crew. Although many were suspicious of the fabricated tales they were delivered by their returning visitors, some lovers and *taio*[21] nevertheless agreed to accompany them to Tubua'i, 480 kilometres to the south.[22] The inhabitants of Tubua'i, however, resisted the would-be settlers for three months.[23] Eventually forced to take to the sea again, the *Bounty* sailed one last time to Tahiti. At that stage, her crew had resolved to split up. One smaller group comprised of Christian

---

17 Dening, 1992, p 62. See also Salmond (2011, p 316) for a comparison with Captain George Vancouver.
18 Islander hostage-taking eventually cost Captain Cook his life, as Bligh witnessed in 1779.
19 6,701 kilometres.
20 Bligh was court-martialled and proven innocent of the loss of His Majesty's ship. See Rutter (1934).
21 A *taio* is a friend with whom one exchanges names and has a long-lasting privileged relationship. For a thorough examination of the concept of *taio*, see Smith (2010).
22 Among them was Hitihiti, who had travelled with Cook in 1773–74, and was later to accompany Bligh on the *Providence* for the second breadfruit mission.
23 For more on the *Bounty* in Tubua'i, see Smith & Thomas (2013, pp 56–87); HE Maude, 'In Search of a Home: From the Mutiny to Pitcairn Island (1789–1790)' (*Journal of the Polynesian Society*, vol 67, no 2, June 1958, pp 104–31); Alecia Simmonds, 'Friendly Fire: Forced Friendship and Violent Embraces in British–Tahitian First Contact' (*Melbourne Historical Journal*, vol 37, 2009, pp 115–36); and Salmond (2011, pp 245–51). It may be noted that among the mutineers' Polynesian lovers was Te'ehuteatuaonoa, a Tubuaian who found herself in the trying situation of supporting the *Bounty* settlers against her own people.

and eight mutineers chose to leave Tahiti forever and roam the Pacific Ocean in search of some remote uninhabited island; with them went six Polynesian men and 12 Tahitian women – some of them abducted – including Mauatua, Christian's wife; and Te'ehuteatuaonoa, known as Jenny, who later provided valuable reports on the events.[24] The other, larger group of 16 *Bounty* men elected to remain in Tahiti – among them the loyalists to Bligh. All were given their share of arms and ammunitions and engaged in what Rod Edmond names 'a mass act of beachcombing'.[25]

Tahitians were now faced with a new kind of European visitor – one who came to stay indefinitely.[26] For the first time also since European contact had occurred 20 years before, the balance of power was unequivocally in the Islanders' favour: the small group of stranded outsiders was vulnerable and depended on Islanders for shelter, food and protection. Tu, or Taina, the chief of Matavai where most of the *Bounty*'s crew were hosted, took control of their much coveted muskets, and made them act as mercenaries. As a result, Tu succeeded in dramatically subduing local rivals and, in the aftermath of the *Bounty* mutiny, the history of Tahiti was changed forever. Tu's son's investiture established the reign of the Pomare dynasty, which lasted until Tahiti and its surrounding islands were annexed by France nearly a century later on 29 June 1880.[27]

Apart from two mutineers who kept attacking Tahitians and were murdered in skirmishes, all the *Bounty* residents in Tahiti were eventually captured in March 1791 by HMS *Pandora*, a warship that had been sent to apprehend them. During her return voyage to England, the *Pandora* ran aground on the Great Barrier Reef, drowning four of the *Bounty* mutineers. The remaining 10 who reached Britain were court-martialled

---

24   Mahuata is also known as Maimiti, or Isabella; and Te'ehuteatuaonoa as Tohimata, or Jenny. The other Polynesian women were Tinafanaea, partner of Tubuaians Tetahiti and Ohu; Mareva, or Moetua, partner of Tahitians Manarii, Teimua and Niau; Toofaiti, or Nancy, partner of Traro; Fa'ahutu; Opuarei; Te'o, or Mary; Teatuahitea, or Sarah; Teraura, or Susannah; Tevarua, or Sarah; and Vahineatua, or Prudence. For biographical information, see Paul J Lareau's *HMS Bounty Genealogies* (Little Canada, MN, PJ Lareau, 1994), which is based on graduate student Pat Bentley's research work at the University of Hawai'i on 'The Women of the *Bounty*'.
25   Edmond, 1997, p 64.
26   American John Brown, who left the *Mercury* on 2 September 1789, just three weeks before the *Bounty*'s ultimate return, was the first beachcomber in Tahiti. See Salmond (2011, pp 255–57).
27   For more on Tahitian colonial history, see Nicholas Thomas, *Islanders: The Pacific in the Age of Empire* (Boston, Yale University Press, 2010); and Bruno Saura, *Histoire et Mémoire des Temps Coloniaux en Polynésie Française* (Papeete, Au Vent des Îles, 2015). On beachcombers, see also HE Maude, *Of Islands and Men: Studies in Pacific History* (Melbourne, Oxford University Press, 1968); and Dening (1980).

in September 1792. Four men were acquitted upon Bligh's written recommendation, two were found guilty but pardoned, one was released on a legal technicality and three were hanged. Bligh did not attend the trial: he was already away on his second breadfruit mission to Tahiti, which he successfully completed on HMS *Providence* that same year.

On the *Bounty*, Christian and eight mutineers, together with the 18 Pacific Islanders, sailed on for three-and-a-half months in search of a suitably off-chart island. On 23 January 1790, they reached Pitcairn, which had been incorrectly charted by Carteret in 1767 and then again by official writer Hawkesworth in 1772 – a combination of errors that proved providential to the mutineers. The island was suitably difficult to find and to land, and it became their final destination. It was also conveniently uninhabited, although the presence of some *marae, papae*,[28] petroglyphs and various stone tools bore testimony to former Polynesian settlements. The mutineers destroyed the *Bounty* to lessen the risk of being found. Within three years, living conditions on Pitcairn dramatically deteriorated, owing to alcoholism, illness and, most infamously, brutal treatment of the Polynesian community: most mutineers abused and exploited the exiled Islanders, denying the men any stake on Pitcairn land and claiming the women for themselves. The resulting bloodshed led to the massacre of all men on the island but two mutineers. When Pitcairn was eventually found by the American *Topaz* in 1808, there were remaining nine Tahitian women (out of the initial 12), one male survivor (mutineer John Adams, enlisted as Alexander Smith) and 25 children. They were living a devout life under the strict rule of Adams, who had grown into a pious patriarch and was granted amnesty by the British Admiralty. In 1817, Te'ehuteatuaonoa was eventually allowed to sail back to Tahiti.

The next generations of 'Anglified natives'[29] lived a self-enclosed, self-sustained life, regulated by unswerving observance of Church of England ritual. The few passing ships that touched at remote Pitcairn invariably marvelled at their unique lifestyle, and spread their renown throughout the world as an Eden-like, close-knit and austerely simple community. The tiny island, however, could not support a rapidly increasing population and, in 1856, 66 years after their forefathers' landing in

---

28   *Marae*: Polynesian place of worship; *paepae*: stone house platform.
29   Vanessa Smith, 'Pitcairn's "Guilty Stock". The Island as Breeding Ground', in Rod Edmond & Vanessa Smith (eds), *Islands in History and Representation*, London, Routledge, 2003.

Pitcairn, the community of 194 people – with only eight surnames among them, including three newcomers[30] – had no choice but to evacuate to the larger Norfolk Island.[31]

Norfolk was less isolated, chillier and, most grievously for the Pitcairners, it was not theirs. They had inherited a strong Polynesian bond to their land: their immediate ancestors, together with their own placenta, lay buried on Pitcairn, so that was where they belonged. It was their *Fenua Maitai*, or Good Land. As early as 1858, one McCoy and two Young families returned to Pitcairn, to be followed by a further four families in 1863:[32] they are the foundations of today's Pitcairn population. Many youths from the ensuing generations moved away from both Pitcairn and Norfolk and spread the names of Christian, Young, McCoy, Adams and the like around the world. Between 1886 and 1890, a large portion of the Pitcairn community became members of the Seventh-day Adventist faith, which remains the Island's dominant creed today.[33] In the second half of the 20th century, scientists started investigating the pre-European Polynesian settlements of Pitcairn and Norfolk.[34] United States, New Zealand and Australian forces used Norfolk as an airbase during World War II and it is now part of the Commonwealth of Australia. In contrast, despite the opening of the Panama Canal and a growing number of visiting ships, Pitcairn has remained relatively isolated. A British colony

---

30   The three outsiders were John Buffet, John Evans and George Hunn Nobbs. Joshua Hill stayed from 1832 to 1838, when he was ordered to leave.
31   There was a previous, failed attempt at moving the Pitcairn community to another island when, in 1831, the whole colony removed to Tahiti, but returned home after only a few weeks: 'a venture that took sixteen Pitcairner lives from the epidemics that were rampant on Tahiti' (my thanks to Herb Ford for privately reminding me of this information). Other island choices (Hawai'i, Huahine in the Society Islands, Juan Fernandez in Chile) were discarded because they did not offer to host the whole Pitcairn community. For more information on 19th-century Pitcairn, see the following publications: John Barrow, *A Description of Pitcairn's Island and its Inhabitants* (New York, Harper & Brothers, 1854); Diana Belcher, *The Mutineers of the Bounty and their Descendants in Pitcairn and Norfolk Islands* (New York, Harper Brothers, 1871); Walter Brodie, *Pitcairn's Island and the Islanders in 1850* (London, Whittaker & Co, 1851); M Burrows, *Pitcairn's Island* (London, Society for Promoting Christian Knowledge, 1853); Rev Thomas Boyles Murray, *Pitcairn: The Island, the People and the Pastor* (London, Society for Promoting Christian Knowledge, 1853); Kirk (2012); ASC Ross & AW Moverley, *The Pitcairnese Language* (London, André Deutsch, 1964); and Smith (2003).
32   For more on the families returning from Norfolk, see Sven Wahlroos, *Mutiny and Romance in the South Seas: A Companion to the Bounty Adventure* (Massachusetts, Salem House Publishers, 1989).
33   My thanks to Herb Ford for informing me about the Seventh-day Adventist faith on Pitcairn. For a relatively recent travelogue account of life on Pitcairn, see Dea Birket, *Serpent in Paradise* (New York, Anchor Books, 1998).
34   First interest in the Polynesian settlements of Pitcairn from the West arose notably with Thor Heyerdahl's 1955 archaeological expedition. See Thor Heyerdahl, *Aku-Aku: The Secret of Easter Island* (Chicago, Rand McNally, 1958). For a more groundbreaking study of Pitcairn's Polynesian settlements, see Kirk (2012).

to this day, with a population of around 50, the legendary island actively campaigns for newcomers, advertising a unique lifestyle inherited from HMAV *Bounty*'s settlers and their Polynesian wives.[35]

Pacific *Bounty* source material

However fascinating the destinies of the *Bounty* officers, mutineers and their descendants might be, it is shocking to realise how prolific Western narratives about the European individuals have been so far, and how few narratives exist about the Polynesians whose lives were severely affected by the *Bounty*. Notably, anonymous hundreds of Islanders were killed in relation to the events. Because, as JM Coetzee argues, 'we can comprehend the deaths of others only one at a time',[36] we need to consider these deaths both individually and collectively. For example, in 1789, one Polynesian in Mangaia in the Cook Islands was murdered by the *Bounty* mutineers while they were searching for a settlement.[37] In 1790, five were murdered by the *Bounty* residents in Tahiti and Moʻorea. Added to those were the collateral casualties of the *Pandora*: two men killed in Tahiti, another one at Nomuka, Tonga, in 1791. These numbers, however, are small compared to the bloodsheds that occurred during the three-month attempt by the *Bounty* escapees to establish a permanent settlement in Tubuaʻi in 1789, and the hundreds of lives lost to firearms among the Paʻae and Faʻaʻa warriors whom the *Bounty* men fought in order to ensure their protector Pomare II's power in Tahiti in 1790. This tragic list continues with the Polynesians who agreed to exile themselves with their *Bounty taio* in Pitcairn. Twenty years or so after the events, the narrative of the only surviving avowed mutineer, John Adams, can hardly be said to have been informative: as Greg Dening muses, 'he told the story of the mutiny to anyone who asked, a little differently to each'.[38] Although Teʻehuteatuaonoa provided valuable information about life on Pitcairn,[39]

---

35   Immigration leaflets were handed out to the general public by a delegation from the Pitcairn Island Government at the first *Bounty* International Festival (Papeete, Tahiti, 25–27 Oct 2013). For more information, see www.immgration.gov.pn and www.pitcairn.pn. For more on Pitcairners, see Harry L Shapiro, *The Heritage of the Bounty: The Story of Pitcairn through Six Generations* (New York, Simon & Schuster, 1936).
36   JM Coetzee, *The Lives of Animals*, London, Profile Books, 1999, p 18. Coetzee makes this argument about humans in this quote.
37   For the *Bounty* mutineers' search for a permanent settlement before Pitcairn, see Maude (1958).
38   Dening, 1992, p 329.
39   Teehuteatuaonoa (Jenny), [Narrative I], *Sydney Gazette*, 17 July 1819; and Teehuteatuaonoa (Jenny), [Narrative II], *United States Service Journal*, 1829, pp 589–93.

can we ever know in detail what happened in Tahiti and on the other islands where the *Bounty* escapees searched for a settlement – Tubuaʻi, the Tongan archipelago, the southern Cook Islands and the southern Lau Group of Fiji? Will the killings of 'the little people from the indigenous side of the beach' ever be fully registered and documented? Will some of those unnumbered Polynesian victims' names come down in history records, too? Other casualties will probably never be fully identified, including the men and women who succumbed to the European diseases spread in Tahiti by the *Bounty* residents, which cut a deadly swathe through the Pacific Island population.

In the South Pacific, history and historicities originally were – and still are, to some extent – transmitted performatively and in local languages, through landscapes and seascapes, mythology, social organisation, people's bodies and memories.[40] To this day, however, most indigenous Pacific Island records of the *Bounty* seem to have been lost. In Europe, what became the European written source material was promptly subjected to the distorting process of influential elites. Because a few personal destinies were at stake, the manner in which the *Bounty* events were reported could mean life or death and can therefore hardly be seen as reliable.[41]

When, at the time of first contacts – shortly before the *Bounty* events – European explorers started recording Tahitian historicities, their conditions could not allow for accurate representations of the Islanders' everyday circumstances: these were extraordinary encounters between mutually unintelligible strangers. The incoming strangers were alien to Tahitian language and culture, and what they were shown and told was obviously filtered and shaped not only by their individual experiences,

---

40   My warm thanks to Christopher Ballard, my colleague at the University of French Polynesia, Tahiti, for allowing me to attend his seminar 'On the Beach: Introduction to Pacific History', Sep–Nov 2016. For more on Pacific history and historicities, see David Armitage & Alison Bashford (eds), *Pacific Histories: Ocean, Land, People* (Basingstoke & New York, Palgrave Macmillan, 2014); Stuart Banner, *Possessing the Pacific: Land, Settlers, and Indigenous People from Australia to Alaska* (Cambridge, MA, Harvard University Press, 2007); Dening (1980); Dening, *The Bounty: An Ethnographic History* (Melbourne University History Monograph no 1, 1988); Dening, 'Ethnography on my Mind', in B Attwood, *Boundaries of the Past* (Melbourne, The History Institute, 1990, pp 14–21); Dening (1992); David Igler, *The Great Ocean: Pacific Worlds from Captain Cook to the Gold Rush* (Oxford, Oxford University Press, 2013); Matt K Matsuda, *Pacific Worlds: A History of Seas, Peoples and Cultures* (Cambridge, Cambridge University Press, 2011); Max Quanchi & Ron Adams (eds), *Culture Contact in the Pacific: Essays on Contact, Encounter and Response* (Cambridge, Cambridge University Press, 1993); Marshall Sahlins, *Islands of History* (Chicago & London, University of Chicago Press, 1985); Thomas (2010).
41   For an excellent and exhaustive *Bounty* bibliography, including *Bounty* source material, see Salmond (2011, pp 490–92, n 1).

but by their collective cultural perspectives as well, and, perhaps most significantly, by what the Islanders were willing to show their visitors in the very peculiar context of those visits. Any written source material from the contact period needs to be contextualised and analysed in an attempt to underscore the writers' cultural foundations. Whenever possible, European documents and perspectives should be compared and contrasted with Pacific Islander views, tales and writings.[42]

The first European written source material on Tahiti was provided by British Captain Samuel Wallis (he stayed over a month in 1767),[43] French Louis-Antoine de Bougainville (nine days in 1768) and James Cook (several stints of many months from 1769 to 1777).[44] A Spanish Catholic mission also temporarily settled on Tahiti (10 months in 1774). After Cook was killed in Hawai'i in 1779, European ships stopped visiting Tahiti, not only because his violent death had belied idyllic representations of South Sea Islanders,[45] but also because most fleets were engaged in the American War of Independence. The first European ships to return to Tahiti were, in 1788, the convict ship *Lady Penrhyn* and, three months later, the *Bounty*. The *Bounty* mutineers provided major written records on Tahiti, because Boatswain's Mate James Morrison and Midshipmen Peter Heywood and George Stewart made on-field observations for approximately one-and-a-half years. Here is Morrison's opinion of the Tahitian records left by Wallis, Bougainville and Cook:

> the Idea formd of this Society and of the Inhabitants of this Island in general by former Voyagers could not possible extend much further then their own opinion, None having remaind a sufficient length of time to know the Manner in which they live, and as their whole system was overturned by the arrival of a ship, their Manners were then as much altered from their Common Course, as those of our own Country are at a Fair, which might as well be given for a specimen of the Method of living in England – and such was always their situation as soon as a ship Arrived

---

42   For penetrating studies of the Polynesians' reactions to Cook and Bligh, see Salmond (2011) and Smith (2010).
43   In the same year, Wallis' *Dolphin*'s companion ship, the *Swallow* – which had become separated from her upon entering the Pacific Ocean – sighted the island of Pitcairn. Captain Carteret marked it down on his British chart as a hardly accessible and presumably uninhabited island, an indication that appealed to Fletcher Christian in 1790.
44   On board Cook's *Endeavour* (1768–71) was Sir Joseph Banks, and on board his HMS *Resolution* (1776–79) was William Bligh – two people who were to set off the *Bounty* mission in the following decade.
45   For more on the myth of Pacific cannibalism, Gananath Obeyesekere, *Cannibal Talk: The Man-Eating Myth and Human Sacrifice in the South Seas* (Berkeley, University of California Press, 2005).

> their whole thought being turnd towards the Visitors, & all Method tryd to win their Friendship. Meantime they were forced to living in a different way of life that they might the better please their New friends.[46]

Although the *Bounty* observers' journals were lost, records from Morrison, together with brief summaries of Heywood and Stewart, were preserved.[47] Morrison's account of Tahitian society, history and culture and Heywood's Tahitian dictionary were rewritten in England from memory. It must be borne in mind that Morrison and Heywood were then awaiting trial for mutiny, and presumably pandered to the British missionaries who could be powerful advocates in the court of public opinion; the budding London Missionary Society (LMS) was eager for any accounts of Tahitian 'savagery' that might encourage their plans to evangelise Tahiti.[48]

After the *Bounty*, Tahiti was never more without European residents, who produced additional written source material. British ships stopped there on their way to or from the nascent penal colony in Botany Bay, New South Wales. They stopped at Tahiti for provisions and, sometimes, as with the *Mercury* in 1790, to dispose of a troublesome crewman. The *Pandora*, Captain George Vancouver's *Discovery* and *Chatham*, and the crew of a shipwrecked British whaler, the *Mathilda*, all touched Tahiti between the departure of the *Bounty* (1789) and the return of Bligh on the *Providence* and the *Assistance* (1792).[49] Whaling and trading also started bringing visitors to the Island, consistently adding to the number of beachcombers. Altogether, 15 ships came to Tahiti in the 30 years after the first contact (1767–97).

And then the missionaries arrived.[50] The LMS's *Duff* was first sighted on 5 March 1797 – a date still celebrated as a national holiday in Tahiti, which gives a measure of the event's lasting impact. In terms of written source material, the first missionaries used the ethnographic information of Heywood and Morrison as a foundation for their own observations on the particulars of the culture they were concomitantly striving to eradicate. The subsequent missionaries' writings were numerous and

---

46 Smith & Thomas, 2013, p 262.
47 For more on Morrison, see Smith & Thomas (2013). For more on Heywood and Morrison, see Du Rietz (1986).
48 See Smith & Thomas (2013); Smith (2010, p 254).
49 For a full examination of Bligh's third stay in Tahiti, see Salmond (2011, chpts 17–21).
50 For more on that period, see Jonathan Lamb, Vanessa Smith & Nicholas Thomas (eds), *Exploration and Exchange: A South Seas Anthology, 1680–1900* (Chicago, University of Chicago Press, 2000); and the London Missionary Society Archives, SOAS, University of London.

some, like William Ellis' *Polynesian Researches* (1829), John Williams' *Narrative of Missionary Enterprises* (1837), and JM Orsmond's information recorded in *Ancient Tahiti* (1928),[51] provide much relied-upon written source material on Tahiti. Because the authors were writing with a mission to prove that the native Islanders were a benighted people in need of Christian salvation, it seems reasonable to assume that their reporting may be prejudiced, self-glorifying and self-exculpatory.

Navigating *The* Bounty *from the Beach*

Just as the *Bounty* mission originated in Tahiti, the project of a collective volume on *The* Bounty *from the Beach* saw the light of day in Tahiti – a vantage point from which to observe the non-universality of the Western position. When the first *Bounty* International Festival was held in Papeete, Tahiti, in 2013,[52] I had been engaged in Pacific Island field research for 14 years at the University of French Polynesia. I introduced students in Anglophone Pacific Island studies to this portion of their history and culture and the way it was represented in literature and movies; they were so actively interested, and so thrilled to contribute to the Festival through round tables, workshops and cultural shows, that I could not refrain from probing the matter further. The groundbreaking Pacific *Bounty* studies of scholars Greg Dening, Rod Edmond, Anne Salmond, Vanessa Smith and Nicholas Thomas inspired me to further contribute to mapping the *Bounty* from this side of the world.

The Bounty *from the Beach*, therefore, takes readers on a discursive Pacific journey along some of the *Bounty*'s routes. As no single book could possibly explore all *Bounty*-related topics, this volume will be partial and selective in its itineraries. It nevertheless aims to follow some of the bearings of the *Bounty*'s course, progressing with the ship through time and space. Just as it crisscrosses the ocean, this discursive journey equally ranges far and wide across disciplines, methodologies and scholarly styles. Its multidisciplinary course strongly contributes to illuminate the multiple ways in which the 'little people on both sides of the beach' cross diverse groups and identities. Its eclectic approaches converge to examine the

---

51   Orsmond's notes were put together by his granddaughter, Teuira Henry, and published after her death.
52   www.bounty-tahiti.net/. See also Delphine Barrais, *La Dépêche* (Papeete, Tahiti, 26 Oct 2013, p 21).

colonial dimension of *Bounty* studies and representations, and highlight how these 'little people' have been silenced across disciplines. Together, our wide-ranging studies make a Pacific Island–centred exploration of the *Bounty* heritage.

In the first chapter, ethno-linguist Jean-Claude Teriierooiterai, who graduated at the University of French Polynesia, reconstructs the lifeworlds and practices of Oceanian Islanders through evidentiary bases: he contextualises the *Bounty* events by embracing both conventional history and vernacular historicities, looking at the *Bounty* from the indigenous side of the beach. Weaving together chronicles and lore, archives and Polynesian cultural practices, he embarks on a maritime history of the South Pacific,[53] comparing and contrasting European documents with Pacific Islander records. He examines the writings of European voyagers on contact history, including during the *Bounty* period, in relation to Pacific Islander non-textual sources. Following Epeli Hau'ofa's dictum that 'We cannot read our histories without knowing how to read our landscapes (and seascapes)',[54] he deciphers seascapes, landscapes and skyscapes, toponyms and unpublished Tahitian legends about the stars that Polynesian navigators used to read to navigate the ocean. Engaging polyphonic voices 'from the indigenous side of the beach', he extends our appreciation of the possibilities of *Bounty* history in the Pacific.

Following this first wide-angle Pacific perspective, the second chapter zooms in on some specific Oceanic journeys and makes a landfall on pre-*Bounty* Pitcairn. Archaeologists and ethno-historians Guillaume Molle and Aymeric Hermann, trained at the University of French Polynesia, investigate the Polynesian settlement of Pitcairn. By highlighting pre-*Bounty* Pitcairn's close contact with the rest of Central Eastern Polynesia, they confirm the ongoing interconnectedness of this region prior to European contact. Complementing Teriierooiterai's argument, they challenge Western perceptions of Pacific Island history by further bringing the historical agency of Pacific Islanders into focus, thereby shedding new light on Pitcairn's alleged social and cultural isolation. Like Teriierooiterai, they look at the *Bounty* from the indigenous side of the beach and try to reconstruct the lifeworlds and practices of Oceanian Islanders through evidentiary bases. But their style and methodology are

---

53   The term 'South Pacific' includes 'not just those islands that lie south of the equator; it covers the whole region, from the Marianas, deep in the North Pacific, to New Zealand in the south' (Hau'ofa, 1998, p 396).
54   Epeli Hau'ofa, 'Past to Remember', in Hau'ofa, 2008, p 73.

distinctly different, prioritising a formal archaeological study. The way this chapter gives voice to 'the little people on the indigenous side of the beach' is, therefore, contrapuntally, more conventionally analytical.

The next leg of journey, in Chapter 3, brings readers forward in time, to consider the Islanders and the *Bounty* sailors in Tahiti just before the mutiny (1789). University of London doctoral student Rachael Utting's critical analysis of museal institutions and culture is largely concerned with hermeneutic perspectives and is, therefore, in turn, keenly distinct in its scholarly approach. The chapter highlights how the strangers from the *Bounty* crossed the beach and 'went native'. It discusses a letter written by Bligh that describes the *Bounty* mutineers' body markings – involuntary markings such as scars and wounds, and voluntary ones such as Polynesian and Euro-American tattoos. The study of *tatau* designs charts some of the ways 'the little people on both sides of the beach', Polynesian and Western, interacted during the *Bounty*'s five-month stay. It highlights how, through acts of body modification, the sailors and prospective mutineers attempted to reclaim their own bodies from the subjectification of the British Royal Navy, while the Islanders asserted their social, political and cultural agency and proved to be predominant in the self-presentation of identities.

Chapter 4 prolongs Utting's discursive call at Tahiti in the years around the *Bounty* mutiny (1788–91), but this time in the mode of a literary critical analysis. This volume's editor parses the way 'the little people on both sides of the beach' – Islanders and *Bounty* beachcombers – are represented in *Mutiny on the Bounty* (1932), a widely read historical novel by Charles Nordhoff and James Norman Hall. Its American authors had both crossed the beach in the 1930s – they were based in Tahiti and had married local *vahine* – and yet their representation of the *Bounty* in Tahiti proves to be predominantly from 'the strangers' side of the beach'. Referring to the works of Pacific historians and anthropologists, critics in colonial studies and narrative theorists, this essay approaches the Tahitian narrative in Nordhoff and Hall's novel from an interdisciplinary, cross-cultural perspective. It highlights the narrative strategies used by the novel's Western authors to focus mostly on the British 'little people on the beach', while occluding the Islanders. The chapter illustrates the textual processes by which the Tahitian characters are merely 'exoticised'[55] through the filter of Western values, producing contingent historical fiction and strongly inflected colonial discourse.

---

55 Jean Bernabé, *Éloge de la Créolité*, with Patrick Chamoiseau & Raphaël Confiant, bilingual edition, MB Taleb-Khyar (trans), Paris, Gallimard, 1989, p 76.

The fifth chapter is also a literary exegesis. It journeys back to Pitcairn, as Sorbonne Professor Jean-Pierre Naugrette revisits post-*Bounty* literary representations of the mutineers and their descendants, through Jack London's short story 'The Seed of McCoy' (1911). By the time London sailed the Pacific Ocean, Pitcairn was democratically governed by James Russell McCoy, a great-grandson of the *Bounty*'s McCoy. In London's fiction, 'Anglified native' McCoy navigates the ocean the ancient Polynesian way, from 'the chart of his memory'.[56] Building on Teriierooiterai's argument, Naugrette illuminates that London concomitantly draws another chart, a richly intertextual one. An expert in Anglophone literature, he demonstrates that London's narrative unfolds in the wake of two of Robert Louis Stevenson's major writings on the Pacific Islands: *In the South Seas* (1896, posthumous) and *The Ebb-Tide* (1894). Stevenson's Pacific works are strongly critical of colonial discourse and policies, vindicating the little people on the indigenous side of the beach.[57] Naugrette's essay, therefore, reads McCoy's cruise as a literary exorcism of the ill-fated *Bounty* mutiny, where the 'little' man from Pitcairn asserts commanding agency and is turned into a potential God-like figure.

Chapter 6 examines the cinematic descendants of Nordhoff and Hall's *Mutiny* novel. Literature and film critics Professor Roslyn Jolly and Dr Simon Petch, from the University of New South Wales and University of Sydney respectively, dissect the nuances of Marlon Brando's performance as Fletcher Christian in MGM's 1962 film *Mutiny on the Bounty*. This sixth essay pits a Wildean, dandified Christian against a cruel and irrational Bligh-in-command. Christian's ironic detachment is seen as existential armour against the absurdities of the postwar world of the film's production, as exemplified by escalating atomic testing in the Pacific Islands. The protagonists' developing conflict leads into an exploration of what it means to be a 'gentleman', albeit 'on the beach',[58] in the 1960s. It also highlights the Cold War colonial powers' deadly contempt for 'the little people on the indigenous side of the beach'.

---

56   Jack London, 'The Seed of McCoy', in *Tales of the Pacific*, Harmondsworth, Penguin Twentieth-Century Classics, 1989, p 94.
57   See Roslyn Jolly, *Robert Louis Stevenson in the Pacific: Travel, Empire, and the Author's Profession* (Farnham, Ashgate, 2009); see also, Sylvie Largeaud-Ortega, *Ainsi Soit-Île. Littérature et anthropologie dans les Contes des Mers du Sud de Robert Louis Stevenson* (Paris, Honoré Champion, 2012).
58   'On the beach' is a 19th-century geolectal expression meaning 'destitute' in the Pacific. See Roslyn Jolly, 'Introduction', *South Sea Tales* (Oxford, Oxford World's Classics, 1996).

The seventh essay, by Princeton University graduate now Denison University historian Adrian Young, takes us back to Pitcairn. The offspring of *Bounty* female Islanders and male British sailors have made a new island, with an indigenous side of the beach that is now hybridised. Through a study of material culture, this final chapter blends together histories and texts. It enhances the Pacific *Bounty*'s 'diversality'[59] by charting the exchange and dissemination of *Bounty* artefacts during the last two centuries, from Pitcairn to the rest of the world. The descendants of the *Bounty* mutineers on Pitcairn and Norfolk islands have given out relics as a means of negotiating their relationship with the outside world. Through them, Pitcairners have fashioned an identity for themselves as romantic, pure, pious and loyal. Once placed in museums and private collections, *Bounty* relics have become sites of captivation, drawing in and retaining the sympathetic interest of collectors while serving as a medium through which outsiders can project their own images of Pacific life. This chapter therefore pulls together the volume's strands of history, historicities and imaginary representations, through a final examination of the records of 'the little people on the beach', their very bodies and surnames sometimes raised to the status of British national treasures. It establishes that, as in ancient Polynesian times, a small-sized Pacific Island like Pitcairn is connected to the wider world through an elaborate network of trades and exchanges – even by the garbage washing onto its shores as a result of the global environmental crisis.

'It is now very strikingly no longer the case that the lesser peoples – formerly colonised, enslaved, suppressed – are silent or unaccounted for', Edward Said wrote in his 1994 Afterword to *Orientalism*.[60] This cross-cultural and cross-disciplinary collection of essays around the *Bounty* capitalises on a widely shared fascination for the *Bounty* story in order to draw scholarly attention to the Pacific Islands. Expanding on an anecdotal occurrence in British maritime history, it highlights the Islanders' powerful agency throughout history, from the times when their ancestors sailed the ocean long before the Vikings started exploring the Northern Hemisphere, through the periods of contact and post-contact with Westerners, to the present. It throws light on the Western colonial discourse that undertook

---

59 'Diversality' is the opposite of 'the totalitarian order of the old world, fixed by the temptation of the unified and the definitive ... it opposes to Universality the great opportunity of a world diffracted but recomposed, the conscious harmonization of preserved diversities' (Bernabé, 1989, p 114).
60 Edward W Said, Afterword, *Orientalism*, New York, Vintage Books, 1994 (1978), p 348.

to stifle and silence this agency, and the neo-colonial policies that have been applied to Oceania, and still are: hegemonic moves that have led to global environmental nuclear and ecological hazards. As a whole, the collection contends that what unfolds in this vast ocean matters: the stakes are high for the whole human community.

1

Contextualising the *Bounty* in Pacific Maritime Culture

Jean-Claude Teriierooiterai
Independent Researcher and
Member of the Tahitian Academy

As described in the Introduction, there have been many narratives – written and filmed – about the *Bounty*. Historical sources are mainly British, and events have been presented mostly from a British perspective. This chapter[1] sheds a somewhat different light on *Bounty* narratives, coming from the perspective of indigenous Pacific Islanders – the perspective of those who stand on 'the other side of the beach', as Greg Dening famously put it. It examines the interactions between European explorers and Pacific Islanders since first contact and, through a close study of late 18th-century Pacific maritime culture and heritage, compares British and Polynesian maritime cultures around the time of the *Bounty*. The aim is to contextualise the *Bounty* from a Polynesian perspective and to give voice to the Pacific Islanders of the past: to those who have long been thought of as 'little'.[2]

---

1   Translated into English by Sylvie Largeaud-Ortega and Meredith Wilson.
2   Greg Dening, 'Writing, Rewriting the Beach: An Essay', in Alun Munslow & Robert A Rosenstone (eds), *Experiments in Rethinking History*, New York & London, Routledge, 2004, p 54.

First European and Polynesian encounters: How the Europeans established their reputation as slayers of men

The Spaniards' first dramatic landfinding

European explorers were constantly amazed by the diversity of the central Pacific islands. Within a maritime area amounting to one-third of the globe's surface, they encountered expansive, towering islands where water flowed from mountains in abundance; and small, ring-shaped, semi-desert sand atolls. Some islands, such as Tahiti, were crowded with inhabitants. According to Tupaia – the Tahitian priest who sailed with James Cook in 1769 – Tahiti had an estimated population of 200,000.[3] The discovery of people on the islands of the Pacific differed from the experience of European navigators exploring the islands of other large oceans – such as the Azores and Madeira in the Atlantic Ocean or the Mascarene and the Seychelles in the Indian Ocean – which were uninhabited. It is more than likely that the European explorers who first ventured into the Pacific Ocean expected to find similarly uninhabited islands.

In 1521, Ferdinand Magellan became the first European to cross the Pacific and the first to encounter the islands of Polynesia. He came across the two tiny atolls of Pukapuka (Isla de los Tiburones) in the eastern Tuamotu, and Flint (Isla de San Pablo) in the Line Islands,[4] both of which appeared to be uninhabited and devoid of evidence of prior settlement. Pukapuka most likely remained uninhabited because it lies at the isolated eastern tip of the Tuamotu Islands and is the last landfall before South America.[5]

The Dutch navigators Jacob Le Maire and Willem Schouten came across Pukapuka atoll in 1616, 95 years after Magellan. While they did not report seeing any inhabitants during their visit, they sighted three dogs on the shoreline. The presence of dogs suggests that people had visited the atoll after Magellan and, therefore, that the Polynesians were continuing to undertake long-distance inter-island voyaging until relatively recently. Magellan eventually made landfall in Guam in the Mariana archipelago

---

3 The current population of Tahiti is no more than 172,000 people.
4 Philippe Mazellier, Eric Monod, Bengt Danielsson & Marie-Thérèse Danielsson (eds), *Le Mémorial Polynésien*, vol 1, *1521–1833*, Papeete, Éditions Hibiscus, 1978.
5 Most Polynesian islands lie between the equator and the Tropic of Capricorn.

of Micronesia, marking the first European–Pacific Islander encounter. In 1526, five years after Magellan's voyage, the Portuguese explorer Jorge de Menezes approached New Guinea from the west, naming it the Islands of Papua (Ilhas dos Papuas).[6] Less than 30 years later, in 1555, Juan Gaetano, a Spaniard, is thought by some to have discovered the Islands of Hawai'i, and therefore to be the first European to have encountered Polynesians.[7] A lack of evidence has led to this claim being strongly contested by historians, and Cook is still regarded as being the first Westerner to discover Hawai'i.

The first known encounter between Europeans and Oceanians of Austronesian origin occurred off the Nui atoll in the Tuvalu archipelago, during the first Pacific voyage of Álvaro Mendaña in January 1568. Although the Tuvalu Islands are Polynesian, the Nui atoll was inhabited by Micronesians.[8] It seems that the Spaniards were not curious explorers, however, and sailed on, merely observing the gesticulating Islanders from their ships as they passed.

Mendaña later reached the Solomon Islands in Melanesia. During a six-month stay, the Spaniards wrote numerous descriptions of the archipelago's inhabitants. As might be expected, their reports were strongly influenced by the racial and religious prejudices of the time.[9] The Spanish agenda in the region was to convert the indigenous peoples to Catholicism, to enslave them and to harvest their gold. The islands were allegedly where King Solomon's fleet had found gold – hence the name given to the archipelago. The Spanish visit involved considerable miscommunication with the Islander communities. There were no religious conversions or enslavements amongst the Islanders, and the Spaniards were refused permission to explore for gold. The Islanders baulked at selling their pigs and forbade the Spaniards access to water sources. The Spaniards did

---

6   Non-Austronesian Papuans have inhabited the islands and the region for at least 30,000 years and are the earliest inhabitants of the Pacific; Austronesian-speaking communities only joined them 3,500 years ago, which is relatively recent on the scale of human history. See Peter Bellwood, *Man's Conquest of the Pacific: The Prehistory of Southeast Asia and Oceania* (Auckland, William Collins Publishers, 1978, p 47). See also JHF Sollewijn Gelpke, *On the Origin of the Name Papua* (Leiden, Kitlv, 1993).
7   The Polynesian Triangle spans from Hawai'i in the north, to Rapa Nui/Easter Island in the east and Aotearoa/New Zealand in the south-west. On the European discovery of Hawai'i, see Oliver L Douglas, *The Pacific Islands* (Honolulu, University of Hawai'i Press, 1989, p 45).
8   Micronesian languages are usually part of the Pacific branch, which also includes Polynesian and Melanesian languages. Only the speakers of the Pacific branch of Austronesian may be considered genuine Oceanians, linguistically speaking.
9   Annie Baert, *Le Paradis Terrestre, un mythe espagnol en Océanie, Les voyages de Mendaña et de Quirós 1567–1606*, Paris, L'Harmattan, 1999.

not understand that these resources were strongly ritualised among the Solomon Islanders and subject to stringent taboos. The visitors accused the Islanders of being cannibals, and violent clashes ensued. The endurance of the Spaniards eventually waned:

> [T]welve [men] were killed in clashes with the natives, ten of whom were attacked and, it is argued, eaten when fetching water at Guadalcanal on 27 May 1568: they were found 'in pieces, some without legs, others without arms, others without heads; all had their tongues cut out, and they had been ripped off their teeth. Those who had not been decapitated had their skulls open, and their brains eaten off …', one of their terrified companions reported. It appears from the various testimonies that the many skirmishes and inevitable retaliations killed about 80 of the native islanders.[10]

Mendaña decided to sail back to Peru, hoping to return later with more resources and stronger armed forces. On his way home, he caught a glimpse of the Marshall Islands and Wake Island in Micronesia.

Mendaña's second attempt to colonise the Solomon Islands, in 1595, proved a turning point in the history of European–Polynesian encounters. It revealed to the European world the existence of the Polynesian people, and the existence of a hitherto-unknown fruit: that of the breadfruit tree, or Tahitian '*uru* – a key feature in the history of the *Bounty*. Mendaña was on his way to the Solomon Islands when, in the late afternoon of 21 July, he sighted an archipelago of mountainous islands. He named it the 'Marquesas de Mendoza' in honour of the wife of the viceroy of Peru. On landing, for the first time in history, a European was facing a Polynesian. It was a shock. Imagine countless warriors, a head taller than the Spanish sailors, brandishing huge clubs, tattooed from head to foot, intrinsically intrepid and inquisitive, clambering aboard the ship and unabashedly snatching whatever they fancied. Muskets were soon firing. The massacre at Tahuata was reported in Spanish journals, as cited by Annie Baert:

---

10 '… douze (hommes) avaient péri dans des heurts avec les indigènes, dont dix furent attaqués et, dit-on, mangés, lors de la corvée d'eau à Guadalcanal du 27 mai 1568 : on les retrouva "en morceaux, certains sans jambes, d'autres sans bras, d'autres encore sans tête ; tous avaient la langue coupée, et on leur avait arraché les dents. Ceux qui n'avaient pas été décapités avaient le crâne ouvert, et on leur avait mangé la cervelle …", rapporta, épouvanté, un de leurs compagnons. Il ressort des différents témoignages que les nombreuses escarmouches et les inévitables représailles firent environ 80 morts chez les indigènes.' (Annie Baert, 'Alvaro de Mendaña (1542–1595), un explorateur du Pacifique sud au destin tragique', *Île en île*, June 2003).

The fact is that different clashes occurred for several reasons – mainly for the soldiers' fear at being largely outnumbered by the natives, as revealed by this anecdote: '… the camp master and two soldiers [left by boat]. Many Indians, approaching on board their canoes, surrounded them and, in order to ensure their own safety, our men killed a few'. As for the Marquesans, they seemed utterly impervious to fear, despite the Spaniards' attempts at arousing it through deliberately fierce acts, such as slashing the bodies of three musket victims with swords and exposing them on shore. According to Quirós, their visit to this island caused the death of 200 Indians, but a detailed survey of the various skirmishes estimates the actual Marquesan death toll between 25 and 70.[11]

Captain Pedro de Quirós, Mendaña's chief pilot, also reported that during the visit some Marquesan women offered themselves to the Spaniards, whose 'hands feasted'.[12] French explorer Louis-Antoine de Bougainville famously recalled a similar interaction between foreign men and local women 171 years later in Tahiti, another Polynesian island.

Quirós was the first to mention the fruit of the breadfruit tree, which he observed in Tahuata. The Spaniards did not record the fruit in the Solomon Islands during their first expedition. As discussed in more detail below, breadfruit was the staple food of the Marquesans and of most Eastern Polynesians. Called *mei* (*Artocarpus altilis*) by Marquesans, the fruit attracted Quirós' attention: he found it 'to his taste' as well as 'healthy and of high value'.[13] He learned that fermented *mei*, called *popoi*, was a favoured food of the Polynesians when they were out at sea, because it could feed the crew of a double canoe, around 10 people, for several months. Unfortunately, Quirós did not include breadfruit in his own crew's menu and, later in the voyage, the Spanish sorely lacked food after precipitately leaving the Santa Cruz Islands – where breadfruit grew – bound for the Philippines (see below).

---

11   'Toujours est-il que se produisirent différents heurts, pour plusieurs raisons, dont la principale fut la peur que les soldats éprouvèrent devant la supériorité numérique des indigènes, comme le révèle cette anecdote : "… le maître de camp et deux soldats [partirent en chaloupe]. Beaucoup d'Indiens, s'approchant sur leurs canoës, les encerclèrent et, pour garantir leur sécurité, nos hommes en tuèrent quelques-uns". Cette peur, que les Marquisiens ne semblaient pas éprouver le moins du monde face à eux, ils voulurent la leur inspirer par des actes délibérément effrayants, comme lorsque les corps de trois victimes des arquebuses furent taillalés à l'épée et exposés sur le rivage. Bien que selon Quirós, cette escale ait causé la mort de 200 Indiens, si on reprend le détail des différentes escarmouches, on peut estimer le bilan réel entre 25 et 70 morts marquisiens.' (Baert, 2003, p 9).
12   Baert, 2003, p 9.
13   Baert, 1999, p 230.

Back in Peru, in a report addressed to King Philip II, Quirós highly recommended this fruit, which he described as '*grande y muy buena*'. And – most appealing to *Bounty* aficionados – Quirós tried to convince the Spanish king to establish a new expedition specifically to fetch the countless resources he had discovered in the Marquesas. The king was apparently not convinced of the merits of this proposal.[14]

Following the discovery of the Marquesas Islands, encounters between Europeans and Polynesians intensified. Each European explorer who sailed across the Pacific took to his credit the discovery of one or several islands up until 1816.[15] Those islands number in the thousands, and span an area roughly 100 million square kilometres. All these islands were either inhabited or had been at some point, such as Pitcairn (see Molle & Hermann, Chapter 2). Gradually, Europeans began to question how the Pacific came to be inhabited. What were these people doing on these tiny islands in the middle of the Pacific? Who were they? How had their forebears managed such vast ocean crossings?

After visiting the Marquesas, Mendaña sailed westward, without stopping, passing the Polynesian atolls of Pukapuka in the Cook Islands and north Niulakita in the Tuvalu archipelago. He then discovered the island of Nendo, which he named Santa Cruz – a name that was later applied to the whole archipelago. Here Mendaña once again encountered Polynesians.[16] Relations between the Islanders and the Spanish were, as usual, initially peaceful until the Spanish opened fire with their muskets. They killed Malope, the Polynesian chief of Nendo, which sparked endless trouble. Mendaña died a month later from malaria, along with about 40 of his crew, and the Spaniards eventually left the island. Under the command of Quirós, the survivors headed for the Philippines. Approximately 50 sailors starved to death during the 12-week journey. The '*uru*, fermented the Polynesian way, might have saved them, if only the Spanish navigators had embraced the preservation practice of the Marquesas. Let it be noted that, when they left Tahiti, neither the crew of the *Bounty*, bound for the West Indies, nor the man-of-war *Pandora*, heading for England, appear to have had fermented '*uru* on board either.

---

14 Baert, 1999, p 231.
15 Otto von Kotzebue discovered Tikehau in 1816.
16 Polynesians lived together with Melanesians on those islands. The two communities sometimes lived on islets that were only a stone's throw from one another, but they were fiercely attached to their idiosyncrasies.

In 1605, Quirós voyaged in search of *Terra Australis* – the great mythical southern landmass imagined by geographers – in order to take possession of it on behalf of the King of Spain. What he discovered first was Henderson and Ducie, two of the Pitcairn Islands, which he named San Juan Baptista and Puesta Luna. While Quirós registered both islands as uninhabited, recent archaeological research suggests that Henderson was settled by Polynesians from the 10th to the 16th centuries (see Molle & Hermann, Chapter 2).[17] Quirós may, therefore, have arrived just after the island was abandoned. Recent research also reveals that the nearby island of Pitcairn had been occupied during the same period. What happened to the people who lived there?

On 10 February 1606, Quirós' fleet arrived at the large Hao atoll, where the first encounter with Pa'umotu Islanders took place.[18] For once, the encounter was peaceful, with gifts exchanged. This atoll's inhabitants must have as yet been unaware of the fatal encounter with the Marquesas a decade earlier.

Quirós' next short visit was at Rakahanga (northern Cook Islands). The lack of fresh water on the island brought his thirsty fleet only temporary solace. While attempting to reach the Santa Cruz Islands, Quirós discovered Taumako – an island of the Duff group located 140 kilometres from Nendo. It was also inhabited by Polynesians from the outliers (i.e. islands outside the Polynesian triangle inhabited by Polynesians who migrated there around a thousand years ago, as in New Caledonia, Vanuatu, Papua New Guinea and the Solomon and Caroline islands). Tumai, their leader, knowing of the Spaniard's fearsome reputation – having heard of their muskets and of Malope's death a decade earlier – did his best to placate them. Responding to Quirós' enquiries about *Terra Australis*, he revealed the existence of an archipelago of more than 60 islands, ranging from the north-west to the south-east of Taumako.[19] The Spaniards immediately set sail again and arrived off the island of Santo (northern Vanuatu), which they took for the northerly tip of the sought-after southern continent. Quirós tried to settle there but, faced with the hostility of the Islanders and disloyal behaviour from his own officers and sailors, he decided to head home.

---

17 Patrick V Kirch, 'Polynesia's Mystery Islands', *Archaeology*, no 41, vol 3, 1988, pp 26–31.
18 Pa'umotu: inhabitant of the Tuamotu Islands.
19 Pedro Fernandez Quirós, *Histoire de la découverte des régions Australes, Iles Salomon, Marquises, Santa Cruz, Tuamotu, Cook du Nord et Vanuatu*, traduction et notes de Annie Berat, préface de Paul de Deckker, Paris, L'Harmattan, 2001.

Several indigenous Islanders were taken from Taumako to be 'educated' in Catholicism in Peru. One of them, who was given the Christian name of Pedro, soon learned enough Spanish to provide valuable evidence about contemporary Polynesian voyages. For instance, he told the Spaniards that a canoe from Vaitupu in the Tuvalu Islands had come to rest in Taumako and that, out of a crew of about 50 people, 10 had survived, including three women. This confirmed that Polynesian women voyaged with men in the traditional ocean-going canoes. Pedro had encountered Polynesians from Tuvalu before; the last time was when a large double canoe sailed from Vaitupu to Sikaiana (500 kilometres north-west of Taumako) with 110 passengers on board.[20] The Tuvalu voyagers reported sighting European ships off Nui, 1,200 kilometres east of Taumako. This was presumably Mendaña's fleet from his first voyage 38 years earlier in 1568.

After the Spanish, the Dutch began to explore the Pacific. They turned out to be more curious, but just as disrespectful, of Pacific Islanders.

The Dutch cross a canoe in the middle of the ocean

In 1616, 15 years after the Spanish, the Dutch navigators Jacob Le Maire and Willem Schouten ventured into the Tuamotu archipelago. After sighting three dogs on Pukapuka, the Dutch proceeded to find other atolls such as Takapoto, Ahe, Manihi and Rangiroa. Throughout their voyage, they were struck by the Islanders' keen interest in iron, nails and bolts. It may safely be conjectured that virtually all the Pa'umotu had heard from the Hao Islanders about the alien metal, and iron was a sought-after commodity in the islands where it did not previously exist. Nails were traded among Pacific Islanders and trade in iron was conducted before recorded European contact. According to Robert Langdon, a Spanish caravel, the *San Lesme*, sank off Amanu in 1526 and the iron from the ship may have been traded in the archipelago and beyond, presumably as far as Tahiti.[21] The Tahitians were already using the word '*auri*' for the metal when the English arrived there in 1767.

---

20   Matthew Spriggs, 'Les éclats du triangle polynésien', in Serge Dunis (ed), *D'île en île Pacifique*, Paris, Klincksieck, 1999, p 38.
21   Robert Langdon, *The Lost Caravel*, Sydney, Pacific Publications, 1978.

1. CONTEXTUALISING THE *BOUNTY* IN PACIFIC MARITIME CULTURE

The Dutch then headed west without deviating from their latitude, like all European explorers of the time. After several days at sea, they came across a double canoe in a remote part of the ocean. The canoe's occupants were travelling between Tonga and Samoa. The contemporary sketches of the vessel indicate that it was a *tongiaki*, a Tongan double canoe, which could carry several dozen people. The lateen sail on these fast vessels appears, at over 20 metres long, disproportionately large. Perplexed by the presence of the craft in the middle of the ocean, the Dutch intercepted it to take a closer look. When the Polynesian navigators ignored their summons, the Dutch opened fire, killing and injuring several people on board. The survivors jumped overboard. Once the canoe was at a standstill, the Dutch examined it more closely and made sketches before sailing away. Those survivors, who were able to return to the canoe, set sail again and, no doubt, decided to reach the nearest land, the islands north of Tonga, where they could tell their misadventure. This is precisely where the Dutch were heading. The assault was bound to have a serious impact on later encounters between the Islanders and Europeans.

Two days after their attack on the *tongiaki*, Le Maire and Schouten landed at Tafahi Island in the extreme north of Tonga. The *tongiaki* survivors must have still been at sea, and the news of the attack had probably not yet reached Tafahi. Le Maire sent a few men ashore with trinkets, which were well received. The Dutch found that, while the Tongans would grab whatever they fancied, they expressed a particular interest in nails. Did the Tongans already know about nails? It is highly likely that the gifts of previous explorers had travelled as far as northern Tonga.

The next day, the Dutch headed to Niuatoputapu, an island visible from Tafahi. To their surprise, a fleet of canoes was awaiting them and launched a fierce attack, but the Dutch managed to ward them off with their muskets. The next day, the island's chief refitted his naval force with 23 double canoes and 45 outriggers, and attacked again. The Dutch fired three cannons to resist their assailants and then sailed away. What caused this sudden change of attitude? Had news of the *tongiaki* survivors reached Niuatoputapu before the Dutch arrived? The chief of Niuatoputapu was certainly prepared to attack, having brought together numerous canoes and put them in order of battle.

The day after the mutiny on the *Bounty*, 180 years later, Captain William Bligh and 18 loyalists landed their overcrowded long boat at Tofua, one of the Ha'apai Islands. This group of islands in northern Tonga was the closest to where the *tongiaki* had been attacked. When the Tofua Islanders saw these scruffy, under-armed white men approach their shores, they knew how dangerous they could be, for their elders had passed on the tale of the *tongiaki* onslaught.

Ten years before the *Bounty* events, James Cook's visit in 1779 had also demonstrated just how dangerous Europeans could be:

> As George Gilbert, one of his midshipmen, remarked, during this visit Cook punished the Tongans 'in a manner rather unbecoming of a European, viz by cutting off their ears; fireing at them with small shot; or ball as they were swimming or paddling to the shore; and suffering the people to beat them with the oars; and stick the boat hook into them; wherever they could hit them.'[22]

Cook had also ordered the flogging of three Tongan Islanders – including chiefly ones – for stealing from the ships, which led to Bligh being attacked by Tongans on one of the *Resolution*'s hunting expeditions. Two days before the *Bounty* mutiny, on 26 April 1789, many Tongans had already badly molested Bligh's watering party, which was led by Fletcher Christian. To retrieve a grapnel stolen from the *Bounty*, Bligh had held four Tongan chiefs hostage – one of whom was the father of a man flogged by Cook – and charged them with degrading, menial tasks. After the mutiny, on 2 May 1789, when the Tongans saw that the British were reduced to a small group cramped into a solitary long boat, they gathered by the hundreds, fiercely determined to attack Bligh and his 18 loyalists. A massacre was only avoided thanks to Bligh's perspicacity, and only one sailor lost his life.[23] He guessed that an attack was eminent; he organised the hasty retreat of his men onto the boat and was able to sail away in the nick of time.

The Dutch discovery of the islands of Tafahi and Niuatoputapu is interesting for the study of Polynesian migration, and may further contribute to the contextualisation of the *Bounty*. Indeed, the lexical notes of the Dutch show that the inhabitants spoke Samoan.[24] Today, however, following their 18th-century annexation by Tonga, they speak Tongan.

---

22 Anne Salmond, *Bligh: William Bligh in the South Seas*, Auckland, Penguin Viking, 2011, p 65.
23 Salmond, 2011, pp 63–65, 218.
24 Willem C Schouten, *The Relation of a Wonderfull Voiage made by Willem Cornelison Schouten of Horne. Shewing how South from the Straights of Magelan in Terra Delfuego: He Found and Discovered a Newe Passage through the Great South Seas, and That Way Sayled Round about the World*, London, Nathanaell Newbery, 1619.

This confirms that, at the time of contact with Europeans, there were still relations and exchange of information between the people of these two archipelagos.

After leaving Niuatoputapu, the Dutch landed in Futuna where, for the first time, Europeans attended a *kava* ceremony offered in honour of the dignitaries from the neighbouring island of 'Alofi. In contrast with the Spaniards, the Dutch were eager to document Pacific canoes and, in addition to sketching the *tongiaki*, they contributed a chart detailing the fleet of 50 double canoes that gathered from 'Alofi to attend the *kava* ceremony. These *vaka foulua*, which is the Futunan equivalent of *tongiaki*, were similar to the Tongan ones and as large as the Dutch ships in Futuna Bay.

Abel Tasman was the next Dutch navigator to explore the Pacific, sailing there from southern Australia in 1642. There he had discovered Tasmania and Aotearoa/New Zealand, approaching the latter from the south and naming it Statenland (Land of the States). Tasman was the first European to make contact with the Maori of New Zealand, the only Polynesians – along with those of Rapa Nui/Easter Island – to settle on subtropical islands where breadfruit trees did not grow. Four of Tasman's men were killed for violating taboo during an encounter with the Maori in the bay where he had anchored. He named the place Moordenaarsbaai (Murderers' Bay). The reputation of the Maori was sealed.

Not wanting to endanger the lives of his men through further encounters with the Maori, Tasman steered away from New Zealand. Heading north, he anchored at the island of Tongatabu, where the crew bartered with the Islanders and collected water in peace. Perhaps the Tongans were unaware of the *tongiaki* and the Niuatoputapu attacks? This is highly unlikely, because Tongatabu was home to the Tuʻi Kanokupolu, a powerful dynasty that had conquered all of Tonga, including Niuatoputapu where Le Maire and Schouten were assaulted in 1616. More probable is that the sovereign was aware of the damage that European weapons could cause and chose to protect his people from such conflict. The Dutch were perplexed by his warm and friendly welcome; when Cook visited the island, 160 years later, he was given a similar reception, leading him to name the archipelago 'Friendly Islands'.

Tasman then headed north-east. He discovered Fiji and compared the inhabitants to Hottentots, owing to their skin colour. He tacked between the many islands of the archipelago – not complaining once about his interactions with the Islanders – before reaching New Guinea.

Before discussing the voyage of the next Dutch explorer to cross the Pacific Ocean, Jacob Roggeveen in 1722, it is important to mention an unusual event that occurred in the Philippines in the meantime, and which highlights the outstanding navigation skills of the Micronesians.

In 1686, Spanish admiral Francisco Lazeano found an island east of the Philippines, which he initially named San Barnabas, but later renamed Carolina in honour of King Charles II of Spain. In 1696, some Pacific Islanders who were shipwrecked in these islands were rescued by Islanders from the Philippines and, as soon as they had learnt enough Spanish, explained that they had sailed from a group of islands to the east. They were asked by the Spaniards in the Philippines to use stone to create a rough map of the islands, which revealed that the shipwrecked Islanders were Micronesians who had travelled over 1,000 kilometres between the Carolina and the Mariana islands. This confirms that, at that time, the Micronesians and Polynesians continued to sail long distances across the Pacific.

Roggeveen sailed into the Pacific via Cape Horn with three ships, following Le Maire and Schouten's route. On Easter day, 5 April 1722, he made landfall on an unknown island. A few Islanders climbed on board his vessel and helped themselves to a small number of items. The next day, Roggeveen organised a punitive expedition, the first of a long series of European massacres on Rapanui, which was renamed Easter Island to mark this event. While Roggeveen explored the unique statues of Rapanui, the island was of no particular interest to him as it did not appear to have any gold or breadfruit. Roggeveen headed west in search of the famed southern continent, sailing through the Tuamotu archipelago – only the second European ship to enter the Dangerous archipelago after Quirós. The *Africaanshe Galey*, one of Roggeveen's three ships, ran aground on the island of Takapoto. The surviving sailors were rescued and dispatched to the other two ships, which departed immediately. This incident was not forgotten by the Islanders. During his onward voyage, Roggeveen noted the discovery of a few low-lying islands, probably Arutua and Apataki, and the south coast of Rangiroa. On 2 June, he sighted more elevated terrain on the Island of Makatea. Some of Roggeveen's boats rowed ashore for fresh food. The first encounters with the Islanders were friendly enough, as long as Roggeveen's men did not attempt to climb the cliffs on the island's shore. When they did, they were met with a hail of stones and some were injured. They retaliated with gunfire, wreaking havoc among the Islanders, and then retreated to their boats.

Why did the people of Makatea attack the Dutch seamen? Probably for the same reasons the Tahitians attacked naval officer Samuel Wallis and his *Dolphin* in 1767 (discussed further below): Makatea belonged to Mihiroa, a cultural area in the Tuamotu that had close cultural and language links with the Society Islands. Like the Tahitians, the inhabitants of Makatea were informed that white people had made violent contact in the Marquesas.

Fleeing Makatea, the Dutch made their way west towards the Society Islands. On 6 June, Roggeveen sighted Bora Bora and Maupiti, which he mistook for Niuatoputapu and Tafahi, recorded by Le Maire and Schouten. While Roggeveen decided against stopping at these islands, it could be argued that the European discovery of the Society Islands should be attributed to the Dutch rather than to British James Cook.[25]

On 13 June 1722, Roggeveen anchored in sight of another group of islands. His ships were soon surrounded by several canoes filled with Islanders whom he described as tall and robust and reminiscent of the people of Rapa Nui. Like them, their naked bodies were covered in 'paintings'.[26] He noted smoke rising from several places on the shore, which suggested that the islands were densely populated. Roggeveen had landed in Samoa. For lack of safe anchorage, however, he sailed on to Batavia. By deciding against making a landfall in Samoa, he probably escaped disaster, for it must be remembered that the *tongiaki* intercepted by Le Maire and Schouten had been sailing from Samoa and the Samoans were bound to have heard of the tragedy. Louis-Antoine de Bougainville also decided against making a landing when he sailed across the archipelago in 1768. His compatriot, Jean-François La Perouse, being more curious, decided to visit the islands in 1787. He paid a high price for his decision, losing his deputy Fleuriot de Langle to hostile Islanders armed with stones and clubs. Four years later, in 1791, the *Pandora*, with 14 *Bounty* prisoners

---

25 Andrew Sharp (ed), *The Journal of Jacob Roggeveen*, Oxford, Clarendon Press, 1970.
26 Marie-Charlotte Laroche, 'Circonstances et vicissitudes du voyage de découverte dans le Pacifique Sud de l'exploration Roggeveen 1721–1722', *Journal de la Société des Océanistes*, vol 38, no 74–75, 1982, pp 19–23.

on board, and her tender the *Matavy* – originally named the *Resolution* by James Morrison, the *Bounty*'s boatswain's mate who had built her in Tahiti – also approached the Samoan archipelago. The Islanders on the small atoll of Nukunonu fled the area overnight to avoid them, whereas, on the larger Tutuila, the crew was attacked by a strong fleet of canoes. At Tutuila, incidentally, the *Pandora* sailors found the uniform of one of La Perouse's murdered men.

These case studies demonstrate that the nature of the encounters between Europeans and Islanders varied between archipelagos, and depended on factors such as how warlike the Islanders were at the moment of contact, their social organisation and religious beliefs, and their population. The inhabitants of high islands, which were generally more populated than atolls, could afford to be more belligerent. The nature of the encounter also depended on the objectives and behaviours of the Europeans: what they had come for and how long they spent on islands. Many 16th- to 18th-century European explorers had strong characters and left a deep and lasting impact on the Pacific Islands that they visited. What may be said about the Spanish and Dutch navigators is that they showed little curiosity about the life, culture and history of the indigenous peoples. While they noticed Pacific Islanders travelling across the ocean at the same time as them – and in spite of the shipbuilding and navigational difficulties they experienced, especially in the 16th century – they did not consider how the remote islands of the Pacific had been settled as early as the Stone Age. There is no way of knowing, for instance, whether the canoes observed by the Spanish in Tahuata were the same as those drawn by Cook on the same spot a century and a half later. Had there been any developments in native shipbuilding? It cannot be ascertained.

The Polynesians kept a close record of all European incursions. Since the first fatal contact in Tahuata, they had been wary of European ships approaching their shores. If any ventured near, they either did their utmost to repel them, or were deliberately submissive to avoid reprisals, knowing that the cannons of the outsiders made them invincible. They showed no mercy, however, in the face of European weakness. This scenario was repeated on each South Pacific island approached by European ships. The navigators who followed the Spanish and the Dutch, including the *Bounty*, paid the price for the actions of their predecessors.

The era of scientific expeditions

The English rediscover breadfruit

The Marquesans cannot but have been unsettled by the tragic episode of the Spanish landfall in Tahuata, which was reported from island to island. The story crossed the South Pacific Ocean and, after travelling through the Tuamotus, eventually reached the Society Islands, 1,500 kilometres away. In 1769, 174 years after the event, Tupaia recounted the story to James Cook. It is no surprise that, being the first Europeans to land in Tahiti in 1767, Samuel Wallis and his crew were not made to feel welcome. Ariʻi Amo, the king[27] of Tahiti, and Queen Purea, his wife, immediately recognised them as the infamous whites described by the Marquesans. The Tahitian army was summoned and their fleet of 100 *pahi tamaʻi* (double war canoes) was gathered. The canoes were loaded with stones before launching an assault on the *Dolphin*. The attack continued for four days without respite, until the *Dolphin*'s cannons shattered the Tahitian fleet and army. Gunshots were fired into the crowd on shore and several houses were destroyed, which caused the Islanders to panic. The Marquesans had been right: these white men were invincible. Ariʻi Amo resolved to surrender. He sent the queen to negotiate with Wallis, and the Tahitians adopted a friendlier approach towards the visitors. In the aftermath, Wallis could not understand why such a welcoming people had initially waged such fierce battle against them. He found them so affable that he later downplayed the battle, reporting no more than four Tahitian casualties. The truth was later revealed by the *Dolphin*'s quartermaster, George Robertson, who provided a full account of the scale of the attacks and of the violence of the British response.[28]

Wallis' *Dolphin* and Philip Carteret's *Swallow* departed together from England in search of *Terra Australis*, but their ships were separated once they sailed into the Pacific. Wallis continued his journey alone and discovered Tahiti, while Carteret sailed on in a southerly direction. On 2 July 1767, Robert Pitcairn, a 15-year-old sailor, sighted an island and it was named after him. Battered by violent breakers, landfall could not be made. The *Bounty* mutineers' ultimate island was then uninhabited, yet

---

27   The terms 'queen' and 'king' were given to the *ariʻi* by European explorers.
28   George Robertson, *An Account of the Discovery of Tahiti. From the Journal of George Robertson, Master of HMS Dolphin*, London, Folio Society, 1955.

Polynesians had lived there, and on neighbouring Henderson, between the 10th and the 16th centuries. They had introduced the *'uru* and several other varieties of trees and had built *marae* (temples).[29] Pitcairn lay on the Polynesian route from Mangareva to Rapa Nui. Tahitian legends about the mythical navigator Rata recall frequent interaction between the Gambier Islands, Pitcairn and the three other islands in the area: Oeno, Ducie and Henderson. All of them were mapped by Tupaia. Mangarevan narratives also testify to heroes calling at these islands when travelling to and from Rapa Nui. Further information concerning the Polynesian settlement of Pitcairn is provided in Chapter 2.

Louis-Antoine de Bougainville landed in Tahiti the year after Wallis, in 1768. Little did he know that his rival British explorer was to thank for the warm welcome he received. He dubbed Tahitians the kindest people on earth, and the Island of Tahiti, 'Paradise regained' or 'New Cythera'.[30]

Given this reputation, it was only natural that the British Admiralty should choose Tahiti as home for a scientific expedition led by Lieutenant James Cook, with an official purpose to observe the transit of Venus in 1769. Two centuries after the Spanish, Joseph Banks, Daniel Carlsson Solander and Sydney Parkinson, all renowned European naturalists, were thus allowed to take a fresh interest in breadfruit, of which they provided detailed descriptions and several sketches. Echoing Quirós, their praise resuscitated interest in the fruit. Like Marquesans, Tahitians were keen on breadfruit, which they called *'uru* (not *mei* as in the Marquesas). As their staple food, its flowering and fruiting determined Tahitian seasons: *tau 'auhune* was the season of plenty, when *'uru* was abundant; and *tau o'e* the season of scarcity. The shift from *tau o'e* to *tau 'auhune* was marked by the rise of a cluster of small stars, *Matari'i* (the Pleiades or 'Small Eyes'). *Matari'i* sparkle at twilight above the horizon around 20 November, when breadfruit trees are in bloom. It was the occasion for Tahitians to celebrate returning abundance: they would serve huge collective meals with breadfruit galore; sing *pāta'uta'u* songs in celebration of the *'uru*; and attend performances by *'arioi* (professional performers and followers of 'Oro, the god of fertility and abundance). Everyone was invited, including deities and the deceased.

---

29   Kirch, 1988, pp 26–31.
30   Louis-Antoine de Bougainville, *Voyage autour du Monde par la Frégate du Roi La Boudeuse et la Flûte l'Etoile (1767–68)*, Paris, La Découverte Poche, 1997 (1771), p 131.

The period of abundance lasted for six months, until late May, when festivities came to an end. Deities and the deceased were urged to return to the spirit world. Breadfruit season was over. Tahitians now had to tap into the fermentation pits where breadfruit was stored. The Pleiades were thus a Tahitian time marker. Their appearance and disappearance at dusk allowed Tahitians to attune their lunar calendar to their astral calendar and to the cycle of seasons.

Cook and his crew stayed in Tahiti at the time of plenty. They noticed that special care was bestowed on breadfruit trees, which provided for the Tahitians' needs. As the Spaniards also observed in the Marquesas, only part of the harvest was consumed during the season of plenty and the surplus was spared for the fermentation pits, in anticipation of the forthcoming season of scarcity. Some time after they had sailed back to England, and at the recommendation of Banks, the British Admiralty decided to harvest and transplant breadfruit saplings to the West Indies to provide cheap food for the slaves of the colonies. The breadfruit mission was entrusted to Lieutenant William Bligh on the *Bounty* in 1788. The English, therefore, embarked on the same mission that Quirós had envisioned and suggested to the king of Spain, to no avail, two centuries earlier.

The origins of the breadfruit tree

The *mei* or *'uru* (*Artocarpus altilis*) tree is of the Moraceae family and originates from South-East Asia.[31] Different species of *Artocarpus* grow naturally in Indonesian forests, and all belong to the jackfruit genus (*Artocarpus heterophyllus*). It is from this species that the three tree varieties found in Oceania derive. The first variety, *Artocarpus camansi*, is native to New Guinea and has spread over to the Philippines. It is closely related to *Artocarpus altilis*, the Polynesian breadfruit tree. Like the latter, its fruit is harvested as a staple food, but it is mainly the seeds, rather than the flesh, that are eaten. *Artocarpus mariannensis*, the second variety, is only grown in Micronesia, also mostly for its seeds. *Artocarpus altilis*, the third variety, is the only species that made it to Polynesia. It is a seedless species and consumed for its flesh. Originally from New Guinea, it was domesticated in Melanesia. Figure 1.1 plots the original distribution areas of the three species of breadfruit.

---

31 Arthur W Whistler, *Plants of the Canoe People*, Lawai, Kaua'i, Hawai'i, National Tropical Botanical Garden, 2009.

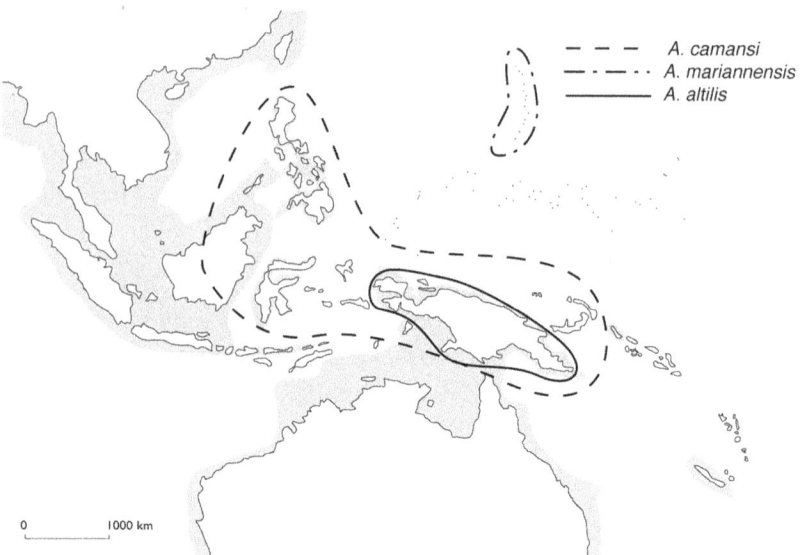

Figure 1.1. Geographic origin of the breadfruit and related species. The shaded areas correspond to the lands that emerged during the last glaciation about 10,000 years ago.
Source: Lebot (2002, pp 114–15).

One needs to distinguish three distribution areas: the area of origin, where the species can be found in the wild; the domestication area, where it was first purposefully replanted; and the diversification area, where careful cultivation has generated several cultivars.[32] Concerning *Artocarpus altilis*, Melanesia is both its origin and domestication area, and Polynesia is its diversification area.[33] Wild species seem to grow only in New Guinea, whereas only cultivated forms can be found elsewhere in Melanesia.[34] Human agency introduced *Artocarpus altilis* into eastern Polynesia, the Marquesas, Hawai'i and other tiny atolls. Without doubt, it has also been repeatedly modified by humans, by means of seeds and suckers,[35] self-fertilisation and cross-fertilisation, as part of a slow, complex and ever-evolving process of domestication and diversification. Because it is a

---

32 A cultivar is a plant variety that has been obtained through growing, generally after selection for its arguably unique characteristics. The selection process might be for aesthetic or technical purposes, or depend on growth speed, resistance to diseases or adaptation to biotopes.
33 Annie Walter, 'Notes sur les cultivars d'arbre à pain dans le Nord de Vanuatu', *Journal de la Société des Océanistes*, vol 88, no 1, 1989, pp 3–18.
34 Vincent Lebot, 'La domestication des plantes en Océanie et les contraintes de la voie asexuée', *Journal de la Société des Océanistes*, 2002, pp 114–15.
35 A sucker is a shoot that springs from the root of a vegetable. It may grow autonomously and be replanted as a new individual. This offspring is genetically identical to its mother plant.

seedless species, it can be extensively cultivated by transplanting suckers. Breadfruit trees found in forests are residues of former plantations. They do not grow in regions outside the tropics, such as Rapa Nui or New Zealand.

It is highly likely that the Lapita populations that spread from northern Melanesia to western Polynesia around 3,000 years ago also spread the breadfruit plant. Linguists have been able to reconstruct a Proto-Malayo-Polynesian (PMP) etymon of *Artocarpus*: **kuluR*, which designates the species that grows naturally in Indonesian forests. As they journeyed to the central Pacific, settlers transplanted the plant and, through selection, created a new species, *Artocarpus altilis*, which has retained **kuluR*, its original Malayo-Polynesian designation, in Proto-Oceanic (POC) language. It is from this etymon that reflections in Polynesian languages are derived.[36] A comparison of cognates of "*ulu*" in Polynesian languages shows that "*uru*', or its cognates in other Polynesian languages, is the generic term for breadfruit in one area of Polynesia. In another area '*mei*' prevails, as in the Marquesas Islands. In Tahiti, the two terms coexist as "*uru*' and '*may-ore*'. The noun "*uru*' is derived from the PMP **kuluR*, while '*mei*' is derived directly from the Proto-Austronesian (PAN) **Kma(ŋ)(s)i*, which is known as **MaRo* in Proto-Remote-Oceanian (PROC). Moreover, '*mei*' prevails in all Micronesian languages.[37] The wide distribution of '*mei*' and "*uru*' across Oceania makes it hard to determine which is the etymon. It may be presumed that one was the generic name in the first place, and that the other designates a variety that gradually supplanted it and thus became a generic term, too. Linguists have not yet resolved this issue.

The cultural uses of breadfruit

Breadfruit trees are mainly used for their food: their edible fruit was formerly the staple food of tropical eastern Polynesia. Polynesians generally steam breadfruit, either in traditional ovens (*umu*) once they have been peeled, or simply on a wood fire with their skin intact: the skin protects the flesh and, once fully charred, is scraped off before the flesh is consumed. The flesh may also be kneaded and mixed with coconut milk, which makes a kind of sweet dough called *ka'aku* in the Marquesas. In anticipation of the season of scarcity, peeled breadfruit is stored for several months in underground silos lined with cordyline sheets

---

36 SJ Greenhill & R Clark, 'POLLEX-Online: The Polynesian Lexicon Project Online', *Oceanic Linguistics*, vol 50, no 2, 2011, pp 551–59, pollex.org.nz.
37 *Micronesian Comparative Dictionary*, www.trussel2.com/mcd/pmc-intro.htm.

for insulation from the soil. This fermented sour dough is called *māhi* in Tahiti and *mā* in the Marquesas. It may be consumed raw during the season of scarcity or on sea voyages. Polynesians, however, seem to prefer it kneaded and mixed with newly plucked and freshly steamed fruit. This dough, called *pōpoi* or *poi*, tastes less bitter and is generally served as a side dish. Cooking methods may vary according to cultivars. For instance, some varieties cannot be cooked on a wood fire, while others have a softer flesh that mixes easily with coconut milk.

In traditional medicine, sap, buds, young shoots, fruit stalks, petioles, mouldy pulp and even the inner bark of young branches were used for various cures. Flowers, for example, were toasted and rubbed on gums to relieve toothache. The white latex sap that flows from the bark was used as chewing gum or cosmetics. Men applied it fresh to flatten their hair back. Women boiled the sap with *monoi* in a clamshell (*pahua*) above a flame before applying it to their hair, too. It was also used to make poultices on sprains, muscle strains and contusions, and to catch birds. Eventually, the bark of young branches came to be used for the production of beige-tinted *tapa* (bark cloth).

Where breadfruit trees proved most valuable was in shipbuilding. In Tahitian forests, one can feel very small in the presence of majestic breadfruit tree trunks that tower 25 metres high, with their fruit completely out of reach. Their timber was once coveted for large canoe building. Polynesians would carve planks of 2–10 metres in length and 0.5–1 metres in width; these were sewn together with sinnet and calibrated and adjusted to make the hulls of canoes. Latex was mixed with coconut fibre and served as pitch to caulk seam holes, seams and cracks. After the *Bounty* mutiny, such Tahitian building techniques were put to good use by James Morrison in the collective building of the *Resolution*, a schooner with which he intended to sail from Tahiti to Batavia before working his way on to England. Shortly after construction, however, the *Resolution* was seized by the British authorities of the *Pandora* and renamed *Matavy*. Under British stewardship, the *Matavy* made a valiant voyage as far as Batavia, where she was sold off to carry on plying the Indian Ocean until a venerable old age. She thus fared much better than the *Pandora*, which ran aground on the Great Barrier Reef with her *Bounty* prisoners on board.

Tahitians were able to build canoes measuring well over 20 metres in length, with the longest recorded by James Cook extending 33 metres. During his second voyage in 1774, Cook recorded a fleet of over

300 canoes in Tahiti, including 160 double canoes. Since this single fleet covered only part of Tahiti and did not include small fishing canoes, the total Tahitian fleet at the time may have numbered in the thousands. The building of those canoes claimed much breadfruit timber. It was therefore necessary to plant tens of thousands of trees to sustain shipbuilding, and the same amount again for food. Under such circumstances, the fact that Tahitians agreed to cede many saplings to help William Bligh fulfil both of his breadfruit missions, first on the *Bounty* and then again on the *Providence*, testifies to one of the principal arguments of this paper. In the absence of alternative methods, Polynesian Islanders were willing to comply with the whims of Europeans rather than confront their wrath.

Figure 1.2. In this painting, modern double canoes built on the model of the old double canoes, are visible in the foreground while, in the background, like ghosts of the past, the silhouette of the old double canoes is evident.

Source: Henri Python (n.d.).

English discovery of Polynesian maritime science

Tupaia tells the English about Mendaña's call at the Marquesas

It was only after James Cook's first visit to Tahiti that the dramatic shifts in Tahitian behaviour towards Samuel Wallis started making sense. The clues were supplied by Tupaia, who narrated the Spanish attack in Tahuata in 1595. Tupaia specifically marked this tragic event on the map that he drew at Cook's request. The map featured all of the lands known to Tupaia, from the Marquesas to Fiji.

Tupaia's map recorded four narratives about European vessels calling at Pacific Islands, including at Tahuata.[38] According to Tupaia, historically four islands were visited by ships similar to those of the English. One of the islands on Tupaia's map that is of particular interest to this essay was spelled 'Ohevatoutouai'. Experts now agree that it corresponds to Tahuata in the Marquesas.[39] The accompanying comment states that a European ship had called there long before. Tupaia did not provide a date, but the Tahitian measure of time was generations, which they called *uʻi*. For instance, any event that had occurred at the time of one's parents was said to be two *uʻi* (two generations old – one's own and one's parents). If the event occurred during the time of grandparents it was three *uʻi* old. If from the time of great-grandparents, it was four *uʻi* old. Tahitians stopped counting beyond four *uʻi*. Events in the deeper past became incorporated into genealogical narratives. Since Tupaia did not date the Tahuata events according to *uʻi* counts, it can be inferred that they occurred in the distant past. His recitation of his genealogy made no sense to the foreigners, who had insufficient knowledge of Tahitian language and culture. The British could not fathom that the seven or eight named ancestors were time markers, and they paid them scant attention.

---

38   Robert Koenig, 'Les navires européens de la carte de Tupaia. Une tentative d'identification', *Bulletin de la Société des études océaniennes*, no 217, 1981, pp 985–91.
39   HAH Driessen, 'Outriggerless Canoes and Glorious Beings: Pre-Contact Prophecies in the Society Islands', *Journal of Pacific History*, vol 17, no 1, 1982, pp 3–28.

In reference to the European call at Tahuata, Tupaia stated: '*maa te taata, pahi rahi, iti te pahi no Britane*'. A form of Tahitian pidgin, the sentence literally translates as either 'food men, ship(s) large, small ship of the British', or 'many men, ship(s) large, small ship of the British'. This in turn may mean 'some men took food, their ships were larger than those of the British', or 'some men were eaten, their ships were larger than those of the British' or, alternatively, 'there was a crowd (on board), their ships were larger than those of the British'. Since no European ships had sailed into this archipelago since Mendaña, Tupaia must have been referring to the four Spanish vessels that had anchored there to restock. Arriving in 1774, Cook was thus only the second European explorer to visit the archipelago, and Tupaia was telling him the narrative of Mendaña's call at the Marquesas. It may be inferred that, when the Tahitians saw Wallis' ship, they assumed the Spaniards had returned and therefore launched an attack.

Tupaia's map contained other valuable information, including one of prime interest to *Bounty* history. While Tahiti stood in the centre of the map, a group of islands with names prefixed by *Hiti* figured on the edges. According to Teuira Henry,[40] the three outermost of these islands, named *Hiti-tautaumai*, *Hiti-tautaureva* and *Hiti-tautauatu*, correspond to Oeno, Henderson and Ducie, east of the Gambier Islands. Henry also claims that Pitcairn Island was called *Hiti-aurereva*. These islands were quoted in Henry's Rata legend[41] (see Molle & Hermann, Chapter 2).

Polynesians were apprised of each passing European vessel

Tupaia also noted that another European ship had sailed past Ra'iatea. The statement on the map referring to Ra'iatea said: '*Tupuna nō Tuapaia, pahi taio*', which literally translates as 'Tupaia grandparents, ship(s) friend(s)'. In other words: 'in the time of Tupaia's grandparents, there was/were (some) friendly vessel(s)'. Tupaia was not yet born when Jacob Roggeveen sailed past Bora Bora and Maupiti in 1722. The English believed that he was in his 40s in 1769, which places his birthdate between 1724 and 1729, and therefore it was not possible for him to have seen the

---

40   Teuira Henry, *Tahiti aux Temps Anciens*, Société des océanistes, no 1, Paris, Musée de l'Homme, 1968, pp 75–76.
41   Henry, 1968, pp 488–500.

ships in 1722. His grandparents, however, may have spotted them on the horizon. As the ships did not stop, they caused no harm and were categorised as 'friendly' ships.

Tupaia also made reference to a European shipwreck near 'Anaa in the Tuamotu Islands: '*Tupaia, ta'ata nō pahi mate*'. This translates as 'Tupaia, people of the ship dead', and may be interpreted as 'in Tupaia's time, the passengers of a ship perished'. Could it have been the *Africaanshe Galey*, one of Roggeveen's three ships that ran aground on Takapoto's reef in 1722? If this was the case, it may seem that Tupaia was mistaken about the date as the shipwreck occurred during his grandfather's time. It must be noted, however, that a couple of years may have elapsed before news of the shipwreck reached Tahiti. A couple of years after the event, in 1724, Tupaia may have been born, in which case the event may indeed coincide with 'Tupaia's time'. What Tupaia did not know was that the ship that was lost in the Tuamotus was part of the same fleet sighted off Ra'iatea and sailed in the same year.

Why did Tupaia locate the shipwreck on 'Anaa and not Takapoto? Once again, Tupaia was not misinformed. At the time, most of the westerly Tuamotu Islands were virtually under the control of the 'Anaa warriors,[42] and Tahitians had no other name for the Tuamotu archipelago than *Fenua 'Anaa*, the 'Land of the people of 'Anaa'.

Tupaia declared that Samuel Wallis was not the first European to have discovered Tahiti; another ship had called there before him. Given that no European nation or explorer claimed to have discovered Tahiti before Wallis, it is impossible to determine to whom Tupaia was referring. According to Tupaia, it was an 'enemy' ship that clashed with the Islanders: '*Metua o te o tupuna Tupaia pahi toa*', which translates as 'at the time of Tupaia's grandparents' ancestors, an enemy ship (appeared)'. Some scholars have speculated that Tupaia was referring to the *San Lesme*, one of Juan Sebastián Elcano's Spanish ships that, according to Robert Langdon, ran aground on the Amanu reef in the Tuamotu.[43] Two ship's guns were excavated from the reef in 1969, which confirmed a shipwreck. Langdon suggests that the ship may have sailed past Tahiti before sinking in Amanu in 1526, 243 years (12 generations) before Tupaia's time. For Tupaia,

---

42   Frédéric Torrente, *Buveurs de Mers Mangeurs de Terres*, Papeete, Te Pito O Te Fenua, 2012.
43   Langdon, 1978.

this went back to ancient times. Langdon's hypothesis is now strongly disputed because recent studies have identified the guns as being of more recent manufacture.[44]

Be that as it may, Tupaia's map is evidence that the European ships that sailed the South Pacific were sighted, recorded and reported to the inhabitants of other islands. Polynesians knew what they had to do as soon as they spotted a European ship on the horizon. This state of affairs even allowed some *tahuʻa* to make prophecies. One of them, Vaita, high priest of Taputapuatea, prophesied shortly before Wallis' arrival that canoes without outriggers would be coming. When he was met with disbelief, he set a *ʻumete* (flat, oblong wooden dish) afloat with stones in the bottom. The craft did not capsize, contrary to the general opinion of the time.[45]

In eastern Polynesia, the last great clash between Europeans and Polynesians occurred in Tubuaʻi, 500 kilometres south of Tahiti, in the Austral Islands. Tupaia reported the existence of Tubuaʻi to James Cook in 1769 while they were off the coast of its neighbouring island Rurutu. In his quest to discover the famed southern continent, Cook took an interest in information about all the lands in the vicinity. Tupaia also informed him of Mutu, an island within a day's sailing to the east, which he recorded on his map. It was not until Cook's third voyage in 1777 that he sailed to this island, known to its inhabitants as Tupuaʻi (Tubuaʻi). The approaching *Resolution* was hemmed in by many canoes and Cook noticed with surprise that the Islanders spoke Tahitian, and were therefore closely related to the people of the Society Islands. One of their chiefs even bore the Tamatoa title, which was held by the most prestigious Society Island *ariʻi*, Opoʻa, in Raʻiatea. Raʻiatea is home to the Taputapuatea *marae*, the international *marae* of which none other than Tupaia was high priest. The people of Tubuaʻi had likely been informed by those of the Society Islands about European visitors. They knew they were a threat and would probably attempt an attack. Cook, however, deeming the pass too hazardous to navigate, decided against laying anchor in the lagoon and sailed away. It may be surmised that he very narrowly escaped an ambush.

---

44   Max Guerout, 'Les vestiges d'Amanu', *Bulletin de la Société des Etudes Océaniennes*, no 292/293, 2002, pp 12–23.
45   Henry, 1968, pp 4–5.

The *Bounty* was not so fortunate when it ventured into the lagoon 20 years later. Carrying Fletcher Christian and his mutineers in search of a safe settlement, Tubuaʻi was Christian's preferred choice. As might be expected, however, the mutineers were not welcome and were ambushed by the Tubuaʻi warriors who allowed the ship to sail into the lagoon before launching an attack with their war canoes loaded with stones. The mutineers returned fire. The bloodshed was such that the location of the battle is known as Bloody Bay.

The *Bounty* headed back to Tahiti to briefly restock and returned to Tubuaʻi on 23 June 1789. Tamatoa gave them a courteous welcome on this occasion, most likely to avoid a repeat of the earlier carnage. Tensions remained high, however, and during one particularly bloody battle, 66 indigenous people lost their lives. Christian eventually had to concede that Tubuaʻi was not the place for them to settle and the mutineers departed in search for a safer location.

European recognition of Polynesians as navigators

It wasn't until James Cook's voyages that the navigation skills of Polynesians became known to Europeans. The turning point was when Tupaia sailed with Cook and, aside from creating his famed map, he imparted a deep knowledge of Tahitian maritime science. It came to be understood that Tahitians had considerable navigational experience and were acquainted with many islands. Joseph Banks noted in his journal on 12 July 1769, on the eve of their departure from Tahiti:

> This morn Tupia came on board, he had renewed his resolves of going with us to England, a circumstance which gives me much satisfaction. He is certainly a most proper man, well born, chief Tahowa or priest of this Island, consequently skilled in the mysteries of their religion; but what makes him more than anything else desireable is his experience in the navigation of these people and knowledge of the Islands in these seas; he has told us the names of above 70, the most of which he has himself been at.[46]

---

46   Joseph Banks, *Banks's Journal: Daily Entries*, 12 July 1769, southseas.nla.gov.au/journals/banks/about.html

According to Banks, Tupaia was a *tahuʻa*,[47] a 'priest' in conjunction with a navigator. His knowledge proved invaluable, both to the continuation of Cook's voyage, and to contemporary understanding of the scientific achievements of 18th-century Polynesians.

Five years after Tupaia's voyage, young Puhoro – another Tahitian navigator who steered the Spanish across the Pacific – was taken to Peru by Captain Jose de Andia y Varela in 1774 and impressed people with his expertise in reading the winds. He divided the horizon into 16 sectors, each bearing a name and showing a different direction, as on a compass board. Andia y Varela noted:

> One of them named Puhoro came to Lima on this occasion in the frigate, and from him and others, I was able to find out the method by which they navigate on the high seas: which is the following. They have no mariner's compass, but divide the horizon into sixteen parts, taking for the cardinal points those at which the sun rises and sets … He knows the direction in which his destination bears: he sees, also, whether he has the wind aft, or on one or other beam, or on the quarter.[48]

Puhoro explained that, to navigate at night, Polynesians read the stars, of which they knew a vast number:

> When the night is a clear one, they steer by the stars; and this is the easiest navigation for them because, these being many [in number], not only do they note by them the bearing on which the several islands with which they are in touch lie, but also the harbours in them, so that they make straight for the entrance by following the rhumb of the particular star that rises or sets over it; and they hit it off with as much precision as the most expert navigator of civilized nations could achieve.[49]

As reported by Andia y Varela, the art of navigating was the preserve of Polynesian master mariners called *faʻatere*: 'There are many master mariners among the people, the term for whom is in their language fatere'.[50] The

---

47   *Tahuʻa*: an expert, one who has special knowledge; for instance, a *tahuʻa vaʻa* is expert in canoe-building; a *tahuʻa fare* is expert in house-building; a *tahuʻa tautai* is expert in fishing seasons; a *tahuʻa räʻau* is a 'doctor', or expert in medicinal plants; a *tahuʻa pure* is expert in prayers and incantations at religious ceremonies; a *tahuʻa marae* oversees the building of *marae*, or religious precincts; a *tahuʻa-nui* or *tahuʻa-rahi* is a high priest in charge of religious ceremonies.
48   BG Corney, *The Quest and Occupation of Tahiti by Emissaries of Spain during the Years 1772–6*, vol 2, London, Hakluyt Society, 1913–19, p 284.
49   Corney, 1913–19, p 284.
50   Corney, 1913–19, p 284.

term *fa'atere* recurs in narratives about the birth of stars.⁵¹ It refers to a star or planet that steered a constellation, which itself symbolised a canoe. *Fa'atere* were experts in this highly developed Tahitian science. One wonders, today, what might have been the full nature of that science.

Language barriers prevented Andia y Varela, Cook, Banks and their fellow travellers from collecting more than fragments of information about traditional Polynesian navigation. To understand how Tahitians used the stars and to make sense of what Tupaia or Puhoro tried to explain to them would have required a mastery of the language. Naturalist Johann Reinhold Forster lamented this fact in his journal in 1774, during Cook's second voyage:

> There is among them in each district one or more Tātā-orrèro who knows their Cosmogony and Theogony (which I could not learn, in so short a time,) who knows their Geography, History, Winds, Stars etc., Almanac.⁵²

Tahitian stellar science was, therefore, not collected and studied by late 18th-century European explorers, and was all but lost by the early 19th century. It was not until 1941 that the American astronomer Maud Makemson⁵³ resurrected the practice through her study of the 'birth of stars', as reported in *Ancient Tahiti* (1928). Only then did the scientific community become aware of the existence of an elaborate science of Polynesian astronomy.

Over his three Pacific voyages, Cook commented on the detail and diversity of Tahitian canoes. Artists commemorated them, too, and depicted the various models such as the *pūhoe*, a small outrigger canoe carved in a single tree trunk; the *pahi*, a double sea canoe made of planks sewn together; the *va'a taurua* or *tīpaerua*, a double canoe with vertical bows for coastal navigation; the *pahi tama'i*, a double war canoe operated by a hundred warriors; the *va'a motu*, a lagoon outrigger; and the *va'a tira*, a double-hulled canoe with long fishing rods at its bow.⁵⁴

---

51 Henry, 1968, pp 368–73.
52 Johann Reinhold Forster, *Observations Made during a Voyage Round the World*, Honolulu, University of Hawai'i, 1996 (1778), p 530.
53 Maud Makemson, *The Morning Star Rises, An Account of Polynesian Astronomy*, New Haven, Yale University Press, 1941.
54 J Neyret, *Les Pirogues Océaniennes*, Association des amis des musées de la Marine, Paris, 1974; A Haddon & J Hornell, *Canoes of Oceania*, Honolulu, Bishop Museum Press, 1975; E Dodd, *Polynesian Seafaring*, Lymington, Hampshire, Nautical Publishing Company, 1972.

When a large naval manoeuvre was organised by *Ari'i Tū* in Matavai Bay in 1774, Cook marvelled at the sight of more than 300 canoes with 7,000 warriors on board, ready to engage in battle with the neighbouring island of Eimeo (Mo'orea). He was told that such canoes sometimes sailed several days to distant islands and ferried back pearls, mother-of-pearl and red feathers. As a navigator, Cook appreciated that the Tahitians were master mariners who, without any instruments, steered by the stars. He noted as much in his journal:

> In their longer voyages, they steer by the sun in the day, and in the night by the stars; all of which they distinguish by names, and know in what part of the heavens they will appear in any of the months during that they are visible in their horizon; they also know the time of their annual appearing and disappearing with more precision than will easily be believed by an European astronomer.[55]

In 1769, Cook and a group of British scientists were commissioned to observe the transit of Venus in front of the sun. Cook elected to land in Matavai Bay, at the same spot visited by Samuel Wallis in 1767. Matavai was a regular destination for British navigators during the 18th century: William Bligh on the *Bounty* in 1788, on which Fletcher Christian briefly returned twice in 1789; Bligh again with the *Providence* in 1792; and London Missionary Society (LMS) missionaries on the *Duff* in 1797. French and Spanish navigators also had favourite landing bays.

Cook's party built an observatory at Tefauroa – which they renamed Point Venus (now known as Pointe Vénus). The site was connected to Polynesian lore and symbolic to Tahitians. Notably, it housed *Te ana-vaha-rau* ('The cave-with-many-holes'),[56] an initiation school for the transmission of consecrated Polynesian knowledge of cosmogony, theogony, genealogies, myths, music, history, oratory, geography, astronomy, medicine, the measurement of time, climatology, shipbuilding and navigation skills.

Most notably, Tefauroa was once home to Hiro, an outstanding legendary Polynesian navigator. Hiro's great deeds were orally transmitted and celebrated throughout eastern Polynesia and his visits are recalled to this day. In Taha'a, for example, a group of rocks bear the name *Te-'ūri-a-Hiro*

---

55 John Hawkesworth, *An Account of the Voyages Undertaken by Order of Her Present Majesty for Making Discoveries in the Southern Hemisphere and Successively Performed by Commodore Byron, Captain Wallis, Captain Carteret and Captain Cook, in the Dolphin …, Drawn up from the Journals …*, London, W Stratham, 1773, p 227.
56 Translation, Henry, 1968, p 81.

('Hiro's dog'). A large oblong stone in Maupiti is known as *Te-pahi-o-Hiro* ('Hiro's canoe') and a cliff, *Te-tūturira'a-a-Hiro* ('Hiro's one-knee support'). In Bora Bora, one may visit *Te-timora'a-a-Hiro* ('Hiro's *timo* game') and *Te-oE-a-Hiro* ('Hiro's bell'). At Huahine, *Te-a-hoe-Hiro* ('Hiro's paddle') can be observed in relief on a cliff. Also in Huahine, as in the Papeno'o valley in Tahiti, peaks carry the name *Te-ure-a-Hiro* ('Hiro's phallus'). In Ha'apape (Mahina) and Tahiti, there is a sand dune built with his own hand, *Te-Mou'a-a-Hiro* ('Hiro's mountain'), and a reef, *To'a-Hiro* ('Hiro's reef'). One of the summits on Ra'ivavae Island is dedicated to him, *Te-Mou'a-o-Hiro* ('Hiro's mountain'). In Rapanui, where Hiro is the god of rain, there is a stone containing a natural hole that the natives call *Pu o Hiro* ('Hiro's horn').

As with all canoe names, the choice of name for Hiro's canoe, *Hōhōio* ('*Intriguing*'), was deliberate. The day it was launched, the star '*Ana-mua* (Antares) sent a gust of wind as a sign of welcome, which meant that the canoe fell under the protection of the gods. Thus imbued with *mana* (supernatural power transmitted by gods), the canoe participated in Hiro's legendary feats, such as towing islands while the Islanders slept (Hiro was forced to flee when the Islanders were alerted by a cock's crow). With Venus as his guide, Hiro sailed around archipelagos, sometimes meeting other heroes like Pai, the Tahitian equivalent of Hercules.

Ironically, Tefauroa has since become the seat of a number of European legends,[57] the most prominent in the early contact period being that Pointe Vénus was Paradise regained. After the *Bounty* mutiny, Bligh himself described the place as 'the Paradise of the World' on account of his men seizing the ship allegedly to the cheers of 'Huzza for Otaheite!'[58] Nowadays, Pointe Vénus is strongly associated with the near-legendary figure in British maritime culture of Cook. Through a process of enduring eulogising and mythmaking, Cook's severe mistreatment of Pacific Islanders during the course of his last voyage has all but been forgotten. At the time of the *Bounty*'s first stay in 1788, even Tahitian chief Tu and his retinue held John Webber's portrait of Captain Cook as 'intensely sacred' and, 'taking no chances' as Anne Salmond puts it, they invoked Cook's *mana* alongside their Tahitian ancestors in order to summon the

---

57   My thanks to Sylvie Largeaud-Ortega for providing the following analytical development of Pointe Vénus's early contact and post-contact history.
58   Bligh, in Owen Rutter (ed), *The Log of the Bounty: Being Lieutenant William Bligh's Log of the Proceedings of His Majesty's Armed Vessel Bounty in a Voyage to the South Seas, to Take the Breadfruit from the Society Islands to the West Indies*, vol 1, London, Golden Gockerel Press, 1937, p 381.

presence of 'Oro, the god of abundance. In the same spirit, they asked Bligh to inscribe on the back of a canvas the 1789 arrival and departure dates of the *Bounty* and of the *Providence* in 1792. Pointe Vénus now boasts a small Captain James Cook memorial, which is visited by tourists from throughout the English-speaking world. Cook's figure has reached such a heroic status that, to many, the British captain could only have been killed by Hawaiians in 1779 because they mistook him for a deity. As proposed by Gananath Obeyesekere in 1992, this form of history writing may tell us more about the West anointing their own deities than anything else.[59]

At Pointe Vénus stands another memorial – a stone erected by the Pitcairn descendants of the *Bounty* mutineers, featuring carvings of the *Bounty* and the faces of mutineers Christian and Adam Smith. Here thrives the legend of European romantic rebels who dared confront abusive authority and chose freedom in the Pacific. Bligh, who is not celebrated at Pointe Vénus, has nevertheless reached similarly legendary status, although of a notorious kind. As discussed in Chapters 4, 5 and 6 of this volume, novels and movies have secured Bligh's global reputation as an inordinately cruel and vicious officer. Pointe Vénus is, therefore, also haunted by the legend of this other British captain.

Pointe Vénus was the place where the first missionaries from the freshly created LMS appeared on the *Duff* on 5 March 1797. The missionaries were bringing dictionaries, compiled for them by *Bounty* prisoners Peter Heywood and James Morrison, with the purpose of spreading the Gospel. It is not within the scope of this chapter to discuss whether Biblical characters may be said to have legendary status; what cannot be gainsaid, however, is that narratives about a single God, Adam and Eve and their descendants surreptitiously became more widely known throughout Polynesia than indigenous narratives of Hiro. The Bible gradually superseded the traditional Polynesian knowledge that was ritually taught at *'Te ana-vaha-rau.* To this day, the sighting of the *Duff* in Matavai Bay has been officially celebrated as a holiday in French Polynesia.

At the foot of the Pointe Vénus lighthouse has sprouted one last, utterly spurious, European legend that revolves around Scottish writer Robert Louis Stevenson (one of his *Bounty*-related fictions is discussed in this

---

59 Gananath Obeyesekere, *The Apotheosis of Captain Cook. European Mythmaking in the Pacific*, Honolulu, University of Hawai'i Press, 1992.

volume, see Naugrette, Chapter 5). A plaque celebrating Stevenson's alleged 'feelings of emotion', as he stood facing the building in 1888, was hung there in 1994. While the quote is apocryphal,[60] it has further contributed to the displacement of original native heroes like Hiro, and to the influx of Western legends associated with Pointe Vénus. Nowadays, many Polynesian organisations are actively reviving Pointe Vénus as a Polynesian cultural hub.

Polynesian maritime science

Tupaia, Captain Cook's Tahitian pilot

What remains of Polynesian maritime science today has partly been transmitted through the notes of European explorers. It is mostly thanks to their written observations and those of the naturalists on board their vessels that Polynesian mastery of the sea can be understood. Tupaia's map provides many valuable clues in this respect. Tupaia himself enumerated 130 islands and Johann Forster identified no less than 84 of them.[61]

After leaving Tahiti, Tupaia wished to visit his relatives once more and he steered James Cook towards the Leeward Islands, which became the explorer's first 'big' Pacific discoveries (Cook was unaware that the Dutch had been there before him). While Cook came to see Tupaia's skills as of use in finding the fabled southern continent, Tupaia was more interested in heading west where, within 10 or 12 days of sailing, several islands he had visited before were located, such as Samoa. He warned Cook that their return voyage north against prevailing winds and currents could take up to 30 days. Cook, however, was intent on abiding by the Admiralty's instructions and headed south regardless. Having discovered nothing of import, except the island of Rurutu (known to Tupaia as Hitiroa), Cook eventually followed Tupaia's advice and veered west in order to reach New Zealand. While he was on board the *Endeavour*, Tupaia was at all times able to identify the precise direction of Tahiti. On the day before he died in Batavia, he was still pointing at *Faupapa*, or Sirius, his native island's zenith star, which he proudly named *fetū roa*, the 'great star'.

---

60   For information on the design of the Pointe Vénus lighthouse, see Robert Veccella, 'Le phare de la pointe Vénus à Tahiti (1767–1868): 100 ans d'histoire de la baie de Matavai', Masters thesis, Université Bretagne Sud, 2016.
61   Forster, 1996, p 310.

In 1768, the year before Cook's arrival, Louis-Antoine de Bougainville also noted the proclivities of the Tahitians for navigation:[62]

> Finally, this nation's educated people – without being astronomers contrary to our gazettes' claims – have classified the most notable constellations; they know their diurnal motions, and they rely on them to steer their way in the open sea from island to island. With this navigation system, they may lose all sight of land sometimes for more than three hundred leagues. Their compass is the race of the sun during the day, and the position of the stars during the nights, which are almost always beautiful in the tropics. (Bougainville 1982: 266)[63]

However observant, Bougainville chose not to heed the desperate pleas of Aoutourou (Ahutoru), the young Tahitian who agreed to sail under his protection. Aoutourou insisted that Bougainville head for Ra'iatea, his native island, so that he might bid his relatives farewell. Had the French explorer complied, he would have discovered the islands of Huahine, Ra'iatea, Taha'a, Borabora and Maupiti – a privilege that was later bestowed on Cook.

During Cook's second voyage in 1772–74, he and naturalists Johann Forster and his son, Georg, verified the accuracy of Tupaia's map by visiting all of the islands that extended from the Marquesas in the east to Fiji in the west. The duration of their stay in Tahiti enabled them to write a valuable 700-entry dictionary registering 18th-century Tahitian lexicon.[64] (Sailing with Cook on his third voyage, William Bligh thus acquired some knowledge of the Tahitian language, which he used to negotiate the *Bounty* mission in 1788.) The Forsters recorded language wherever they landed and, across the vast ocean area traversed, they discovered that people shared idioms from the same family. Johann Forster even managed to register dialectal differences between Polynesian languages. He found that, in the Society Islands, there were variations between the Leeward Islands (Tahiti) and the Windward Islands (Borabora). Like Cook and

---

62   Louis-Antoine de Bougainville, *Voyage autour du monde par la frégate du Roi, 'La Boudeuse' et la flûte 'l'Etoile'*, Paris, Gallimard, 1982.
63   'Au reste, les gens instruits de cette nation, sans être astronomes, comme l'ont prétendu nos gazettes, ont une nomenclature des constellations les plus remarquables; ils en connaissaient le mouvement diurne, et ils s'en servent pour diriger leur route en pleine mer d'une île à l'autre. Dans cette navigation, quelquefois de plus de trois cents lieues, ils perdent toute vue de terre. Leur boussole est le cours du soleil pendant le jour, et la position des étoiles pendant les nuits, presque toujours belles entre les tropiques' (Bougainville, 1997).
64   KH Rensch, *The Language of the Noble Savage, the Linguistic Fieldwork of Reinhold and George Forster in Polynesia on Cook's Second Voyage to the Pacific 1772–1775*, Canberra, Archipelago Press, 2000.

Banks, he also observed the closeness of Maori and Tahitian customs and concluded that these islands were unquestionably interrelated. But, without any instruments of navigation, how could the inhabitants have travelled such long distances?

Two other Europeans of the early contact era spent considerable time in Tahiti: Maximo Rodriguez stayed 10 months at Tautira between 1774 and 1775;[65] the *Bounty*'s James Morrison spent a year and a half in Matavai between 1788 and 1791 (before and after the mutiny), and was involved in local shipbuilding.[66] Their journals are of great ethnographic value, but provide scant detail about Polynesian astronomical science. The journals of Samuel Wallis, Bougainville, Cook and Bligh also lack information on the topic. Reviewed by editors, these journals were at times stripped of information that may have been crucial for reconstructing traditional knowledge.[67]

Few astronomical clues have been handed down via Polynesian oral tradition. While genealogies, myths, fables and legends narrate the voyages of gods and demigods, they fail to offer practical details that align with modern-day scientific standards. When these oral communications are confronted with the testimonies of explorers, however, and when they are examined from a linguistic perspective, they yield highly valuable information.

Most of what is now known about ancient Polynesian astronomy may be traced back to testimonies from the LMS. Reverend John Orsmond's work, in particular, is a major source of information – collected from Tahitian King Pomare II and other witnesses to ancient Tahitian maritime science and astronomy from 1817 onward. Orsmond's original manuscript, which was given to Governor Charles Lavaud and was later lost in Paris, was partially rewritten by Teuira Henry, Orsmond's granddaughter. It was published in English in 1928 under the title *Ancient Tahiti*, and is particularly valued for its unique collection of Tahitian texts. Henry's censorship of certain aspects of Orsmond's original work resulted from her 'shock [at] pagan practices, especially polytheism, infanticide,

---

65 M Rodriguez, *Les Espagnols à Tahiti (1772–1776)*, Paris, Société des Océanistes, 1995.
66 James Morrison, *Journal de James Morrison*, Papeete, Société des Etudes Océaniennes, 1981.
67 Many of these journals are now available online at the National Library of Australia website southseas.nla.gov.au.

human sacrifice and the exuberance of the time'.[68] Fortunately, this censorship spared the sections of the manuscript that dealt with the less controversial themes of astronomy and navigation.

Europeans navigating with instruments in contrast with Polynesians navigating with stars

Given what we now know about the ancient Polynesian art of landfinding, to conclude this chapter I briefly compare European and Polynesian navigation skills during the period of early contact with Europeans and around the time of the *Bounty* events. The aim is to provide a fresh perspective on the *Bounty* drama and, perhaps, tip the balance of hitherto predominantly Western narratives. The point I would like to make here is that nautical and scientific achievements are not always found where we expect.

During the earliest contact period, European navigators used a range of instruments to determine their courses and positions, including compasses, astrolabes, quadrants and arbalestrilles. In the 18th century, these were superseded by octants and sextants. The magnetic needles of compasses could be trusted to point north. Other instruments would measure how high the sun or stars stood above the horizon, or help them to determine latitudes. This explains why the Spanish and the Dutch, then the English and the French, sailed across the Pacific along imaginary lines parallel to the equator. They would position their ships at a specific latitude and sail on, making sure that they held their course. Whenever they found an island they reported its latitude. The only means for them to locate that island again was to retrace their course along the same latitude and trust their luck, which often proved fickle because of the limitations of their instruments and the inconsistent accuracy of existing navigational records.

---

68 '… choquée qu'elle fut des pratiques païennes et en particulier par le polythéisme, l'infanticide, les sacrifices humains et l'exubérance des mœurs de l'époque' (Alain Babadzan, *Mythes Tahitiens*, Paris, Gallimard, 1993, p 10).

Longitudes were even more difficult to measure. Contrary to latitudes, which could be referenced in relation to the equator and the poles, longitudes have no natural bearings and are calculated through angular 360-degree measurements based on reference meridians. Europeans were desperate to invent a precise and sturdy clock able withstand the hazards of sea voyaging, and whose measurement of time would be independent enough from geographical locations. This was finally achieved in England in 1734 (see Young, Chapter 7). Before then, European explorers could only estimate the distance travelled since leaving port in order to attempt to calculate an island's longitude. The margin of error was such that locating an island on a subsequent voyage was virtually impossible. This problem was not remedied until the English sailed into the Pacific.

Polynesians had worked things out in their own way, without instruments. Tahitians could navigate without instruments because they had conceived of pillars and star trails. Those pillars and star trails were stored within the myth of the 'Birth of celestial bodies', a myth that has only recently been reconstructed.[69] For Polynesians, there were two kinds of stars by which they could navigate. The first were stars that would endlessly emerge from specific 'wells' located below the horizon, and would then draw a *rua* (star trail), across the sky; there were a dozen such stars, each recognisable by means of a *ta'urua* star. On the other hand, there were stars that positioned themselves one after the other high in the sky; these successive positionings would make a *pou* (meridian/pillar) that could be referenced to another star north or south. A dozen such stars were identified, each recognisable by means of an *'ana* star.

By memorising their positions from the zenith stars, Polynesians could return to locations at any time. They were able to locate an island from any location within the Pacific, as Tupaia demonstrated to the British in Batavia.

Navigating with the environment

Navigating with stars may have been efficient, but it was not sufficiently accurate to give a focal range greater than about 170 nautical miles, or 315 kilometres. With this method alone, it was all but impossible

---

69   Jean-Claude Teriierooiterai, 'Mythes, astronomie, découpage du temps et navigation traditionnelle: l'héritage océanien contenu dans les mots de la langue tahitienne', PhD thesis, Université de Polynésie française, 2013.

to find a particularly remote island such as Pitcairn. Pacific Islanders, however, had a raft of additional devices and data to refine their voyaging and become more accurate at targeting particular islands. These devices and data were found in their environment, and the methods of deciphering them have been closely studied and tested by David Lewis.[70]

One of the navigation devices used by Polynesians was to expand targets by aiming at a group of islands instead of a single island. Beyond a 25- or 30-nautical-mile radius, a high island is not visible from the open sea. Groups of islands expand the radius through addition or overlapping, and therefore expand the target area. Once a group of islands was reached, it was not difficult to navigate to other islands within the group. For instance, from Tahiti, it was easier to reach Hao, in the centre of the Tuamotu Islands, by navigating towards the archipelago as a whole. North to south, the Tuamotu Islands extend over 1,500 kilometres, whereas Hao is only about 30 kilometres wide. With a few exceptions, the islands of the Pacific cluster into archipelagos, making this navigational technique effective across the region.

A second device used by Polynesian navigators was observation of the ocean's hues. The ocean's colours vary according to depth and the lighter coloured deep reefs in the middle of the oceans are excellent markers for navigation. Reefs close to an island or archipelago indicate the sailing distance required before reaching a target.

Flotsam was also used as navigational devices. At sea, flotsam is ferried from land by currents and provides clues regarding the distance from its destination. For instance, a dry coconut drifting with the current can be assessed in terms of the sourness of the coconut water, or the degree to which the sinnet is soaked. Both of these factors indicate the length of time that the coconut has been at sea and, depending on the speed of the current, how far it has drifted from land. The same method was applied to coconut fronds and other plant debris.

---

[70] David Lewis, *We, the Navigators: The Ancient Art of Landfinding in the Pacific*, Honolulu, University of Hawai'i Press, 1972.

Another landfinding device was to observe the swell. A swell that meets no obstacle will remain steady. Any obstacle will send a reflected secondary swell or will alter its shape, bending it near the coast or causing turbulence in the rear. Depending on the shape of the swell, navigators could locate an island even before they could see it.

Polynesians could identify atolls by the colour of the clouds above them. The lagoons of some atolls can shine so brightly that their colour reflects on the clouds above. This phenomenon is called *paku* in the Tuamotu Islands and *pa'u* in Tahiti; hence the name Pa'umotu given by Tahitians to the archipelago in the past and to its inhabitants today. The reflection of the lagoon around 'Anaa is particularly spectacular; being so bright that it can be sighted from over the horizon.

Polynesians would also look for cumuli cloud formations generated by the heat of high islands, or large clouds that cling to island peaks and hang still over a landmass. The presence of a stable cumulus cloud formation amidst otherwise moving clouds indicates a landmass.

The flight of birds and their flying range also gave navigational clues in that some sea birds leave land in the morning to reach their fishing grounds and fly back at night. Their morning and evening flight paths therefore point to islands, and even provide some indication of how far away those islands may lie. Some species, like phaetons, fly within a range of approximately 170 kilometres and sighting one suggested an island lay somewhere within that distance.

It is possible that some of these indigenous navigation methods were familiar to Europeans before they sailed into the Pacific. Tropical island environments had been known to the Spanish since the voyages of Christopher Columbus, and the Spanish were already familiar with sailing in the Caribbean and the Indian Ocean as far as the Philippines. The Dutch owned outposts in the Caribbean and Indonesia, so they were also used to navigating tropical island regions.

It was not until the voyages of Jose de Andia y Varela and James Cook that the Europeans expressed any interest in Polynesian navigation. Puhoro educated the Spanish as to how Tahitians used the wind as a compass, while Tupaia taught the British how to read clouds, winds and stars for direction and weather forecast. Mahine, who embarked with Cook on his second voyage, used bird flight to calculate the distance of an island. On Cook's third voyage, Tahitian Ma'i (Omai) returned home on the

Resolution – William Bligh was mate on this voyage. It was not reported whether Bligh and Maʻi spoke during the journey, but they are bound to have done so at some point given the length of the voyage. Maʻi was not a navigator and nor was he as knowledgeable as the other indigenous travellers but, like all Polynesians, he would have been a fisherman and therefore able to share the basics about sailing.

Cook interacted with Polynesians often enough to integrate the Polynesian navigating methods of Tupaia, Mahine and Maʻi into his own voyages. Bligh, in turn, was able to observe Cook's methods. While Bligh's notes on Tahitian customs and language are valuable – for example, he was the first to notice the taboos applied to the syllables that made up the name of a *ariʻi* and that, once Pomare became king of Tahiti, the words *po* and *mare* were banished from everyday language, and replaced by *hota* and *ruʻi* – he did not include specific observations about the Polynesian arts of navigating and landfinding.

Bligh's concern for the health and wellbeing of the *Bounty* crew was largely misconstrued as harshness. The lessons he learned from Cook about navigating in the tropics, however, saved his life and those of his men. On the *Bounty* long boat that took him 3,620 nautical miles (6,700 kilometres) from Tonga to Timor, Bligh followed the same latitude up to Australia, like Polynesians using *rua*. Indeed, he may have relied on Polynesian expertise in making allowance for 'leeway, effect of currents and the speed made through the water', since the charts he produced from his surveys on the *Bounty* launch turned out to be 'considerably more accurate for scale and orientation than Cook's'.[71]

The untimely demise of the Polynesian art of navigation caused by the influx of Europeans

After James Cook, the number of European visitors to the Pacific increased and with them came another way of looking at the sky. Venus lost her poetic name, *Taʻurua-nui-horo-ahiahi* ('Great-celebration-that-runs-in-the-evening'), and it was replaced by *Venuti*, a phonetic adaptation of Venus into Tahitian. *Taʻurua-nui-i-tuʻi-i-te-pōrou-o-te-raʻi* ('Great-celebration-that-

---

71 ACF David, 'The Surveyors of the *Bounty*: A Preliminary Study of the Hydrographic Surveys of William Bligh, Thomas Hayward and Peter Heywood and the Charts Published from Them', Royal Navy Hydrographic Department, Ministry of Defence, Taunton, Somerset, 1982, p 23, quoted in Salmond, 2011, p 225.

hits-the-zenith-of-the-sky') became simply *Iupiti*, a rendering of Jupiter. Sirius, which was paramount to Tahitians because it shone at their island's zenith, was known as *Taʻurua-faupapa* ('Celebrations-of-the-first-great-leaders') until it disappeared altogether from the Tahitian lexicon and, it might be said, from the Tahitian sky.

Between 1822 and 1840, Louis Isidore Duperrey,[72] Jules Dumont d'Urville,[73] François-Edmond Pâris[74] and René Primevère Lesson[75] lamented the decline of Polynesian navigation and the disappearance of *Ariʻi* Tū's fleet of double canoes, which had been so fervently praised by Cook in 1774. Pâris, who sailed with Dumont d'Urville on the *Astrolabe* in 1826–29, made an inventory of Tahitian canoes. He wrote this bitter note:

> We took advantage of our long stay with them to have a look at the canoes; all the large ones were extinct, but we are glad that we could find the detailed drawing of one from Captain Cook's second navigation as he witnessed the gathering of a whole fleet, which may give a favourable impression of what Taïti (Tahiti) used to be like, in those days.[76]

Pâris' drawing of a contemporary canoe reveals that its appearance had changed from the ancient *vaʻa* and it was now constructed as a hybrid of traditional canoes and certain recently introduced European boats. A sailing sprit had replaced the bird wings that once characterised Tahitian *vaʻa* with a triangular sail. Lesson, surgeon on board Duperrey's *Coquille* during the 1822–25 scientific circumnavigation, had a few years earlier bemoaned the Tahitian neglect of the art of shipbuilding:

---

72   Louis Isidore Duperrey, *Voyage autour du monde: exécuté par ordre du roi, sur la corvette de Sa Majesté, la Coquille, pendant les années 1822, 1823, 1824 et 1825*, Paris, Arthus Bertrand Libraire Editeur, 1826.

73   Jules Dumont d'Urville SC, *Voyage pittoresque autour du monde*, Papeete, Haere Po No Tahiti, 1988.

74   E Pâris, *Essai sur la construction navale des peuples extra-européens ou collection des navires et pirogues construits par les habitants de l'Asie, de la Malaisie, du Grand océan et de l'Amérique dessinés et mesurés pendant les voyages autour du monde de l'Astrolabe, La Favorite et l'Artémise*, Paris, Arthus Bertrand, 1841.

75   RP Lesson, *Voyage autour du monde entrepris par ordre du Gouvernement sur la Corvette La Coquille*, Paris, Pourrat Frères, 1839.

76   'Le long séjour que nous fîmes parmi eux put être utilisé pour les pirogues; toutes les grandes ont disparu, mais nous sommes heureux d'en trouver un plan exact dans le second voyage du capitaine Cook, qui vit réunie une flotte propre à donner une idée avantageuse de ce qu'était alors Taïti (Tahiti) …' (Pâris, 1841, p 32).

> One of the arts that modern Tahitians seem to be dropping is that of nautical architecture. Their fertile topsoil has made it less necessary for them to go sailing. These islanders, however, have a perfect knowledge of the islands which surround them on all sides, and which they used to sail to more often, either as friends or foes. The early navigators who landed the Society Islands have left us prints of canoes decorated with very ornate iconic carvings, which are nowhere to be found nowadays.[77]

European-style boats now sailed between islands. The use of compasses, stopwatches, octants and sextants put an end to a 2,000-year-old navigational practice. All that was left for Polynesians were their reminiscences, transmitted in the form of glorifying myths and legends that recounted the great deeds of their epic heroes.

Another unfortunate consequence of the upheaval of this contact period was the extinction of Tahitian astral calendars. Calendars showed how Tahitians had solved the crucial problem of fitting together lunar months and natural cycles. They determined rituals that anticipated the first '*uru* harvests and the first bonito fishing parties. Three stars would successively come into play at different times in the year to synchronise lunar months with seasons: *Rā*, the sun at solstices and equinoxes; *Matariʻi*, the Pleiades at their evening heliacal rise before the start of the austral summer and their evening heliacal setting before the start of the southern winter; and *Rehua*, Pollux, at its heliacal evening setting. It may be reasonably argued that Tahitians had developed elaborate concepts about time and astral movements. The only remnant of Polynesian calendrical systems today is a lunar calendar used by fishermen and farmers.

Traditional Tahitian culture collapsed in the early 19th century, along with traditional forms of astronomy. European voyagers have even wondered whether Polynesians ever had any such science, despite there being no other way to account for the settlement of Polynesia, located 6,000 kilometres from the nearest continent. Jacques Antoine Moerenhout,[78] who did not think highly of the Islanders' sailing skills in the 1830s, wrote that they

---

77 'Un des arts que les Tahitiens modernes semblent négliger est celui de l'architecture nautique. La fertilité de leur sol leur a rendu moins nécessaires les navigations lointaines. Ces insulaires, cependant, ont une parfaite connaissance des îles qui, de toutes parts, les entourent, et qu'ils visitaient plus fréquemment autrefois, soit comme amis, soit comme ennemis. Nous voyons en effet, dans les gravures que nous ont laissées les premiers navigateurs qui abordèrent aux îles de la Société, les pirogues ornées de sculptures emblématiques très soignées, dont on ne découvre nulle trace en ce moment' (Lesson, 1839, pp 386–87).
78 Jacques-Antoine Moerenhout, *Voyages aux îles du grand Océan*, 2 vols, Paris, Adrien Maisonneuve, 1837.

were incapable of sailing from one island to the next without European support. He suspected, however, that Tahitians were the heirs of a brilliant civilisation:

> First, I am convinced that, at the time when they were discovered by Europeans, Polynesian people had reached a state of absolute decadence. Second, I believe that prior to that discovery, probably from a very early date and over a certain period of time, they may have gone through a stage of civilization and relatively advanced political splendour.[79]

He further declared:

> To me, it cannot be gainsaid that Polynesians went through a second stage when, to some extent, they practised arts, sciences and navigation. This may have lasted for quite a while in some islands, before it gradually changed to the situation I have mentioned before.[80]

Not unlike Reverend William Ellis, who thought that Tahitians might have originated from Mount Meru in India, Moerenhout speculated that the original land of their civilised noble ancestors was part of a sunken continent lying deep down on the ocean floor. To him, contemporary Tahitian people were merely survivors of a decadent culture.

Moerenhout was in touch with Reverend John Orsmond and relied heavily on *Ancient Tahiti* in writing up his research as *A Voyage to the Great Ocean Islands*. Not being a missionary, he was not burdened with Orsmond's moral qualms about Tahitian culture. Despite not being proficient in Tahitian – neither written or spoken – and even though his Tahitian quotes are incomplete, his interpretation of Tahitian ways of life were less subject to religious prejudice and were, in the fields of spirituality or morality, more explicit than Orsmond's.[81] His description of Tahitian calendar rituals, for example, is central to our modern understanding of traditional Tahitian year divisions.

---

79 'Je suis convaincu d'abord, que les peuples de la Polynésie étaient, à l'époque de leur découverte par les Européens, dans un état de décadence absolue. Je crois en second lieu, qu'antérieurement à cette même découverte, ils ont dû, pendant plus ou moins longtemps, et, probablement depuis une époque déjà fort ancienne, connaître un état de civilisation et de splendeur politique relativement très avancé' (Moerenhout, vol 2, 1837, p 176).
80 'Il me paraît donc certain qu'il y a eu une seconde époque pendant laquelle les Polynésiens cultivaient jusqu'à un certain point les arts, les sciences, et se livraient à la navigation. A cet ordre de choses, qui a dû se prolonger beaucoup dans quelques-unes des îles, aura insensiblement succédé celui dont j'ai parlé' (Moerenhout, vol 2, 1837, p 219).
81 Moerenhout, vol 2, 1837, p 11.

Although other missionary narratives from the same period may be of great value, they include few Tahitian writings. Their authors mostly provided their own translations, which they adapted to suit their religious views. For example, Ellis, provides a detailed description of Tahitian customs. However, the reliability of his work cannot be ascertained, as the original Tahitian texts are not referenced. Of particular interest here, however, is Ellis' description of a personal experience during a voyage between Tahiti and Huahine in 1820, when his companions relied on Tahitian navigation methods using the stars:

> The natives of the islands were, however, accustomed in some degree to notice the appearance and position of the stars, especially at sea. These were their only guides, in steering their fragile barks across the deep. When setting out on a voyage, some particular star or constellation was selected as their guide in the night. This they called *aveia* [*'avei'a*], and by this name they now designate the compass, because it answers the same purpose. The Pleiades were favourite *aveia* with their sailors, and by them, in the present voyage, we steered during the night.[82]

This document shows that, in the 1820s, Tahitians could still read the stars, and used them to sail between the Society Islands. Sailing was not just instinctive, but based on firm empirical knowledge. Polynesian navigators understood the complexities of star motions, and climatic, ecological and biological cycles.

Conclusion

This chapter has contextualised the *Bounty* from the Polynesian side of the beach, focusing on traditional Pacific maritime culture. Its survey of a series of early encounters with Europeans accounts for the ways that Europeans were received by Pacific Islanders between the 16th and 18th centuries, including the contrasting receptions given to William Bligh and Fletcher Christian in Tahiti, Tonga and Tubua'i. The particular emphasis of this chapter on pre-contact inter-island connections paves the way for the detailed archaeological, historical and cultural study of pre-contact Pitcairn in the chapter that follows (see Molle & Hermann, Chapter 2).

---

82 William Ellis, *Polynesian Researches, During a Residence of Nearly Eight Years in the South Seas Islands*, vol 2, Newgate, Fisher, Son, & Jackson, 1928, p 412.

Since most *Bounty* narratives extoll the achievements of British navigators – and deservedly so – in this chapter it has been my humble purpose to draw contrapuntal attention to the outstanding navigational expertise that Polynesians developed and perfected over many generations before Europeans arrived. It is unlikely that the Tahitians who sailed with Christian to Pitcairn were well versed in navigation, as it seems that there were no *tahu'a* on board. An expert *fa'atere va'a* might have steered the *Bounty* to a more appropriate island, such as any of the other three in the Pitcairn group, which were more welcoming, had been recorded in myths and were reported on Tupaia's map.[83] It should be noted, however, that around 1794, in the spirit of their valiant ancestors, many of the *Bounty* Tahitian women in Pitcairn took to the sea on their own, in an attempt to escape from Pitcairn on a boat that, being leaky, sank off the coast.

In pre-contact times, while there was some variation between the navigation concepts and methods developed in each Polynesian archipelago, there was also remarkable similarity in the techniques used across the region. With European intrusion, these techniques were rapidly lost, as was the technique for building large double canoes. Europeans brought with them a new navigation system based on highly developed mechanical instruments, and they introduced a new form of single-hulled vessel. Star navigation expertise was lost for several generations. Oral transmission of traditional navigation methods was disrupted and the introduced religions strove to ban the traditional rituals and chants that accompanied the myths associated with navigation, and the local terms that conveyed scientific concepts.

It appears that none of the elements of Polynesian navigation expertise have survived. Nowadays, most Tahitians are unaware of the skills of their forebears. They find it hard to believe that their ancestors had managed to traverse such vast ocean distances and that their scientific approach to astronomy, navigation and time division was so refined. Modern navigation methods using a sextant, the measurement of angles and ephemeris, rendered traditional navigation methods obsolete. Simple-to-use Western calendars and the introduction of Christian religions led to the replacement of the Tahitian calendar that was founded on lunar and astral cycles.

---

83 The British knew that those islands existed but they did not know where they were.

There was no other way for Polynesians to exchange with their neighbours but to master the ocean. They achieved this through the interpretation of astronomical and natural phenomena. The traditional navigation skills of these people, who have been thought of as 'little', are unrivalled. In addition to their ability to read the signs of their environment, the genius of Polynesian navigators lay primarily in their understanding of celestial movement. Developing a system of celestial pillars and star trails made them genuine astronomers. The stars were an integral part of their lives. Their deified ancestors had themselves grown into stars, and thus, their relationship to the stars was extremely intimate. While Polynesians may not have known how to write, they certainly knew how to read their natural environment.

2

Pitcairn before the Mutineers: Revisiting the Isolation of a Polynesian Island

Guillaume Molle
The Australian National University

Aymeric Hermann
Max Planck Institute for the Science of Human History

Introduction[1]

The myth of Pitcairn, building on the destiny of the *Bounty* mutineers, focuses on the recent history of this island as the epitome of marginality and isolation. Human occupation of the island, however, occurred long before the *Bounty* settlement, and Pitcairn provides a fascinating example of Polynesian sustainability that is little known to the general public. Located at the eastern fringe of Central Eastern Polynesia, the Pitcairn group includes the volcanic island of Pitcairn (4.5 square kilometres), the elevated limestone island of Henderson (37.2 square kilometres) and the two small atolls of Oeno and Ducie (Figure 2.1). Situated approximately 400 kilometres east of the Gambier Islands and 1,700 kilometres west of Rapa Nui/Easter Island, this island group is one of the world's most geographically isolated.

---

1   We would like to thank Sylvie Largeaud-Ortega for accepting our chapter for this volume, for her assistance with English and for her useful comments on our first draft. We thank Meredith Wilson for her comments that helped us improve the manuscript.

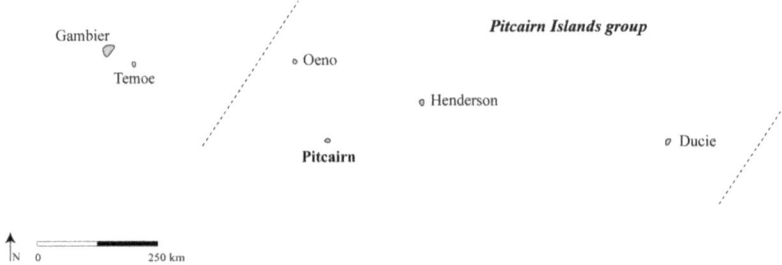

Figure 2.1. Location of Pitcairn Islands in relation to the Gambier Islands.
Source: Guillaume Molle & Aymeric Hermann.

While Pitcairn was uninhabited when the *Bounty* mutineers landed on 23 January 1790, subsequent exploration of the island by the mutineers, and later by scholars, provides strong evidence of previous Polynesian occupation. For this reason, Pitcairn is often referred to as one of the 'Mysterious Islands' of the Pacific; this expression, conceived by Peter Bellwood,[2] defines a group of approximately 25 atolls and high volcanic islands that were devoid of human habitation at the time of European discovery. The so-called 'Mysterious Islands' also include Nihoa and Necker in the Hawaiian archipelago, several islands amongst the Line and Phoenix groups, as well as Norfolk, Kermadec and Raoul in south-east Polynesia.[3] Different environmental and cultural hypotheses have been proposed to explain why these islands were abandoned before Westerners arrived.

This chapter reviews and synthesises various kinds of archaeological information that document the ancient occupation of Pitcairn and its position within Central Eastern Polynesia (see Teriierooiterai, Chapter 1). In pre-European times, before the *Bounty* mutineers chose the island as a refuge on which to hide from the British Navy, the Pitcairn community was involved in a complex set of inter-island relations. The Pitcairn case, therefore, illustrates two ways in which to perceive insularity, which are

---

2   Peter Bellwood, *The Polynesians: Prehistory of an Island People*, rev edn, London, Thames & Hudson, 1987, pp 109–10.
3   See Geoffrey Irwin, *The Prehistoric Exploration and Colonization of the Pacific* (Cambridge, Cambridge University Press, 1992); Patrick V Kirch, 'Polynesia's Mystery Islands' (*Archaeology*, vol 3, no 41, 1988, pp 26–31); Patrick V Kirch, *On the Road of the Winds. An Archaeological History of the Pacific Islands before European Contact* (Berkeley & Los Angeles, University of California Press, 2000); Paul Wallin & Helene Martinsson-Wallin, 'When Migration Failed. On Christmas Island and Other "Mystery Islands" in the Pacific', in Paul Wallin (ed), *Migrations and Exchange in a Historical Perspective* (Kon-Tiki Museum, No Barriers Seminar Papers, no 3, 2000, pp 10–13); Atholl Anderson, 'No Meat on that Beautiful Shore: The Prehistoric Abandonment of Subtropical Polynesian Islands' (*International Journal of Osteoarchaeology*, vol 11, 2001, pp 14–23).

discussed from a long-term historical perspective. By doing so, we are attempting to breach the common Western narrative on Pitcairn Island. While building on Greg Dening's approach,[4] this case further advocates that the agency of ancient Polynesians be reconsidered at the core of this historical trajectory.

Polynesians on Pitcairn: A long-term archaeological perspective

Traditional knowledge of the island

Few oral traditions are available for Pitcairn. While people now use the name 'Petania' – an abbreviation of 'Peretania', the Polynesian transliteration of 'Britannia' – the island was known by other names before the arrival of Europeans. Peter Buck[5] recalls the name of Heragi in the Mangarevan version of the legend of Hina and Tinirau. Teuira Henry[6] uses the name Hiti-au-rereva ('the edge of passing clouds') to refer to Pitcairn, but its use is restricted to this single source.

Ethnographic research conducted by Père Jacques-Désiré Laval in the Gambier Islands provides details of Mangarevan oral traditions relating to Pitcairn. Prior to the arrival of Europeans, inhabitants of the Gambier Islands found themselves in a near-constant state of warfare, with defeated chiefs often forced into exile. Taratahi, one of these chiefs, was sent to an island called Mata-ki-te-ragi (possibly 'beginnings of the skies'), which could be Pitcairn.[7] While it is not clear whether Taratahi fled with his men or if the land had already been settled by another group, it is reported that the island's Meriri people eventually rose up against him, leading to the destruction of the breadfruit trees. One of Taratahi's grandsons, Te Agiagi, who still lived on Mangareva, had a vision of this disaster and decided to travel to Mata-ki-te-ragi with his father and two of his brothers. Heading south, they encountered three small, uninhabited atolls before reaching their destination, a high volcanic island on which it was extremely difficult

---

4   Greg Dening, *Islands and Beaches: Discourse on a Silent Land, Marquesas 1774–1880*, Melbourne University Press, 1980.
5   Peter H Buck (Te Rangi Hiroa), *Vikings of the Pacific*, New York, FA Stokes Co, 1938, p 224.
6   Teuira Henry, *Tahiti aux Temps Anciens*, Paris, Musée de l'Homme, Publication de la Société des Océanistes, no 1, 2000, p 75.
7   Honoré Laval, *Mangareva, l'Histoire ancienne d'un peuple polynésien*, Pape'ete, Haere Pō, 2013 (1938), p 10.

to make a landing. Te Agiagi went ashore alone and found Taratahi dead in a creek. He replanted breadfruit and banana trees all over the island, which he then divided into two parts, one for each of his brothers. Rua-kai-tagata went to Puniga and Rua-toga went to Marokura. Several years later, the resources of the island attracted Ragahenua, another chief living on Mangareva. Ragahenua sailed with 500 warriors on his canoes to Kai-ragi (an abbreviation of Mata-ki-te-ragi) and built a fortified place on the highest peak. After defeating Puniga and Marokura, Ragahenua took possession of the island. Four fugitives fled back to Mangareva during the conflict and reached the archipelago after a short trip for which they took no provisions. One of them went to the chief of the Taku district in Mangareva and told him about the war on Mata-ki-te-rangi. This event is said to have taken place prior to the late 14th century, and there appears to be no further mention of the island in Mangarevan oral traditions.

There has been continuous debate about whether Mata-ki-te-rangi is Rapa Nui or Pitcairn. Laval raised this question at a time when Mangarevans argued that Mata-ki-te-rangi was Rapa Nui. When the traditions were transcribed for Laval by the Mangarevans themselves, however, the text specified '*Pe a kaiga ko Petania noti reka*', which can be translated as 'this land looked like Pitcairn'.[8] Other scholars agree that these traditions do refer to Pitcairn on the basis of the following evidence:[9] first, Pitcairn is the closest high island to the Gambier Islands. It can be reached faster from Mangareva, which is also consistent with the narrative of the last fugitives who did not carry any provisions on their short canoe trip. Moreover, it is known that landing on Pitcairn is extremely difficult, while Rapa Nui possesses some large beach areas. Finally, breadfruit trees are prevented from growing on Rapa Nui by severe climatic conditions. These aspects of the oral traditions provide compelling evidence that the island of Mata-ki-te-rangi was indeed Pitcairn, a place that Mangarevans knew of and to which they travelled. This story does not contradict the well-known traditional account of Rapa Nui being settled by King Hotu-Matua from Mangareva.[10] Archaeological work in the region currently supports the idea that all of these easternmost Polynesian islands were discovered and settled during a single pulse of colonisation that occurred around a thousand years ago.

---

8   Laval, 2013, no 18.
9   Buck, 1938; Henri Lavachery, 'Contribution à l'étude de l'archéologie de l'île de Pitcairn', *Bulletin de la Société des Américanistes de Belgique*, vol 19, 1936, pp 3–42.
10   Alfred Métraux, 'Ethnology of Easter Island', *Bernice P Bishop Museum Bulletin*, no 160, 1940, p 33.

The settlement of Pitcairn

Most of the archaeological work on Pitcairn has consisted of survey and artefact collection, and has been focused on the more recent past. In the absence of archaeological excavation, access to information about the timing and nature of the early settlement of Pitcairn is not yet available.[11] Archaeological data from the Gambier Islands, Henderson Island and Rapa Nui, however, may help in generating an estimate for the date of settlement of Pitcairn.

Lying at the south-eastern margin of French Polynesia, the Gambier Islands occupy a key position at the confluence of the Tuamotu and Austral chains that is the most likely point of departure to Rapa Nui.[12] While a lack of data[13] caused the Gambier Islands to be neglected in early settlement models, investigations conducted since the early 2000s have provided insight into the chronology of human occupation there. Several sites have now been excavated and dated, such as Onemea on Taravai, Nenega-iti on Agakauitai,[14] and a few locations on Kamaka. Results show an intensive occupation of these localities from around AD 1200 until the arrival of Westerners in the late 18th century. The initial Polynesian settlement is demonstrated by a series of significant anthropogenic impacts on the island environment, including the hunting of seabird

---

11 Yosihiko Sinoto has identified only two radiocarbon dates for Pitcairn ('An Analysis of Polynesian Migrations based on Archaeological Assessments', *Journal de la Société des Océanistes*, vol 76, 1983, p 61). The dated samples were recovered by Sinoto from an adze workshop, however, which was probably in use by the 14th century. While this means that a group definitely occupied the island at this time, the period of initial colonisation has not yet been confirmed.

12 Roger C Green, 'Linguistic Subgrouping within Polynesia: The Implications for Prehistoric Settlement', *Journal of the Polynesian Society*, vol 75, 1966, pp 6–38; Roger C Green, 'Rapanui Origins Prior to European Contact: The View from Eastern Polynesia', in Patricia Vargas Casanova (ed), *Easter Island and East Polynesian Prehistory*, Santiago, Universidad de Chile, 1998, pp 87–110; Patrick V Kirch & Éric Conte, 'Mangareva and Eastern Polynesian Prehistory', in Éric Conte & Patrick V Kirch (eds), *Archaeological Investigations in the Mangareva Islands (Gambier Archipelago), French Polynesia*, Archaeological Research Facility, no 62, Berkeley, University of California, 2004, pp 1–15.

13 Yosihiko Sinoto, 'A Tentative Prehistoric Cultural Sequence in the Northern Marquesas Islands, French Polynesia', *Journal of the Polynesian Society*, vol 75, no 3, 1966, pp 286–303; Yosihiko Sinoto, 'An Archaeologically Based Assessment of the Marquesas as a Dispersal Center in East Polynesia', in Roger C Green & Marion Kelly (eds), *Studies in Oceanic Culture History*, Pacific Anthropological Records, vol 11, 1970, pp 105–32; Patrick V Kirch, 'Rethinking East Polynesian Prehistory', *Journal of Polynesian Society*, vol 95, no 1, 1986, pp 9–40.

14 Conte & Kirch, 2004; Patrick V Kirch, Éric Conte, Warren Sharp & Cordelia Nickelsen, 'The Onemea Site (Taravai Island, Mangareva) and the Human Colonization of Southeastern Polynesia', *Archaeology in Oceania*, 45, 2010, pp 66–79; Patrick Kirch, Guillaume Molle, Cordelia Nickelsen, Peter Mills, Emilie Dotte-Sarout, Jillian Swift, Allison Wolfe & Mark Horrocks, 'Human Ecodynamics in the Mangareva Islands: A Stratified Sequence from Nenega-iti Rock Shelter (Site AGA-3, Agakauitai Island)', *Archaeology in Oceania*, vol 50, no 1, 2015, pp 23–42.

and the introduction of *Allopeas* snails and Pacific rats (*Rattus exulans*). Two early radiocarbon dates indicate that this human occupation may have occurred around AD 950.[15]

The pre-European contact history of marginal Henderson Island has also been well documented, first in a preliminary study by Yosihiko Sinoto,[16] then through extensive work conducted by Marshall Weisler.[17] The island's constrained environment and its depleted terrestrial and marine resources exemplify human adaptation pushed to its limit. The centre of the uplifted limestone island is formed by karstic depressions and is not suitable for human habitation. As a consequence, many north-eastern coastal caves and rock shelters were occupied for domestic purposes, as shown by the presence of artefacts, firepits and bone remains. Along with these habitation sites, gardening areas were established nearby in rare pockets of arable soil.[18] Burials were also discovered in close proximity to habitation sites. Surveys and excavations demonstrate a long-term human occupation of the island rather than short-term visits. In total, 31 radiocarbon dates are available to reconstruct the cultural sequence for Henderson.[19] Weisler first argued that the colonisation of the island could have taken place as early as the 8th century AD, taking into account the maximum range of the oldest sample.[20] Although not impossible, this assertion is at variance with the results obtained for Mangareva that suggest a later occupation. On the other hand, many coastal rock shelters certainly provide evidence of occupation by the 12th century, leading Weisler to propose, more convincingly, that Henderson might have been settled around AD 1050.[21] This assumption is in keeping with the most recent results for the Gambier Islands.[22]

---

15   Kirch et al, 2010, p 72.
16   Sinoto, 1983, p 59.
17   Marshall Weisler, 'Henderson Island Prehistory. Colonization and Extinction on a Remote Polynesian Island', in TG Benton & T Spence (eds), *The Pitcairn Islands: Biogeography, Ecology and Prehistory, Biological Journal of the Linnean Society*, vol 56, nos 1–2, 1995, pp 377–404.
18   Mark Horrocks & Marshall I Weisler, 'Analysis of Plant Microfossils in Archaeological Deposits from Two Remote Archipelagos: The Marshall Islands, Eastern Micronesia, and the Pitcairn Group, Southeast Polynesia', *Pacific Science*, vol 60, no 2, 2006, pp 261–80.
19   Weisler, 1995, tbl 2, p 389.
20   Marshall Weisler, 'The Settlement of Marginal Polynesia: New Evidence from Henderson Island', *Journal of Field Archaeology*, vol 21, 1994, pp 83–102.
21   Roger C Green & Marshall Weisler, 'The Mangarevan Sequence and Dating of the Geographic Expansion into Southeast Polynesia', *Asian Perspectives*, vols 41–42, 2002, pp 213–41.
22   Kirch et al, 2010; Kirch et al, 2015.

Rapa Nui, the easternmost Polynesian island, has a long history of archaeological research and has been integrated into various models of colonisation. More recent studies propose initial settlement from around AD 1200.[23] As mentioned earlier, Polynesian migration traditions attribute the settlement of Rapa Nui to the legendary King Hotu-Matua, high chief of Marae-erenga, who landed on Anakena beach after sending scouts to discover the island.[24] Following the chiefly genealogies, cultural anthropologist Alfred Métraux suggests that this episode took place around the 12th century.[25] While Métraux previously proposed that Hotu-Matua originated from the Marquesas, it now seems more likely that Hotu-Matua departed from Mangareva following a land dispute.

Outside the south-eastern region, archaeologists now have at their disposal new data sets from other central Polynesian archipelagos that further illuminate our understanding of the colonisation of east Polynesia. Human presence is attested on both Mo'orea in the Society Islands and on Mangaia in the Cook Islands by the 11th century AD,[26] and Ua Huka in the Marquesas by the 10th century AD.[27] With this in mind, it appears that a wide-ranging and rapid movement of migration occurred by the end of the 1st millennium AD, departing from Samoa. The discovery of the Gambier Islands, probably around AD 1000, could have led rapidly to further voyages eastwards. From this perspective, we might hypothesise that Polynesian navigators located the Pitcairn group around the same period, during exploration voyages to Rapa Nui. Based on the dates available for the region, it is possible that Pitcairn was first settled between AD 1000 and 1200.

---

23 Terry L Hunt & Carl P Lipo, 'Evidence for a Shorter Chronology on Rapa Nui (Easter Island)', *Journal of Island and Coastal Archaeology*, vol 3, no 1, 2008, pp 140–48; Janet M Wilmshurst, Terry L Hunt, Carl P Lipo & Atholl J Anderson, 'High-Precision Radiocarbon Dating Shows Recent and Rapid Initial Human Colonization of East Polynesia', *Proceedings of the National Academy of Sciences*, vol 108, 2011, pp 1815–20.
24 Thomas S Barthel, *The Eighth Land: The Polynesian Discovery and Settlement of Easter Island*, Honolulu, University Press of Hawai'i, 1978.
25 Métraux, 1940, p 33.
26 Jennifer G Kahn, 'Coastal Occupation at the GS-1 Site, Cook's Bay, Mo'orea, Society Islands', *Journal of Pacific Archaeology*, vol 3, no 2, 2012, pp 52–61; Patrick V Kirch (ed), *Tangatatau Rockshelter (Mangaia, Cook Islands): The Evolution of an Eastern Polynesian Socio-Ecosystem*, Los Angeles, Cotsen Institute of Archaeology Press, Monumental Archaeologica series, 2017.
27 Éric Conte & Guillaume Molle, 'Reinvestigating a Key-Site for Polynesian Prehistory: New Results from Hane Dune Site, Ua Huka, Marquesas', *Archaeology in Oceania*, vol 49, 2014, pp 121–36.

Temporal issues aside, the finer details of the settlement process are difficult to resolve. Biological affinities have been demonstrated between the Rapa Nui and Henderson populations,[28] which imply either ancestor–descendant relationships (from the Gambier Islands to Henderson then Rapa Nui) or sister populations descending independently from the same founding group, presumably Mangareva. These two possible patterns must be evoked in the case of Pitcairn due to its position midway between Mangareva and Henderson. While it is impossible to solve this problem without further work, a simultaneous discovery and settlement of Pitcairn and Henderson remains the most convincing hypothesis because it supports the idea of a quick development of inter-island interactions, as outlined below. As for remote Rapa Nui, the population of which probably originated from the Gambier Islands via the Pitcairn group, linguists have demonstrated that it became rapidly isolated from other Central Eastern Polynesian islands.[29]

'Marked in stone': Remains of an active community

As previously discussed, archaeological work has been limited on Pitcairn in comparison with other islands in the region. This is due largely to the island's geographical isolation and relative difficulty to reach by ship. The first anthropologists working on Pitcairn stopped only for brief visits on their return from Rapa Nui. In 1915, Katherine Routledge, who conducted pioneer work on Rapa Nui, stayed on Pitcairn for five days before returning to Tahiti.[30] Archaeologist Henri Lavachery and anthropologist Alfred Métraux, on the Franco-Belgian expedition to Rapa Nui, spent just two days on Pitcairn in 1935.[31] The short accounts available from these visits mention petroglyphs and destroyed *marae*, the locations of which had already been reported by earlier visitors.[32] During the

---

28   Sara L Collins & Marshall I Weisler, 'Human Dental and Skeletal Remains from Henderson Island, Southeast Polynesia', *People and Culture in Oceania*, vol 16, 2000, pp 67–85; Vincent H Stefan, Sara L Collins & Marshall I Weisler, 'Henderson Island Crania and their Implication for Southeast Polynesia Prehistory', *Journal of the Polynesian Society*, vol 111, no 4, 2002, pp 371–83.
29   Green, 1998; Steven R Fischer, 'Mangarevan Doublets: Preliminary Evidence for Proto-Southeastern Polynesian', *Oceanic Linguistics*, vol 40, no 1, 2001, pp 112–24; Mary Walworth, 'Eastern Polynesian: The Linguistic Evidence Revisited', *Oceanic Linguistics*, vol 53, no 2, 2014, pp 256–72.
30   Katherine Pease Routledge, *The Mystery of Easter Island: The Story of an Expedition*, London, Hazell, Watson and Viney, 1919, pp 305–15.
31   Lavachery, 1936.
32   Frederick W Beechey, *Narrative of a Voyage to the Pacific and Beering's Strait*, London, Colburn & Bentley, 1831; Jacques-Antoine Moerenhout, *Voyage aux îles du Grand Océan*, Paris, Arthus Bertrand, 1837; Walter Brodie, *Pitcairn Island and the Islanders in 1850*, London, Whittaker & Co, 1851.

2. PITCAIRN BEFORE THE MUTINEERS

Norwegian expedition of 1956, Thor Heyerdahl directed excavations in two cave sites, together with a general survey of the island.[33] As part of the Polynesian archaeological research program led by the Bernice P Bishop Museum of Honolulu, an expedition composed of a number of specialists was led by Peter Gathercole (University of Otago, New Zealand) from January to March 1965. This was the first and only intensive archaeological project ever undertaken on Pitcairn. Unfortunately, only a preliminary report is available despite the large amount of data collected over a three-month field season.[34] Nonetheless, the report includes a map of recorded archaeological sites. Little archaeological work has been conducted on Pitcairn since, with the exception of Yosihiko Sinoto's excavation of a pit area in 1971,[35] and Marshall Weisler's samples of different quarry sources for geochemical analysis.[36] More recently, Nicholas Erskine focused on the historical archaeology of the *Bounty* mutineers' settlement.[37] While certainly of interest, this study does not provide any further information about pre-European settlement.

Despite the relative scarcity of information, a detailed review of available sources helps to trace the pre-European history of Pitcairn prior to its abandonment and 'rediscovery' by the *Bounty* mutineers (Figure 2.2). Two questions arise regarding past occupation of this marginal island: did the early inhabitants use the natural resources of the island sustainably, and was occupation temporary or permanent? One must consider these questions with respect to the desertion of the island prior to the arrival of the *Bounty* settlers.

---

33   Thor Heyerdahl & Arne Skjölsvold, 'Notes on the Archaeology of Pitcairn Island', in Thor Heyerdahl & Edwin N Ferdon (eds), *Reports of the Norwegian Archaeological Expedition to Easter Island and the East Pacific*, vol 2, *Miscellaneous Papers*, Stockholm, Monographs of the School of American Research and the Kon-Tiki Museum, no 24, part 2, 1965a, pp 3–7.
34   Peter Gathercole, *Preliminary Report on Archaeological Fieldwork on Pitcairn Island*, Jan–Mar, University of Otago, Department of Anthropology, 1964.
35   Sinoto, 1966; Sinoto, 1983.
36   Kenneth D Collerson & Marshall I Weisler, 'Stone Adze Compositions and the Extent of Ancient Polynesian Voyaging and Trade', *Science*, vol 317, 2007, pp 1907–11; Marshall I Weisler, 'Prehistoric Long-Distance Interaction at the Margins of Oceania', in Marshall I Weisler (ed), *Prehistoric Long-Distance Interaction in Oceania: An Interdisciplinary Approach*, New Zealand Archaeological Association Monograph 21, 1997a, pp 149–72; Marshall I Weisler & Jon D Woodhead, 'Basalt Pb Isotope Analysis and the Prehistoric Settlement of Polynesia', *Proceedings of the National Academy of Sciences*, vol 92, 1995, pp 1881–85.
37   Nicholas Erskine, 'The Pitcairn Project: A Preliminary Report of the First Integrated Archaeological Investigation of the Mutineer Settlement of Pitcairn Island', *Bulletin of the Australian Institute for Maritime Archaeology*, vol 23, 1999b, pp 3–9; Nicholas Erskine, 'The Historical Archaeology of Settlement at Pitcairn Island, 1790–1856', PhD thesis, James Cook University, 2004.

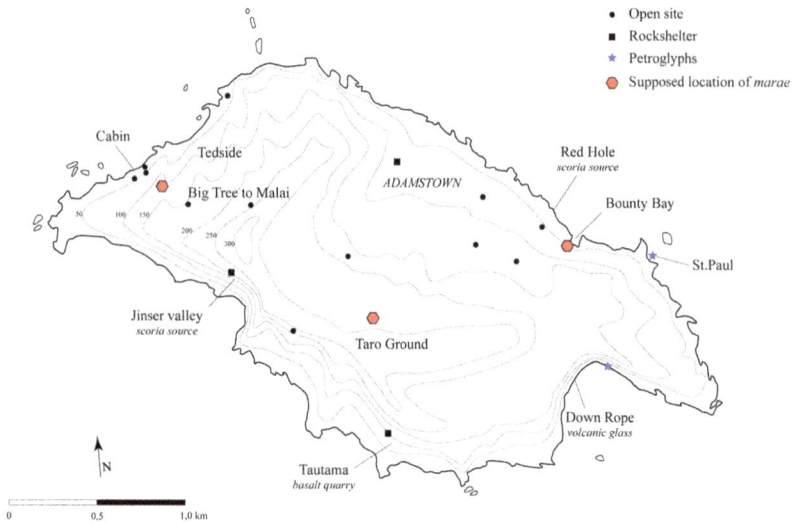

Figure 2.2. Location of archaeological sites on Pitcairn.
Source: After Weisler (1995).

Exploitation of stone resources

Peter Gathercole's report noted that 'the whole of Pitcairn island is a "site", in the sense that over much of its surface can be found flakes of basalt, and to a lesser degree pitchstones, fragments of worked tuff, hewn stones and carted beach boulders'.[38] All visitors highlight the importance of stone implements, both in the archaeological landscape and in museum collections. Along with Eiao in the northern Marquesas, Pitcairn offers one of the finest sources of good-quality basalt in Central Eastern Polynesia. For this reason, these two islands constituted major sources in the past, allowing ancient Polynesians to produce various types of valued stone implements. On Pitcairn, these tools include mostly adzes but also side-hafted axes, picks, drills, chisels, gouges, stone balls and projectile points.[39]

---

38   Gathercole, 1964, p 19.
39   Kenneth P Emory, 'Stone Implements of Pitcairn Island', *Journal of the Polynesian Society*, vol 37, 1928, pp 125–35; Heyerdahl & Skjölsvold, 1965a; Heyerdahl & Skjölsvold, 'Artifacts Collected on Certain Islands in Eastern Polynesia', in Heyerdahl & Ferdon, 1965b, pp 155–68; Gonzalo Figueroa & Eduardo Sanchez, 'Adzes from Certain Islands in Eastern Polynesia', in Heyerdahl & Ferdon, 1965, pp 169–254.

2. PITCAIRN BEFORE THE MUTINEERS

In the early years of Polynesian archaeology, distinctive morphologies and styles of adze blades were used as cultural markers to identify connections between islands and to further hypothesise migration routes.[40] Pitcairn's archaeological assemblages show great typological variability. Nearly all of the types of East Polynesian adzes and axes identified by Roger Duff[41] are present on the island. Both types 1 and 2 (Figures 2.3a & 2.3b) are widespread in all archipelagos and correspond to a formative period in Eastern Polynesian societies. In contrast, types 3E and 4A show morphological specificities that are unique to Pitcairn, such as the great flare towards the cutting edge in type 3E (Figure 2.3c), the thinness of type 4A (Figure 2.3d) and a tendency towards symmetrical bevels. Most adzes in those two categories are of exceptional size (between 30 and 50 centimetres in length) and, therefore, may have been prestige goods used in ceremonial contexts.

One can argue that these various types of adze blades were likely to have been produced by local specialists excelling in stone knapping. Indeed, the use of percussion to shape these fine tools, rather than 'easier' techniques such as pecking or hammering[42] would seem to argue in favour of advanced knowledge in the manufacture of stone tools. In Pitcairn assemblages, the work of specialists is even more likely where stone hammer percussion was used for fine shaping. Tremendous skill was involved in all stages of the production process, from the roughing out to finishing phases of the blade production process.

A series of sites has been explored and partly tested by archaeologists. The most prominent of these, located at Tautama on the south-east shore, encompasses an area of approximately 1 hectare stretching between the base of a cliff and the sea. Polynesian-introduced banyan trees in the vicinity indicate the presence of cultural remains. The entire surface is covered with flaked debris of hard, dark-grey, fine-grained basalt that was collected downslope and quarried at Tautama.[43] The high density of flakes and roughouts in this area probably corresponds to a first stage

---

40   Kenneth P Emory, 'East Polynesian Relationships as Revealed through Adzes', in I Yawata & Y Sinoto (eds), *Prehistoric Culture in Oceania, A Symposium*, Bishop Museum Press, 1968, pp 151–70.
41   Roger S Duff, *The Moa-Hunter Period of Maori Culture*, 3rd edn, Wellington, Government Printer, 1977.
42   Emory, 1928, p 127; Figueroa & Sanchez, 1965, p 178; John FG Stokes, 'Stone Implements', in Robert T Aitken (ed), *Ethnology of Tubuai*, Honolulu, BP Bishop Museum Bulletin, vol 70, 1930, pp 139–40.
43   Gathercole, 1964, p 40.

of manufacture, while the completion process took place elsewhere. A small rock shelter located 20 metres away from the quarry contains the remains of human occupation, including several charcoal layers, shells and bones. Gathercole collected samples but no radiocarbon date has ever been published. One might suppose, however, that the site was occupied by small groups of adze makers working at Tautama.

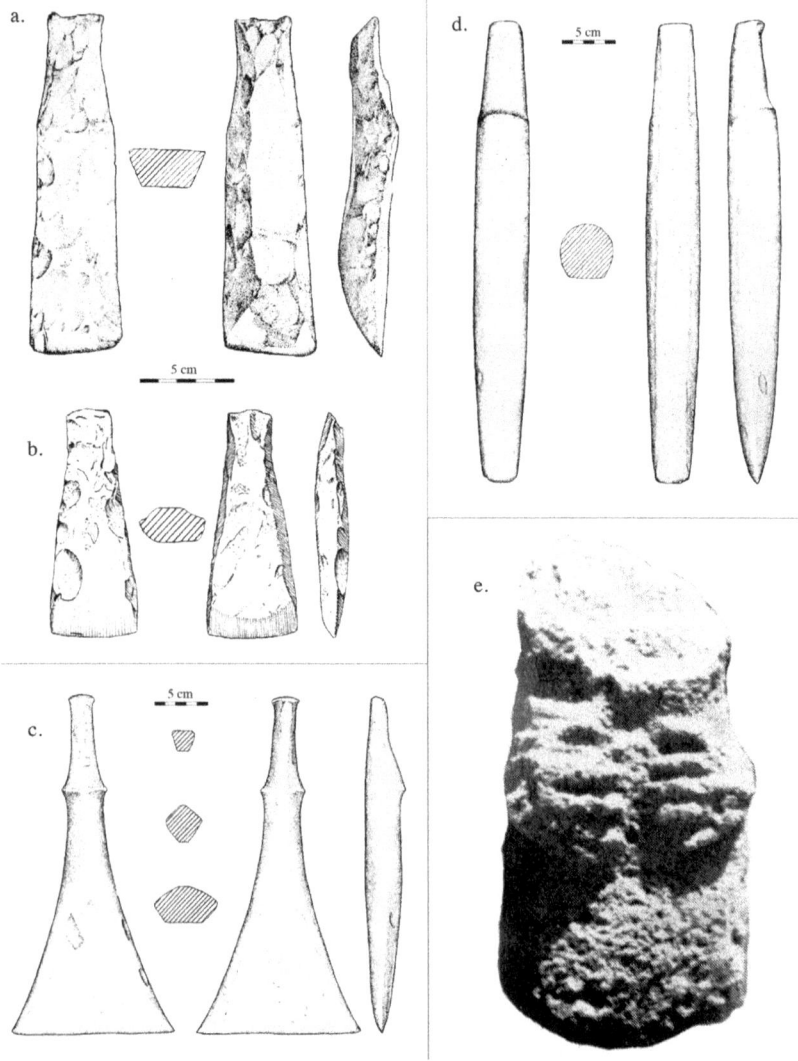

Figure 2.3. Typical stone adze blades and a tiki from Pitcairn.
Source: a–d: After Figueroa & Sanchez (1965); e: After Heyerdahl & Skjölsvold (1965a).

2. PITCAIRN BEFORE THE MUTINEERS

Aside from the Tautama source, which provides among the best quality basalt in south-eastern central Polynesia, Pitcairn offers other geological resources. Red volcanic tuff is found in at least two locations: Red Hole on the north-east shore near Bounty Bay, and in the Jinser valley on the south-west edge of the island (Figure 2.2). The latter was investigated by Thor Heyerdahl and Gathercole.[44] This cave is difficult to access as it is located in a cliff and situated 50 metres above the sea. It contains a zone of red scoria underlain by vesicular basalt and other basalt dykes. Volcanic tuff was used on many islands for stone carving: on Rapa Nui, the *pukao* hats of the *moai* were made of tuff from Puna Pau; while, in the Marquesas, white, yellow and red tuff called *keʻetu* was carved with *tiki* and displayed on *meʻae* temple sites. On Pitcairn, the red tuff from Jinser valley could have been employed for the same purpose, as discussed further below. It is also possible, however, that tuff was used as an abrader to polish and hone basalt, as noted by the geologist Robert M Carter from the Gathercole expedition.[45] This idea is consistent with the discovery of such fragments found in association with basalt flakes and finished tools in many locations across the island.

Also of note is the presence of a volcanic glass source on Pitcairn situated near Down Rope in the south-west of the island. The source consists of ignimbrite with patches of welded grey and black glass.[46] This material is often referred to as obsidian, to which it is petrographically close. It is rarely found in Polynesia, except on Rapa Nui where it was widely used to manufacture projectile points called *mataʻa*.[47] Such artefacts have been recovered from excavations on Henderson Island, where they must have been imported from Pitcairn.

Living, surviving or adapting?

During the 19th and the 20th centuries, a large number of stone tools from Pitcairn were purchased by different museums (see Young, Chapter 7). Given the potential to generate an income from these objects, post-*Bounty* Pitcairners began to systematically collect objects, without regard for their

---

44   Heyerdahl & Skjölsvold, 1965a, p 6; Gathercole, 1964, p 50.
45   Gathercole, 1964, p 54.
46   Weisler, 1995, p 394.
47   William Mulloy, 'The Ceremonial Center of Vinapu', in Heyerdahl & Ferdon, 1965, pp 93–180; Michel Charleux, 'L'outillage lithique de l'île de Pâques. Considérations générales. Contribution à l'étude technologique et typologique de l'outillage pédonculé en obsidienne: les *mataʻa*', Masters thesis, Université Paris I Panthéon-Sorbonne, 1986.

archaeological context.[48] This caused a detrimental loss of information, hindering attempts to reconstruct the processes of raw material acquisition, tool manufacture and use. Archaeological data recovered from excavations on quarry sites, however, are insufficient to ascertain the nature of the Polynesian occupation in these areas. This question requires consideration of other categories of archaeological evidence.

Several excavations took place at different locations near Tedside, a place on the western side of Pitcairn where a stone platform was discovered.[49] The platform was constructed using vesicular basalt and beach boulders, the latter delineating a semicircular area where basalt points were manufactured, and may have been part of larger pavements that served as domestic sites. Another platform of 15 x 3 metres was discovered at a higher point on the slope. A few structures were also found further down the valley, at a location called Cabin. These appear to have been hearths, although their antiquity has not yet been determined. It is indeed interesting to note the presence of various remains in this area situated around 60 metres from a small sand beach. This embayment is one of two safe landing spots on Pitcairn (along with Bounty Bay) and 'may have been a convenient place to bring fine-grained basalt adze preforms from the Tautama quarry for finishing and grinding'.[50] In agreement with Peter Gathercole, Marshall Weisler interpreted the area as a place favoured for canoe manufacturing, as it provides a good launching spot. This argument was also supported by Henry Maude[51] who considered Pitcairn's timber resources to be the finest in the region. It is possible, therefore, that Pitcairn was visited because of its suitability for canoe construction.[52]

In addition to its wood resources, Pitcairn provided a fertile environment for growing various food crops and plants introduced by Polynesians over the course of their occupation. Teehuteatuaonoa – also known as Jenny, one of the Tahitian women amongst the *Bounty* settlers – reported the discovery of several species during the first days after their arrival on the island, including *taro* (*Caladium esculentum*), *autī* (*Cordyline fruticosa*) and, ironically enough, breadfruit (*Artocarpus altilis*). Paper mulberry (*Broussonetia papyrifera*) was also on the island, which proved useful in

---

48 Gathercole, 1964, p 6.
49 Gathercole, 1964, p 61.
50 Weisler, 1995, p 384.
51 Henry E Maude, 'The History of Pitcairn Island', in ASC Ross & AW Moverley (eds), *The Pitcairnese Language*, London, André Deutch, 1964, p 46.
52 Gathercole, 1964, p 81.

the first years of the post-*Bounty* settlement, as it allowed the Tahitian women to maintain their cultural tradition of *tapa* production[53] and provide clothing to the settlers.

Also relevant to the subject of resource availability is that the *Bounty* Pitcairners discovered a burial site on a *marae* (see below) in which the individual lay on his back with his head resting on a mother-of-pearl shell. Mother-of-pearl is scarce in Pitcairn's archaeological records. Thor Heyerdahl reports finding a pearl-shell scraper and two partially worked pieces of pearl shell.[54] At a place known as Bills Ground III, Gathercole's team uncovered the only pearl-shell fishhook ever discovered on the island.[55] The scarcity of pearl-shell artefacts may be explained by a bias in archaeological sampling due to insufficient survey of coastal areas where they are usually found. Moreover, Pitcairn's acidic soil conditions do not favour the preservation of this material.[56] Importantly, however, *Pinctada margaritifera* pearl shell does not grow in Pitcairn's waters and was more likely imported from the Gambier lagoons, where it is abundant (Figure 2.4).

That being said, and supposing that Pitcairn was once inhabited by a large population, they did not import pearl shells in numbers large enough to manufacture fishhooks, a major item in the Polynesian tool kit. People must have turned to other local resources to overcome this constraint, developing stone fishhook manufacturing instead. Indeed, as we mentioned earlier, several stone hooks are found in museum collections.[57] Although stone hooks are more common on Rapa Nui (and in New Zealand), the Pitcairn specimens evince a different system in tying the line to the head. Geochemical analysis has not been run on these fishhooks in order to ascertain a basalt source, but we hypothesise that their makers chose the Tautama fine-grained stone to manufacture them. This highlights two points of interest that are explored further below: the importation of pearl shell, and Polynesian adaptation to local resources.

---

53   Erskine, 2004, p 175.
54   Heyerdahl & Skjölsvold, 1965b.
55   Gathercole, 1964, p 76.
56   Weisler, 1997, p 157.
57   Bengt Anell, *Contribution to the History of Fishing in the Southern Seas*, Uppsala, Studia Ethnographica Upsaliensia, vol 9, 1955, p 105; Henry Skinner, 'A Classification of the Fishhooks of Murihiku, with Notes on Allied Forms from Other Parts of Polynesia', *Journal of the Polynesian Society*, vol 51, 1942, pp 208–21, 256–86; Roger C Green, 'Pitcairn Island Fishhooks in Stone', *Journal of the Polynesian Society*, vol 68, no 1, 1959, pp 21–23.

Religious practices

One of the most challenging aspects of Pitcairn's pre-European history lies in the assumed existence of *marae*, the traditional Polynesian temple sites. Several early visitors, including Frederick Beechey and Henri Lavachery, report having seen *marae* remains in different places. Descriptions differ between accounts and, in the absence of detailed maps, it is now impossible to locate these sites with precision. Moreover, shortly after their arrival, the *Bounty* mutineers destroyed the *marae* for religious reasons, and some of their descendants later participated in their final destruction.[58] It is likely that the stone material employed in *marae* construction, such as hewn tuff slabs and boulders, was removed by later Pitcairners for building cisterns, house thresholds and steps.[59]

The main site, identified as site no 1 by Lavachery, was located at the eastern edge of Adamstown, on a cliff overlooking Bounty Bay. It is not clear, however, if it was lying at the Edge, as claimed by Lavachery, or further east of the bay at Ships Landing Point, which would fit Beechey's account.[60] Beechey was told that the *Bounty* mutineers had found four stone statues, about 1.8 metres in height, standing on a platform. At that time, only one statue had been preserved but it was later thrown down the cliff when the site was destroyed by later Pitcairners, perhaps in the early 20th century. In 1919, Katherine Routledge made observations in the area designated by Beechey as the location of this *marae*. She noted a 3.6-metre-high human-made embankment at the edge of the cliff. While its seaward face was vertical, the landward face formed an inclined plane extending over 12 metres in length. Routledge assumes that both sides were paved with marine boulders, and eventually compares the general arrangement of the site with the semi-pyramid *ahu* she had previously documented on Rapa Nui.[61] In 1935, Lavachery did not find any remains of the sanctuary but gave a rough reconstruction based on Routledge's comments.[62] Unfortunately, Routledge's personal notes have never been published so we must rely on her brief description. The architectural similarities between the Pitcairn site and the Rapa Nui *ahu* are interesting, as they could provide evidence for the potential transfer of forms from

---

58   See Knight's report in Gathercole, 1964, p 28.
59   Gathercole, 1964, p 52.
60   Beechey, 1831, vol 1, p 112.
61   Routledge, 1919, p 313.
62   Lavachery, 1936, fig 2.

2. PITCAIRN BEFORE THE MUTINEERS

one island to the other. Both Routledge and Lavachery, however, though excellent archaeologists, may have been influenced by their experience on Rapa Nui, and thus inclined to make potentially overhasty regional comparisons.

Of the four statues formerly standing on site no 1, only one fragment remained during Lavachery's visit in 1935. It had been picked up from the base of the cliff at Bounty Bay and was now used as the supporting pillar of a house. The owner refused to allow Lavachery to transport it to Belgium, so the archaeologist took a photograph and described it in detail.[63] The statue was eventually sold in 1936 to the Dunedin Museum of Otago, where it is currently displayed (Figure 2.3e). The headless statue carved from red tuff is 76 centimetres high, 33 centimetres wide and 30 centimetres thick. Its large hands almost meet in front of the abdomen, which is a traditional posture in Polynesian statuary.

Lavachery located site no 2 inland, within the Taro Ground area, but there were no architectural features present at the time of his visit, and local informants reported that there were no stone statues on this site. Lavachery also noted the existence of a third site, which he did not visit, on the western part of the island in the Tedside area. His informants stated that a statue had stood on this *marae*, built on a cliff above Pitcairn's other primary landing area, but unfortunately the *marae* was now destroyed. There are contradictions between the information provided by different authors, and it is unclear if the *marae* was situated at Cabin or Big Tree to Malai, two localities that might have been visited by Beechey and Routledge.[64] Jacques-Antoine Moerenhout stated that he and his guides walked for a long time through several cultivated fields and across a valley to finally reach a high peak where the trail was rough and hazardous. Unlike Lavachery and Peter Gathercole, we propose that the site described by Moerenhout could be the one located at Tedside. Moerenhout's itinerary, and his description of a *marae* 'of considerable extent, ornamented at each corner with a statue of about 2.5 to 3 metres/8 to 10 feet in height, raised on platforms of stone masonry still very well joined together'[65] might apply to site no 3, and not site no 1, which is located close to Bounty Bay and is of easier access. It is therefore highly likely that the only stone image Moerenhout saw there was the same one that Lavachery was told about.

---

63   Lavachery, 1936, p 13.
64   Gathercole, 1964, p 37.
65   Moerenhout, 1837, p 53.

Furthermore, the existence of an ancient temple in this area would make sense in light of other remains discovered during Gathercole's expedition (see above).

The existence of at least three *marae* sites on Pitcairn points to a long-term occupation of the island rather than short-term visits. Indeed, the amount of effort put into the construction of *marae* and the carving of statues indicates a permanent settlement, which is also confirmed by associated burial sites discovered by later Pitcairners during their process of *marae* destruction. The ancient practice of burying individuals on *marae* (supposedly persons of higher rank) is attested elsewhere in Polynesia, especially in the Tuamotu archipelago[66] and on Temoe atoll in the Gambier Islands.[67] In this context, connecting the ancestors to the land is significant and further reveals the existence of a complex organisation in Pitcairn's ancient society.

In addition to religious sites, petroglyphs have been recorded at two locations. The most famous are situated at the base of Down Rope cliff at the rear of the beach. The panel of tuff on which they were incised measures 11 x 3.8 metres. First published partly by Walter Brodie,[68] then Léon Seurat,[69] they were studied in more detail by Lavachery.[70] The Down Rope site includes 22 figures representing human bodies, animals – supposedly chickens and maybe a dog and a pig – some features interpreted as tools, a canoe, and geometric figures. The other location, a cave facing St Paul's rock, east of Bounty Bay, shows eight figures including one human representation. Analysis of rock art is a delicate matter in Polynesia as figures can only be interpreted in relation to their general archaeological

---

66   Éric Conte & Kenneth Dennison, *Te Tahata. Etude d'un* marae *de Tepoto (Nord), Archipel des Tuamotu, Polynésie française*, Puna'auia, Les Cahiers du CIRAP, vol 1, 2009; Guillaume Molle, *Ancêtres-Dieux et Temples de corail: Approche ethnoarchéologique du complexe* marae *dans l'archipel des Tuamotu*, Tahiti, Collection Cahiers du CIRAP, vol 3, 2015; Guillaume Molle, 'Exploring Religious Practices on Polynesian Atolls: A Comprehensive Architectural Approach towards the *Marae* Complex in the Tuamotu Islands', *Journal of the Polynesian Society*, vol 125, no 3, 2016, pp 263–88.

67   Pascal Murail & Éric Conte, 'Les sépultures de l'atoll de Temoe (archipel des Gambier)', *Les Dossiers d'Archéologie Polynésienne*, no 4, 2005, pp 164–72; Guillaume Molle & Pascal Murail, *Recherches archéologiques et anthropologiques sur l'atoll de Temoe, archipel des Gambier. Rapport de la campagne 2010*, Punaauia, Université de la Polynésie française-CIRAP, 2012; Guillaume Molle, Pascal Murail & Aymeric Hermann, *Recherches archéologiques et anthropologiques sur l'atoll de Temoe, archipel des Gambier. Rapport de la campagne 2013*, Punaauia, Université de la Polynésie française-CIRAP, 2014.

68   Brodie, 1851, p 14.

69   Léon G Seurat, 'Sur les anciens habitants de l'île Pitcairn', *L'Anthropologie*, vol 15, 1904, pp 369–72.

70   Lavachery, 1936.

context.⁷¹ In Pitcairn, the two sites are independent of one another and neither archaeological structures nor any other remains have been found in either vicinity. It is therefore very difficult to interpret the significance of the figures. They might have been engraved for some ritual purpose for which we have no details.

Pitcairn in its regional context: Nuancing the isolation

Tracing ancient inter-island mobility and exchange in south-east Polynesia

Prior to the development of computer simulations and experimental voyaging,⁷² which established that Polynesian seafarers had the skills and abilities to navigate long distances, some researchers suggested that the colonisation of Pacific Islands was accidental or resulted from drift voyages, and that societies consequently evolved in total isolation on remote lands.⁷³ Recent studies, however, offer new evidence for previously unsuspected patterns of exchange between Polynesian islands during pre-European times and put into question the idea of isolation (see Teriierooiterai, Chapter 1). Geochemical analyses of volcanic rocks used for tool manufacture allow archaeologists to source the provenance of artefacts. These analyses have largely developed over the past two decades and the sourcing of Polynesian adzes has become a major focus of archaeological research.⁷⁴ Provenance studies have shown, in contrast to the idea of isolation, that Polynesian communities remained in contact for several centuries after their initial colonisation of islands, by exchanging

---

71 For Marquesan cases, see Sidsel Millerstrom, *Gravures rupestres et archéologie de l'habitat de Hatiheu à Nuku Hiva (Iles Marquises, Polynesie française)* (Puna'auia, Collection les Cahiers du Patrimoine – Archéologie, 2003).
72 Irwin, 1992; David Lewis, *We, the Navigators: the Ancient Art of Landfinding in the Pacific*, 2nd edn, Honolulu, University of Hawai'i Press, 1994; Ben Finney (ed), *Pacific Navigation and Voyaging*, Wellington, Polynesian Society Memoir, vol 39, 1976.
73 Andrew Sharp, *Ancient Voyagers in Polynesia*, Auckland, Paul Longman, 1963.
74 Collerson & Weisler, 2007; Weisler, 1997; Marshall I Weisler, 'Hard Evidence for Prehistoric Interaction in Polynesia', *Current Anthropology*, vol 39, 1998a, pp 531–32; Marshall I Weisler & Patrick V Kirch, 'Interisland and Interarchipelago Transport of Stone Tools in Prehistoric Polynesia', *Proceedings of the National Academy of Sciences*, vol 93, 1996, pp 1381–85; Weisler & Woodhead, 1995.

basalt artefacts as well as various other types of goods.[75] Inter-island communication indeed played an important role in political alliances that were sealed through inter-community marriage and the exchange of prestige items. Inter-archipelago transfers of commodities took place within interaction spheres of different scales in Central Eastern Polynesia.

Marshall Weisler[76] has been at the forefront of geochemical studies by conducting intensive research in the Gambier and Pitcairn island groups. Drawing on analyses of both raw material and finished artefacts, Weisler identified reciprocal exchanges of utilitarian items within the south-east region of Central Eastern Polynesia (Figure 2.4). Pitcairn provided fine-grained basalt and volcanic glass to Henderson and Mangareva for tool-making purposes. In return, abundant black-lipped pearl shell (*Pinctada margaritifera*), vesicular basalt used as oven stones, maybe *porites* coral files and abraders, and a variety of economically useful plants[77] originated from the Gambier Islands, while green sea turtles (*Chelonia mydas*) and red feathers of lory (*Vini stepheni*) or fruitdove (*Ptilinopus insulariis*) were imported from Henderson.[78] These rare red feathers were used by Polynesian chiefs as prestige items reflecting a divine nature, and were therefore intensively exchanged through specific networks that generally included high islands and atolls (like Society–Tuamotu or southern Cook–Austral–Society). The transfer of feathers and turtles, however, has never been ascertained archaeologically within the Pitcairn group.

---

75   Barry V Rolett, 'Voyaging and Interaction in Ancient East Polynesia', *Asian Perspectives*, vol 41, no 2, 2002, pp 182–94; Marshall I Weisler, 'Centrality and the Collapse of Long-Distance Voyaging in East Polynesia', in Michael D Glascock (ed), *Geochemical Evidence for Long-Distance Exchange*, Westport, Bergin & Garvey, 2002, pp 257–73; Mark Eddowes, 'Etude archéologique de l'île de Rimatara (Archipel des Australes)', *Dossiers d'Archéologie Polynésienne*, Puna'auia, Ministère de la Culture de Polynésie française, 2004; Collerson & Weisler, 2007; Aymeric Hermann, 'Production et échange des lames d'herminette en pierre en Polynésie centrale', in F Valentin & G Molle (eds), *La pratique de l'espace en Océanie: Découverte, appropriation et émergence des systèmes sociaux traditionnels*, Paris, Séances de la Société Préhistorique Française, no 7, 2016, pp 205–21.
76   Weisler, 1997; Weisler, 1998a; Marshall I Weisler, 'Issues in the Colonization and Settlement of Polynesian Islands', in Patricia Vargas Casanova (ed), *Easter Island and East Polynesian Prehistory*, Universidad de Chile, 1998b, pp 76–86; Weisler, 2002.
77   There is no doubt that the cultigens brought to Pitcairn originated from the Gambier Islands. Plant remains identified in archaeological contexts on Henderson could, however, have been introduced from both Pitcairn and Mangareva. Whether they were introduced during the initial settlement of the island or over the course of four centuries of inter-island interaction in the region remains unknown. The same issue occurs for introduced fauna, including pigs (*Sus scrofa*), chickens (*Gallus gallus*) and rats (*Rattus exulans*). See Horrocks & Weisler (2006).
78   Weisler, 1997.

2. PITCAIRN BEFORE THE MUTINEERS

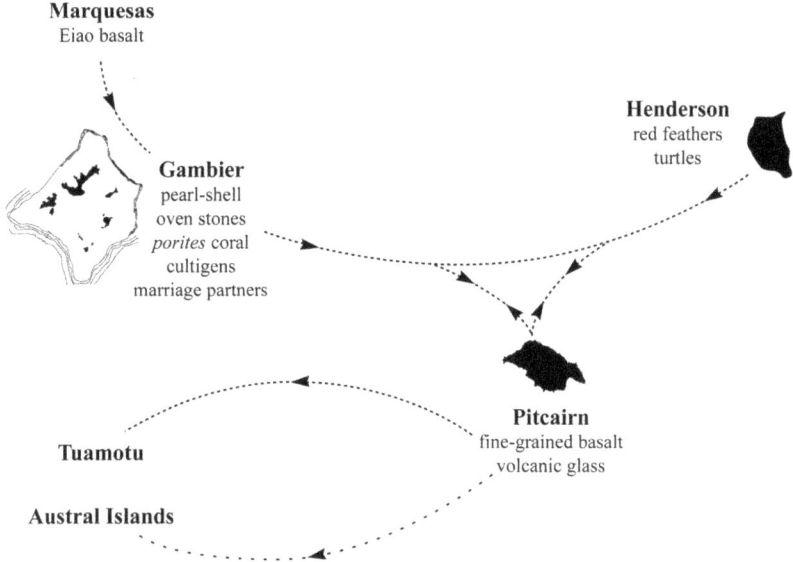

Figure 2.4. Patterns of interaction involving Pitcairn and the Gambier islands.
Source: After Weisler (1995, 1997, 1998a); Collerson & Weisler (2007); Hermann (2013).

In addition to these items, marriage partners were also exchanged. Maintaining connections between islands, particularly those inhabited by small isolated communities, both favoured their development and helped populations face harsh ecological conditions. The case of Henderson provides a striking example of the role of inter-island exchange and voyaging in sustaining small communities in an extremely impoverished environment.[79]

Given its central position within the south-east region, Pitcairn might have played the role of an intermediary in the exchange of items. It may be seen as a hub in a 'down-the-line' network pattern extending from the Gambier Islands in the west to Henderson in the east. Other recent data show that stone resources from Pitcairn were also distributed outside the south-east sphere of interaction identified by Weisler: an adze collected on the atoll of Katiu in the Tuamotu archipelago has been sourced to Pitcairn's Tautama basalt quarry,[80] and primary analysis of two volcanic glass flakes discovered in the Atiahara site on Tubua'i Island (Austral archipelago) show

---

79   Weisler, 1997, p 170.
80   Collerson & Weisler, 2007.

a geochemical signature matching the Down Rope outcrop in Pitcairn.[81] Indeed, recent investigations provide information to reconstruct an extensive sphere of interaction including all archipelagos from the Cook Islands to Pitcairn and the Marquesas, through the Societies, the Australs and the Tuamotu archipelago (Figure 2.4) during the first centuries of Polynesian presence in the region.[82]

The abandonment of Pitcairn: Why, when and how?

An examination of archaeological data shows evidence of long-term human occupation on Pitcairn Island. Given that the island was deserted when the *Bounty* mutineers landed in 1790, however, Peter Bellwood was led to classify Pitcairn as one of the 'Mysterious Islands' of the Pacific, reinforcing the idea of its isolation. Several researchers have tackled this question and proposed different hypotheses to explain the abandonment of Pitcairn.

The desertion of the island was first presented as a consequence of decline in inter-island voyaging and exchanges in Central Eastern Polynesia by the 15th century, a phenomenon also referred to as the 'contraction' of interaction spheres.[83] Exchanges did not stop suddenly, nor completely, but rather decreased in intensity and became confined to geographically limited networks within archipelagos, as described in oral traditions. Patterns observed in the Cook and the Marquesas islands demonstrate a similar sequence of an interruption in long-distance exchange and a consequent adaptation to local resources.[84] Within the Mangareva–Pitcairn sphere, such a sequence is revealed through archaeological records, especially on Henderson where artefacts produced after the 15th century were no longer made of imported material (such as basalt from Pitcairn or pearl shell from the Gambier Islands) but of local material

---

81 Aymeric Hermann, 'Les industries lithiques pré-européennes de Polynésie centrale: savoir-faire et dynamiques techno-économiques', PhD thesis, University of French Polynesia, 2013, p 184.
82 Collerson & Weisler, 2007; Hermann, 2013; Andrew McAlister, Peter J Sheppard & Melinda S Allen, 'The Identification of a Marquesan Adze in the Cook Islands', *Journal of the Polynesian Society*, vol 122, no 3, 2014, pp 257–74; Barry Rolett, Eric W West, John M Sinton & Radu Lovita, 'Ancient East Polynesian Voyaging Spheres: New Evidence from the Vitaria Adze Quarry (Rurutu, Austral Islands)', *Journal of Archaeological Science*, vol 53, 2015, pp 459–71.
83 Rolett, 2002; Weisler, 2002.
84 Richard Walter, 'The Southern Cook Islands in Eastern Polynesian Prehistory', PhD thesis, University of Auckland, 1990; Barry Rolett, 'Hanamiai: Prehistoric Colonization and Cultural Change in the Marquesas Islands (East Polynesia)', *Publications in Anthropology*, no 81, 1998.

instead, including *tridacna* shell adzes and *isognomon* shell fishhooks.[85] Archaeological records on Pitcairn are still insufficient to demonstrate such a pattern, although it is clear that neither basalt from the Tautama quarry nor volcanic glass from Down Rope has ever been recovered from other Polynesian islands after AD 1450, which indicates an interruption in exports.

The Henderson population maintained their autonomy after the 'collapse' of inter-island voyaging, and eventually left permanently by AD 1600.[86] There is no chronological data available to date the actual abandonment of Pitcairn. As its environmental conditions are more favourable than those of Henderson, however, it is highly probable that a sustainable occupation was maintained there for at least as long as on Henderson. Moreover, the construction of *marae* on Pitcairn might date from a relatively recent period, probably post-16th century, based on what we know about the regional development of ceremonial architecture. Although further investigation is needed, we can assume that the island was abandoned during the 17th century or maybe at the beginning of the 18th century. Given this, the contraction of interaction spheres cannot be the only cause for deserting the islands. The exact reasons for contraction have not been entirely established, but it is likely that a combination of different ecological and sociopolitical factors led to the abandonment of Pitcairn and Henderson.

Environmental fragility due to anthropogenic pressure has been proposed by several authors as a reason for abandonment. Jared Diamond[87] and Atholl Anderson[88] have described these islands as highly vulnerable to faunal depletion through over-exploitation. They have also argued that local populations were unable to overcome these environmental constraints through the development of agriculture. This could explain the situation on Henderson where the over-predation of nesting birds led to avian extinction and extirpation.[89] On the other hand, prehistoric faunal

---

85 Weisler, 1995.
86 Weisler, 1995.
87 Jared Diamond, 'Why Did the Polynesians Abandon their Mystery Islands?', *Nature*, vol 317, 1985, p 764.
88 Anderson, 2001; Atholl Anderson, 'Faunal Collapse, Landscape Change and Settlement History in Remote Oceania', *World Archaeology*, vol 33, no 3, 2002, pp 375–90.
89 Susan E Schubel & David W Steadman, 'More Bird Bones from Archaeological sites on Henderson Island, Pitcairn Group, South Pacific', *Atoll Research Bulletin*, vol 325, 1985, pp 1–13; Graham M Wragg & Marshall I Weisler, 'Extinctions and New Records of Birds from Henderson Island, Pitcairn Group, South Pacific Ocean', *Notornis*, vol 41, 2004, pp 61–70.

extinction has not yet been recorded on Pitcairn. Unlike Henderson, the high island of Pitcairn and its maritime environment provided its inhabitants with other food resources, through fishing and the cultivation of various prehistorically introduced crops (see above). Pitcairn did, however, face episodes of ecological degradation as it was partly deforested and eroded when the *Bounty* mutineers arrived.[90] It is therefore likely that the island's ability to regenerate was significantly reduced. Water resources are relatively limited on the island and, therefore, extended periods of drought could have destabilised the local hydrographic system and impacted on the inhabitants.[91] In the absence of further investigation, it is difficult to evaluate the role of environmental change on the abandonment of Pitcairn.

Mangareva turns out to be pivotal within the organisation of the south-east interaction sphere, as exchanges were likely controlled by the chiefdoms of the Gambier Islands. Given that Mangareva was a gateway to remote archipelagos such as the Marquesas and the Society islands, the Pitcairn group was likely to be highly dependent on Mangareva for long-term survival. This dependency became even more critical after the interruption of long-distance voyaging and connections with the Marquesas. As a result, the role of the Gambier Islands as a node in the region was reinforced after the 15th century, and sociopolitical development in Mangareva would have impacted neighbouring islands. According to Irving Goldman, prior to European contact, the people of Mangareva participated in a 'stratified society' that was riddled with rivalries and almost constant warfare.[92] From this perspective, Marshall Weisler hypothesises that, by the 16th century, Mangareva reached an untenable sociopolitical situation, 'withdrawing from servicing the Pitcairn group', which eventually led to the abandonment of the islands.[93]

While explaining the abandonment of the 'Mysterious Islands' remains challenging given our limited understanding of local settlement histories, this brief review of existing hypotheses shows that the desertion of Pitcairn did not happen suddenly but consisted of a final, and somehow inevitable, response to both internal and external factors. Pitcairn's Polynesian

---

90 Weisler, 1995.
91 Gathercole, 1964.
92 Irving Goldman, 'Status Rivalry and Cultural Evolution in Polynesia', *American Anthropologist*, vol 57, no 4, 1955, pp 680–97.
93 Weisler, 2002, p 268.

community remained on the island in a state of relative autonomy after the collapse of the south-east interaction sphere and adapted to local environmental conditions.

Conclusion

The early prehistoric occupation of Pitcairn was probably motivated by the exploitation of valued local resources, and succeeded due to a network of interaction with neighbouring islands and archipelagos that continued for at least five centuries after initial colonisation. Evidence for inter-island voyaging in the south-east region shows that the Polynesian community on Pitcairn was not isolated but maintained constant relations with allied groups that were easily reachable by short canoe trips. Even after the interruption of long-distance exchanges by the 15th century, archaeological data tends to support the idea that a sociopolitical group lived on Pitcairn for longer.

By 1790, however, the island was deserted. Pitcairn was the perfect answer to the *Bounty* mutineers' search for a remote place outside the travel routes of Western ships that might allow them to escape British pursuit.[94] Moreover, it had been wrongly charted, both by Philip Carteret, the first Westerner to sight the island, and by John Hawkesworth who transcribed the British navigators' *Voyages* (see Young, Chapter 7). Nicholas Erskine's investigation of the historical archaeology of the island also demonstrates that the *Bounty* colonists' initial settlement in the Adamstown area was directed by a 'fundamental concern for concealment'.[95] The destruction of the vessel further removed all chances of leaving the island.[96] The isolation they sought on a remote island was reinforced by their decision to burn the ship, leaving these new islanders with no means of communication with the outside world.

By taking a long-term historical view of Pitcairn Island we are confronted by two intriguingly distinctive perceptions of insular 'isolation': Polynesian and European. In both cases, geographic isolation determined social evolution on the island. The different contexts of settlement and distinct

---

94 Henry E Maude, 'Tahitian Interlude. The Migration of Pitcairn Islanders to the Motherland in 1831', *Journal of Polynesian Society*, vol 68, no 2, 1959, pp 115–40.
95 Erskine, 2004, p 148.
96 Erskine, 2004, p 2.

cultural backgrounds have, however, led these groups to comprehend isolation in different ways. For Polynesians, the ocean was mostly seen as a facilitator of communication with other lands and groups. This idea remains strong today among Pacific Islanders, as demonstrated by the work of historian Paul D'Arcy.[97] In contrast, Europeans[98] on Pitcairn voluntarily subjected themselves to isolation in a bounded territory whose maritime perimeter served as a protective barrier to communication with the outside world.

The *Bounty* mutineers' extreme isolation lasted for 18 years until the *Topaz*, an American sealing vessel, arrived and heralded the beginning of a new period in the modern history of Pitcairn. Even though the post-1790 settlement survived, difficulties were numerous and adaptation to the unfamiliar environment was challenging for the Europeans, who mostly relied on materials salvaged from the *Bounty* to maintain a semblance of Western life.[99] From the 1820s, the mutineers' descendants began to open up to the world in response to more frequent visits to the island by whalers and commercial vessels (see Naugrette, Chapter 5). As a direct consequence, opportunities for trade developed and Pitcairners obtained a large range of utilitarian items in exchange for water and food as well as other *Bounty* relics (see Young, Chapter 7). This system of trade soon became regulated, and eventually led the British Government to grant the island the status of a British protectorate (see Young, Chapter 7). It is noteworthy that the increasing trade severely impacted the environment of the island through the exploitation of timber resources, production of agricultural surpluses, and associated land clearance and catastrophic erosion.[100] In 1853, an episode of drought brought the trading to an end and revealed the vulnerability of the island. Three years later, an official decision was made to relocate the community to Norfolk Island, resulting once again in the abandonment of Pitcairn.

---

97 Paul D'Arcy, *The People of the Sea: Environment, Identity, and History in Oceania*, Honolulu, University of Hawai'i Press, 2006.
98 We refer to the *Bounty* settlement here as European, reflecting the fact that the Polynesian members of the group were never allowed to take part in any decision-making concerning the development of the colony. In the first years of the settlement, the Polynesian men were almost reduced to slaves by Englishmen.
99 Erskine, 2004, p 207.
100 Erskine, 2004, p 212.

Following the discovery of the *Bounty* survivors and descendants, an entire literature emerged that included popular fiction and historical novels (see Jolly & Petch, Chapter 6; and Naugrette, Chapter 5). This genre of Crusoe-like island adventure narratives, whose characters face extreme environmental conditions, has highlighted and reinforced the isolated nature of the island in Western minds. Conversely, the long-term occupation of Pitcairn exemplifies the efflorescence of sustainable communities in the most marginal islands of Polynesia prior to European arrival. Similarly, the reconstruction of inter-island exchange networks reveals how Greg Dening's 'little people', who first settled this remote island, remained connected with other groups through regional spheres of interaction for several centuries. As Scott Fitzpatrick and Atholl Anderson[101] remind us, there is a real challenge in endeavouring to assess how various degrees of interaction and isolation may have shaped island societies at various points in their historical trajectories. In Polynesia, as in most Pacific Islands, shores were reached and beaches were crossed many times, long before European explorers, missionaries or even mutineers entered the scene.

---

101 Scott M Fitzpatrick & Atholl Anderson, 'Islands of Isolation: Archaeology and the Power of Aquatic Perimeters', *Journal of Island and Coastal Archaeology*, vol 3, no 1, 2008, pp 4–16.

3

Reading the Bodies of the *Bounty* Mutineers

Rachael Utting
Royal Holloway, University of London

On 15 October 1789, Lieutenant William Bligh wrote a damning letter to the British Admiralty in which he described the physical characteristics of the mutinous so-called pirates who cast him and 18 others adrift from the HMAV *Bounty* in a 7-metre open boat. Bligh and his launch crew covered nearly 4,000 nautical miles between Tofua and Coupang (now known as Kupang), in Timor, South-East Asia, in what is widely considered to be one of the most impressive and inspirational episodes in open-boat sea survival. They arrived at Coupang, weak and exhausted after six weeks at sea, on 14 June, 'perhaps a more miserable set of beings were never seen' who could 'not have existed a week or a day longer'.[1] Remarkably, only one of their number had died, not from the rigours of the journey but from an attack by Islanders on the shores of Tofua, a small island where they had briefly found respite from their voyage (see Teriierooiterai, Chapter 1). A further four members died of disease in the ports of Coupang and Batavia (Jakarta). In the weeks and months after Bligh and his crew arrived in port, he was alight with indignation and penned a series of letters, both to the families of those mutineers

---

1   18 Aug 1789, ADM 1/1506 (9), The National Archives, London (TNA). This reference number covers all of Bligh's letters held in this file. Unhelpfully, several of these were written on the same day. Wherever possible dates have been added to aid archival research.

who had betrayed his trust and to the authorities, outlining his version of events. In an attempt to vindicate himself for the loss of his ship in the obligatory court martial he knew he would face on his return to England, Bligh ensured every member of the launch crew signed an exculpatory affidavit witnessed by the governor of Batavia, William Adrian Van Este.[2] This stated that Bligh was in no way responsible for the 'unforeseeable and unpreventable' loss of the *Bounty* and would 'use his utmost exertions to appear before their lordships and answer for the loss of his majesty's ship'.[3] After recuperating at Coupang, Bligh and his remaining crew sailed to Batavia and, from there, in separate vessels on to England via the Cape of Good Hope. The day before he sailed on the Dutch packet SS *Vlydte*, Bligh wrote what was effectively a wanted poster for the mutineers. This revealing letter, now housed in the National Archives, London, intimately describes the bodies of those individuals whom Bligh sought to capture.[4] Based on an earlier version written during the open-boat voyage, the letter outlines their markings in the form of tattoos, scars, effects of disease and wounds, and physical anomalies. These were described from Bligh's own memory and 'from the recollections of the persons with me, who were best acquainted with their marks'.[5]

This chapter does not investigate the guilt or innocence of those involved in the mutiny; this has been discussed at length in print and film over the last 200 years. Rather, its aim is to dissect Bligh's letter, to use the body as the primary focus of investigation and to discuss the physical characteristics of the *Bounty* mutineers.[6] The document identified involuntary markings such as scars and wounds, and voluntary ones such as Polynesian *tatau* and Euro-American tattoos, the presence of which is a key factor in criminalising the mutineers within the Western consciousness. The chapter questions how these markings function

---

2   Greg Dening, *Mr Bligh's Bad Language: Passion, Power and Theatre on the Bounty*, Cambridge, Cambridge University Press, 1992, p 108.
3   18 Aug 1789, ADM 1/1506 (9), TNA.
4   18 Aug 1789, ADM 1/1506 (9), TNA.
5   18 Aug 1789, ADM 1/1506 (9), TNA.
6   The *Bounty*'s crew members are identified in two groups: those that accompanied Bligh in the launch (the launch crew), and those that remained with the ship (the mutineers). This distinction is not indicative of guilt or innocence, and is provided merely for clarity within the text. The crew of the *Bounty* are broadly referred to as Euro-American, rather than their specific nationalities. This identifies them as falling under the umbrella of Western philosophy, teachings and religions whilst 'differentiating them from those who can be regarded as non-European in cultural and ideological terms' (S Williams Milcairns, *Native Strangers; Beachcombers, Renegades and Castaways in the South Seas*, Auckland, Penguin Books, 2006, p 16). Where quoting directly from the sailors, I have kept to their original, somewhat individual spelling and grammar. Any idiosyncrasies are their own.

in a communicative context and highlights how, through acts of body modification, the mutineers attempted to reclaim their bodies from the subjectification of the British Royal Navy and integrate into Tahitian life.

Bligh's marked men

William Bligh's 'description list of the pirates' is one of several versions. The first was drafted in his notebook during the open-boat voyage when he and his subordinates certainly had plenty of time to trawl their collective memory for details, and one assumes their vitriol was at its highest.[7] In addition to this, whilst recuperating in Batavia, Bligh wrote a version for Governor Van Este and gave another to the governor-general of India, Lord Cornwallis. These were to be distributed to 'their different settlements to detain the ship wherever she may be found' as 'it is impossible to say where a set of piratical people may go'.[8] Van Este's copy was translated into Dutch and was clearly intended for the widest distribution possible.[9] Bligh also took the opportunity to send a description of the mutineers to the newly formed Australian penal colony of Port Jackson.[10] This illustrates the scope of such letters to migrate across geographic and linguistic boundaries and reach any number of European colonial outposts, spreading and reaffirming the view of what 'criminals' looked like, particularly ones who bore the distinct characteristics of a sailor. As maritime historian Marcus Rediker states, 'jack tar's body often gave away his line of work … much to the delight of the press gangs that combed the port towns'.[11] His body was deeply tanned with a face that had 'withstood the most obstinate assaults of the weather', due to the nature of his work he often had broken or disfigured hands. He had marks of warfare and violence, a distinct way of speaking and walking, 'swinging [his] corps like a pendulum and believing it the most upright steady motion'.[12] All of these distinct characteristics were found upon the bodies of the *Bounty* mutineers, from

---

7   W Bligh, 'Notebook and List of Mutineers', 1789, MS 5393, nla.gov.au/nla.ms-ms5393-2.
8   18 Aug 1789, ADM 1/1506 (9), TNA, p 26.
9   W Bligh, *A Voyage to the South Seas, Undertaken by Command of His Majesty for the Purpose of Conveying the Breadfruit Tree to the West Indies in His Majesty's Ship the Bounty*, London, P Wogan, 1792, p 362.
10 Sven Wahlroos, *Mutiny and Romance in the South Seas; A Companion to the Bounty Adventure*, Massachusetts, Salem House Publishers, 1989, p 89.
11 M Rediker, *Between the Devil and the Deep Blue Sea. Merchant Seamen, Pirates, and the Anglo American Maritime World, 1700–1750*, Cambridge, Cambridge University Press, 1987, p 12.
12 N Ward, 1756, quoted in Rediker, 1987, p 11.

the bow-leggedness of Fletcher Christian to the damaged arm of Henry Hillbrant whose 'left arm [is] shorter than the right, [where it] has been broke', to the 'dark' or 'high brown' complexions of Edward Young and John Millward amongst others.[13]

Although Bligh's letter forms part of a chain of private correspondence, details of the mutiny soon appeared in the national press. Bligh's racial terminology was typical of that used in the emerging print culture of the era. The newspapers used a rich visual language to describe individuals at large, whether runaway slaves, servants, military absconders or everyday criminals. In order to facilitate an arrest, this necessarily concise language contained a 'verbal shorthand' focused on those features most easily recognisable by the public.[14] The height, skin colour and demeanour of miscreants were obvious starting points on which to build a public image of a formerly private body.[15] Bligh's letter is in keeping with this literary tradition, listing these attributes for each mutineer in addition to their ages, scars, wounds and tattoos. In order to describe skin tone, he used a palette ranging from 'sallow' to 'pale' and 'high brown' to 'dark brown' and, finally, 'blackish', which he reserved for Christian. These terms were not *necessarily* indicative of ethnic background; darkened skin was the mark of career sailors. It was an easily recognisable side effect of their profession. They were terms that could also be used to indicate the sense of dirt and moral laxity associated with the British lower classes from which the bulk of maritime workers were drawn. It was within these lower classes that tattooing was principally associated, having been used to mark criminals and deserters from the British army (a practice begun in 1717 and not rescinded until 1879) and, with increasing popularity, nomadic social groups such as soldiers and sailors.[16] Within the consciousness of the literate upper classes the fact that tattooing had been used for largely

---

13   18 Aug 1789, ADM 1/1506 (9), TNA.
14   G Morgan & P Rushton, 'Visible Bodies: Power, Subordination and Identity in the Eighteenth-Century Atlantic World', *Journal of Social History*, vol 39, no 1, 2005, p 42.
15   The term 'private' is used with restraint as by the late 18th century the bodies of the populous were undergoing increasing scrutiny from bureaucratic sources. Workhouses, hospitals, asylums and jails kept increasingly detailed records for public and private uses. See Douglas Hay, Peter Linebaugh, John G Rule, EP Thompson & Cal Winslow (eds), *Albion's Fatal Tree: Crime and Society in Eighteenth-Century England* (London, Allen Lane, 1975); H Maxwell Stuart & J Bradley, '"Behold the Man": Power, Observation and the Tattooed Convict' (*Australian Studies*, vol 12, no 1, 1997, pp 71–97).
16   See, for example, the 'Branding tool for marking deserters, London, 1810–1850' in the collection of the Science Museum, London, obj no A627067, broughttolife.sciencemuseum.org.uk/broughttolife/objects/display?id=92953 See also, Ira Dye, 'Tattoos of Early American Seafarers, 1796–1818' (*Proceedings of the American Philosophical Society*, vol 133, no 4, 1989, pp 520–21).

punitive purposes encouraged an association between tattoos and the criminality of the proletariat masses. In addition to this, the popularity of voyage narratives with their descriptions and illustrations of 'painted natives' ensured that indigenous tattoos had become the sign of the exotic other, the identifying mark of natives and savages.[17] That the *Bounty* mutineers were described as being so heavily tattooed only incriminated them further; as if the act of mutiny wasn't bad enough, they had taken up with island women and gone native. The *General Evening News* reported:

> The most probable conjecture is, that, being principally young men they were greatly fascinated by the Circean blandishments of the Otaheitean women, they took this desperate method of returning to scenes of voluptuousness unknown, perhaps in any other country. (16 March 1790)

These men illustrated the power of island living to subvert the supposedly superior Western mind. Their crimes were made worse by the fact that, as white men, they had known Christian salvation and willingly chose to throw it off. In contrast with the unmarked, light-skinned and clothed Christian body, native skin was dark, tattooed and uncovered. By darkening their skin with marks of 'cultural treason' the *Bounty* sailors confused the clear definition of coloniser and colonised within the Western mind.[18] That Bligh reserves the term 'blackish' to describe Christian indicates his antipathy towards the mutineer. This terminology, in addition to the statement that Christian sweated profusely and 'soils everything he touches', could be read as an attempt to portray him as a physically and morally degenerate character. Comparison of the version written in the launch notebook and the later one to which this chapter refers reveals minor deviations between the two documents, which indicates that the passage of time and memory had led Bligh to

---

17 In 1595, almost 200 years before Sir Joseph Banks, naturalist on Cook's voyage, described Polynesian tattooing, the Spanish navigator Pedro Fernandez de Quiros observed that the inhabitants of Fatu Hiva in the Marquesas were 'naked, without any part covered: their faces and bodies in patterns of a blue colour, painted with fish and other patterns' (Quiros, 1595; quoted in B Douglas, '"Curious Figures": European Voyagers and Tatau/Tattoo in Polynesia 1595–1800', in N Thomas, A Cole & B Douglas (eds), *Tattoo: Bodies, Art and Exchange in the Pacific and the West*, London, Reaktion Books, 2005, p 33). In 1590 (five years prior to de Quiros' description), the engravings of Theodore de Bry were published in Thomas Harriot's *A Briefe and True Report of the New Found Land of Virginia*. Based upon John White's original watercolours of New World Indians, these engravings included imagery of indigenous 'types', including tattooed 'Picts of Ancient Britain', and had catapulted visions of tattooed men and women into the public eye (see K Sloan, *A New World: England's First View of America*, London, British Museum Press, 2007). This textual reporting of tattoos was also reinforced by the exhibition of individuals. Beginning in the late 16th/early 17th century, there were occasional and much publicised exhibitions of tattooed 'natives' who were kidnapped or coerced from their New World homes.
18 Williams Milcairns, 2006, p 30.

change his descriptions of Christian. In the launch notebook, Christian is described as having a dark swarthy complexion; in the later versions, this is amended to a 'Blackish or very dark brown Complexion'. This subtle shift of wording indicates a level of embellishment that should make us wary of the veracity Bligh's descriptive language. Bligh is in no way impartial and issues of memory, audience and narrative reliability must be acknowledged when reviewing historical source material such as this. With regard to reliability, however, if his letter were not an accurate description of the bodies (rather than demeanour or colour) of the runaway sailors, then it would fail in its primary purpose, which was to allow them to be identified with sufficient certainty as to lead to their apprehension. Their arrest and subsequent trial would exonerate Bligh from any responsibility for the mutiny and, therefore, the failure of the voyage.[19] We can only assume that Bligh and his co-castaways are honest as far as possible about the *physical* marks (scars, wounds, tattoos) they mention; however, their assertions that certain mutineers were 'dark', 'raw boned' or had a 'rather a bad look' should be treated with caution. After all, how does one define a 'rather bad look'?

Eighteenth-century sailor tattoos

William Bligh's description is of typical sailors of the late 18th century, men physically altered by their vocational and pathological experiences. The list of injuries, largely compliant with a seafaring vocation (although of course other interpretations are possible) includes multiple broken or disfigured fingers or toes and damaged limbs. Marks of violence include scars from stabbing and a musket-ball wound. The impressive list of diseases that left their marks on the bodies ranges from multiple cases of small pox, scrofula (tuberculosis of the lymph glands, known as the king's boil), rotten or missing teeth (a symptom of the poor dental hygiene of the era but also a side effect of scurvy), to the excessive sweating of Fletcher Christian, which is possibly the result of hyperhidrosis.[20] To differentiate these men from the thousands of other sailors exhibiting

---

19 As Captain Cook's former sailing master on HMS *Resolution*, Bligh was hopeful of his future prospects within the Navy. Cook's untimely death made it imperative for Bligh's career that Sir Joseph Banks' breadfruit mission was a success. Only the successful court martial of the mutineers would ensure Bligh's reputation remained intact. See Caroline Alexander, *The Bounty: The True Story of the Mutiny on the Bounty* (London, Harper Perennial, 2003, pp 46–48).

20 For a discussion of Christian's possible medical condition, see D Williams, *Mutiny on the Bounty & Pandora's Box* (Lulu.com, 2015).

3. READING THE BODIES OF THE *BOUNTY* MUTINEERS

similar marks of disease and violence, Bligh relied on the scale and variety of their Euro-American tattoos and their adoption of Tahitian *tatau*. The following information is extracted from Bligh's letter.

Table 3.1: Tattooed markings on the bodies of the 25 *Bounty* mutineers

Types of markings
four mutineers have no tattoos
three mutineers have date markings, but no *tatau*
three mutineers are marked with the heart motif, two of which are embellished with darts
seven mutineers have *tatau* designs
five mutineers are described as 'tattooed'
six mutineers are described as 'very much tattooed' or in 'several parts of the body'
three mutineers have examples of both tattoo and *tatau*
Motifs
three hearts
four dates
one set of initials
one name
one Order of Garter and motto 'Honi soit qui mal y pense' (Shame on him who thinks this evil)[1]
one Manx tattoo known as a triskelion and motto 'Quocunque Jeceris Stabit' (Whithersoever you throw it, it will stand)
four stars on the left breast
three examples of Tahitian buttock tattooing (*taomaro*)
one Tahitian feather breast plate (*taumi*)
11 miscellaneous

[1] For information about the Order of Garter, see www.royal.uk/order-garter.

The onomatopoeic Polynesian term *tatau* was introduced to the English language in the late 18th century via the early contact voyage narratives of Samuel Wallis, Louis-Antoine de Bougainville and James Cook (and the evidence upon the skin of Cook's crew). This was not the origin of the activity of tattooing, however, only of the name.[21] The Anglicised term tattoo became synonymous with a pre-existing practice previously

---

21   This theory is supported in the following works: J Caplan (ed), *Written on the Body: The Tattoo in European and American History* (London, Reaktion Books, 2000); CP Jones, '*Stigma*: Tattooing and Branding in Graeco-Roman Antiquity' (*Journal of Roman Studies*, vol 77, 1987, pp 139–55); SP Newman, 'Reading the Bodies of Early American Seafarers' (*The William and Mary Quarterly*, 3rd series, vol 55, no 1, 1998, pp 59–82; Dye, 1989, pp 520–54).

known to Euro-Americans by terms such as 'inking' or 'sailor's marks'. The stereotypical sailor's marks of the era included religious motifs such as angels and crosses, and maritime imagery such as anchors, ships, fish and stars. Also included were images of hearts, dates, Masonic symbols and national emblems such as eagles or flags.[22] Although voyage narratives reinvigorated the activity, the tattooing of seafarers is thought by some to be a 'common and well-established practice at the time of Cook's voyages and probably long before'.[23] That 84 per cent of the mutineers described by Bligh had tattoos (whether acquired on the *Bounty* voyage or not) indicates an overwhelming interest in body modification throughout the ship's company, from the below decks' able seamen to the quarterdeck, the exclusive preserve of the officers and gentlemen. If this level of tattooing is representative of a trend amongst late 18th-century sailors, it seems to support the theory that tattooing was already a well-established practice amongst seafarers.

Historian Ira Dye carried out an exhaustive analysis of American seafarers and their tattoos through two sets of primary data extending over 22 years from 1796–1818.[24] These two sources – the Philadelphia Seamen's Protection Certificate applications (SPC-A), held at the US National Archives; and the General Entry books of American prisoners of war, 1812–15, held at the National Archives, London – represent the only detailed data on American seafaring tattooing of that period.[25] SPC were issued as proof of nationality for American sailors (or those that had been naturalised), who wished to avoid being forcibly impressed into the British Navy. The British authorities argued that British citizenship was enduring and, as such, American individuals could justifiably be impressed when the Navy was shorthanded. It was in the sailors' interest to ensure that their defining features were clearly and accurately described, including their tattoos. This has left historians with a wealth of body historiographies to analyse with regard to ages, heights, injuries, literacy and body modification.[26] Dye's research into the 9,772 surviving SPC-A records (38 per cent of the total issued) shows that 979 individuals were

---

22   Newman, 1998, pp 69–71.
23   Dye, 1989, p 523.
24   Dye, 1989, p 523. The multicultural nature of maritime communities, whether based at sea or at liberty on land, created the perfect breeding ground for tattooing and shared tattoo iconography to spread. It is likely, therefore, that the tattoo designs of American sailors were broadly speaking comparable with their European counterparts. The obvious exception is that British bodies may have displayed patriotic tattoos, such as James Morrison's Order of the Garter, and lacked the American revolutionary tattoos sported by some older Americans.
25   Dye, 1989, p 532.
26   Newman, 1998, p 60.

tattooed with a total of 2,354 tattoos. Of these 979 men, 40.1 per cent had only one tattoo (usually their initials) and the number of men with multiple tattoos dropped sharply as tattoo numbers increased.[27] Between 1796 and 1803, 20.6 per cent of sailors were marked and, by 1801, this figure had increased to 27.8 per cent.[28] Amongst the 2,354 sailor tattoos identified by Dye, there is not one *tatau* or mark identified as being of Polynesian or, to use mutineer Peter Heywood's term, 'curious' origin.[29] Although it is known that some members of Cook's crew acquired markings in Polynesia, there is limited evidence to suggest that this activity was on the same scale as shown by members of the *Bounty* crew. The adoption of Tahitian *tatau* amongst the crew of the *Bounty*, therefore, represents an evolution in the practice of early sailor tattooing as it deviated from the conventional format of the era, which was limited in the number of designs and bodily locations.

Island interactions: Tattoos and *tatau*

Table 3.2: Description of mutineer's tattoos

1	Fletcher Christian	Star on left breast, *tatau* on backside
1	George Stewart	Star on left breast, *tatau* on backside, heart with darts and date on arm
1	Peter Heywood	Very much tattooed, three-legged emblem of Isle of Man and motto
2	Edward Young	Heart with dart, date 1788 [or possibly 1789] and initials EY
4	Charles Churchill	Tattooed in several parts of the body
1	James Morrison	Star on left breast, Order of the Garter, Knight of Garter and motto
3	John Mills	Not tattooed
1	John Millward	*Tatau* under pit of stomach, a Tahitian breast plate
4	Matthew Thompson	Tattooed
4	William McKoy	Tattooed
1	Matthew Quintal	*Tatau* on backside and 'other places'
4	John Sumner	Tattooed in 'several places'
4	Thomas Burkitt	Very much tattooed

27 Dye, 1989, pp 535 (number of tattoos), 542 (information on initials).
28 Dye, 1989, p 533.
29 Edward Tagart, *A Memoir of Captain Peter Heywood, R.N., with Extracts from his Diaries and Correspondence*, London, F. Wilson, 1832, p 82.

1	Isaac Martin	Star on left breast
4	William Muspratt	Tattooed in 'several places'
4	Henry Hillbrant	Tattooed in 'several places'
4	Alexander Smith	Very much tattooed
4	John Williams	Tattooed
4	Richard Skinner	Tattooed
2	Thomas Ellison	Name, October 25th 1788 on arm
4	William Brown	Tattooed
3	Michael Byrne	Not tattooed
2	Joseph Colman	Heart tattooed on arm, also the date 5–7–77[2]
3	Thomas McIntosh	Not tattooed
3	Charles Norman	Not tattooed

1 = has *tatau*

2 = has tattoos

3 = not tattooed

4 = miscellaneous

[2] The information in this table is extracted from Bligh's letter to the Admiralty, 15 October 1789 (ADM 1/1506 [9], TNA), in keeping with Bligh's order of mutineers. The specifics of Coleman's tattoo and details of his previous voyage with Cook are taken from Alexander, 2003, p 250.

Table 3.2, extracted from William Bligh's letter, outlines the range of imagery inscribed upon the mutineer's skin and the textual details of the marks described. It indicates the scale of body modification amongst the mutineer crew. Of the 25 mutineers, only four had not indelibly inked their skin.[30] The iconography falls into two groups, which this chapter refers to separately. These are tattoos: marks originating from the Euro-American design spectrum; and *tatau*: marks that Bligh identifies as being of Polynesian origin. Tattoos range from hearts, alphanumeric characters and marks of regional and national affiliation, such as Peter Heywood's Isle of Man emblem (the Manx triskelion) and James Morrison's symbol of the Order of the Garter and associated French motto. *Tatau* include Able Seamen John Millward's 'Taoomy or Breast plate of Otaheite'; the extensive buttock tattooing known as *taomaro*,

30 It is striking that, of the four members who Bligh indicated were innocent of mutiny, 'these two last McIntosh and Norman declared as Coleman had done [that they had taken no part]. Michael Byrne, I was told had no knowledge of what was doing'. Only one of these four crew members, Joseph Coleman, had a tattoo; it was an inoffensive heart and date. The other three had neither tattoos nor *tatau*. They were described as both innocent and unmarked. I question how far Bligh felt, or was using, the presence of *tatau* as a marker of criminality amongst his mutineers.

which appear on the bodies of Fletcher Christian, George Stewart and Matthew Quintal; and the star motif found on the left breast of Christian, Stewart, Morrison and Isaac Martin. This star motif is identified as being of Tahitian origin because it was also adopted 15 years before by the crew of James Cook's ship, HMS *Resolution*. There are also ambiguous references to individuals being 'very much tatowed' or 'Tatowed on Several places'. These are tantalising descriptions that offer insight into the scale of sailor tattooing in the late 18th century, but lack the description adequate for useful analysis. Therefore, the mutineers described as such are set aside to concentrate on those who bear clearly defined markings.

Second skins

The Tahitian tattooing process was clearly not a ritual to be undergone lightly; early reporters of the practice commented on the extreme levels of pain endured,[31] which were so great that to undergo the operation 'a stranger would suppose it was doing [*sic*] against their will and that they were forced to suffer it contrary to their inclinations'.[32] William Bligh's description, discounting the 11 'very much tattooed' individuals, indicates three – Fletcher Christian, George Stewart and Mathew Quintal – who had aquired *taomaro*. *Taomaro* consisted of a series of extended arches stretching across the hips and buttocks, as can be seen on the body of the Tahitian woman in Figure 3.1, a detail from a painting by William Hodges draughtsman on Cook's second voyage.

Within the Tahitian *tatau* tradition, extensive buttock tattooing was a way of controlling the delicate balances of *tapu* (sacredness) and *mana* (potency) associated with the childhood phase of life.[33] The tattooing of

---

31 JC Beaglehole (ed), *The Endeavour Journal of Sir Joseph Banks 1768–1771*, vol 2, Sydney, Angus and Robertson Ltd, 1963; Tagart, 1832.
32 James Morrison, *The Journal of James Morrison*, London, Golden Cockerel Press, 1935, p 21.
33 Any discussion of *tatau* must also incorporate the principles of *mana* and *tapu*, both terms that lack a direct translation. *Mana* is described as:
> Not so much a mystical abstract power which people possess, but rather an efficacy manifested in specific outcomes such as fertility, health or success. It is a means by which divinity manifests its presence in the world through particular persons and things. Being of divine origin, *mana* is a problematic potency, dangerous, life creating and life destroying, and must be managed with care. (S Hooper, *Pacific Encounters: Art and Divinity in Polynesia 1760–1860*, London, British Museum Press, 2006, p 37)

Tapu was a state of being in opposition to *mana*. It referred to things that were 'restricted', 'holy', a 'state of a person, a thing, a place or a time period when *mana* is present' (Hooper, 2006, p 37). Any contact with *tapu* objects or individuals must be avoided or controlled.

a *taomaro* in adolescence was part of a complex process of deconsecrating rites, known as *amoʻa*. The performing of *amoʻa* rites during early adolescence acted to progressively lessen *tapu* status associated with this phase of life. *Amoʻa* allowed children to engage in increasingly higher levels of social relationships, ultimately marking the end of childhood and the availability for sexual relations and fertility.[34] James Morrison noted that girls 'never conceive themselves company for weomen – being only counted as children till they have their tattowing done'.[35]

Figure 3.1. Detail from William Hodges, *A View taken in the bay of Oaite Peha [Vaitepiha] Otaheite [Tahiti]* ('Tahiti Revisited'), 1776.
Source: National Maritime Museum, collections.rmg.co.uk/collections/objects/13872.html.

The tattooing of *taomaro* was described at length in Morrison's diary:

> The Hips of Both sexes are Markd with four or five Arched lines on each side, the Upper most taking the whole sweep of the Hip from the Hip bone to the Middle of the Back where the two lines Meet on one, which is drawn right a Cross from one hip to the other and on this all the other lines begin and end; under this Center line are generally four or five more, sweeping downwards, but Most Woeman have that part blacked all over with the Tattowing.[36]

---

34 M Kuwahara, *Tattoo: An Anthropology*, Oxford, Berg, 2005, pp 12, 35.
35 Morrison, 1935, p 221.
36 Morrison, 1935, p 221.

According to anthropologist Alfred Gell, author of *Wrapping in Images* (1993) – the seminal work on the subject of Pacific tattooing – the name translates as *tao* (spear) and *maro* (girdle) indicating the protective capacity of *taomaro*.[37] Any contact with *tapu* objects or individuals had to be avoided or controlled. Cosmological tattooing such as *taomaro* involved protecting or controlling the principles of *po* – the world of darkness, the gods and 'sacredness' – from *ao* – 'the world of light, of the senses, and of ordinary existence'.[38] These opposing cosmological states were created by the god Ta'aroa who, by cracking his shell, created the *ao* world. As Gell suggests, Tahitian cosmology 'was centred on the idea of crusts and shells, so that all phenomenally real things were defined as shells within shells, and so on'.[39] The skin represented an interactive zone upon which *tatau* markings provided an additional shell. These markings placed the wearer within Tahitian social hierarchy, which consisted of *ari'i* (the chiefly class descended from gods), yeomen and commoners. Specific *tatau* also indicated that the bearer belonged to one of the eight grades of the revered *Arioi* religious group.

As the body is born with skin and therefore pre-wrapped, tattooing represents the creation of a second skin encasing the *mana* within the body whilst protecting individuals and keeping Tahitian society in the appropriate balance of *po* and *ao*. This boundary status on the skin is described as a way of wrapping the body, not so much to form a secondary skin as to be a skin itself.[40] Therefore *tatau* has a trans-dermal quality, able to be both within the skin and on the skin. For the Tahitian, 'not just the person, but the whole world was a skin, a fragile integument, through which a precarious two-way traffic had to be maintained'.[41] This dichotomy of wrapping and revealing – controlling the visibility of the flesh – did not go unnoticed by the mutineers. As Morrison described in his diary, Fletcher Christian clearly appreciated this as, post-mutiny, he had the studding sails cut up to make uniforms for all hands:

> Observing that nothing had more effect on the minds of Indians as a uniformity of Dress. Which by the by has its affect among Europeans as it always betokens *discipline* especially on board British Men of War.[42] (Morrison's own emphasis)

---

37 Alfred Gell, *Wrapping in Images: Tattooing in Polynesia*, Oxford, Clarendon Press, 1993, p 145.
38 Gell, 1993, p 125.
39 Gell, 1993, p 124.
40 Gell, 1993, p 38.
41 Gell, 1993, p 126.
42 Morrison, 1935, p 48.

The fact that the crew had to be dressed around their superiors, just as the Tahitian had to be *uncovered* in the presence of their chiefs, indicates that the importance of wrapping permeated throughout Tahitian culture. The wrapping of individuals in bark cloth, sometimes great quantities of it, was an integral part of the ritualised activities at key events such as birth, dancing, tattooing, fighting and ultimately death. It was also part of the *taio* exchange ritual in which individuals with whom friendship relationships were expressed in name exchange, would wrap their *taio* in bark cloth. Tinah, Bligh's *taio*, wrapped him in a 'large quantity of cloth, we joined noses and exchanged name, he taking the name of Bligh … and I that of Tinah'.[43] *Taio* exchange relationships integrated Bligh and many of the crew into Tahitian life and, as it would transpire, politics. By allowing *taio* partners reciprocal access to goods, labour and kinship relations in the form of adoption and sexual relations with a *taio* partner's wife, the custom of name exchange blurred the lines of personal identity and ownership.[44] Bligh makes it clear in the ship's log, however, that the relationship could be a little one-sided: 'I am sorry to say my friend Tynah [Tinah] although I have loaded him with riches is not very grateful in return'.[45] Tinah made repeated requests for arms and it was the access to weaponry afforded to the Islanders by these relationships that ultimately changed the face of island politics (see Largeaud-Ortega, Chapter 4).

Tattooing and name exchange represented a means to avoid transgressing *tapu*, and exposing oneself to potentially destructive *mana*, but on a wider societal level it was a way of maintaining social cohesion and reproduction. It was a way of keeping the Tahitian world in balance. Morrison suggests that a person who was deficient of *tatau* was 'publically reproached'.[46] His description of *taomaro* is interesting because he states that the design, in parts, is open to personal choice:

> evry one pleases their own fancy in the Number of lines or the Fashion of them, some making only one broad one while others have 5 or 6 small ones ornamented with stars and sprigs &c.[47]

---

43   Extract from the logbook HMS *Bounty*, kept by Captain W Bligh, 16 Aug 1787– 20 Aug 1789 (*Bounty*, Log), 28 Oct 1788, ADM 55/151, TNA.
44   Kuwahara, 2005, p 46.
45   *Bounty*, Log, 18 Nov 1788, ADM 55/151, TNA.
46   Morrison, 1935, p 221.
47   Morrison, 1935, p 221.

The indication that there was a degree of choice in design suggests that it was not just the design that carried the protective capacity, but the application of the *tatau* itself – the ritual creating of Gell's second skin. The women trading sex and island produce for Western goods on the *Bounty*'s arrival were not peturbed by the sailors' lack of *taomaro*. As Bligh wrote in the ship's log, the Tahitians 'crowded on board in vast numbers … and within minutes I could scarce find my own people', so we assume that the benefits of trade outweighed the fear of the foreigner's uncontained *mana*.[48] Without *tatau*, however, the crew were unstable entities. To leave them unmarked was to risk leaving the *tapu* associated with individuals who were essentially alien beings from across the sea unrestrained and dangerous. The interaction between the tattooist (*tahuʻa*) and a sailor involves the transfer of motif onto the body and the absorption of the stranger into Tahitian life: it can be seen as a transformative ritual in which the visible structure supported an invisible one. The amalgamation of the forces of the land (Tahitians) and the sea (foreigners) through marriage alliance or sociopolitical office was a recognised practice. It produced a stronger society in terms of its *mana* because the whole is more than the sum of its parts; the forces of Sea and Land were united to create a stronger entity. The tattooing of the crew represented a means of integrating them into Tahitian life, thereby facilitating social cohesion. It can also be seen as an assertion of indigenous agency: tattooing the sailors or encouraging them to engage in *taio* exchange pacts allowed easier access to tradable goods and, more importantly, firepower. The deeply asymmetrical relationship of boat versus beach was levelled slightly by the act of name exchange and the adoption of *tatau*.

In January 1789, three sailors deserted Bligh's crew, demonstrating that several crewmembers were committed to adopting Tahitian life. Charles Churchill, William Muspratt and Millward must have relied on a significant amount of help from their Tahitian friends and their *taio*. They deserted at a time when most of the sailors were living at ease, some ashore. It was several months before they were due to leave and, given departure was not imminent, the log of the *Bounty* informs us that Bligh allowed women to stay with the men on board the ship at night.[49] The men's food was not rationed and life was significantly more pleasant than during the difficult

---

48 *Bounty*, Log, 26 Oct 1788, ADM 55/151, TNA.
49 *Bounty*, Log, 27 Oct 1788, ADM 55/151, TNA.

voyage to Tahiti.⁵⁰ The deserters' planned escape, relying on indigenous help and language skills, suggests a considerable level of interaction with their hosts. According to Bligh, Millward had an extensive *tatau* on his lower abdomen in the form of a Tahitian breastplate, or gorget, known as a *taumi*. See Figure 3.2 for an example.

Figure 3.2. Tahitian Gorget (*taumi*). Crescent-shaped breast ornament decorated with feathers, hair and shark's teeth.
Source: 1887.1.392, Pitt Rivers Museum, University of Oxford.

The *taumi* was a visually striking breast adornment worn by warriors. Its distinctive shape was thought to represent the jaws of a shark and imbued the wearer with the qualities of said animal.⁵¹ These high-status objects covered most of the bearer's chest and were often highly decorated with feathers and shark teeth. *Taumi* formed part of the exchange relations played out between high-status Islanders and senior visiting mariners. During his investiture as an elite 'Erree of Oparre', Bligh was offered 'a Tahaumee or Breast plate' in addition to long swathes of red-stained

---

50 Bligh outlined this ordeal in a letter to the Admiralty from the Cape of Good Hope on 24 May 1788 (ADM 1/1506 (9), TNA).
51 Hooper, 2006, p 185.

bark cloth.⁵² Cook was also given a *taumi* when he was on Tahiti.⁵³ *Taumi* were not normally found (or not recorded by European visitors) within the *tatau* design lexicon. The adoption of this design by Millward, therefore, directly allied him with the material culture of a warrior and represented a particularly assertive statement in self-representation. It is suggested that this use of the *taumi tatau* is an example of what Gell describes as 'scheme transfer', a tradition within Polynesian tattooing of the adoption/adaptation of a material object into *tatau* designs.⁵⁴ While the Tahitians developed new *tatau* iconography based on Western goods – such as guns, animals, swords and compasses – Tahitian designs were being adopted by the Euro-Americans.

All three deserters were soon recaptured. Millward and Muspratt were sentenced to four dozen lashes and Churchill to two dozen, to be dealt out on two separate occasions. Considering desertion was a capital offence, all three can be said to have got off lightly. The sailors would have been stripped to the waist and lashed to a latticed frame on deck, with all hands mustered to witness the flogging (see Figure 3.3). Flogging was an occupational hazard for sailors, often dealt out by harsh captains with little restraint. It was largely considered part of the initiation of sailors, 'who prided themselves on their courage and toughness, [and] felt profound shame if they were ever made to appear less than heroic'.⁵⁵ If Millward acquired his *taumi* prior to flogging, it would have been on display during this disciplinary encounter. Its visibility would have been important in imparting a message to the Tahitians whom Bligh tells us were present and deeply distressed by the flogging. It may also have fuelled Millward's courage. As Blanchard suggests, a tattoo acts as 'a form of exo-skeletal defence: it can serve as a charm protecting the tattooee or giving him or her special benefits in the immediate environment'.⁵⁶ The disfigurement caused by flogging occurred within the same zone as the apotropaic capacity of *tatau*, the skin. Even 'dressed' as a warrior, Millward was no match for the brutal British Navy. Via the act of flogging,

---

52 *Bounty*, Log, 13 Feb 1789, ADM 55/151, TNA).
53 For a discussion of the exchange of goods and curiosities, see J Newell, 'Exotic Possessions: Polynesians and their Eighteenth-Century Collecting' (*Journal of Museum Ethnography*, vol 17, 2005, pp 77–88).
54 Gell, 1993, p 101; J White, 'Marks of Transgression: The Tattooing of Europeans in the Pacific Islands', in Thomas, Cole & Douglas, 2005, p 77.
55 Isaac Land, *War, Nationalism, and the British Sailor, 1750–1850*, Basingstoke & New York, Palgrave Macmillan, 2009, p 38.
56 M Blanchard, 'Post-Bourgeois Tattoo: Reflections on Skin Writing in Late Capitalist Societies', in L Taylor (ed), *Visualising Theory: Selected Essays from the VAR 1990–1994*, New York & London, Routledge, 1994, p 288.

Bligh issued a strong physical and visual reassertion of naval power and there was a performative element to Millward's lashes that would not be lost on those who spoke another language.

Figure 3.3. George Cruikshank, *A Point of Honor*.
Source: Old Sailor & G Cruikshank (1826).

If we consider this alternative, that Millward engaged in his *tatau* sometime after his final flogging, then his adoption of warrior iconography could be read as a none too subtle statement of Tahitian alliance and a gesture of defiance toward the Navy. Unfortunately, no record has come to light as to when Millward acquired his unusual *tatau*. Whatever the timescale, however, in his choice of *tatau* Millward transcended the role allocated to him on board the *Bounty* and attempted a form of social leapfrogging. He allied himself with imagery of status and power that was far removed from his shipboard role as an able seaman.[57] This was not done exclusively

---

57 The wreck of the *Bounty* was excavated in 1997 by members of the Pitcairn Project, a team of maritime archaeologists from James Cook University who extensively surveyed the wreck site and the island. It is interesting to note that, amongst the items salvaged from the wreck, was a pearl-shell gorget of Polynesian workmanship. Four Aitutaki Islanders presented Bligh with a large mother-of-pearl gorget with a suspension cord of human hair when he came upon their island not long before the mutiny. However, Erskine attributes this find to the crew and their collection of 'curios' (Nicholas Erskine, 'Reclaiming the *Bounty*', *Archaeology*, vol 52, no 3, 1999a, pp 34–43). That Millward went so far as to have himself tattooed with the image of a *taumi* suggests the crew's engagement with the Tahitian material culture was more nuanced than the ad hoc collection of 'curios'. See Newell (2005) for sailors' collecting practices.

through *tatau*, which signified the deserters' commitment to Tahitian life; the choice of *taio* also had an impact on the sailors' role on the Island. Bligh seemed unable to describe the markings of the mutineers unless they fell within a recognisable Western canon. Hearts, dates and French or Latin mottos posed no problem for his descriptive powers, but he was at a loss to fully describe the indigenous marks. He made no attempt to describe Peter Heywood's 'curious' Tahitian designs but does mention his Manx triskelion. The only *tatau* he named was Millward's *taumi* – which Bligh could recognise because he had previously received such a breastplate as a gift – and the star on the left breasts of Christian, Isaac Martin, Edward Young and Morrison. The log of the *Bounty* is full of rich ethnographic description but Bligh failed to mention *tatau* – either amongst the Islander population or amongst the crew. The fact that Fletcher Christian acquired *tatau* and, as master's mate, he and Bligh interacted regularly and often dined together, make it surprising that Bligh makes no reference to the practice. Greg Dening suggests the amount of space both the crew and Bligh had on board was compromised by the boat's adaptation into a floating greenhouse and that Bligh's quarters may have been separated from those of the crew only by a canvas sheet.[58] This would have led to an unusual level of physical intimacy between captain and crew, and yet he makes no attempt to fully describe their markings, nor to record the practice from an ethnographic point of view. This in itself is not unusual. Ira Dye noted a similar phenomenon with regard to Cook who, although he recorded the practice of *tatau*, did not compare it to any marks adopted by his crew. But, as Dye suggests, Cook was 'reporting on exotic Polynesian customs not the familiar habits of the British sailor'.[59]

The extended stay in Tahiti allowed an unprecedented level of sustained cultural immersion for the crew of the *Bounty*. Friendship bonds were formed, lovers were taken and discarded, *heiva* were witnessed, and the full gamut of Tahitian life was experienced – but from a totally alien perspective. For the crew of the *Bounty* the skin became a contact zone, a social space 'where disparate cultures clash, and grapple with each other'.[60] Out of that grappling came a new skin, a different person. The skin proclaims experience and skin marked by *tatau* was a clear indicator of 'South Seas' experience. An anchor, for example, might mark

---

58 Dening, 1992, p 20.
59 Dye, 1989, p 523.
60 ML Pratt, *Imperial Eyes: Travel Writing and Transculturation*, London, Routledge, 1992, p 7.

you out as a sailor, but Heywood's 'curious indigenous marks' betray a level of interaction with the Islanders that would be viewed with suspicion by the majority of the gentlemanly class back home.[61] Corporal John Ledyard of the Marines on Cook's third voyage, remarked that back in England 'the [Tahitian] marks on my hands procure me & my Country-men the appellation of "wild men"'.[62] Amongst the sailing fraternity, *tatau* spoke of island living and sexual freedom and was the mark of a seasoned sailor, but, for members of the upper classes, such as Heywood's mother, it may have been a different matter altogether. Heywood wrote to her describing his appearance when apprehended on board the HMS *Pandora*, which was sent by the Admiralty to round-up the mutineers.

> Being dressed in the country manner, tanned as brown as themselves [the Tahitians] and I tattooed like them in the most curious manner, I do not wonder at their [the *Pandora* crew] taking us for natives.

His sense of boyish pride is tempered with 'I was tattooed, not at my own desire, but theirs'.[63] Heywood's description of being mistaken for a Tahitian betrays the ability of the skin to be a register of similarity and difference. When his pale European skin became tanned and familiar tattoo symbols were mixed with Tahitian designs, boundaries became blurred. By acquiring a mixture of Tahitian and Western tattoos, mutineers such as Heywood, Stewart and Morrison became amorphous beings in the eyes of their compatriots.

Bligh did not mention Heywood having *tatau*; rather, he is described as 'very much tattooed'. Heywood refers to himself as having curious tattoos 'like them'. The implication here is that these were indigenous designs as worn by the Tahitians; standard sailor tattoos of the era would not appear curious to fellow Europeans on the HMS *Pandora*. In addition to this, Bligh's letter tells us that on Heywood's right leg 'is tatowed the Legs of Man as the impression on that Coin is. At this time he had not done growing and Speaks with the Isle of Man Accent'. The three-legged Manx symbol represented the stability and robustness of the Manx character (see Figure 3.4). That Heywood should choose such distinctly nationalistic

---

61   There were examples of 'gentlemanly' tattooing, such as those on the skin of Sir Joseph Banks and Sydney Parkinson, but these were upon the arms and therefore discreet enough to be covered by the clothing of the day. Kuwahara tells us that Banks made no mention of being tattooed himself (2005, p 47).
62   Kuwahara, 2005, p 47.
63   Tagart, 1832, p 82.

iconography shows his affinity with his homeland. In doing so he was not solely choosing to define himself vocationally as Midshipman Heywood but as someone anchored within a terrestrial identity as well. His tattoo and *tatau* acted as a map of his travels, marking him out as a sailor, an adventurer and a proud Manxman. Even if the reasoning behind the voyage of the *Bounty* was largely mercantile (breadfruit would produce cheap food for slaves in the West Indies), it was sanctioned by the Royal Society and led by Sir Joseph Banks himself. With the addition of two dedicated botanists, one a veteran of all three Cook voyages (David Nelson), it had all the trimmings of a voyage of discovery.[64] Whilst the majority of their maritime colleagues were engaged in trade or warfare, the crew of the *Bounty* were embarking on a voyage to the edges of the known world. To these sailors, their *tatau* were the stamp of experience and proof of their adventures.

Figure 3.4. The triskelion emblem, on a Manx coin dating from 1733.
Source: © Paul Richards, CoinQuest.com.

Just as Heywood's triskelion offers us scope for analysis, likewise, Morrison's Order of the Garter tattoo can be read as a revealing choice. The Order was founded by King Edward III in 1348 and consisted of 25 knights, of aristocratic rank, chosen as a mark of Royal favour. The insignia of the Order became increasingly elaborate over the centuries and, by Morrison's day, it included a garter with the motto embroidered or bejewelled upon

---

64 Wahlroos suggests that Morrison accepted a career demotion from his previous role as midshipman to the lesser post of boatswain's mate on the *Bounty* because of his desire to go the South Seas (1989, p 326).

it; a gold collar with badge depicting St George and the Dragon; a broad riband; and the star, an eight-pointed silver badge depicting the cross of St George, surrounded by a depiction of the Garter. Drawing from this elaborate regalia, Morrison's tattoo took the form of the garter, wrapped around his left leg and inscribed with the Order's motto. It is unimportant whether Morrison acquired this tattoo prior to the voyage, or on the Island using indigenous skill; what matters is what it says about him. Morrison was a 28-year-old boatswain's mate, not a knight of the realm. That he chose a tattoo of a distinctly British institution, an ancient order of chivalry sanctioned directly from the Crown, hints at a proud patriotic streak, or a profound sense of irony. As a sailor in the Royal Navy he was on the lower rungs of the famously hierarchical Georgian society, and yet his tattoo spoke of an allegiance to the highest rungs of power and influence. By adopting the regalia of the aristocrat he would never be, there was a sense of aping one's betters.

Morrison also sported a star *tatau* on his left breast, a motif that he shared with Christian, Stewart and Martin. This star *tatau*, also adopted by Cook's crew onboard HMS *Resolution*, was used to identify the *arioi* elite from other Islanders.[65] As Midshipman John Elliot explained:

> All our mess conceived the idea of having some mark put upon ourselves, as connecting us together, as well as to commemorate our having been at Otaheite. For which purpose we determined on having a compleate Star drawn then tattowed with black, the same way as the Natives are tattowed, upon our left Breast, and painful as this operation was, we all underwent it, and have each a very handsome Black Star on our left Breast, the size of a Crown Piece.[66]

Cook's crew used the star *tatau* in a commemorative capacity as a memento of their voyage and their shared experiences. We do not know the exact reasons for its adoption by the *Bounty* crewmen – multiple readings are possible and all are conjecture, but that the motif appears on the bodies of the four sailors suggests a viral tendency of mark-making amongst the crew. Midshipman Elliot tells us the star *tatau* soon spread throughout the wider crew of the *Resolution*. There is no reason why this would not be the case on the *Bounty*; it was, after all, a distinguishing vocational motif of the Euro-American seafaring community but with the added

---

65 White, 2005, p 74.
66 Elliot (1773) in White, 2005, p 74.

cross-cultural appeal of being a Tahitian *tatau*.[67] The sharing of this star motif between crew mates suggests an indelible bond, allying them to each other and, in its capacity as a vocational marker, reaffirming the sense of belonging to a wider seafaring collective; as a *tatau*, it associated them with an elite Island class and it therefore acted as a multipurpose signifier. As Bligh states, Christian was one of the first to move ashore and one could question how far the adoption of a design such as this and his *taomaro* helped to ease the shift of allegiance from ship to shore at a time of uncertainty in the face of an unknown culture.[68] That this indigenous design, with its cosmological and societal meanings, was adopted by the crew confirms it as a shared memento and a vocational marker. In undergoing the painful process of tattooing, they cemented the bonds of masculinity forged in the fo'c's'le[69] and affirmed the collective sense of sailor unity. Where Morrison's Order of the Garter tattoo speaks of individuality, the star *tatau* speaks of collective belonging and memory.

The tattoos of dates – such as those of Joseph Coleman, Thomas Ellison and Young – can clearly be read as chronological markers, but also mementos of experiences. Ellison's tattoo commemorates the *Bounty*'s first sighting of Tahiti on 25 October 1788. By permanently altering himself, he used the date to define himself as separate from the person he was before. His tattoo reflected a momentous event in his life. Ellison's (likely) use of indigenous skill to impart an alphanumeric tattoo rather than a Tahitian *tatau* extends and complicates our understanding of the sailor/*tahu'a* interaction. Considering the ebb and flow of design-sharing between Islanders and sailors, and the very obvious skill of the Tahitian *tatau* priests, it is unlikely that Ellison would have asked a crewmate to act as tattooist when he could draw on the prodigious talent of the Tahitians. His choice of numbers and letters as opposed to imagery is interesting as he was illiterate at the time of embarkation. Bligh had given instructions to his clerk John Samuel to teach the boy 'Writing and Arithmetick' and stated that 'Tom Ellison is improving and will make a very good seamen [sic]'.[70] By tattooing himself with the alphabetised date (rather than numeric such as Coleman's 5–7–77) and his full name rather than just initials, Ellison was clearly displaying his hard-earned literacy for all to see.

---

67 White, 2005, p 74.
68 *Bounty*, Log, 10 Oct 1788, ADM 55/151, TNA.
69 Fo'c'sle: the forward part of a ship below the deck, traditionally used as the crew's living quarters.
70 Alexander, 2003, p 270.

Young's and Coleman's tattoos depicted dates accompanied by a heart, a motif that was also tattooed on Stewart. The heart, which is today considered to be a feminine motif, occurs relatively often in Dye's data set, accounting for 201 (8.5 per cent) of the total number of tattoos recorded.[71] Amongst the *Bounty* mutineers, these hearts were the only recognisable symbols of love and acknowledgement of domestic relations left behind. As Newman suggests:

> Tattoos recorded connections with people and communities ashore, they functioned as deeply gendered badges of professional identity, proclaiming those who worked under harsh and dangerous conditions in a world from which women were almost completely absent.[72]

Bligh wrote in his log that 'every night I order all the natives on shore, except the women as soon as the sun is down'. One could therefore suggest that the bonds formed on the outward voyage in an exclusively male environment were reconstituted on arrival by the introduction of women into the fo'c's'le.[73] By marking themselves with symbols of love, the sailors acknowledged relationships elsewhere and made reference to a life outside of the ship, either at home or on shore. They were not just sailors: they were husbands, lovers, brothers or family men. While it was common practice for older hands to tease younger crew for their attachments to women left behind at home, it would be a brave man who teased dangerously violent troublemaker Quintal for (re)naming his Tahitian partner after his mother, who died when he was a boy. The knowledge that each of his Tahitian children were named after his English relatives betrays an attachment to the memory of a family far away that sits awkwardly with the image of an aggressive, abusive drunk. He was the first to be flogged aboard the *Bounty* for insolence and contempt, and the man who attempted to deny Bligh the compass after forcing him and his men into the launch boat, an act that would have greatly compromised their chances of survival.[74]

The issue of naming, renaming and owning Polynesian women is pertinent within the *Bounty* story. Women were taken as consorts either voluntarily or violently on Tahiti, Tubuaʻi and Pitcairn and given European names

---

71 Dye, 1989, p 544.
72 Newman, 1998, p 73.
73 *Bounty*, Log, 27 Oct 1788, ADM 55/151, TNA.
74 Alexander, 2003, p 278. For background information on Quintal, see thepeerage.com/p15758.htm (accessed June 2018).

pronounceable to the English tongue. This act of renaming disassociated them (if only orally) from the Tahitian lineages that were discernible in their Polynesian names.[75] It is unclear how far the mutineers appreciated the genealogical importance of the women's Polynesian names, and the renaming of their lovers either equates to the endearing bestowal of a nickname or an oppressive act of social control. That John Adams, who signed up under the name of Alexander Smith, tattooed his Tahitian lover, Teehuteatuaonoa (known as Jenny), with his alias implies an indelible mark of ownership that outstrips even the act of renaming.[76] Names could be dropped as easily as adopted, as he well knew. To name is to control the description of something or, as in this case, someone, but to tattoo someone with a name is a statement of irrefutable *possession*. We have no knowledge of whether this was a brutal act of oppression – inking one's name into another's flesh, or if Teehuteatuaonoa voluntarily elected to bear Adams' initials as a mark of affection. That he enlisted under an alias and later reverted to his former name implies a level of subterfuge within his character and would perhaps explain why he chose to bestow his initials upon his lover, rather than on his own body.

The tattooing of oneself with initials has been likened to the use of military dog tags to preserve sailors from anonymity in death – for example, in the event of shipwreck.[77] Dye's research into Seamen's Protection Certificates revealed that the majority of sailors in this group had only one tattoo and that, of these, 38 per cent were tattooed with their initials. It would seem that, for many seamen, tattooing one's initials not only represented the first tentative steps into the world of tattooing, but also acted as assertive marks of identity, a theory borne out by the bodies of Young (aged 22) and Ellison (aged 17), but bucked spectacularly by the highly ornamented bodies of Heywood (aged 17) and Quintal (aged 21).[78] Considering the scale of tattooing amongst the crew and if the inking of initials upon the skin really did represent a 'gateway' tattoo preceding further skin embellishment, it is surprising that only two identified themselves by tattoos of their names or initials. The dog tag analogy is particularly apt

---

75 Pauline Reynolds, 'The Forgotten Women of the *Bounty* and their Material Heritage', paper presented at the Māori and Pacific Textile Symposium, 10–11th June 2011, Museum of New Zealand Te Papa Tongarewa, 2010, p 2, academia.edu/5830921/The_Forgotten_Women_of_the_Bounty_and_their_Material_Heritage.
76 D Oliver (ed), *Justice, Legality and the Rule of Law: Lessons from the Pitcairn Prosecution*, Oxford, Oxford University Press, 2009, p 45.
77 Maxwell Stuart & Bradley, 1997, p 83.
78 Dye, 1989, p 537.

for nomadic populations such as soldiers and sailors, as the possibility of dying unidentified and so far from home was a real and constant threat. Death at sea would have been ever present in the minds of the *Bounty* sailors especially following the death of Able Seaman James Valentine on 10 October 1788. His few possessions were distributed amongst those that had cared for him 'with great care and affection' and he was buried at sea with 'all the decency in our power'.[79] That he was cared for so sensitively by his crewmates acknowledged the bonds formed under such physically demanding and dangerous conditions. His carers were given his shirts, which were his only possessions. Valentine died of an infection caught whilst being bled by the surgeon for a separate complaint. Although he lacked any tattoos, and is therefore not mentioned in Bligh's letter, he is relevant here because his death highlights how the simple act of cutting the skin led to a painful and drawn out death. This was a real risk with tattooing. That the sailors knew of the extreme levels of pain and swelling tattooing caused and yet still engaged in the process indicates their commitment to redefining their bodies and the way others saw them. It could also show an appreciation of the importance of *tatau* to the Tahitians, and what the crew stood to gain, as Heywood explains:

> It was my constant endeavour to acquiesce in any little custom which I thought would be agreeable to them, though painful in the process, provided I gained by it their friendship and esteem.[80]

Through their choice to engage with body modification, the crew of the *Bounty* took ownership of how they wished to be seen by others. With little personal space and very few belongings, tattooing was a way for 'little people' (as Greg Dening puts it)[81] to assert their individuality within an institution as rigid as the British Navy. The space restrictions experienced by the sailors on the *Bounty*, which were by no means unique, are suggested by Bligh's need to refer to his fellow castaways to trawl their collective memories for it was they 'who were best acquainted with their [the mutineers] marks',[82] suggesting an intimate knowledge of each others' bodies acquired through months of living cheek by jowl.

---

79   *Bounty*, Log, ADM 55/151, TNA.
80   Tagart, 1832.
81   Greg Dening, 'Writing, Rewriting the Beach: An Essay', in Alun Munslow & Robert A Rosenstone (eds), *Experiments in Rethinking History*, New York & London, Routledge, 2004, p 52.
82   18 Aug 1789, ADM 1/1506 (9), TNA.

Conclusion

Prior to the voyage, the sailors' details were noted by the Royal Navy in the Ships' Muster Roll.[83] As the voyage progressed, details of any medical treatment, how much tobacco they consumed, who owed money and whose moral fibre had been found wanting by the action of desertion were all listed with uncompromising factuality. The bureaucratic data-gathering of the Admiralty reduced men to subjectified bodies who were measured, assessed and documented. However, this documentation of the sailor reveals little, if anything, of the men trapped inside the muster rolls. In contrast, Bligh's letter offers us a springboard with which to build a visual picture of the mutineers and extract a sense of the sailor's voice within the *Bounty* narrative. This voice offers a counter balance to the view of a mutinous, criminal crew, as presented via their repeated cinematic personas. The bowlegged and perpetually sweaty (and, by implication, anxious) figure of Fletcher Christian is no one's idea of a Hollywood movie star (see Jolly & Petch, Chapter 6). The letter acts as propaganda for Bligh, but nowhere in it does he criminalise the act of tattooing *per se*. His silence on the practice before the mutiny, raising it only after the event, implies that tattooing played a role in converting the crew to the Tahitian way of life. In contrast to the typical wanted advertisements placed in media of the era for criminals and runaways, the bodies of the *Bounty* mutineers were not described as wearing any clothing. They were textually laid bare for all to see, 'clothed' only in tattoos. As the literate masses viewed tattoos as marks of criminality, their presence upon the skin of the mutineers was indicative of their moral decline and untrustworthy nature.

Bligh's letter is revealing of the cross-cultural appeal of tattooing between sailors and their Polynesian hosts; however, it is not just the tattoos that build a picture of these individuals. His descriptions of the markings of vocation and disease form an enlightening picture of seafaring life in the 18th century. Injuries, 'remarkable' scars, crooked and maimed fingers, multiple scaldings and severely damaged limbs due to breakages tell of the dangers that these working men faced throughout their lives. It is interesting to note, however, that there is no mention of scars from flogging. It is hard to believe that the bodies of 18th-century sailors failed to exhibit symbols of authority such as these. William Muspratt, who received 36 lashes over two separate floggings within one month, *must*

---

83   *Bounty*, Royal Navy Ships' Musters, ADM 36/10744, TNA.

have exhibited evidence of this on his skin. Flogging was an accepted part of their vocation, and Bligh's silence in relation to any 'official' ownership of the body is revealing of just how normal this casual, if theatrical, violence was.

The body is engaged in a lifelong process of growth. It responds both to external factors such as nutrition, disease or violence, and internal ones such as the need to recast and reinvent oneself as a consequence of experience. The mutineers' experiences of indigenous contact were expressed upon their skin in the form of Tahitian *tatau*, but they also carried markings identifiable with their own cultures, such as hearts, dates and initials. These tattoos marked them out as sailors, practically the only group to engage in tattooing during this period. They also identified them as individuals grounded within shore-based institutions, whether geographic, such as Peter Heywood's Manx triskelion; or sociocultural, such as James Morrison's Order of the Garter. Edward Young's tattooed initials show how sailors combatted their fears about mortality through their bodies, which must have been a very real fear since marks of disease, disfigurement and injury were present in almost every member of the crew. Death was a clear occupational hazard.

The ages and ranks of the mutineers indicate that many of them had made multiple voyages during which they may have acquired the tattoos described by Bligh. Thomas Ellison, just 15 years old when he sailed on the HMAV *Bounty*, had already served under Bligh in the West Indies. John Mills had served in the Navy on the HMS *Mediator* and, presumably, to reach the rank of gunner's mate, several other vessels as well. Morrison had eight years' Royal Navy service to his name. Research suggests, however, that only Joseph Coleman whose date tattoo stemmed from an earlier voyage with Cook, had visited the Pacific.[84] By acquiring more tattoos on successive voyages, such marks became 'visible indicators of long service at sea', confirming the men as 'professional' seafarers.[85] That such a high proportion of the crew should be engaging in tattooing, only 20 years after the introduction of the term *tatau* into the English language, suggests that indelibly inking the skin was already an established practice prior to these voyages. Although it is possible they acquired (Western)

---

84 Alexander, 2003, p 250.
85 Newman, 1998, p 61.

tattoos prior to arriving in Tahiti, any Tahitian *tatau* were acquired in the five months between the *Bounty*'s arrival in October 1788 and departure the following April.

While carrying out their work – fetching water, food and wood – the sailors made inroads into the island itself. In doing so, their interactions with, and reflections upon, the Tahitians were made from a unique standpoint. The examples given by Bligh of buttock tattooing, the adoption of the Tahitian star motif, Millward's *taumi* and Ellison's date tattoo indicate that the skin acted as a transitional space allowing new island identities to be formed and crew relationships to be reconstituted through the sharing of motifs and the painful process of tattooing.[86] By regarding the surface of the skin as an interface between sailor and Islander that allowed or sanctioned integration into island life, an analysis of the skin encourages a deeper understanding of sailor/Islander relations in early contact Tahiti. That three mutineers, Christian, Stewart and Quintal, who Bligh identified as the main players in the mutiny, should engage in the lengthy, repeated and highly painful activity of *taomaro*, a requirement for social and, perhaps more importantly, sexual relations, indicates a commitment to and understanding of their host culture. We can surmise, from Morrison's extensive ethnographic descriptions and Peter Heywood's admission of having been tattooed at the desire of the Tahitians, that tattooing, either in passive witnessing or active participation, formed a significant part of the interaction.[87]

---

86 See Greg Dening, *Islands and Beaches: Discourse on a Silent Land, Marquesas 1774–1880* (Melbourne University Press, 1980, pp 20–34) for a discussion of liminal transitional spaces.
87 Tagart, 1832, p 82.

4

Nordhoff and Hall's *Mutiny on the Bounty*: A Piece of Colonial Historical Fiction

Sylvie Largeaud-Ortega
University of French Polynesia

Introduction

Various *Bounty* narratives emerged as early as 1790. Today, prominent among them are one 20th-century novel and three Hollywood movies. The novel, *Mutiny on the Bounty* (1932), was written by Charles Nordhoff and James Norman Hall, two American writers who had 'crossed the beach'[1] and settled in Tahiti. *Mutiny on the Bounty*[2] is the first volume of their *Bounty Trilogy* (1936) – which also includes *Men against the Sea* (1934), the narrative of Bligh's open-boat voyage, and *Pitcairn's Island* (1934), the tale of the mutineers' final Pacific settlement. The novel was first serialised in the *Saturday Evening Post* before going on to sell 25 million copies[3] and being translated into 35 languages. It was so successful that it inspired the scripts of three Hollywood hits; Nordhoff and Hall's *Mutiny* strongly contributed to substantiating the enduring

---

1   Greg Dening, 'Writing, Rewriting the Beach: An Essay', in Alun Munslow & Robert A Rosenstone (eds), *Experiments in Rethinking History*, New York & London, Routledge, 2004, p 54.
2   Henceforth referred to in this chapter as *Mutiny*.
3   The number of copies sold during the Depression suggests something about the appeal of the story. My thanks to Nancy St Clair for allowing me to publish this personal observation.

myth that Bligh was a tyrant and Christian a romantic soul – a myth that the movies either corroborated (1935), qualified (1962; see Jolly & Petch, Chapter 6) or tried to mitigate (1984).[4]

The axiom adopted here is that a historical novel is a piece of writing whose authors, when reconstructing some past period or event, 'make their best to ensure that their work is historically accurate'.[5] Through reference to the works of historians, anthropologists, critics in colonial studies and narrative theorists, this chapter explores the gap between what Nordhoff and Hall knew of the *Bounty*'s historical facts[6] and the facts they chose to deliver in their fiction, in order to raise questions about the novel's literary discourses and genre. Their choice of a fictional white male narrator and protagonist is probed in terms of its impact on their reconstruction of life in Tahiti. Their *mise-en-abyme* structure, with an older narrator relating the tale of his younger self, raises further questions of narrative reliability and relativism. The overarching purpose of this chapter is to demonstrate that Nordhoff and Hall's discourse is predominantly colonial,[7] which makes their *Mutiny* narrative highly partial and contingent historical fiction.

Roger Byam, imaginary protagonist and narrator

The most blatant invention by Nordhoff and Hall is their replacement of historical Midshipman Peter Heywood with imaginary Midshipman Roger Byam. As the main protagonist and narrator, Byam delivers the *Bounty* narrative in the form of a memoir written in his old age –

---

4   For information about the commercial success of Nordhoff and Hall's *Mutiny*, and a more extensive presentation of the movies, see Greg Dening's *Mr Bligh's Bad Language: Passion, Power and the Theatre on the Bounty* (Cambridge University Press, 1992, pp 346–79 (henceforth referred to as *BBL*)). My thanks to Daniel Margueron for privately supplying further information on the commercial success of Nordhoff and Hall's novel.
5   Sarah Johnson, 'Defining the Genre: What are the Rules for Historical Fiction?', Associated Writing Programs annual conference, New Orleans, Mar 2002.
6   For an exhaustive presentation of Nordhoff and Hall's source material, see their end notes to *Mutiny on the Bounty* (New York, Boston & London, Back Bay Books, Little, Brown & Company, 2003 (1932), pp 382–83).
7   For colonial and postcolonial studies, see the seminal works of Bill Ashcroft, Gareth Griffiths & Helen Tiffin (eds), *The Empire Writes Back: Theory and Practice in Post-Colonial Literature* (London, Routledge, 1989); Homi K Bhabha, *The Location of Culture* (London & New York, Routledge, 1994); Edward Said, *Orientalism* (London, Penguin, 1985); Gayatri Chakravorty Spivak, 'Can the Subaltern Speak?', in Patrick William & Laura Chrisman (eds), *Colonial Discourse and Post-Colonial Theory: A Reader* (Hennel Hempstead, Harvester Wheatsheaf, 1993).

in hindsight and as a first-person narrative. *Mutiny* is the only volume in the *Bounty Trilogy* that has an imaginary homodiegetic narrator.[8] What might the authors have hoped to achieve through this choice? One possibility is that it gives the impression of neutrality. Since it is impossible to establish objectively what happened on the *Bounty* and in Tahiti, the reporting might as well be entrusted to an imaginary character – an outsider who might be presented as neither pro-Bligh nor pro-Christian.

Byam, however, is unmistakably based on historical Heywood. Every single historically known officer and crew from the *Bounty* is present in *Mutiny*, except for Heywood, who has been replaced by the non-historical Byam. Heywood and Byam share the same profile: each is a young midshipman who claims that he was held on the *Bounty* against his will at the time of the mutiny, is court-martialled, sentenced to death, finally has his life saved and pursues a brilliant career in the Navy. While Heywood took sides in the Bligh–Christian opposition, he shifted alliances: during the court martial, he protested his utter respect for Bligh – his own life depended on doing so – but, after the court martial, 'the moment he was free of the constraints of appearing innocent',[9] he was clearly pro-Christian. Given that the *Bounty*-related experiences of the historical Heywood and non-historical Byam are so similar, why did Nordhoff and Hall elect to use an imaginary protagonist/narrator? What other differences exist between Heywood and Byam that might hint at the grounds for their decision? Why opt for an older narrator reporting on his younger self's experiences? To what extent does this narrative strategy alter facts and shape readers' responses to the text?

From the start of the narrative, Byam is presented as flawless and vulnerable, rather more so than his historical role model. For instance, his birthplace is Somerset, not the Isle of Man where the Heywoods and the Christians were distant relatives,[10] thus precluding any likelihood of a pre-existing Byam–Christian connivance. Nor can Byam be suspected of belonging to any self-governing island boasting its own

---

8   A homodiegetic narrator is both narrator and a character in the narrative. For illustrations, see Gérard Genette, *Figure III* (Paris, Seuil, 1972, pp 225–66). The narrator in *Men against the Sea* is Thomas Ledward, the historical surgeon acting on board the *Bounty* launch. In *Pitcairn's Island*, the narrator is an anonymous omniscient extradiegetic narrator, which means that s/he stands outside the narrative altogether. S/he reports historical Adam Smith's embedded narrative in fictional direct speech in the last chapters.
9   Dening, 1992, pp 257–58.
10 Both families had been established on the Isle of Man for centuries, and had known each other well for generations.

flag and triskelion emblem (see Utting, Chapter 3): Byam is a true-blue Englishman. He is the only son of a solitary widowed mother and his late father was a maritime scientist held in such high esteem that Sir Joseph Banks himself recommends Byam to Bligh. When Byam embarks on the *Bounty*, he is a young man who has never been away from home and is innocent of sea life – which is one of the reasons for his dismay at the time of the mutiny.

In reality, Heywood had 10 brothers and sisters, and both of his parents were alive when he departed for Tahiti. Heywood's father was an estate agent with a record blemished by embezzlement.[11] Heywood was recommended and awarded the privileges of a junior officer, not by Banks, but by Bligh's father-in-law. Finally, like many other young men of that time, Heywood had entered sea service at an early age,[12] which meant that he possessed significant experience of ship life before he embarked upon the *Bounty*.

Nordhoff and Hall introduce another major imaginary aspect to Byam: he is a young man with a mission that he alone can accomplish, and is commissioned by none other than Banks. Here is how Bligh introduces the topic in the early pages of *Mutiny*:

> [Sir Joseph Banks] has solicited me most earnestly to employ my time in Tahiti in acquiring a greater knowledge of the Indians and their customs, and a more complete vocabulary and grammar of their language, than it has hitherto been possible to gather. He believes that a dictionary of the language, in particular, might prove of the greatest service with the mariners in the South Sea.[13]

Bligh confesses that he has no gift for languages and so, with Banks' enthusiastic support, the task is bequeathed to the providential Byam. In reality, the historical Bligh had already learnt some Tahitian during Cook's third voyage and, back in Tahiti with the *Bounty*, 'Bligh was able to converse quite freely with the Tahitians'.[14] What is more, there was no linguistic mission on the historical *Bounty*: Banks' concern was only for the transfer of breadfruit to the West Indies and the maritime exploration

---

11   For further information on Peter Heywood's life and career, see WH Smyth, 'A Sketch of the Career of the later Capt. Peter Heywood, RN' (*United Service Journal and Naval and Military Magazine*, vol 1, 1831a, pp 468–81).
12   At seven, Heywood was captain's servant on the *Halifax* and, at 14, a trainee on harbour-bound HMS *Powerful*.
13   Nordhoff & Hall, 2003, p 10. Further references to this text list page number only.
14   Anne Salmond, *Bligh. William Bligh in the South Seas*, Auckland, Penguin Viking, 2011, p 169.

of the Endeavour Straits.[15] Actual plans for Heywood's Tahitian dictionary did not start until 1792, at the instigation of the budding London Missionary Society.[16]

Nordhoff and Hall's invention of a linguistic mission is fraught with narrative consequences, all of which converge on one point: the aggrandisement of their protagonist/narrator. First, the younger Byam does not just travel to the South Seas; he is asked by Banks to render a 'great service [to] the mariners' of his Majesty's Navy. Second, Byam is a unique and indispensable character with a monopoly on writing; the very valuable proto-ethnographic notes on Tahiti that were taken by historical George Stewart, James Morrison and Bligh[17] are not mentioned in *Mutiny*. Third, the young midshipman is propelled to an intellectually (and therefore, albeit unofficially, hierarchically) higher level: he is exceptionally talented where his superior is a self-confessed dunce. Bligh is deficient where Byam is proficient, and thus the Bligh–Byam relationship is under challenge even before the *Bounty* departs. That challenge concerns the mastery of language – which is quite ironic since, as Greg Dening demonstrates in his decisive *Bounty* study, historical Bligh's most serious flaw was his 'bad language'.[18] Fourth, the lurking Bligh–Byam rivalry becomes obvious when Bligh eventually fails in his *Bounty* mission, while Byam succeeds in his. The breadfruit are lost, but the dictionary lands safely in the lap of Banks who declares: 'It is excellent, Byam; precisely what is needed' (338). Fifth, to

---

15   The Endeavour Straits were indeed strategically placed in relation to the eastern routes and the colony of New South Wales, and Bligh did chart them during his passage in the *Bounty* launch.
16   On the history of the London Missionary Society (LMS) Tahitian mission, see John Davis, *The History of the Tahitian Mission 1799–1830*, CW Newbury (ed) (Hakluyt Society & Cambridge University Press, 1961); Neil Gunson, *Messengers of Grace: Evangelical Missionaries in the South Seas 1797–1860* (Melbourne, Oxford University Press, 1978); KR Howe, *Where the Waves Fall: A New South Sea Islands History from First Settlement to Colonial Rule* (Honolulu, University of Hawai'i Press, 1988); Richard Lovett, *The History of the London Missionary Society 1795–1895* (London, Henri Froude, 1899).
17   On Heywood's notetaking, see Rolf Du Rietz, *Peter Heywood's Tahitian Vocabulary and the Narrative by James Morrison: Some Notes on their Origin and History* (Banksia 3, Uppsala, Sweden, Dahlia Books, 1986). On Morrison's note-taking, see Vanessa Smith & Nicholas Thomas (eds), *Mutiny and Aftermath: James Morrison's Account of the Mutiny on the Bounty and the Island of Tahiti* (Honolulu, University of Hawai'i Press, 2013, pp 5–21): 'Only Morrison both lived among the Tahitians and wrote of what he found … In fact, Morrison might be said to be the first European participant observer of Tahitian society' (p 9). For Bligh, see Salmond (2011): 'Although Joseph Banks has sometimes been called the father of Pacific ethnography, William Bligh's accounts of life in Tahiti are more detailed and astute than anything Banks was able to accomplish – no doubt because of his repeated visits to the island. As his understanding of the language became more fluent and subtle, his reports grew more accurate and insightful. Since Bligh was able to converse quite freely with the Tahitians, he shared more experiences with them; and because Po'e'eno and his father Moana, and Tu and his wife 'Itia, were his bond friends, they were obliged to answer his questions and share their knowledge (even sacred information) with him' (p 169); on Stewart's journal, see this volume's Introduction.
18   See Dening, 1992, pp 57–81.

modern readers, Bligh's mission appears much less commendable than Byam's 'philosophical' one: the former – helping plantation slave-owners and spurring racial exploitation – epitomises archaism and prejudice; the latter – probing into indigenous Pacific languages – epitomises progress and enlightenment, and heralds ethnographic studies. There is, therefore, little doubt as to whom modern readers will trust. The final point to be made here, giving Byam extra credence in his role as narrator, is that as a master of language (unlike Bligh) he can be relied upon to tell the *Bounty* story (thereby casting doubt on all other *Bounty* narratives). Indeed, if on the diegetic level, Banks entrusts the younger Byam with a writing mission, it seems only natural that, on the extradiegetic level, Nordhoff and Hall should entrust the older Byam with a mission to write the *Bounty* narrative.[19] When it comes to writing/narrating, Byam stands out as most reliable – or so it seems. He is also, incidentally, endowed with all of the attributes of a worthy young white male hero, as befits the genre of popular historical novels.

Life on board HMAV *Bounty*

What does Roger Byam narrate of life on board HMAV *Bounty*? The backbone of the story is true to history: the ship's course, the major dates and the food rationing are consistent with historical records. Byam's portrayal of William Bligh's character, however, impacts upon the tale of life on board.

Byam does praise Bligh's navigational skills – those could hardly be gainsaid, given Bligh's outstanding achievement in making the *Bounty* launch's passage to Timor. The way Byam delivers his praise is, however, worth a close reading: '*in justice to an officer whose character in other respects was by no means perfect, I must say* that there was no finer seaman and navigator afloat at the time' (29, my italics). The eulogy is heavily counterbalanced, with faults and merits weighing against each other. The tone sounds so constrained that the reader cannot help but feel the antiphrastic value of the rhetorical 'I must say'. Byam's use of the word 'justice' seems equally reluctant. The same semantic pattern of begrudged

---

19 Diegetic level: narrated level, or the fiction world. Extradiegetic level: writing level, or the real world – with real people, like writers Nordhoff and Hall, and flesh and blood readers. For more detailed definitions of both terms, see Genette (1972, pp 225–66).

justice and the same counterpoise often recur in the narrative where Bligh is concerned, which evinces how difficult it is for Byam to sound impartial to Bligh.

From the start of the novel, the older Byam presents Bligh as uncouth and violent. The *Bounty* is still at Spithead when Bligh introduces the younger Byam to sea law by having him attend the flogging around the fleet of a man who has just died under the lashes: 'From neck to waist the cat-o'-nine-tails had laid the bones bare, and the flesh hung in blackened, tattered strips' (23). After witnessing the flogging of the corpse with a smile, without a transition Bligh proceeds to take 'his soup with relish, and sounds better fitted to the forecastle than aft' (25). Indiscriminate flogging and 'masting' subsequently become part of the voyage. In a chapter entitled 'Tyranny', there is a vivid description of the first *Bounty* flogging:

> A great red welt sprang out against the white skin, with drops of blood trickling down on one side. Mills was a burly ruffian and he endured the first dozen without crying out, though by that time his back was a red slough from neck to waist. (52–53)

And yet, Greg Dening counters, 'the cat rarely broke the skin in a dozen lashes'.[20] The same chapter depicts the 'masting' of young Midshipman Tinkler on an 'icy cold' night, from which he comes down 'blue with cold, unable to stand up or to speak' (56). In history, it was Peter Heywood, not Tinkler, who was thus 'masted'.[21] In *Mutiny*, Bligh also has a midshipman (Edward Young) flogged, which 'was almost without precedent' (61). There seems to be no historical record of that particular flogging.

It might therefore come as a surprise that Byam's reports of subsequent punishments should be true to record. Master-at-arms Charles Churchill is given 'two-dozen lashes', and Able Seamen John Millward and William Muspratt 'four-dozen each' (105) for jumping ship in Tahiti. What the narrative fails to say, however, is that desertion was a capital offence (see Utting, Chapter 3) so the punishment was lenient. This is true also for Midshipman Thomas Hayward, who was only disrated for being

---

20   Dening, 1992, p 64.
21   Heywood reported this 'masting' to WH Smyth only years later, so it may have been altogether spurious. Glynn Christian – a descendant of Fletcher Christian by five generations – signals that Heywood made no mention of it in the long letter he wrote from the Cape of Good Hope, a few weeks after the alleged event. Christian conjectures that Heywood may have made this late addition in order to demonise Bligh. See WH Smyth, 'The *Bounty* Again!' (*United Service Journal and Naval Military Magazine*, vol 3, 1831b, p 305); and Glynn Christian, *Fragile Paradise: The Discovery of Fletcher Christian Bounty Mutineer* (Boston, Little, Brown, 1982, in Dening, 1992, pp 67–69, 312).

asleep at watch during the desertion. Predictably enough, *Mutiny* does not indicate that, contrary to the practices of Captain Cook, Bligh neither took Tahitians hostage, nor did he have their ears cut off.

Older narrator Byam may therefore be said to deliberately construct the fantasy of a violent captain Bligh. And it *is* a fantasy, Bligh was not a physically violent man: 'Bligh's passions were verbal, not physical'[22] (see this volume's Introduction). The purpose of this chapter is not to examine Bligh, nor to apportion blame for the mutiny. Neither is it to disentangle what Heywood actually did during the mutiny: he claimed during his trial that he had meant to leave the *Bounty* in the launch, but a series of circumstances prevented him from doing so – a situation in which the younger Byam also finds himself.[23] Rather, this chapter aims to reflect upon narrative strategies. So far, the differences between Heywood and Byam all contribute to make the younger Byam appear blameless. Unlike Heywood, Byam has never done anything wrong – he has not even been 'masted', so he cannot be suspected of bearing any personal grudge against Bligh. He is an innocent young man with a clean record. In Byam's narrative of life on board HMAV *Bounty*, Nordhoff and Hall create a seemingly flat, two-dimensional protagonist who is likely to appeal to a wide readership of popular literature. By allowing narrator Byam to replicate the Heywood party's skewed perspective, the authors also contribute strongly to the myth of Bligh as a violent man.

Life in Tahiti: *Vahine* and sex

What about Roger Byam's narrative of life in the Pacific Islands? *Mutiny* devotes less than two pages to the mutineers' three-month stay in Tubua'i (165–67): 'I shall give [Tubuaians] no more space than they deserve' (165), the narrator spurns. In those three months, however, there was constant fighting because Tubuaians were unwaveringly hostile to the *Bounty*'s would-be settlers (see Teriierooiterai, Chapter 1). The narrative strategy of avoiding commentary on the interaction between mutineers

---

22   Caroline Alexander, *The Bounty: The True Story of the Mutiny on the Bounty*, London, Penguin Books, 2003, p 138.
23   See Heywood's Letters in Donald A Maxton & Rolf E Du Rietz (eds), *Innocent on the Bounty: The Court-Martial and Pardon of Midshipman Peter Heywood, in Letters by Peter Heywood and Nessy Heywood* (Jefferson, NC, McFarland, 2013).

and the Islanders actually speaks volumes: *Mutiny* will not dwell on any representation of Eastern Polynesians that might stain the stereotype of the Noble Savage.[24]

The narrative of life in Tahiti introduces two major differences between Heywood and Byam. The first one bears on sex and romantic love. The resounding successes of Louis-Antoine de Bougainville's *Voyage* (1771),[25] John Hawkesworth's *Voyage* (1773)[26] and the pamphlets and parodies of Joseph Banks' sexual adventures in Tahiti[27] had nurtured collective European fantasies that Tahiti was a hotbed of unbridled erotic pleasure. The *Bounty* company succeeded in living out this fantasy. After their first five-month stay in Tahiti, 40 per cent of them, including Fletcher Christian and Peter Heywood, had caught 'the venereals'. *Mutiny*, however, tells a different tale. It gives no hint of Christian's reputation from his previous voyage as 'one of the most foolish young men I ever knew in regard to the sex', recorded by Edward Lamb from the *Britannia*.[28] *Mutiny* confirms Edward Christian's contention in the *Pamphlet* 'Appendix' that Christian had 'no traffic with the women who infested the ship' (92). Instead, Christian forms in time an exclusive 'attachment to Maimiti … of the tenderest description' (107). Historical Mauatua was indeed Christian's lover and, after the mutiny, she willingly went away with him to both Tubua'i[29] and Pitcairn. Too little is known,

---

24 In contrast to Eastern Polynesians, Western Polynesians are the stereotypical Ignoble Savages, as demonstrated in *Mutiny* by the serious troubles experienced on the Friendly Islands and, in *Men against the Sea*, all islands west of Tahiti. The distinction was first made by early European explorers like Bougainville and Cook. For the stereotype of Tahitians as Noble Savages, see AO Lovejoy & G Boas, 'Islands of the Blest', in *Primitivism and Related Ideas in Antiquity* (New York, Octagon Books, 1980, pp 290–367).
25 Louis-Antoine de Bougainville, *Voyage autour du Monde par la Frégate du Roi La Boudeuse et la Flûte l'Etoile (1767–68)*, Paris, La Découverte Poche, 1997 (1771), pp 138–53.
26 Hawkesworth's *Voyage* dramatically revamped Samuel Wallis, Banks and Cooks' Tahitian notes. For more on Bougainville, Cook and Hawkesworth, see Anne Salmond, *Aphrodite's Island. The European Discovery of Tahiti* (Berkeley & Los Angeles, University of California Press, 2009); and Salmond (2011, pp 17–19); Rod Edmond, *Representing the South Pacific: Colonial Discourse from Cook to Gauguin* (Cambridge, Cambridge University Press, 1997, p 69); Serge Tcherkézoff, *Tahiti – 1768. Jeunes Filles en Pleurs. La face cachée des premiers contacts et la naissance du mythe occidental* (Pirae, Au Vent des Îles, 2004); Sylvie Largeaud-Ortega, 'Stevenson's *The Ebb-Tide*, or Virgil's *Aeneid* Revisited: How Literature May Make or Mar Empires' *(Victorian Literature and Culture,* vol 41, 2013, pp 567–69); *Ainsi Soit-Île. Littérature et anthropologie dans les Contes des Mers du Sud de RL Stevenson* (Paris, Honoré Champion, 2012, pp 35–118).
27 For a discussion of contemporary comments on Banks' pranks, see Colin Roderick, 'Sir Joseph Banks, Queen Oberea and the Satirists', in Veit Walter (ed), *Captain James Cook: Image and Impact. South Sea Discoveries and the World of Letters* (Melbourne, Hawthorne Press, 1972, pp 67–89).
28 Dening, 1992, p 311.
29 The *Bounty* briefly called at Tahiti before heading for Tubua'i. See Smith & Thomas (2013, pp iii–xv).

however, to ensure that she was his one and only partner in Tahiti. In contrast with Heywood, Byam remains a virgin during his first Tahitian stay. This narrative choice confirms that, at the time of the *Bounty* mutiny, Byam was an inexperienced, innocent young man with very high moral standards. He cannot be suspected of being prompted by either love or lust to return to Tahiti, unlike the mutineers who famously cheered: 'Huzza for Tahiti!' (141).[30]

It is only during the second stay in Tahiti, *after* the mutiny, that Byam 'cease[s] to be a boy and be[comes] a man' (173). Like Heywood, Byam settles down to a 'life of tranquil happiness' (189) and, unlike Heywood, he fathers a daughter.[31] His love story, however, starts in a dramatic way. It is requited love at first sight and, on the day the two exchange their first few words, they decide to wed. Once again, the guiding principle seems to be that there should be nothing illegitimate about Byam, at least from a European perspective (Tahitians saw no harm in free unions). Also, Byam is made to become a literary heir to Christian: with Christian now gone forever, Byam becomes the next romantic figure on Tahitian soil. Christian is a sombre Hamlet-like doomed figure:[32] 'the ardour of his nature, his handsome person and changing moods, made him what women call a romantic man' (93). Byam is a blissful prelapsarian character, beatifically repeating himself: 'It means little to say that I was happy with Tehani' (189), 'That year of 1790 was the happiest and seemed the shortest of my entire life' (203). Both white male archetypes in their own ways allow the popular cliché of South Sea romanticism to endure.

Female characters, on the other hand, seem to be the type of the South Sea *vahine* redeemed. Nordhoff and Hall's narrator is an ardent vindicator of the virtue of Tahitian women, in reaction against their reputation as 'wanton'.[33] He acknowledges that 'as regards the possibilities of dissipation, to which seamen are given in every port, the island could only be described as a Mohammedan paradise' (89). Repeating James

---

30 In his 21st-century *Mutiny on the Bounty* historical novel, John Boyne turns the scale against Heywood, by having aptly named Turnstile, the young cockney first-person narrator, call 'scrawny, pimpled Heywood' a 'scut'. He accuses him of being a liar, a Peeping Tom and a deliberate homewrecker (London, Black Swan, 2008, pp 341–43).
31 'No child of Heywood is mentioned' in any source material (Alexander, 2003, p 309).
32 See Edmond (1997, p 75).
33 See John Hawkesworth, *An Account of the Voyages Undertaken by Order of Her Present Majesty for Making Discoveries in the Southern Hemisphere and Successively Performed by Commodore Byron, Captain Wallis, Captain Carteret and Captain Cook, in the Dolphin ..., Drawn up from the Journals ...* (London, W Stratham, 1773).

Morrison's journal almost word for word, however, he argues that 'to form an impression of the ladies of Tahiti from the women who visited his ships would be like judging the virtue of Englishwomen from a study of the nymphs of Spithead' (83).[34] Against Bougainville, Hawkesworth and collective South Sea phantasmagoria – and, more importantly still, against American anthropologist Margaret Mead's recently published and bestselling *Coming of Age in Samoa* (1928) – older Byam declares 'this is, perhaps, a fitting place to say a word for the Indian ladies, so often and so shamelessly slandered by the different navigators who have visited this island' (82). In a brave display of cultural relativism, the authors have their narrator contend that '[n]o women in the world are more modest than the ladies of Tahiti, but they bare their breasts as innocently as an Englishwoman shows her face' (90).

Tahitian Tehani, Byam's wife, is a stunning beauty, an orphan and the favourite niece of a childless chief depicted as the most powerful in Tahiti. She develops a deeply romantic and mutually loving relationship with Byam, bears him a loving daughter and dies soon after he is forced to return to England. In that respect, Tehani is a character who is much flatter than Byam. She stands in the line of Herman Melville's Fayaway in *Typee* (1846), or Pierre Loti's Rarahu in *Le Mariage de Loti* (1879): a lovelorn figure, she is left behind to die a romantic death 'in the moon of Pipiri, when [Byam is] three months gone' (378). However well documented Byam's narrative may be on Tahitian gender issues, Tehani is no more than a type. In *Mutiny*, the *vahine* fails to be much more than a foil to the European male protagonist. She is but a loving, faithful wife, dignified and respectable, and yet unsubstantial enough to be allowed to die, and disappear from the narrative altogether, as soon as her lover departs. As Rod Edmond argues, the *vahine* '*is* the island'.[35] *Te hani* in Tahitian means 'the land', 'the earth'; as a verb, *hani* can be used to describe 'a bond with the island', and the expression *Ua hani te fenua ia 'oe* may translate as 'the land has made you hers'. This strongly supports the idea that Tehani *is* the island.[36] Like the island, she is eventually left and longed for by a self-indulgent and nostalgic European protagonist – a *locus amoenus* of colonial discourse.

---

34   Morrison's words are: 'the ladys who act these [licentious practices] are not to be taken as a standard for the Whole no more then the Nymphs of the Thames or Syrens of Spithead are to be taken as Samples of our own fair Country Weomen', in Smith & Thomas (2013, p 264). Observations of the same kind were made by various other early commentators including Johann Reinhold Forster and Cook.
35   Edmond, 1997, p 75.
36   My warm thanks to Joudy Clark-Tefau, 2017–18 second-year undergraduate student at the University of French Polynesia, for her valuable information on the meaning of *hani*.

Life in Tahiti: Island ceremonies

Roger Byam's wedding, the major Tahitian ceremony in *Mutiny*, might be a departure from the novel's dominant colonial discourse. Veihiatua – Tehani's uncle and tutor, and the highest Tahitian chief – readily gives his assent to his favourite niece's wedding. Tehani, he claims, is 'a royal gift in truth. For three and seventy generations she can count her ancestors back to the gods!' (183). In comparison, Midshipman Byam confesses he is '[a] very small [chief in his own land], perhaps' (178). What looks like a glaring social mismatch devised to suit the erotic and racial fantasies of colonial discourse, may have been viewed by Tahitians as an excellent match. They may have thought that intermarriage with early contact foreigners come from 'beyond the sky' would increase their own spiritual force, or *mana*.[37] This apparent foray into ancient island culture can suggest a postcolonial reading for *Mutiny*. Byam does indeed seem to fleetingly present the wedding from the Tahitian 'side of the beach':[38]

> The priest ... called upon the mighty chiefs and warriors whose skulls stood before us, giving each man his full name and resounding titles, and calling upon him to witness and bless the union of Tehani with *the white man from beyond the sea.* (188, my italics)

But the narrator does not proceed to explain that, for Tahitians, the expression 'white man from beyond the sea' is much more than exotic poetry. Byam does not *account* for the wedding from a Tahitian perspective. He reduces it to the folkloric crowning of a romantic love bond, as Westerners would have it. Readers consequently must accept as appropriate that the European male protagonist should marry into the most powerful Tahitian family, and that the wedding should be an occasion for much pomp and circumstance. The Tahitian wedding ceremony is accordingly described in some length over four pages (185–88). It does provide interesting, relatively accurate ethnographic information,[39] but the fact that the European bridegroom should be so complacently

---

37 Dening, 1992, pp 160–61; Tcherkézoff, 2004, p 19. This theory was originally presented by Marshall Sahlins about Hawaiian and Fijian societies in *Islands of History* (Chicago & London, University of Chicago Press, 1985).
38 Dening, 2004, p 54.
39 For the description of a historical native wedding ceremony between a Tahitian woman and a European sailor (1792), see 'Extracts from a Log-Book of HMS *Providence*, kept by Lieut Francis Godolphin Bond RN, on Bligh's second Breadfruit Voyage, 1791–3' (*Journal of the Royal Australian Historical Society*, vol 46, no 1, pp 24–57, in Salmond, 2011, p 365).

the focus of all attention once again brackets the narrative as colonial discourse. Any attempt at sketching Tahitian identity is defeated by an overruling assertion of colonial British identity.

The major island ceremony that took place during the historical *Bounty* beachcombers'[40] Tahitian sojourn was Pomare II's investiture. It celebrated the victory of the Pomares over their rivals. Morrison draws a clear picture of Tahitian political rivalries at the time. Three main groups had been struggling for hegemony:

1. The Seaward Teva. Vehiatua at their head, based in Taiarapu.
2. The Landward Teva. Purea at their head, based in Papara.
3. The Porenu'u. Tu, *alias* Teina, or the Pomare line at their head, based in Pare-Arue-Matavai.[41]

In *Mutiny*, island rivalries are only fleetingly mentioned: the reader is told that 'Vehiatua is the king of the smaller island – the most powerful of the Indian princes. His realm is richer and more populous than those of his rivals' (69), but this only serves to enhance the prestige of Byam's father-in-law. At one point, Charles Churchill makes a flippant allusion to serving as a mercenary to Vehiatua, to fight against the chief's rivals:

> 'I like the old chief – your father-in-law, whatever he is – and he seems to like me. He's a fighting man, and so is the other chief, Atuanui. We were planning a bit of a war last night. He says if I'll help him he'll give me a piece of land, with a young wife thrown in.' (196)

But it all sounds rather hypothetical, and Churchill is killed before any war breaks out. Local warfare is mostly presented as a backdrop, a kind of theatrical stage prop: '[o]f furniture there was scarcely any: … a stand of weapons hanging on one of the pillars which supported the ridgepole, including my host's ponderous war club' (81).

---

40   'Beachcombing [is] the act of repudiating Western civilisation by jumping ship, crossing the beach and attempting to join an island culture' (Edmond, 1997, p 17).
41   A map of these rival groups may be found in Smith & Thomas (2013, pp 88–134, 185–219). See also Dening (1992, pp 179–80); Salmond (2011, pp 268–77).

Mutiny thus fails to show how fierce Tahitian wars were, and how dramatically the *Bounty* residents 'shaped events in Tahiti, in ways disproportionate to their numbers'.[42] As recorded in Morrison's journal,[43] the beachcombers' firepower transformed local warfare, destroyed an ancestral balance of power and radically changed the face of island history.

> The mutineers from the *Bounty* offered their services as mercenaries and furnished arms to the family which became the Pōmare Dynasty. The chief Tu, *alias* Teina, or Pōmare, knew how to use their presence in the harbors favoured by sailors to his advantage. As a result of his alliance with the mutineers, he succeeded in considerably increasing his supremacy over the island of Tahiti.[44]

In *Mutiny*, however, this historical watershed is stymied into wishful thinking. Upon the *Pandora*'s arrival, high chief Teina ingenuously conjectures:

> that Cook and Bligh, if the latter chanced to be with him, would now decide to remain permanently at Tahiti; he [Teina] would urge them to do so, and would set aside great tracts of land for their use and provide them with as many servants as they might want; with their help he would bring the whole of Tahiti under subjection; then we would all proceed to the island of Eimeo, and on to Raiatea and Bora Bora, conquering each of these islands in turn. And he promised that Stewart and I [Byam] should be made great chiefs, and that our children should grow in power after us. (209)

William Bligh had tricked Tahitians into believing that James Cook was still alive but, by 1789, they knew that he was dead.[45] The imagined consequences of the arrival of Cook and Bligh on the *Pandora* are indeed described here as delusory (with the repeated use of 'would' and 'should'), but the aim is to imply that prospects of British-supported wars never materialised in Tahiti. The narrator's tone is condescending to Teina, as if the primitive high chief should be excused for indulging in such wild dreams. This presentation of things is blatantly at odds with the historical truth. Also, the narrative exonerates the beachcombers of any mercenary

---

42 Nicholas Thomas, *Islanders: The Pacific in the Age of Empire*, Boston, Yale University Press, 2010, pp 21–22.
43 Smith & Thomas, 2013, pp 115, 116.
44 Alexander, 2003, p 12.
45 Tahitians were informed of Cook's death first in 1788 (three months before the *Bounty*'s first call) by seamen from the *Lady Penrhyn*, and again in 1789 (one month before the *Bounty*'s last call) by the captain of the *Mercury*.

4. NORDHOFF AND HALL'S *MUTINY ON THE BOUNTY*

meddling by transferring the onus – albeit virtually – onto British officers Cook and Bligh. Since Cook and Bligh consistently refused to take part in local warfare,[46] it may be surmised that the authors wish to keep most *Bounty* mutineers – and more specifically their hero – clear of any moral stain, as in typical popular fiction.

Teina's victory did occur, with the decisive help of the *Bounty* beachcombers. He gradually took control of most Society Islands, an unprecedented achievement, and the Pomare dynasty remained in power until the French abolished the native monarchy in 1880.[47] The *Bounty* residents, as well as Bligh during his second Tahitian stay, were able to witness the six-month-long ceremony of young Pomare II's investiture, over 'weeks of extravagant feasting'. Morrison reports gruesome details about 'rows of human sacrifices, thirty of them':

> [the priest] took an Eye out of each, with a Piece of split bamboo, and placing them on a leaf took a Young Plantain tree in one hand, and the Eyes in the Other Made a long speech holding them up to the Young King, who sat above him with his mouth open … [T]he reason that the King sits with his Mouth open, is to let the Soul of the Sacrafice enter into his Soul, that he may be strengthened thereby, or that His Tutelar deity or Guardian Angel presides to receive the Soul of the Sacrafice … [T]he Human sacrifices offered this day were 30, some of which had been Killd near a Month.[48]

This pharaonic ceremony could hardly have escaped the beachcombers' notice, nor easily been forgotten. Yet Pomare II's investiture is conspicuously absent from *Mutiny*. The figure of the Noble Savage remains untainted. As far as Tahitian ceremonies are concerned, Byam's wedding stands alone to the fore – colonial discourse prevails.

---

46 On Cook, see James Cook & James King, *A Voyage to the Pacific Ocean. Undertaken, by the Command of his Majesty, for Making Discoveries in the Northern Hemisphere. Performed Under the Direction of Captains Cook, Clerke, and Gore, in his Majesty's Ships the* Resolution *and* Discovery. *In the Years 1776, 1777, 1778, 1779, and 1780. In Three Volumes*, vol 1 (London, 1784, pp 190–201). On Bligh, see Salmond (2011, p 79).
47 See Jean-François Baré, *Le Malentendu Pacifique. Des premières rencontres entre Polynésiens et Anglais et de ce qui s'ensuivit avec les Français jusqu'à nos jours* (Paris, Hachette, 1985); Bruno Saura, *Histoire et Mémoire des Temps Coloniaux en Polynésie Française* (Pirae, Au Vent des Îles, 2015).
48 Smith & Thomas, 2013, p 132.

Life in Tahiti: Going native

The second main difference between the Tahitian narratives of Peter Heywood and Roger Byam lies in their choice of a residence in Tahiti. Like most of the *Bounty* beachcombers, Heywood only 'crossed' part of 'the beach': he chose to live in Matavai, the port of call of all British ships. He first moved in with Scottish Midshipman George Stewart, and then settled down with his Tahitian wife nearby, on the land of Stewart's wife. Nearly all of the *Bounty* residents remained in groups of two to five. Except for occasional short trips to other villages, they were never isolated from one another for long.[49]

Like many of the *Bounty* beachcombers, Heywood once took a trip to Taiarapu, Vehiatua's stronghold at the other end of the island. Like James Morrison, William Muspratt, Thomas Burkitt, Charles Churchill and others, he was offered the chance to settle down there. These invitations were proffered in the context of local warfare, with a mind to coaxing more beachcombers to Taiarapu – but Heywood declined the offer.[50] He remained in Matavai where he adopted a Tahitian lifestyle: he agreed to be further heavily tattooed, he learnt the Tahitian language and he gained considerable insight into the Tahitian way of life. Like all the *Bounty* beachcombers, he was wholly dependent on his *taio* and the Tahitian *ari'i*'s[51] goodwill: it was 'their relationship to the highly ranked Tahitians that kept at bay much ordinary envy and anger at their presence'; they were given land, shelter and protection, in return for duties like acting as mercenaries.[52]

Two notorious troublemakers, *Bounty* Master-at-Arms Churchill and Able Seaman Matthew Thompson, became 'the epitome of the licentious and roguish beachcomber'.[53] Part of their historical tale must be told to underscore the differences with Byam's narrative. Thompson raped a young girl, then;

---

49 Most of the *Bounty* beachcombers lived in Matavai or neighbouring Arue and Pare.
50 Smyth, 1831b, pp 102–05, 304–05.
51 *Taio*: Tahitian word for friend. For an extensive study of the word's meaning, see Vanessa Smith, *Intimate Strangers: Friendship, Exchange and Pacific Encounters* (Cambridge, Cambridge University Press, 2010). *Ari'i*: Tahitian word for a nobleman, or high chief.
52 Dening, 1992, pp 213–58.
53 Dening, 1992, p 217.

[he] shot a man dead, together with the infant he was carrying. The man was a visitor from another island, totally innocent and ignorant of what had happened in relation to the girl. In the disorder that followed, Churchill … volunteered to be the general of [the beachcombers'] army and the men's captain. It was an offer that the others refused, and, by gifts and diplomacy, they quieted the situation. As a result, Churchill went off with Thompson to Taiarapu, at the other end of the island. There his ambition to be a leader of some sort, a passion for command that had bedevilled them since the day of the mutiny, was fulfilled. His *taio*, Vehiatua, the *ari'i* of the Seaward Teva, died and, in some way, Churchill was made *ari'i* in his place.

… Aware that Thompson was bitterly jealous of his honours and fearful of the dangers in that, Churchill had Thompson's weapons stolen. Thompson then returned to Matavai, persuaded the others to lend him a musket and returned to Taiarapu, where he killed Churchill. Enraged that he had killed their chief, one of the Teva … battered him to death.[54]

In *Mutiny*, unlike Heywood, Byam chooses to 'cross the beach' further, by living away from Matavai and all the other *Bounty* beachcombers. He agrees to settle down in his wife's village – precisely in 'Taiarapu, at the other end of the island'. When Vehiatua welcomes fugitive Churchill and Thompson, Byam declares that this is done on his own account: 'Vehiatua, *supposing him to be one of my friends*, had welcomed [them]' (195, my italics). Older Byam's narrative does not account for the fate of Churchill and Thompson from a Tahitian perspective. As a result, first, Vehiatua is stripped of his political acumen, and reduced to the blindly obliging Tahitian stereotype, a feature of the Noble Savage. Second, the narrative focus shifts onto Byam's younger self, giving the European protagonist all the credit for a decision of the most powerful Tahitian *ari'i*'s. In a blazingly colonial kind of discourse, Byam is made to wield supreme authority over Vehiatua, both as older narrator and as younger protagonist.

Byam explains that Churchill and Thompson had to look for a place far away from Papara whose leaders were 'allied with the clan to which the murdered man belonged' (195). But he fails to say that the two fugitives' choice of Taiarapu was not due to distance only. More importantly, they sought refuge in the bulwark of the 'hostile alliance'[55] against Papara, under the protection of Vehiatua who was glad to be friendly with his

---

54   Dening, 1992, pp 217–18. For further information on these events, see Douglas Oliver, *Ancient Tahitian Society* (Honolulu, University of Hawai'i Press, 1974, chpt 28).
55   Salmond, 2009, p 84.

foes' foes. The narrative also significantly fails to signal that Churchill was raised to the ranks of Vehiatua's *taio* and of *ari'i*. In the novel, the old chief's good health endures, so Churchill does not inherit his title. Ironically enough, at the extradiegetic level, rivalries are displaced here, from historical Tahitian chiefs to non-historical European characters: in *Mutiny*'s Taiarapu, Byam shall be the one and only 'white man from beyond'. Nobody shall vie for his position of honour.

Byam's choice of a residence miles away from all the other *Bounty* mutineers illuminates the figure of a white man solitary among natives – i.e. gone native. Here is a dialogue between Byam and Stewart, who once pays his friend a visit:

> [Stewart:] 'What a place for a hermit's meditations!'
>
> 'Would you like to live here?' I asked.
>
> 'Perhaps. But I would miss the sight of English faces. You, Byam, living alone among the Indians, do you never miss your own kind?'
>
> I thought for a moment before I replied: 'Not thus far.'
>
> Stewart smiled: 'You are half Indian already.' (201)

There is dramatic irony in Stewart's comment that Byam is 'half Indian'. Byam does not quite go native: throughout the Tahitian narrative he says that he is not there to stay. He constantly reminds the reader of his twin duties to Britain: his mother, and Joseph Banks' Tahitian dictionary. He has a 'civilised' excuse for going native: even in the places farthest removed from European civilisation, he has 'not a care in the world, save the making of [his] dictionary' (85). Although there was no tradition of writing in Tahiti, Byam's gentle *vahine* 'leav[es him] free to do [his] writing' (189–90). Coincidentally, Byam never debases himself to the duties of a mercenary:[56]

> The loss of Churchill was accepted as an unfavourable omen by Vehiatua's priests, and the expedition planned against the people of the south coast of Eimeo was given up. I was secretly glad to be freed from the duty of taking up arms against men to whom I bore no ill-will, and settled down with relief to a tranquil domestic life and my studies of the Indian tongue. (197)

---

56 Heywood did fight in several skirmishes, see Peter Heywood's letter to this mother, 20 Nov 1791, Batavia, ML M 3075, in Salmond (2011, p 400).

Mutiny is no postcolonial Pacific *Heart of Darkness* – Tautira is a far cry from the upper Congo River, and Byam and Kurtz go native in dramatically different ways. Byam's life is the Western fantasy of island life at its most idyllic. Crusoe-like, Byam is immersed in exotic nature but with enough Western culture to preserve his British identity.

The finale of colonial discourse in the narrative of life in Tahiti coincides with the *Pandora*'s arrival. As soon as the Tautirans sight the *Pandora*, they launch their canoes and reach Matavai much before her; yet, 'news of the ship precede[s]' the Tautiran sailors to the port of call. There might be an allegorical reading to this race: however well-performing the Tahitian society, or whatever their nautical, cultural, political, and other achievements, they are subdued by 'news' or narratives. It is a colonial narrative that shapes the readers' representations of Tahiti. As Byam sails back to Matavai on board Tuahu's canoe, he gives what sounds like a farewell song, a litany of Tahitian place names: 'Pueu … Hitiaa … Tiarei'. When he finally reaches Matavai, he stops at Tahara'a – renamed 'One Tree Hill' by Samuel Wallis (204). 'One Tree Hill' are the closing words of the chapters on Tahiti. *Nomen est omen*: the British place name, and colonial discourse, triumph in the narrative of Tahitian life.

Roger Byam's court martial and closing framing narrative

Older narrator Byam is allowed to warp Tahitian history so as to make the European male protagonist, his younger self, the undivided centre of narrative focus. The question asked at the court martial of younger Byam,[57] whether his tale of the mutiny is reliable, may therefore sound ironical. This intriguing *mise en abyme* of narrative reliability in *Mutiny*, however, raises fresh questions about literary discourses and genres. But first, what are the main differences between Peter Heywood's and Byam's experiences of a court martial?

---

57 This study deliberately leaves out the eventful voyage back home, the narrative of which is largely historically accurate in *Mutiny*.

Younger Byam returns to England an orphan, because his mother and only remaining family has been dealt a fatal blow by William Bligh's scathing letter about his 'baseness … beyond all description' (224). Those were indeed historical Bligh's words to Mrs Heywood, but they did not kill her: she was spared reading them by a wide, caring circle of family and friends.

Peer Heywood and Byam both made/make emotional pleas. They appeal/ed to the court's feelings of pity with regards to their extreme youth and innocence. Here are extracts from Heywood's plea:

> My parents (but I have only one left, a solitary and Mournful Mother who is at home weeping and trembling for the event of this day) [should be considered, to determine] the consolation or settled misery of a dear mother and two Sisters who mingle their tears together and are all but frantic for my situation.[58]

One of the sisters, Nessy, did do 'frantic' lobbying. She appealed to a powerfully affluent and influential network of close relatives and friends.[59]

Byam's plea reaches even higher emotional peaks, by expanding on the image of a wronged orphan and noble boy victim. His sole support (not lobbyist) and eventual saviour is Banks – which is ironic because historical Banks patronised Bligh all along.

In history, Heywood and James Morrison were found guilty of the charge of mutiny, sentenced to death and pardoned by King George III. William Muspratt was released on a legal technicality. In *Mutiny*, Morrison, Muspratt and Byam are all found guilty. Morrison and Muspratt are pardoned. Byam, on the other hand, is proved innocent after a tense 22-page-long suspense involving fictional events: Robert Tinkler, given for lost, reappears at the 11th hour and bears testimony just before the hanging. As a result, the court 'are convinced of [Byam's] entire innocence of the crime of mutiny' (352). The protagonist is once again singled out for his moral values, the only *Bounty* beachcomber to be proved 'as innocent as Sir Joseph' (363). Thus put on an equal footing with Banks, Byam's national identity is clearly outlined. This leaves little doubt as to the *Mutiny*'s literary discourse and genre: a colonial narrative that preserves British morality. An epitome of popular literature, it delivers gripping

---

58   Owen Rutter (ed), *The Court Martial of the 'Bounty' Mutineers* (Edinburgh & London, William Hodge, 1931, pp 147–48).
59   See Maxton & Du Rietz (2013).

melodrama. As to younger Byam's reliability, the court acknowledges 'the truth of every statement' he has made. To the readers' emotional relief, his narrative of the mutiny is deemed reliable.

The tale delivered at court martial, however, is but a short one embedded within several other tales. It is a tale within Byam's tale of the *Bounty* events, embedded within Byam's journal. The journal itself is embedded within the framing narrative of older Byam's tale, delivered 55 years after the events. This *mise en abyme* raises issues of validity, owing to distance and added reports. Any attempt to determine this historical novel's degree of contingency must thus question the reliability of narrator Byam – not the younger narrator, but the older one.

The *Mutiny*'s Epilogue briefly states that Byam fights the Napoleonic wars, and his valiant role at Trafalgar earns him the rank of captain. This peremptorily confirms the hero's British identity and ultimate recognition by his British peers. Deeply nostalgic, however, middle-aged Byam manages to call back at Tahiti in 1810, on a passage to New South Wales where 'Bligh was once more the central figure of a mutiny' (371).[60] In Tahiti, Byam finds nothing but desolation: in the last 20 years, most of his friends and family have succumbed to the so-called 'fatal impact' of their contact with Westerners.[61] His daughter, a rare survivor, has grown into a replica of his twin lost loves: 'she had all her dead mother's beauty, and something of my mother as well' (379). Feeling that he no longer belongs there, Byam chooses not to make himself known to her, and leaves Tahiti forever. Byam and Tahitians, including his own daughter and grandchild, have become irretrievable strangers to one another.

The Epilogue evinces significant changes from the source material. Unlike Byam, Heywood enjoyed speedy promotion to the highest rank of post-captain, thanks to his influential friends. He never sailed back to Tahiti. He left the Navy to become Admiralty hydrographer, got married and died in 1831, aged 58.[62] In comparison, Byam's military record is

---

60   The Rum Rebellion: Bligh was then governor of New South Wales, and the object of a rebellion from the military officers. *Mutiny* fleetingly shows Bligh in one of his outbursts, still the same uncontrollably violent speaker in 1810. For further information on the Rum Rebellion, see Salmond (2011, Epilogue).
61   South Pacific postcolonial literature decries the 'fatal impact' argument: see, for example, fictions like Keri Hulme's *The Bone People* (1984), Patricia Grace's *Potiki* (1987), Alan Duff's *Once were Warriors* (1990) and Albert Wendt's *The Mango's Kiss* (2003).
62   For more detailed information on Heywood's subsequent career compared to that of other *Bounty* members, see Smyth (1831a, pp 468–81).

more glorious and, by remaining single, the hero retains the status of romantic lover required by this genre of popular literature. The Epilogue also delivers colonial discourse where otherness is clearly delineated: there can be no more cultural or ethnic bridging in the Tahiti of 1810, no more talk of crossing the beach and going native. Native culture itself is moribund. Banks' reaction against freshly acquitted Byam's plan to return to Tahiti proves literally right: 'the islands … no, my lad!' One only goes there to 'bury [one]self' (363). The novel's closing words, 'the place was full of ghosts, – shadows of men alive and dead, – my own among them' (379), illuminate what Rod Edmond defines as the twin colonial mantras of nostalgia for a place of perfect happiness forever lost, and of a Pacific island people doomed to become extinct after the West's fatal impact.[63]

Roger Byam's opening framing narrative

What about the opening frame's all-encompassing narrator? The year is 1843; 73-year-old Byam is about to deliver his embedded *Bounty* narrative in the form of an analepsis. So the beginning is actually the end, and the Epilogue is a false end. From the start, readers are thus alerted to ambivalences. Ambivalence characterises the narrator–protagonist also: he is both an older narrating 'I', and a younger narrated 'I'. May there be more to Byam than meets the eyes, after (or before) all? Whereas the younger voice recounts the events, the older voice reflects on those to-be/have-been events. It also hints at the untold tale of Byam's life since 1810 – a life of emptiness and profound nostalgia, which remains unsaid. What matters may lie in this other, untold tale.

The opening narrative (3–5) may prove decisive to this chapter's argument: an underlying feeling of oppression and a craving for liberty run through its lines. In conservative, never-changing Britain, the old man complains: 'Forty years of this life have made a *slave* of me' (my italics). Older Byam's freedom may only be gained through writing about the past – 'to be *free* to wander in the past' (my italics) – and, more specifically, about Tahiti. The opening frame thus operates a gradual shift, through writing, from oppression to freedom, from the present to the past, and

---

63 Countering the 'fatal impact' argument, Edmond writes: 'Pacific historians and anthropologists have emphasised the resilience and continuity of Pacific societies in the colonial period. Far from being wiped out, they adapted and survived, often conceding less than contemporary missionary accounts, for example, were prepared to admit' (Edmond, 1997, p 14).

from Britain to Tahiti. In that respect, the opening narrative foreshadows the main narrative, since writing is presented as a means of liberation throughout the novel: in Tahiti, 'the making of [his] dictionary [gives Byam] sufficient occupation to prevent ennui' (85); on the *Pandora*, the same writing activity lifts 'the prohibition' against speaking Tahitian (242); in jail, the 'manuscript pages' allow Byam's mind to wander off to 'Tahiti' (342); and it is finally his own written plea of innocence that results in his avoiding hanging. The opening framing narrative, with its focus on the liberating virtues of writing, might therefore be seen as a miniature mirror image of the main narrative.

Older Byam's tale of oppression, however, sounds almost comic: his gaoler is 80-year-'old Thacker', the family's 'housekeeper' who 'will listen to no hint of retirement'. Byam's self-mocking tone, his 'inward amusement' may indicate dramatic irony: the older narrating 'I''s ironical distance from his own narrated 'I' may give readers a hint to follow suit and be critical of Byam's overall representations of things. Older Byam clearly invites readers to relativism, as he puts to the test a number of 18th-century hierarchies. His very first words challenge national hierarchies: 'The British are frequently criticized' – which gives him an excuse to decry Britain and the British Navy as a narrow-minded, self-enclosed set. Life in Britain's West Country, he argues, 'conform[s] to the patterns of a *simpler age*' (my italics), which looks, one might think, intriguingly similar to life in primitive places. Likewise, Byam begs to be 'pardoned a *not unnatural* tenderness towards the scene of *his* youth' (my italics): first, the stress on his own *natural* side makes him once more singularly akin to 'natural' Tahitians (7); and, second, the fact that Byam speaks of himself in the third person clearly marks distancing. With the male master 'a slave' to the female servant, Byam further questions gender and social hierarchies. He carries on challenging racial hierarchies when he notes that 'Seven generations of Byams have lived and died in Withycombe [but] at my death what remains of our blood will flow in the veins of an Indian woman in the South Sea' (5). This next confession again strongly urges relativism: 'Insignificant in the annals of the Navy, and even more so from an historian's point of view, [the *Bounty*] incident was nevertheless the strangest, the most picturesque, and the most tragic of my career'.

Older Byam's voice of relativism may urge readers to put his embedded narratives into perspective. 'It makes me smile to-day to think of [my past candidness]' (15), he later engagingly says. He acknowledges that his perceptions as a younger man may have been deceiving:

> [At court martial] We were objects of curiosity to everyone, and many of the officers stared at us as though we were wild animals. At least, so it seemed to me, but no doubt I was unusually sensitive at that time, and imagined insolence and hostility on faces which revealed nothing more than natural curiosity. (321)

While awaiting hanging, Byam ponders the effects of changing lights and changing mental perspectives:

> Even the common objects in my small cabin, – the locker, the table, and the inkwell before me, – seen in various lights at different hours of the day, I found beautiful and wondered that I had failed to notice such things before. (340)

At times, he is a self-confessed deficient narrator: 'I never felt that I truly understood the workings of [Bligh's] mind and heart' (141); or a self-confessed censor: 'Of my interview with his mother I shall not speak' (367). In terms of literary genres, this double voice allows the character of popular fiction to evolve into the rounder character of a *Bildungsroman*. It also calls for metaliterary relativism: in a kind of self-commentary, or relativism *mise en abyme*, *Mutiny* invites readers to ponder over the issue of narrators' reliability:

> It was my opinion at the time of the court-martial, and it is so still, that [Hayward] arranged his recollections of what had taken place [during the mutiny] so as to put his own actions in the most favourable possible light. (315)

That is relativism with a vengeance, exposing older Byam's opinion on younger Byam's opinion on Thomas Hayward's opinion on the *Bounty* mutiny. Equally interesting is this conversation in New South Wales in 1810, when Byam discusses William Bligh and the Rum Rebellion:

> [Pascoe:] 'What have you heard of all this in England?'
>
> [Byam:] 'Only rumours; we know nothing of the truth.'
>
> [Pascoe:] 'The truth is hard to get at, even here. No doubt there is justice on both sides.' (372)

The Rum Rebellion being another 'mutiny' (371), such balance in pronouncing judgement on Bligh is arresting.

It seems that, all along, older Byam knows that, since his narrative is autobiographical, it will be biased. That is exactly what the opening frame seems to alert readers to. Framing narratives can, and often do, play a vital role in the narratives they frame:[64] it might apply here. Why should there be a relativist opening frame in *Mutiny*, if not to deliver a tongue-in-cheek variation of the main narrative's leitmotiv on oppression, and thereby tone it down? '[O]ld Thacker', the so-called tyrannical housekeeper, is clearly a parody of tyrannical Bligh. This parodic introduction might hint that the embedded description of Bligh's tyranny is also exaggerated – that narrated Bligh is also a parody of historical Bligh. While reading over older Byam's shoulder, readers may ponder old Thacker's *and* Bligh's tyrannical ways. Likewise, the self-derisively overstated metaphor, 'a slave', applied to older Byam, may announce another possibly equally overstated metaphor, 'hell' (153), which historical Fletcher Christian claimed he suffered under Bligh's command.

Another of older Byam's whimsical confessions is a paragon of self-derision and ambivalence: 'I continue, almost against my will, to live by the clock' (4). While talking about his life in Withycombe, is he not also hinting at his failure to leave the *Bounty* at the time of the mutiny? Indeed, he comically presents himself as the passive victim of outside animation out of his control – in Withycombe: 'seven finds me dressing', 'my copy of the *Times* would reach me at ten'; similarly, on the *Bounty*, the mutiny finds him 'too late' to board a launch that 'had drifted astern' seemingly of its own accord (139). It is as if older Byam were nudging readers into caution when he protests that he cannot be blamed for his own actions, neither now nor then. It is as if he were urging them to deride him. All he seems to have retained from his life experiences is a commitment to punctuality – funnily enough, 'too late' – of derisory value in retired life. Self-mocking Byam gives *Mutiny* additional literary interest: hovering over the flat protagonist of popular fiction, there is a more nuanced and challenging older narrator, a rounder character who is likely to attract a more analytical kind of readership. The multiplicity of narrative voices might orient the narrative away from the popular historical novel towards a higher, more reflexive and more thought-provoking literary genre.

The all-encompassing older narrator might also be said to challenge colonial discourse in *Mutiny* as a whole. Owing to the framing narrative, Byam appears as a fragmented self, which is a result of having 'crossed the beach'. His self might be too fragmented to give a unified and coherent representation of the British. His voices might be too many to sound an

---

64   See H Porter Abott, *The Cambridge Introduction to Narrative* (2nd edn, Cambridge, Cambridge University Press, 2009, pp 28–39).

unequivocal hymn to the Navy. Cultural relativism hints that otherness might be found at home, too. When Byam finds himself free again in London, he mourns, 'I was alone, among strangers, for the first time in five years' (356). Likewise, in the following quote, the word 'savage' and the use of the demonstrative 'those' marks the narrator's distance from his own culture:

> Sea Law. Just – yes; just, savage, and implacable. I would have given the whole of the Articles of War and all those who wrote them to have had Tom Ellison [one of the hanged mutineers] sitting, in the flesh, opposite me in that seat in the London coach. (355)

Older Byam's criticism of Britain, his longing for the South Sea and his overall relativism contribute to questioning the narrative of a British unitary identity.

Mutiny's colonial discourse, however, remains unchallenged. However fragmented, the European self is the undisputed narrative focus. Although he has 'crossed the beach', older Byam's moralising voice never questions the wisdom of Joseph Banks' insistence on a linguistic mission being sent to Tahiti, which facilitated Western settling in the Pacific. Not once does he reflect on his own active role in the fatal impact he decries: with the other *Bounty* beachcombers, he unwittingly participates in Pacific island depopulation through the spread of European diseases, guns and British lifestyle. His profound nostalgia for Tahiti remains self-centred and only serves a colonial mantra. However relativist, *Mutiny* remains a Eurocentric and egotistic narrative. Writing imprisons the older narrator in the narrative of his own past. The narrating 'I', writing his memoirs about the narrated 'I' writing his journal, produces nothing but a cyclical, self-enclosed and self-centred narrative. Writing thus *mise en abyme* binds the writing narrator in endless repetition. The 'camphor-wood box' wherefrom older Byam retrieves his journal in 1843 is but another 'Pandora's box': it tightens the chains around him. In this way, older Byam is bound to repeat the same plea for forgiveness: 'an old man … may be pardoned a not unnatural tenderness' (3). His plea for 'pardon' and excuse of extreme 'old' age echoes younger Byam's plea and excuse of 'extreme youth' at court martial. Older Byam still craves the same need for self-exculpation and identification to blameless British peers:

> It has long been my purpose to follow the example of other retired officers and employ the too abundant leisure of an old man in setting down, with the aid of my journal and in the fullest detail, a narrative of some of the episodes of my life at sea. (5)

What eventually matters in *Mutiny*'s whole narrative is colonial discourse founded on British identity, however subjected to criticism that identity may be.

Nordhoff and Hall, like older Byam, were constantly and sometimes excruciatingly balanced between home in the United States and Tahiti.[65] Like older Byam, they turned to writing in an attempt to define their own selves. But while writing 'from the beach' in Tahiti, they chose to adopt a British narrator's viewpoint. Their narrative choices in *Mutiny* buttress Byam's colonial discourse. Like him, they longed for things Western, since they elicited to represent *Tahiti* from a British perspective, with a strong focus on the British protagonist. They failed to practise their older narrator's preaching in cultural relativism. This might ultimately explain their choice of an imaginary white male narrator–protagonist: they created Byam in their own image – a Byam with their own bias.[66]

Their narrative of the *Bounty* was mostly a commercial venture, urged by Ellery Sedwig, the editor of the *Atlantic Monthly*, who convinced them that the story would sell well. Writing about Tahiti was, to a certain extent, a variant of colonial exploitation. Somewhat like Banks' self-styled civilising missions to transfer breadfruit to slave-owners and to write a Tahitian dictionary for British mariners, their narrative of *Mutiny* further contributed to the stereotypically colonial representation of Tahiti as a carefree island where natives lived in 'a timeless, myth-ridden, ahistorical haze'.[67] Their South Sea narrative is conventionally romantic and their purpose in writing was to sell, not to make a breakthrough in the history of Pacific literature. Nor did they aim to write highbrow or innovative literature. Whatever their forays into narrative strategies, what they wrote was colonial discourse in the genre of a popular novel parading as historical.

---

65 For a detailed biography of Nordhoff and Hall, see Paul L Briand, Jr, *In Search of Paradise: The Nordhoff–Hall Story* (Honolulu, Mutual Publishing Paperback Series, 1966).
66 Nancy Hall does not know where Roger Byam's name comes from: 'As far as she thought, it was made up.' Personal communication from Cindy Overhardt, James Norman Hall's granddaughter, reporting her mother's answer to my written enquiry, 21 Mar 2014. I find the Byam-bias paronomasia rather tantalising.
67 Salmond, 2009, p 33.

Conclusion

At times, *Mutiny* fleetingly strikes a postcolonial stance. By vindicating the Tahitian *vahine*, it makes a genuine attempt at discarding a prevailing Tahitian stereotype and delineating some features of Polynesian identity. By fragmenting the narrator's identity, it likewise invites cultural relativism. Yet, colonial discourse prevails in the way the narrative deals only incidentally and superficially with local politics, culture and gender issues, and does not balk at reconstructing the *Bounty* mutiny and Tahitian history to the advantage of the British protagonist. In keeping with colonial discourse, Tahitians are stereotypes of Noble Savages, while Roger Byam stands out as the archetypal British romantic. He may go temporarily 'half native', but his main concern is constantly to reaffirm a clearly defined British national identity. Byam returns home and his lovelorn Tahitian lover and her island soon perish, according to the sweepingly colonial fatal impact argument. While writing *Mutiny*, Nordhoff and Hall were gazing at far-away Britain from Tahiti, and their narrative strategies converged to produce colonial discourse in a popular romantic novel. Whereas *Mutiny on the Bounty* was acclaimed as a historical novel, it turns out to be mostly fictionalised history. As such, it has widely contributed to spreading enduring myths, not only about William Bligh but also, in collective Western representations, about Tahiti. Illustrating this resilience, John Boyne's more recent popular historical novel, *Mutiny on the Bounty* (2008), does strive to restore Bligh's name, but still shows little concern for Tahiti. For instance, in blatant dismissal of Tahitian culture, it describes the breadfruit – a key element to any *Bounty* narrative – as 'an extraordinary thing … growing in the soil'.[68] Such misinformation and neglectful documentation in the age of internet clearly pertains to colonial discourse. To echo Greg Dening and Gérard Genette, a popular, postcolonial *Mutiny on the Bounty* remains to be written 'from the indigenous side of the beach', 'where the British would be seen, described and judged by Polynesians' and where 'thematic and axiological viewpoints' would be duly inverted.[69]

---

68   Boyne, 2008, p 213.
69   The original quote is 'a *Friday*, where Crusoe would be seen, described and judged by Friday' (my translation), in Gérard Genette, *Palimpsestes, La Littérature au Second Degré* (Paris, Seuil, 1982, pp 419, 424).

5

A Ship is Burning: Jack London's 'The Seed of McCoy' (*Tales of the Pacific*, 1911), or Sailing Away from Pitcairn

Jean-Pierre Naugrette
University of Sorbonne-Nouvelle Paris 3

A major writer never sails away alone, without any reference or book at hand. Even at the far end of the world, there is always a literary reminiscence, the trace of a volume, a library of sorts, in his cabin, guiding him on his way, like the wake of a ship. When sailing up the Congo River, André Gide had quite naturally Joseph Conrad's *Heart of Darkness* (1899) in mind, and Robert Louis Stevenson's novel *The Master of Ballantrae* in his luggage:[1] his *Voyage au Congo* (1926–27) is dedicated to 'the memory of Joseph Conrad' and includes, on the same page, a quotation from John Keats: 'Better be imprudent moveables than prudent fixtures', which may serve as a motto for adventure. This was also the case with Jack London when he left San Francisco and the devastation caused by earthquake (18 April 1906), sailing away on board his ketch the *Snark* on 23 April 1907: he was embarking on a cruise 'in the wake of' such famous literary predecessors as Herman Melville, Mark Twain and Robert

---

1   Gide's trip to the Congo is contemporary with Macmillan's publication of the Tusitala Edition of Stevenson's works (1924a, 1924b & 1924c).

Louis Stevenson,[2] with Charmian as his mate – both in the sentimental and sailing sense of the term. Later, between Hawai'i and the Marquesas, during a solitary, two-month crossing where the winds prove whimsical and the doldrums exhausting, he will read out loud, in the evening, the beloved authors of his youth, the very Melville, Stevenson or Conrad who had been, together with Rudyard Kipling, his literary models.[3] In such a literary wake, his cruise turned out to be, quite naturally, a pilgrimage of sorts. At Nuku Hiva, in the Marquesas, he rented the very house in which Stevenson stayed a few years before, and rode on horseback to Hapaa valley, the paradise described by Melville in *Typee*. After having left Tahiti on 4 April 1908, when London reached the bay of Apia on the Samoan island of Upolu, he insisted on seeing the celebrated grave of Stevenson, tucked away in the jungle on top of Mount Vaea, the only grave in the world, according to him, that was worth visiting.[4] Whereas Stevenson's literary correspondent, admirer and friend Marcel Schwob had failed, only six years before, in his attempt at visiting the grave – when reaching Apia, he was so sick and bedridden that he had to stay in his cabin – London and Charmian managed to hack their way up to the top of the place where Stevenson was carried in state, like a tribal chief, by the Samoan natives who had nicknamed him 'Tusitala', the teller of tales. Samoans indeed held Stevenson in high esteem for having 'crossed the beach', or been willing to be 'transformed' by contact with Polynesian culture, as Greg Dening puts it[5] (see Introduction). Preceding Dening's calls to take a fresh look at 'the little people on the beach', Stevenson said – against the grain, in the colonial era – that Samoans were 'like other folk, lazy enough, not heroes, not saints, ordinary men, damnably misused'.[6] During the Samoan civil war, he daringly supported Prince Mata'afa, a fierce opponent of Western hegemony. This, and his anticolonial articles, pamphlet and fiction, earned Stevenson *mea-alofa*, the Samoan gift of love.

---

2   Andrew Sinclair, *Jack: A Biography of Jack London*, London, Weidenfeld & Nicolson, 1978, p 139.
3   Andrew Sinclair, 'Introduction to Jack London', in *Tales of the Pacific*, Harmondsworth, Penguin Twentieth-Century Classics, 1989, p 7.
4   Alex Kershaw, *Jack London: A Life*, London, Harper Collins, 1997, pp 197–98.
5   Greg Dening, 'Writing, Rewriting the Beach: An Essay', in Alun Munslow & Robert A Rosenstone (eds), *Experiments in Rethinking History*, New York & London, Routledge, 2004, pp 30–55.
6   Robert Louis Stevenson, letter to Vailima Colvin, 6 Sep 1891, in Ernest Mehew (ed), *Selected Letters of Robert Louis Stevenson*, New Haven & London, Yale University Press, 1997, p 465.

5. A SHIP IS BURNING

London's South Pacific cruise proved to be catastrophic and disastrous from a personal point of view. When in Tahiti, he learned that his Californian ranch was a financial failure, and had to steam back in haste to California in order to sort out his affairs, then back to Tahiti to resume his trip. His health also began to deteriorate:

> London was sick from many tropical illnesses including yaws and ulcers and a skin disease which seemed to be leprosy caught at Molokai. His elbows became silvery and his hands swelled to the size of boxing-gloves and their skin fell away, layer after layer.[7]

Molokaʻi was a leper colony located on an islet off Honolulu that Stevenson had also visited: traces of this visit can be found in his story 'The Bottle Imp' (1893, in *Island Night's Entertainments*), where leprosy, called the 'Chinese Evil', is treated on the magic or fantastic mode, and related fears charmed away.[8] London's more serious, embedded fear of his own contamination is echoed in several stories of his *Tales of the Pacific*,[9] like 'Good-By, Jack', 'Koolau the Leper' or 'The Sheriff of Kona', which bear on 'the horror' attached to a disease taking seven years to incubate, and potentially undermining an apparently sound, beautiful body.[10] The personal obsession is so overwhelming here that, according to London himself in a letter to Lorrin A Thurston dated 1 February 1910,[11] his Pacific tales about leprosy cannot match Stevenson's pamphlet *Father Damien, An Open Letter to Reverend Dr Hyde of Honolulu* (1890), in which Stevenson vigorously vindicated the memory of Father Damien, a Catholic priest who had nursed the lepers before dying of leprosy himself, and had been accused of consorting with his patients. In comparison, London's tales sound haunted by *memento mori*, by the frailty of appearances, by the debated issue of diagnosis, and by Kipling's horrifying story 'The Mark of the Beast' (1890), which also deals with leprosy. The image of 'the mark of the beast' is thus used about Lyte Gregory in 'The Sheriff of Kona' to

---

7   Sinclair, 1989, p 9.
8   Jean-Pierre Naugrette, 'La lèpre comme métaphore. Questions de diagnostic et détection traumatique dans des nouvelles de Rudyard Kipling, Jack London et Sir Arthur Conan Doyle', in Caroline Bertonèche (ed), *Bacilles, Phobies et Contagions. Les métaphores de la pathologie*, Paris, Michel Houdiard, 2012, pp 17–40.
9   All references to London's *Tales of the Pacific* are to Andrew Sinclair's Penguin edition (1989), and are abbreviated *TP*. Further references list page numbers only.
10 On Stevenson's and London's stories on leprosy, also see Sylvie Largeaud-Ortega, *Ainsi Soit-Île. Littérature et anthropologie dans les Contes des Mers du Sud de Robert Louis Stevenson* (Paris, Honoré Champion, 2012, pp 243–49).
11 Jack London, letter to Lorrin A Thurston, 1 Feb 1910, in vol 2, Earle Labor, Robert C Leitz & Milo Shepard (eds), *The Letters of Jack London* (Stanford, Stanford University Press, 1988, pp 870–71).

describe the sudden apparition of the disease in a man who, so far, had displayed all the signs of health and strength (*TP*, 127). In other words, following in the wake of predecessors may also prove dangerous and risky if inheritance has to do with promiscuity, atavism and contamination.

'The McCoy of the *Bounty*'

'The Seed of McCoy' is written from a completely different, less personal perspective, because sailing in the wake, this time, is a means of achieving some sort of redemption. First published in April 1907 in the 77th issue of *Century* magazine, before being collected with London's other *Tales of the Pacific*, it can be described as a 'tale of humble certainty mastering brute terror and adversity' in which 'London set down his rare hope for his own future and for those who could still command their fate'.[12]

The first sentence of the story can be read as a good instance of Conradian reminiscence, a tribute to the famous incipit of *Heart of Darkness* (1899) where the *Nellie*, a 'cruising yawl', is described as swinging to her anchor before being 'at rest':

> The *Pyrenees*, her iron sides pressed low in the water by her cargo of wheat, rolled sluggishly, and made it easy for the man who was climbing aboard from out a tiny outrigger canoe. As his eyes came level with the rail, so that he could see inboard, it seemed to him that he saw a dim, almost indiscernible haze. (*TP*, 80)

The visitor, described as a 'ragged beach-comber, in dungaree trousers and a cotton shirt' (*TP*, 81), wearing a 'worn straw hat' failing 'to hide the ragged gray hair' (*TP*, 82), soon realises what is the matter with this ship, which has 'hoisted the signal of distress' (*TP*, 80), prompting his climbing aboard. His bare feet, indeed, enable him to formulate a kind of diagnosis: the dull warmth pervading the deck is enough to signal that the *Pyrenees* is burning. When he asks Captain Davenport how long she has been afire, the captain, who obviously resents the ragged, shabby appearance of the newcomer, answers 'Fifteen days'. When Davenport asks the stranger his name, he answers 'McCoy'. When he asks him if he is the pilot, McCoy gives an evasive answer: 'I am as much a pilot as anybody … We are all pilots here, Captain, and I know every inch of these waters.' When the

---

12   Sinclair, 1978, p 9.

diffident captain insists on talking to the proper authorities, McCoy replies, 'in a voice that was still the softest and gentlest imaginable' (*TP*, 81), that he is 'the chief magistrate' of the so far unnamed island he has paddled from.

A first literary wake appears here. McCoy's all-embracing, sweeping gaze across the deck as he climbs aboard, the kind of diagnosis he formulates about the ship's 'distress' – not a contagious disease, as opposed to his previous fears about the health of his 'happy islanders' (*TP*, 80) – is indeed reminiscent of Captain Delano's at the beginning of Herman Melville's *Benito Cereno* (1855), as he boards the *San Dominick*, a ship he first views as 'in distress':[13] the newcomer also embraces a mystery, from which he might well be excluded. The name of the ship chosen by London, the *Pyrenees*, may be derived from Melville's sea novella, in which the ship is compared to 'a whitewashed monastery after a thunderstorm, seen perched upon some dun cliff among the Pyrenees' (*BC*, 674), while the black slaves are viewed as Black Friars pacing cloisters.[14] But, whereas Delano needs the whole length of the story to see through appearances and realise the kind of threat prevailing on board after the black slaves' mutiny against their Spanish commander, McCoy's perception of Davenport's predicament is not distorted or biased, since the latter's 'gaunt face and care-worn eyes made no secret of the trouble, whatever it was'. Instead of hiding a covert, treacherous purpose like the black sailors 'picking oakum' in Melville, the image of a sailor 'calking the deck' points to a rather successful control of the slow-burning fire: a 'faint spiral of haze' curls, twists, and is gone (*TP*, 80). The secret, which in *Benito Cereno* is materialised by a Gordian (sea) knot to be cut after a long, complicated, delayed decoding,[15] is an open one here: it can, indeed, be easily deduced from the symptoms of a postponed, protracted combustion of the cargo, of which only faint, elusive exterior signs are to be perceived at this early stage. When Davenport thinks that the newcomer is the 'pilot' who will take him to Pitcairn Island where, after a fortnight's cruise, the exhausted,

---

13 Herman Melville, *Benito Cereno*, in *The Piazza Tales*, New York, The Library of America, 1984, p 674. Further references to this text are abbreviated *BC* and list page numbers only.
14 Melville may have been inspired by Prosper Mérimée's story *Tamango* (1829), which deals with black slaves rebelling on board the brig *L'Espérance*, an ironic name since the slaves prove unable to steer the ship they have taken over from Capitaine Ledoux, and are doomed to starve. 'Tamango', published just a few years after Byron's poem on Fletcher Christian, can be read as a severe critique of the slave trade, and the related reactions it induces: Tamango first sells his own wife, and his mutiny proves a disaster.
15 Ian Watt, *Conrad in the Nineteenth Century*, London, Chatto & Windus, 1980.

shattered crew wish to cast themselves, McCoy answers that he is its chief magistrate, or governor. When the captain asks him if he is 'Any relation to the McCoy of the *Bounty*', he answers that the said McCoy was, indeed, his great-grandfather (*TP*, 82) (on historical governor McCoy, see Young, Chapter 7).

McCoy's sweeping glance at the desperate crew is compared to a 'benediction, soothing them, wrapping them about as in a mantle of great peace' (*TP*, 80), a sharp contrast to the sailors' hysterical outbursts against the prospect of the sudden, unpredictable unleashing of fire on board. As a connoisseur of 'these waters', McCoy explains that Pitcairn is a bad choice: there is no place where the burning ship can be beached. The islanders do not keep any boats; they carry their canoes to the top of the cliff – an eerie image that can be traced down to Werner Herzog's film *Fitzcarraldo* (1982), where a steamboat is being slowly, but steadily carried on top of a hill. Pitcairn is, indeed, an inhospitable, forbidding island,[16] which explains why the descendants of Fletcher Christian's crew could still be found there, at the beginning of the 20th century, more than a century after they had taken refuge on it. But whereas the mutineers of the *Bounty*, as years went by, had indulged in all kinds of excesses, and had killed each other off, McCoy, the 'bare-footed beachcomber', seems characterised by his 'high-sounding dignity' (*TP*, 80); he, indeed, looks like a composed, serene descendant, ready to help and rescue his fellow mariners, to bestow his 'benediction', and find the proper place where to beach their burning ship. The voice and face of this 'little' man from 'the beach'[17] exude 'peace and content' (*TP*, 81), inner strength, knowledge of charts, currents and causes, self-command and spirituality. He will need those qualities when obliged to explain to the reluctant crew that, Pitcairn being excluded, their next and best choice lies nearly 500 kilometres away, at Mangareva: 'There is a beautiful beach there, in a lagoon where the water is like a mill-pond' (*TP*, 82).

---

16   This feeling is well conveyed by Jean-Yves Delitte's recent graphic version of the story. The volume opens on the image of a ship approaching Pitcairn and finding the island inhospitable in February 1790 – i.e. after Christian and his men have landed there. This is confirmed by Michel Pérez in his comprehensive article, stressing what to western eyes is the remoteness of Pitcairn – its isolation, inaccessibility, its lack of beaches, port and mooring, so that cruising ships, if any, have still to cast anchor off-shore. See Michel Pérez, 'Pitcairn. Au bout du monde, au bout des rêves', in Serge Dunis (ed), *D'Île en Île Pacifique* (Paris, Klincksieck, 1999, pp 235–77, 237–38).

17   Dening, 1980, p 54.

From smouldering mutiny to charting a new literary course

After McCoy has convinced him that Mangareva is what they should aim at, Captain Davenport calls the crew aft and explains the situation. A shrill Cockney voice remonstrates against McCoy – who seems to ignore what sailing on board this 'floatin'' 'ell' implies (*TP*, 84). The voice sounds like an echo from Stevenson's South Sea novel *The Ebb-Tide* (1893), in which the character of Huish, another Cockney, embodies the lower instincts of greed and revolt against the aristocratic, tyrannical figure of Attwater who rules with an iron grip on his island. This Cockney sailor is in fact the spokesman for the general feeling of rebellion that smoulders on board the *Pyrenees* in much in the same way as the fire in the hold, a haunting image for London, who had sailed away from San Francisco after the earthquake had devastated the city. In *Benito Cereno*, Captain Delano also wonders: 'might not the *San Dominick*, like a slumbering volcano, suddenly let loose energies now hid?' (*BC*, 698). Even McCoy admits that the crew are starving. Davenport speaks to the crew again, 'and again the throat-rumbling and cursing arose, their faces convulsed and animal-like with rage'. The second and third mates join the captain, and stand behind him at the break of the poop: 'Their faces were set and expressionless; they seemed bored, more than anything else, by this mutiny of the crew':

> 'You see,' the captain said to McCoy, 'you can't compel sailors to leave the safe land and go to sea on a burning vessel. She has been their floating coffin for over two weeks now. They are worked out, and starved out, and they've got enough of her. We'll beat up for Pitcairn.' (*TP*, 85)

The prospect of a mutiny suggests that History might repeat itself. The *Pyrenees* is, indeed, in very dangerous waters, those off and around Pitcairn, the very island where Christian and his fellow mutineers of the *Bounty* took refuge. To put it in the terms of the Prologue to *Romeo and Juliet*, the risk is that 'ancient grudge' should:

> … break to new mutiny,
>
> Where civil blood makes civil hands unclean.[18]

---

18 William Shakespeare, *Romeo and Juliet*, Prologue, l. 3–4, London, Penguin Popular Classics, 2017 (1594), p. 2.

Obviously, Davenport has no intention of reliving the fate of his predecessor Captain William Bligh, and facing a civil war on board his burning ship – he thus beats up for Pitcairn.

'But the wind was light, the *Pyrenees*' bottom was foul, and she could not beat up against the strong westerly current' (*TP*, 85). When asked for advice, McCoy calmly replies: 'I think it would be better to square away for Mangareva. With that breeze that is coming, you'll be there to-morrow evening' (*TP*, 86). It seems, then, that the breeze, the current and McCoy's placid, confident attitude cannot be resisted. The captain addresses the crew again, and explains the situation. Ironically enough, he now presents the newcomer as 'the Honorable McCoy, Chief Magistrate and Governor of Pitcairn Island'. The effect of his speech is different from his first one: 'This time there was no uproar. McCoy's presence, the surety and calm that seemed to radiate from him, had had its effect' (*TP*, 86). The paradox, then, is that it is McCoy, the great-grandson of 'McCoy, of the *Bounty*', the ship on board of which, in April 1789 (just a few months before the French Revolution), a revolution[19] of sorts took place regarding who should embody law and order, peace and legitimacy, guidance and reason.[20] By advising the *Pyrenees* to sail away from and not towards Pitcairn, he first takes the risk of fuelling the fire of mutiny on board the *Pyrenees*, but he also diverts the ship from the course followed by Fletcher Christian, who, on arriving at Pitcairn on 23 January 1790, had to burn the *Bounty* so as to leave no trace of the ill-fated ship.[21] Confronted with the 'signal of distress' hoisted by the *Pyrenees*, with the sense of urgency shared between officers and crew, with the impending explosion of both mutiny and fire, the present-day McCoy embodies a completely different attitude as far as time and space are concerned. Instead of advocating immediate action, he will defend a willing suspension of time as well as an extension of space. This suspension and this extension are instrumental

---

19   London may also have taken the mutiny motif from Stevenson's novel *The Master of Ballantrae* (1889), which was completed in Waikiki, Hawai'i. In Chapter 9, entitled 'Mr Mackellar's Journey with the Master', the house-steward, Mackellar, tries to push the master overboard, an attempt that leaves him 'overcome with terror and remorse and shame' (London, Macmillan, Tusitala Edition, vol 10, 1924a, p 171). Allusions to the French Revolution can be found in the fact that Mackellar deposits his manuscript 'this 20th day of September Anno Domini 1789' (Stevenson, 1924a, p xxii).
20   Jean-Pierre Naugrette, 'A la recherche de La Pérouse: Dumont d'Urville et le voyage second', in *Les Français et l'Australie. Voyages de découvertes et missions scientifiques de 1756 à nos jours*, Nanterre, Université Paris X-Nanterre, 1989, p 82. See also Pérez (1999, p 248).
21   Jean-Yves Delitte, *La Bounty. La Mutinerie des Maudits*, Grenoble, Glénat, 2014, p 46.

5. A SHIP IS BURNING

in creating the suspense of the story: if immediate measures are not taken, the obvious risk is that the *Pyrenees* may burst into flames, in mid-ocean, at a moment's notice, 'with her cargo of fire' (*TP*, 90).

Whereas officers and crew sound anxious to find an easy way out of their predicament, after 15 days spent on board what First Mate Konig calls 'the anteroom of hell' (*TP*, 84), McCoy seems in no hurry at all: he promises that he will escort them to Mangareva – but he must first return to Pitcairn and ask permission from his fellow islanders. When the captain bursts forth and asks 'Don't you realize that my ship is burning beneath me?', McCoy, 'as placid as a summer sea', explains that it is the usual custom. The governor must ask permission to leave the island, and the people 'have the right to vote their permission or refusal' (*TP*, 87). Abiding by a democratic rule of government, he must make arrangements for the conduct of the island during his absence. He will return in the morning, with two canoe loads of food – dried bananas will be best. Which he does, in due time.

Other tensions and suspensions, postponements and extensions appear as far as space is concerned. A first tension appears between 'the big general chart' (*TP*, 92) in the captain's cabin, and the concrete, first-hand knowledge of McCoy. When the latter mentions an alternative solution, Davenport retorts: 'I have no chart of Mangareva. On the general chart it is only a fly-speck. I would not know where to look for the entrance into the lagoon. Will you come along and pilot her in for me?' (*TP*, 86). In the Tuamotus, some islands are uncharted and, even then, currents often drive you away from the linear, ideal course traced by the abstract computing of courses. Jack London follows here in the literary wake of Robert Louis Stevenson. In *Treasure Island* (1883),[22] Captain Smollett, when sighting shore in Chapter 12, asks if any of the men has 'ever seen that land ahead?'. Although he has a map of the island, he needs the first-hand experience of Long John Silver, who alone is able to give the lie of the land. Silver warns Smollett and the other gentlemen against a strong current that 'runs along south, and then away nor'ard up the west coast' (*TI*, 63–64). No map would indicate those crucial data. In *The Ebb-Tide*, the Findlay directory, when looked up by Captain Davis and his fellow adventurers, proves extremely vague about the precise bearings of New Island, 'which from private interests would remain unknown'. The very

---

[22] Robert Louis Stevenson, *Treasure Island*, Oxford, Oxford University Press, 1998b. Further references to this text are abbreviated *TI* and list page numbers only.

existence of the island 'is very doubtful, and totally disbelieved in by South Sea traders'.[23] Stevenson himself owned a copy of Findlay's *Directory for the Navigation of the South Pacific Ocean*.[24] In a letter to Charles Baxter, he writes that Findlay's *Pacific Directories* are 'the best of reading anyway, and may almost count as fiction' (*ET*, 284), a statement supported by Lloyd Osbourne, Stevenson's stepson, for whom he wrote *Treasure Island*, when reminiscing about 'Stevenson at Thirty-Eight':

> Ah, the happy times we had, with outspread maps and *Findlay's Directories of the World!* Findlay who, in those massive volumes, could take the sailor anywhere, and guide him into the remotest bay by 'the priest's small, white coral house on a cliff bearing N.N.E.'; or a 'peculiarly shaped rock, not unlike a stranded whale and awash at high tides which, when in line South half West with the flagstaff on the old calaboose, ensures an absolutely safe entrance into the dangerous and little-known harbour of Greater Bungo'.[25]

The paradox is that Findlay's directories are so precise, so circumstantial, that they eventually partake of what Stevenson, in his essay 'A Gossip on Romance' (1882), calls 'the poetry of circumstance', which, according to him, is a defining trait of 'romance'.[26] Lloyd's quotation from Findlay and Flint's indications as to where the treasure is buried seem to echo each other.[27] If maps, charts and directories 'may almost count as fiction', how can they be trusted?

What should have been a linear crossing, a mere trip from A (Pitcairn) to B (Mangareva), soon turns into a desperate kind of cruise, as if B, in a kind of Kafkaesque remoteness, were perpetually postponed; despite Davenport and Konig's computing, the *Pyrenees* misses Mangareva by a long shot, on the day after. McCoy sounds unperturbed: 'Why, let her drive, Captain. That is all we can do. All the Paumotus are before us. We can drive for a thousand miles through reefs and atolls. We are bound to fetch up somewhere' (*TP*, 91–92). As the captain mentions Acteon Islands, which are only 60 kilometres away, McCoy provides

---

23 Robert Louis Stevenson, *The Ebb-Tide*, in *South Sea Tales*, Oxford, Oxford University Press, 2008, p 185. Further references to this text are abbreviated *ET* and list page numbers only.
24 Alexander George Findlay, *A Directory for the Navigation of the South Pacific Ocean*, 5th edn, London, Richard Holmes Laurie, 1884 (1851).
25 Stevenson, 1924a, p xi. See also Mehew (1997).
26 Stevenson, 'A Gossip on Romance', in *Memories and Portraits*, London, Macmillan, Tusitala Edition, vol 29, 1924c, p 120.
27 'Tall tree, Spy-glass shoulder, bearing a point to the N. of N.N.E.', Stevenson (1998b, p 34).

a detailed, comprehensive description, at the end of which he dismisses them for having 'no entrances', a point that drives the captain frantic. While Davenport still relies on his charts and reads chapters from his naval *Epitome*, McCoy proves to be the worthy heir to his navigating Polynesian ancestors, as he seems to have a metaphorical chart in his mind: 'All these islands, reefs, shoals, lagoons, entrances and distances were marked on the chart of his memory' (*TP*, 94). Borne along by the conflicting currents, the *Pyrenees* will miss them all: Moerenhout, Hao, Resolution, Barclay de Tolly, Makemo, Kation, Raraka – as elusive as mirages in the desert, treacherous and remote, out of reach. The captain wanders about 'like a lost soul' (*TP*, 90), as if his current-driven ship were that of 'The Rhyme of the Ancient Mariner'. 'This cursed current plays the devil with a navigator', he complains to McCoy, who replies that 'The old navigators called the Paumotus the Dangerous Archipelago' (*TP*, 92), an answer that shows, in response to the ancient mariner haunting the captain, he has a precise 'old navigator' in mind:

> You never can tell. The currents are always changing. There was a man who wrote books, I forget his name, in the yacht *Casco*. He missed Takaroa by thirty miles and fetched Tikei, all because of the shifting currents. You are up to windward now, and you'd better keep off a few points. (*TP*, 95)

Besides being a living naval directory and knowing those islands by heart,[28] McCoy proves to be a sea library as well. The 'man who wrote books' in the yacht *Casco* is none other than Stevenson,[29] who, in the chapter of his book *In the South Seas* (1891) devoted to the Tuamotus (Paumotus) (Part II), describes the 'Dangerous Archipelago' in the following terms:

> The huge system of the trades is, for some reason, quite confounded by this multiplicity of reefs; the wind intermits, squalls are frequent from the west and south-west, hurricanes are known. The currents are, besides, inextricably intermixed; dead reckoning becomes a farce; the charts are not to be trusted.[30]

McCoy's reference to Stevenson's book will prove crucial in his effort to stop the crazy course of the *Pyrenees*, whose deck is described as so hot that, in order to move from one spot of the ship to another, crew

---

28 In the way that Polynesian *tahuʻa* or expert *faʻatere vaʻa* used to (see Teriierooiterai, Chapter 1).
29 See Stevenson's letter to Charles Baxter from on board the *Casco*, in which he mentions 'the Dangerous Archipelago' (6 Sep 1888), in Mehew (1997, p 379).
30 Stevenson, *In the South Seas*, London, Macmillan, Tusitala Edition, vol 20, 1924b, p 124.

members have now to run as fast as they can. It will constitute a mooring, an anchorage of sorts. In the second chapter of this part devoted to the Tuamotus, Stevenson describes at length 'Fakarava: an atoll at hand', and praises its entrance: 'the lagoon has two good passages, one to leeward, one to windward'.[31] Eventually, as the fire begins to spread so dangerously that 'the *Pyrenees* was an open, flaming furnace' (*TP*, 107), it is at Fakarava that she will find her final place of destination – i.e. in Stevensonian waters. Boats are lowered, the ship sails alone on her course in the lagoon, and, at long last, burns. If McCoy dismisses charts, he thus remembers *In the South Seas* and Stevenson's cruise on board the yacht *Casco* in the Tuamotus (1888–89) to chart another course for the *Pyrenees*, an intertextual one. The Tuamotus are not only, as Captain Davis puts it in *The Ebb-Tide*, a 'wide-lying labyrinth' (*ET*, 158), but a palimpsest on which literary lines intersect;[32] not so much a labyrinth in the nautical, as in the Borgesian sense. Stevenson's text is used as a new kind of map, which can still be performative a few years later. While Davenport's mind is still *Bounty*-oriented, McCoy's is that of a Stevensonian reader, sailing according to *In the South Seas*, whose descriptions of the Tuamotus, its atolls, lagoons and entrances, are taken at their literal value. Quoting from, and sailing by the book is a reckoning of sorts, a means of following in the wake of a predecessor who charted those waters in more detail than the official, deficient maps.

As they drift along, it seems that the story of the *Bounty* has still to be exorcised, especially when 'despair and mutiny' are looming again on the smoking deck and, at one point, the crew refuse duty. Some members even spring to the boats, proceed to swing them out, and 'to prepare to lower away'. It is only when McCoy's 'dovelike, cooing voice' begins to speak that the mutineers pause to hear (*TP*, 100). The contents of his speech are not given – the narrative only mentions the soft, lulling quality of his voice, which Konig describes as having 'hypnotized' the rebellious crew. Once again, the 'trouble' has been averted (*TP*, 101). This rings a bell, the reminiscence of another 'trouble', another mutiny. Davenport asks McCoy to tell him 'what happened with that *Bounty* crowd after they reached Pitcairn? The account I read said they burnt the *Bounty*, and that they were not discovered until many years later' (*TP*, 102).

---

31   Stevenson, 1924b, p 132.
32   On *The Ebb-Tide* as palimpsest, and rewriting of Bunyan's *Pilgrim's Progress* or Virgil's *Eneid*, see Jean-Pierre Naugrette (ed & trans), Introduction to *Le Creux de la Vague* (Paris, GF-Flammarion, 1993, pp 21–24); and Largeaud-Ortega (2012, pp 89–118).

McCoy willingly complies, and tells a tale full of sound and fury, 'serenely cooing of the blood and lust of his iniquitous ancestry' (*TP*, 102–03). Instead of indulging in a Byronic, idyllic, romantic version of the story (*The Island, or Christian and His Comrades*, 1823), McCoy spares no sordid detail: the picture he gives corresponds to what Michel Pérez calls a 'Descent into hell'.[33] His own great-grandfather, he explains, had 'made a still and manufactured alcohol from the roots of the ti-plant. Quintal was his chum, and they got drunk together all the time. At last McCoy got delirium tremens, tied a rock to his neck and jumped into the sea' (*TP*, 103).[34] Seed of McCoy, but the question is, which seed? In the descendant's version, the root, plant and seed motifs are explicitly related to the excesses of alcohol, and subsequent degradation. As opposed to this 'iniquitous ancestry', the governor of Pitcairn sounds like *the real McCoy*, an idiom referring to what is genuine, first-rate, of high quality; it may be used to designate an excellent brand of whisky, for instance, but the pilot of the *Pyrenees* seems to have transcended and redeemed the explosive nature of his male ancestor, who was associated with mutiny, the burning of the *Bounty*, the fateful ship as an image of individual combustion – as it is the case, for instance, in Zola's *L'Assommoir* (1877). It is no coincidence if the seed image should be found again in the very cargo of the *Pyrenees*, this 'cargo of wheat' that is burning – but burning slowly, so slowly that the present-day 'Anglified native'[35] McCoy, as opposed to his great-grandfather and his fellow-mutineers before him, thinks in terms of the island community, and is in a position to take all the time he needs. The title of the tale is thus more ironic than meets the eye: the governor of Pitcairn, who feels the need to consult his fellow Islanders before leaving for a few days, does not take after his hubristic, transgressive Scottish ancestor, William McCoy (c 1763–98). Telling the ill-fated story of the Pitcairn mutineers is thus a means of subduing, of soothing the incipient mutiny on board the *Pyrenees*: as a talking cure, the function of the embedded, *Bounty*-related story is clearly apotropaic, a means of telling the captain and the crew members that they are right

---

33 Pérez, 1999, pp 263–67.
34 Pérez mentions the fact that when women found William McCoy's body at the bottom of the cliff, his hands and feet were bound. As he puts it, the isle of refuge had turned into a prison, and a grave. Ten years after the mutineers' arrival on Pitcairn, only one sailor, Alexander Smith, had survived, along with 10 Tahitian women and a group of children.
35 Vanessa Smith, 'Pitcairn's "Guilty Stock". The Island as Breeding Ground', in Rod Edmond & Vanessa Smith (eds), *Islands in History and Representation*, London, Routledge, 2003.

in sailing away from Pitcairn, even if their ship is burning – or perhaps because it is burning – it should avoid following in the wake of the *Bounty* before them.

Although she is burning, what is remarkable is that McCoy's presence and directions should introduce some sort of balance, a stabilisation of sorts. Balance between combustion and conflagration – although the latter, we guess, is only postponed. Balance between drifting at random and following in the wake, thanks to the Stevenson intertext, which charts an intermediary (inter)course, on board the yacht *Casco*, between the *Bounty* and the *Pyrenees*. Balance between the impending destruction and the long, protracted cruise that carries the danger away from Pitcairn, across the 'Dangerous Archipelago'. Balance between time, which Davenport and the crew members experience as pressing, and space, which McCoy views as extensive – a clever, if devious, means of suspending present time by relying on literary predecessors. London may have found one in Jules Verne and his sea novel *Le Chancellor* (1874), in which the eponymous ship is also described as burning, a cargo of cotton whose combustion is compressed, repressed, delayed, because the bales are so tightly packed in the hold that the air, which any kind of fire needs to burst forth, is missing. 'You see, when we discovered the fire, we battened down immediately to suffocate the fire', Davenport explains (*TP*, 85). In his reading of Verne's novel, Michel Serres highlights those 'figures of balance' or 'syzygies' as so many stationary, if not stable, points, where a certain amount of balance is reached between contradictory elements. In Verne's novel, this stationary point of balance, even if it moves from one stage to another, is fully respected and maintained since the danger of fire is driven away by a storm and the reefs that stop the drifting ship in its erratic course: 'the static balance overcomes the thermic ending'.[36] The smouldering bales of cotton follow a kind of autonomous spiralling pattern of combustion, or 'positive feed-back loop', which makes each stage progress, but each time towards a new balance of elements and forces.[37]

Although the protracted course of the ever-burning *Pyrenees* follows a similar pattern, the nature of McCoy's intervention is quite different in London's story. When McCoy boards the ship, he notices that the pumps are not working, but he will not attempt to reactivate them, a reaction that would be impossible in a Verne novel, where any dedicated

---

36 Michel Serres, *Jouvences sur Jules Verne*, Paris, Ed de Minuit, 1974, p 117.
37 Serres, 1974, p 114.

captain would try. For McCoy, the forces of balance and composure are elsewhere to be found than in the fire/water equation, or the syzygy of elements. The issue at stake is not to prevent the *Pyrenees* from burning – she will, in the end, burn, there is no doubt about that. But only in the end. For the time, she 'is burning', as Davenport puts it, an '-ing' form or present participle, which suggests a process, not a statement of fact. The kind of spiral or 'positive feed-back loop' McCoy relies on as a pilot is of a different nature. It has nothing to do with the laws of natural physics or dynamics, but with the balance to be found in and between previous narratives, which unfold on board the *Pyrenees* as she sails away from Pitcairn; between the embedded reminder of the original story of 'the McCoy of the *Bounty*' and the charting of a Stevensonian course ruled after *In the South Seas*, McCoy appears as the one who can 'govern' the island or 'pilot' the burning ship in literary waters. Hence the image of the 'faint spiral of haze' that he first sees when boarding her. There is no point in trying to compress the burning cargo in order to smother the smouldering fire by want of air. The spiral cannot be changed into a full circle. The repressed cannot be fully caulked.

Ships are burning: Between combustion and conflagration

When devising the spectacular, long-expected finale of his story, Jack London may have followed in the wake of two predecessors, who also described burning ships to dramatic effect.

The first is Robert Louis Stevenson and the 'Tail-Piece' of *The Ebb-Tide*, on which the novel closes like a curtain, in a highly cinematic scene. While repentant Captain Davis, who has converted himself to Attwater's religion and rule, is described as 'praying on the sand by the lagoon beach', the Englishman Herrick's skiff, in a zooming-in effect, is spotted 'tacking towards the distant and deserted *Farallone*' (*ET*, 250), the schooner that brought the trio of adventurers to Attwater's New Island from Pape'ete. While still in Tahiti, Davis presents the vessel as the 'last chance' of the trio, although it seems plagued by its past:

> She's the *Farallone*, hundred and sixty tons register, out of 'Frisco for Sydney, in California champagne. Captain, mate, and one hand all died of the small-pox, same as they had round in the Paumotus, I guess … (*ET*, 146)

When they board her, she is moored 'well out in the jaws of the pass' and branded as 'an outcast': she has indeed hoisted 'the yellow flag' of quarantine, 'banished to the threshold of the port, rolling there to her scuppers, and flaunting the plague-flag as she rolled' (*ET*, 152). When the third member of the trio, Huish, begins to remonstrate, Davis retorts that he is prepared to signal a man-of-war and send him 'ashore for mutiny' (*ET*, 154). In the next chapter, 'The Cargo of Champagne', Davis charts a clear course for the *Farallone*:

> Now, if this South East Trade ever blew out of the S.E., which it don't, we might hope to lie within half a point of our course. Say we lie within a point of it. That'll just about weather Fakarava. Yes, sir, that's what we've got to do, if we tack for it. Brings us through this slush of little islands in the cleanest place: see? (*ET*, 158)

At this 'point', Stevenson's *In the South Seas* and *The Ebb-Tide* intersect: both voyages and fiction confirm that Fakarava is 'the cleanest place', a safe destination to steer by. Sailing as he was in the wake of Stevenson's South Sea works,[38] London may have remembered those elements for 'The Seed of McCoy' – the signal of distress, the sense of isolation, the motif of the doomed ship that can only bring bad luck to her crew, the risk of mutiny, the Tuamotus and the atoll of Fakarava.

In the 'Tail-Piece', while Davis is still praying on the sand, with his eyes closed, Herrick is bent on a specific mission:

> and presently the figure of Herrick might have been observed to board her, to pass for a while into the house, thence forward to the forecastle, and at last to plunge into the main hatch. In all these quarters, his visit was followed by a coil of smoke; and he had scarce entered his boat again and shoved off, before flames broke forth upon the schooner. They burned gaily; kerosene had not been spared, and the bellows of the Trade incited the conflagration. (*ET*, 250–51)

London will use the same word, 'conflagration', at the end of his story. But the burning of the ship is voluntary here: while Davis is praying, Herrick sets fire to the schooner, which embodies illness, ill-fate and mishap, a reminder of 'Herrick's picture of the life and death of his two

---

38   Sometimes edited and collected as part of a whole, like in the German edition *In der Südsee, Erzählungen und Erlebnisse Mit Illustrationen von Wolfgang Würfel* (Berlin, Verlag Neues Leben, 1972). The edition includes *The Beach of Falesá*, 'The Bottle Imp', 'The Isle of Voices' and *In the South Seas*. (Thanks to Manfred Diehl.)

predecessors; of their prolonged, sordid, sodden sensuality as they sailed, they knew not whither, on their last cruise' (*ET*, 170) – an image that may be related to the *Bounty* sailing towards Pitcairn, and to the *Pyrenees*, whose 'bottom' is described as 'foul' (*TP*, 88). The *Farallone* must be sacrificed, purified, so that a new kind of adventure, a more spiritual one, perhaps, a kind of redemption, may take over. But, unlike what happened to the *Bounty* when reaching Pitcairn, burning one's boats does not mean cutting oneself off from society, so as to escape pursuit: 'There she burns! and you may guess from that what the news is', a triumphant Herrick explains to prayer-bound Davis (*ET*, 251). In fact, a new ship, the *Trinity Hall*, has been sighted half an hour ago, and Herrick means to use it on his trip home – a far cry from Fletcher Christian and his comrades' isolation on Pitcairn.

Another influence may be traced back to Joseph Conrad's story 'Youth', first published in *Blackwood's Magazine* in 1898, whose second part deals with the *Judea*, and her cargo of coal, beginning to burn in the Indian Ocean, while bound for Bangkok:

> The cargo was on fire.
>
> Next day she began to smoke in earnest. You see it was to be expected, for though the coal was of a safe kind, that cargo had been so handled, so broken up with handling, that it looked more like smithy coal than anything else. Then it had been wetted – more than once. It rained all the time we were taking it back from the hulk, and now with this long passage it got heated, and there was another case of spontaneous combustion.[39]

Like in the case of the *Chancellor*, the captain tries 'to stifle this 'ere damned combustion by want of air', but this proves to be of no avail, the smoke keeps on 'coming out through imperceptible crevices; it forced itself through bulkheads and covers; it oozed here and there and everywhere in slender threads … This combustion refused to be stifled' (*Y*, 109–10). The rest of the story is suspended to whether this 'spontaneous combustion' of the cargo will keep on smouldering and wait until the *Judea* reaches a safe haven, or suddenly burst forth into flames in mid-ocean, while the crew is unprepared. At one point, an 'explosion' takes place, but Marlow describes it in slow motion, in a series of fractured, split impressions, a narrative technique that London will remember for

---

39 Joseph Conrad, 'Youth', *Heart of Darkness and Other Tales*, Cedric Watts (ed), Oxford, Oxford University Press, 1990, p 109. Further references to this text are abbreviated *Y* and list page numbers only.

the ending of his story. Eventually, as smoke is more and more visible on board, a steamer is seen far astern, and the *Judea* hoists two flags, 'which said in the international language of the sea, "On fire. Want immediate assistance"' (*Y*, 116) – a motif also taken up by London, this time at the beginning of his story. After the steamer, the *Somerville*, has taken the *Judea* in tow, fire is seen for the first time: 'The speed of the towing had fanned the smouldering destruction' (*Y*, 119). The final description of the burning ship is highly poetic, as may be expected from a sailor like Marlow who has 'a complete set of Byron's works' (*Y*, 106) at hand:

> Between the darkness of earth and heaven she was burning fiercely upon a disc of purple sea shot by the blood-red play of gleams; upon a disc of water glittering and sinister. A high, clear flame, an immense and lonely flame, ascended from the ocean, and from its summit the black smoke poured continuously at the sky. She burned furiously; mourning and imposing like a funeral pile kindled in the night, surrounded by the sea, watched over by the stars. A magnificent death had come like a grace, like a gift, like a reward to that old ship at the end of her laborious days. The surrender of her weary ghost to the keeping of stars and sea was stirring like the sight of a glorious triumph. (*Y*, 125)

The image of the 'funeral pile' might be read as a reminder of PB Shelley's pyre being lit by his friend Trelawney and Lord Byron after he drowned off Leghorn on 8 July 1822. The 'death' of the *Judea* is described as a kind of ceremony, a magnificent, romantic ritual of burial at sea eventually transcending the original introduction of the ship as being 'all rust, dust, grime – soot aloft, dirt on deck', but consistent with the 'touch of romance' that makes Marlow 'love the old thing – something that appealed to my youth!' (*Y*, 95).

In that respect, even if the waters are clearly Stevensonian, the ending of 'The Seed of McCoy' is highly Conradian. The last movements of the *Pyrenees* into the lagoon of Fakarava, until she strikes bottom, are described as if in slow motion, or at least the fire spreading to the sundry parts of the ship suggests some sort of slow explosion, 'exploding-fixed':[40] 'Shreds and patches of burning rope and canvas were falling about them and upon them' (*TP*, 119). Thanks to McCoy's advice and wise piloting, the final 'conflagration that had come to land' (*TP*, 119) has nothing to do with the hasty, reckless burning of the *Bounty* by Christian and his iniquitous ancestor, or, for that matter, with the swift, joyful spreading

---

40   André Breton's 'explosante fixe', also the title of a musical piece by Pierre Boulez (1972–93).

of kerosene on the *Farallone* for the sake of purification. Like in 'Youth', the spontaneous combustion of the cargo, if not stifled or mastered, has been displaced, postponed, extended as far as possible. 'Following the sea', as the phrase goes, in the wake of Herman Melville, Jules Verne, Stevenson and Conrad is a means for London of exorcising the ill-fated story of the *Bounty*, and perhaps of his own cruise on the *Snark*: the benevolent, calm, radiant, gentle, smiling, blessing, soothing, peaceful, tender, compassionate, dignified, sweet, placid, serene, persuasive, simple, gracious, blissful, ragged – and ultimately, Christ-like – figure of McCoy, governor and beachcomber, has managed to take and tuck away the burning ship to her final, 'beautiful bed' (*TP*, 109).

6

Brando on the *Bounty*

Roslyn Jolly
University of New South Wales

Simon Petch
University of Sydney

Film studio MGM's 1962 film *Mutiny on the Bounty* (hereafter *1962*) accords with no one's assumptions about the events that occurred on HMAV *Bounty* in 1787–89, and Marlon Brando is nobody's idea of Fletcher Christian. This may be why the film is impossible to see at the cinema, why it never gets shown on television, and why the DVD version is harder to find in libraries than MGM's earlier film of the same title, which was released in 1935 (hereafter *1935*). That film, starring Clark Gable as Christian and Charles Laughton as William Bligh, won the 1936 Academy Award for Best Picture, and remains the canonical cinematic version of the mutiny on the *Bounty*. The 1962 film (with Trevor Howard as Bligh) was nominated for seven Academy Awards at the 1963 Oscars, but was blown out of the water by David Lean's *Lawrence of Arabia*. Like another contentious epic, John Milton's *Paradise Lost*, *1962* was delayed by 'long choosing, and beginning late'.[1] Its production spanned two years and went through several writers and directors, including the uncredited Carol Reed. Although it did reasonably well at the box office, the film failed to recover its costs – a failure for which Brando (whose contract

---

1   John Milton, *Paradise Lost*, *Milton: Poetical Works*, Douglas Bush (ed), 2nd edn, London, Oxford University Press, 1966 (1674), Book 9, line 26.

gave him control over the script, who is reputed to have done much of the directing, and to whom the delays and budget blow-out have been attributed) has been exclusively blamed.

Neither of MGM's versions of *Mutiny on the Bounty* has any serious claim to historical accuracy, or draws consistently on the extant documentary sources of the mutiny and its aftermath. The courts martial, of Bligh on his return to London without his ship in 1790, and of the mutineers in 1792, are matters of public record; and, in addition to Bligh's official log and his private journal, there are eyewitness accounts from two *Bounty* crew members, Ship's Master John Fryer and Boatswain's Mate James Morrison. Both films cite a novel, *Mutiny on the Bounty*, by Charles Nordhoff and James Norman Hall (1932), among their writing credits and, therefore, as a 'source' for their content. This novel is narrated in the first person by one Roger Byam, a fictional creation based upon aspects of the character of *Bounty* Midshipman Peter Heywood.[2] From our perspective, Byam's main function in the novel is to be a friend and confidant to Christian. On Tahiti, he is Christian's interpreter, in the literal sense of translating the Tahitian language for Christian's understanding; but he is also the interpreter of Christian in the broader sense of his proximity to Christian supposedly affording him insight into Christian's motivation for the mutiny. Such insight, of course, is purely fictitious. Byam's presence and perspective are retained in *1935*, to which they are central, but *1962* does without him. This exclusion leaves Brando space in which to explore the dramatic possibilities of the mysterious character who is both the mutiny's prime mover and its black hole.

Most reviewers in 1962 were still well-disposed towards Brando, but they were puzzled by his performance in this film. Christian may have led a mutiny, but the character created by Brando bore no identifiable relationship to the earlier and more explosively rebellious characters of his career: Stanley Kowalski, Emiliano Zapata, Terry Malloy and Johnny Strabler. The main reason for the puzzlement was that Brando's performance could not be placed, for his career offered no model for what he did in *1962*. Subsequent commentators have responded more harshly to the challenge of Brando's Christian, dismissing his performance as extravagant and self-indulgent. Most recently, Dan Chiasson has said that in Brando's many historical roles – and he specifically mentions

---

2   For a comprehensive analysis of this novel, and an especially penetrating discussion of Byam's narratorial and cultural functions within it, see Chapter 4 of the present volume.

this one – his brilliance is 'crusted over badly with deposits of silliness', and lost in 'the wilds of period accents'.[3] Brando's English accent in this film is routinely regarded as risible, but, in the early 1960s, 'mumbling' was generally admitted to be the hallmark of his acting style. Here, his precisely articulated diction is the absolute opposite of mumbling, and the accent with which it is inflected is the most potent sign of the class to which the film assigns him. It is also, incidentally, a sign of historical accuracy, for it acknowledges the fact that Christian was an Englishman, a significant advance on *1935*, in which neither Gable nor Franchot Tone (Byam) attempted an English accent.

The 1962 film, and its central character, Christian, are better understood in the contemporary social context of the early 1960s than in relation to events in the South Seas in 1787–91. It may be fanciful to see, in the elegance and style of Brando's very English Christian, a reflection of the qualities of the recently elected US President John F Kennedy. It is equally fanciful, however tempting, to read the mutiny as both Christian's Bay of Pigs[4] (1961) and his Cuban Missile Crisis (1962), both of which were encompassed by the period of the film's production. But it is less fanciful to sense, in Bligh's resentment of Christian's sophistication, which he can never attain, something of Richard M Nixon's bitterness towards the playboy senator from Massachusetts, rising from a milieu of money and privilege that was light years away from the California backwater where Nixon grew up. (Nixon was Kennedy's opponent in the 1960 presidential election.) Nor is it fanciful to see, in Bligh's blind commitment to 'the Admiralty', the ideology of The Organization Man. This collective mindset has been identified by William H Whyte as a dominant social ethic in middle-class American society in the 1950s. It was promoted and sustained by '[those] of our middle class who have left home, spiritually as well as physically, to take the vows of organization life, and it is they who are the mind and soul of our great self-perpetuating institutions'.[5] As a principle of collective ideology to which Bligh subscribes, it can easily be placed in opposition to the nonchalant individualism of Christian.

---

3   Dan Chiasson, 'Where's Brando?', *New York Review of Books*, vol 62, no 1, 8 Jan – 15 Feb 2015, p 18.
4   'Pig' is a charged word in this film. 'You remarkable pig,' Christian says to Bligh after the mutiny. 'You can thank whatever pig-god you pray to that you haven't quite turned me into a murderer.' This echoes Rio's furious outburst at Bob Amory, 'you scum-suckin' pig', at an equally tense moment of rebellion in Brando's own *One-Eyed Jacks*. On Pitcairn, Matthew Quintal refers to Bligh as 'the old pig'. A willing participant in this porcine plenitude, Bligh refers to the mutineers as 'these swine'.
5   William H Whyte, *The Organization Man*, London, Jonathan Cape, 1957, p 3.

Whyte interprets Herman Wouk's novel *The Caine Mutiny*, on which the 1954 film of the same name is closely based, as 'the problem of the individual versus authority … raised to the nth degree';[6] and the script of this film, which may be *1962*'s strong precursor, draws on *Bounty* material.[7] But we need to look beyond the United States, because the film's insistent concern with class took it, with Brando's accent, across the Atlantic, which is why his performance, washed away in trans-Atlantic currents to become one of the many 'lost' Brando performances,[8] should be seen from an English, indeed a European, as well as from an American perspective.

The historical Fletcher Christian came from an impoverished if established family and, as a representative of the genteel poor, and so obliged to work for a living, he would certainly not have enjoyed the leisured lifestyle glimpsed through *1962*'s representation of him. The eternal British obsession with class, accent and gentility was as tangible as ever in the early 1960s, when a postwar meritocracy – self-styled, of course – began to fancy its chances of attaining power and authority. From 1951 until 1964, Britain was governed by the Conservative Party, the party of the establishment. When Churchill, aged 80, resigned as prime minister in 1955, he was succeeded in that office by a line of Old Etonians – Anthony Eden, Harold Macmillan, then, astonishingly, by an Old Etonian who was also a Peer of the Realm, Baron Home of the Hirsel. The principles upon which the governing party apparently chose its leaders cut hard against a burgeoning popular culture, and the first Beatles film, *A Hard Day's Night* (1964), poked good-natured fun at the Home Counties' establishment by celebrating new ways of being and by promoting new ways of talking. The tribulations of the Conservative Government's final years reflected such stresses in the British, and more particularly the English, social order. The judicial proceedings that followed from the Profumo affair, in which a minister was revealed to have lied to parliament about an affair that may also have been a security risk, opened the lid on a Pandora's box of

---

6   Whyte, 1957, p 243.
7   Lt Tom Keefer (Fred MacMurray) compares Captain Queeg to Bligh, and Queeg's obsession with missing strawberries is a reworking of Bligh's obsessive concern, immediately prior to the mutiny, with apparently stolen coconuts. See Caroline Alexander, *The Bounty: The True Story of the Mutiny on the Bounty* (London, Harper Perennial, 2003, p 424). The coconut episode is well documented; see Alexander (2003, pp 134–35). Crucial to both Nordhoff and Hall and *1935*, it is significantly omitted from *1962*.
8   For a discussion of Brando's neglected work in the 1960s, his decade of disasters, see Simon Petch & Roslyn Jolly, 'Brando in the Sixties' (*Heat,* new series, vol 10, 2005, pp 157–72).

licentiousness at the highest levels of society. In 1964, Harold Wilson, who both was, and sounded as though he was, a Yorkshireman, led the Labour Party to power. The class conflicts simmering beneath this changing demographic are brilliantly realised in Harold Pinter's script for Joseph Losey's *The Servant* (1963), when the servant (Dirk Bogarde) barks angrily to his master (James Fox) the unforgettable line: 'I'm a gentleman's gentleman, and you're no bloody gentleman!' Less dramatic, if equally challenging, was Al Alvarez's introduction to Penguin's famous 1962 anthology *The New Poetry*.[9] Alvarez, who edited the book and who was himself an Englishman, identified 'the gentility principle' as the crippling weakness of contemporary English poetry.

Susan Mizruchi has claimed that 'the most important dramatic change' introduced by Brando in his ongoing work on the 1962 script is 'the emphasis on class',[10] and his accent surely supports her claim. With its contemporary inflection, the 1962 *Mutiny on the Bounty* is less a remake of the 1935 film than a series of riffs occasionally inspired by the earlier movie. In one such riff, *1962* turns a phrase from *1935* into a major theme. When Christian and Bligh meet aboard the *Bounty* in *1935*, it is explicit that they have sailed together before, for Bligh has specifically requested Christian as one of his crew; as he puts it, 'I like having a gentleman as my subordinate, being a self-made man'. This provocative statement is incidental in *1935* and, while it is not repeated in *1962*, its implications are developed into the class principle that governs the Bligh/Christian relationship. As a matter of historical record, Christian and Bligh had sailed together before, and Bligh had indeed requested Christian's presence on the *Bounty* expedition. But, in *1962*, Bligh and Christian meet for the first time when Christian arrives on board in all his finery, and their initial encounter seethes with class-conscious tension between the dandified gentleman and the professional sailor. A minor chord in *1935* is amplified, in *1962*, into a major sequence that drowns out historical fact.

Our contention in this paper is that MGM's 1962 version of *Mutiny on the Bounty* offers a unique interpretation of the *Bounty* story, an interpretation that is significantly and demonstrably linked more to the historical context of the film's production than to the documented events

---

9   Al Alvarez (ed), *The New Poetry*, Harmondsworth, Penguin, 1962.
10   Susan Mizruchi, *Brando's Smile: His Life, Thought, and Work*, New York, WW Norton, 2014, p 161.

of 1787–89. That context involves two postwar phenomena: changing British feelings in the early 1960s about class; and the emergence, in Europe, of Existentialist philosophy.

The appearance of the dandy

'What's this, a royal visit?' asks William Bligh acerbically as Fletcher Christian's fine carriage draws up on the Portsmouth dock. Christian (Marlon Brando) emerges from the carriage looking like a Cavalier who has lost his way amongst the Roundheads. He wears a finely decorated suit of silvery-grey material topped off with a splendid scarlet cloak, carries a cane under his arm, and is accompanied by two Gainsborough-style beauties who are also sumptuously dressed. Something odd is going on, sure enough, and we need the benefit of hindsight to discover it: the extravagant, even baroque gesture with which Christian doffs his top hat – an oddly Puritan-style appurtenance, as Susan Mizruchi has observed[11] – is a preamble to the elaborate play with his naval hat that is a feature of Brando's performance. But at this early stage in the film, the viewer simply doesn't have a clue.

Brando's appearance in the film is startling. The discrepancy between Christian's foppish self-presentation and the naval context of discipline and danger into which he must somehow fit is matched by the discrepancy between viewers' expectations about a Brando performance and the extraordinary spectacle now presented to us. This highly artificial self-styling, so different from the attractively virile personas created earlier by Clark Gable (1935) and later by Mel Gibson (*The Bounty*, 1984) in the same role, prompts the question: what, as an actor, is Brando doing? Unfortunately, most critics of the film have not attempted to answer this question; rather, they have been, like Bligh, affronted. Donald A Maxton, knowledgeable as he is about *Bounty* representations, gets himself on the wrong foot by appealing to 'history': after a promising, historically informative start, he says, 'the film begins to go downhill when Christian arrives in a splendid coach, dressed in foppish, un-seamanlike clothing and accompanied by two French-speaking women. Brando speaks his lines in a peculiar, distracting accent that makes it difficult to regard

---

11   Mizruchi, 2014, p 162.

his character seriously'.[12] To seasoned film critic David Thomson, Brando's 'Fletcher Christian from Harrods' 'ruined' the simple but effective outlines of the adventure story conveyed by *1935*.[13] Perhaps it is not surprising that no one has taken any notice of Bosley Crowther, a contemporary reviewer who found himself at the wrong end of the right point when he complained that Brando's character was 'more a dandy than a formidable ship's officer'.[14]

If we entertain the possibility that Brando is offering a serious interpretation of the character, not merely an absurd caricature, we must consider not only why *Brando* should choose to act this way, but also why he should choose to have *Christian* act this way. For everything we see of Christian in this scene is a pose; not merely the actor, but the character also, is acting a part. He dresses and speaks like an aristocrat, although he is in fact not one. (His companions in this first scene are a 'Comtesse' and a 'Lady', although he is plain 'Mr' Christian.) This may shed some light on the accent that Brando adopts, which has been the object of so much critical scorn and ridicule. Unusually for the time among Hollywood actors, Brando was perfectly capable of producing a standard (Received Pronunciation) English accent, as he had shown in *Julius Caesar* (1953) and would show again in *Burn!* (1969) and *A Dry White Season* (1989). So, why should he choose to speak in this clearly artificial and affected way? One answer is that the accent is an affectation for the character, one of many that constitute his persona as no mere fop, but a dandy with the full force that 19th-century artists and 20th-century philosophers have given to that term.

To quote Jules Barbey d'Aurevilly's classic *Anatomy of Dandyism* (1845), this Fletcher Christian has 'the Dandy's assurance in conduct, the sumptuous impertinence, the preoccupation with exterior effect, and perpetually present vanity'.[15] All these qualities are evident in the opening scene. Christian's 'assurance in conduct' is shown in the way he carries off the impropriety of turning up to work in this frivolous garb. Although his first words after introducing himself are 'please forgive my appearance',

---

12   Donald A Maxton, *The Mutiny on H.M.S. Bounty: A Guide to Nonfiction, Fiction, Poetry, Films, Articles and Music*, Jefferson, NC, McFarland, 2008, p 217.
13   David Thomson, *'Have You Seen …?': A Personal Introduction to 1,000 Films*, New York, Knopf, 2008, p 584.
14   Crowther is quoted by Mizruchi (2014, p 162; she gives no reference for the comment).
15   Jules Barbey d'Aurevilly, *The Anatomy of Dandyism, With Some Observations on Beau Brummell*, DB Wyndham Lewis (trans), London, Peter Davies, 1928 (1845), p 17.

this is in no sense an apology, for his tone and carriage make clear that he does not care whether he is forgiven or not. He may have offended naval protocol by reporting for duty thus attired, but he remains secure in his sense of social superiority to everyone else aboard the *Bounty*. Furthermore, his explanation – that he came straight from the country house where he was a guest – serves to emphasise the social inequality from which will spring his conflict with Bligh. Similarly, the favour he asks, to introduce his fashionable lady friends to the captain, brings out another difference in status and education: Bligh cannot speak French.[16] One of the ladies coquettishly calls this 'uncivilised', lightly passing a judgement on Bligh that will resonate seriously as the plot unfolds.

'Sumptuous impertinence' is the keynote of Brando's performance as Christian in all his dealings with Bligh, and it is well established in this first scene. Christian shows disrespect for the captain's and the Navy's values when he refers to the *Bounty*'s mission to collect breadfruit from Tahiti as 'a grocer's errand' and asks, 'Does it really matter when these vegetables arrive in Jamaica?' He presents himself as carelessly indifferent to Bligh's goals, accurately, but dismissively, characterising the captain as motivated by a desire for 'promotions, even honours, and all that'. At the end of the scene, he uses Bligh's own description of the gardener, Brown, as 'the most important man on the ship' to imply his lack of regard for his commanding officer's authority.

In this first scene, Christian's elaborate costume and manners demonstrate his 'preoccupation with exterior effect', while every speech and gesture expresses the 'perpetually present vanity' that makes him condescend to his commanding officer. The scene also introduces two further aspects of dandyism: its problematic relation to the concept of profession, and its aspiration to spiritual aristocracy. Before even speaking to Christian, Bligh impugns his professionalism by labelling him 'a career fop'. This brings the captain strangely close to Charles Baudelaire, who wrote that the dandy's 'solitary profession is elegance'.[17] In a study of the greatest dandy, Beau Brummell, Jules Barbey d'Aurevilly also found that the 'vocation' of

---

16   In Nordhoff & Hall, this failure to know French is a sympathetic disadvantage for Bligh. He has been told of Jean-Jacques Rousseau's ideas, he says, 'but unfortunately I left school too young to learn French' (*The Bounty Trilogy*, Boston, Little, Brown & Company, 2003 (1936), p 9). In *1962*, Bligh's Francophone deficiency is a social disadvantage for which he can only apologise, and so an unsympathetic humiliation.

17   Charles Baudelaire, *The Painter of Modern Life and Other Essays*, Jonathan Mayne (trans & ed), London, Phaidon, 1964, p 26.

dandyism was not often compatible with the more utilitarian conception of profession[18] – for, he declared, '[a] Dandy cannot admit eager interest in or anxiety about anything on earth'.[19] When questioned by Bligh about his choice of career, Christian replies, 'One must do something' – he appears to speak straight from the well of modern *ennui* that, according to d'Aurevilly, was the origin of all dandyism.[20] But, although he appears not to take seriously the idea of a career, he insists that he will perform his duties as a naval officer conscientiously and that an officer can, indeed should, also be a gentleman. The dandy's mindset – although not necessarily his bloodline – is aristocratic: one must at least appear not to be motivated by bourgeois values of effort and ambition. Brummell expressed his disavowal of bourgeois society in the utter incompetence he brought to the only real 'job' he ever had, as British consul in Caen. Brando's Christian, on the other hand, manifests his 'aristocratic' superiority by succeeding effortlessly as a naval officer, without seeming to care about that success. As Baudelaire observed:

> Dandyism does not even consist, as many thoughtless people seem to believe, in an immoderate taste for the toilet [self-grooming] and material elegance. For the perfect dandy these things are no more than symbols of his aristocratic superiority of mind.[21]

It is his own conception of this aristocratic superiority of mind that Brando's *Mr* Christian expresses through the mixture of carelessness and impertinence with which he establishes his anomalous presence on the *Bounty*.

This opening sequence of *1962* establishes the clash of personalities between Christian and Bligh, and sets up class difference as a major source of the conflict that leads to the mutiny.[22] It also establishes Christian in the persona of the dandy, who, like any good actor, knows that dress, tone and gesture are as important as dialogue in creating a character. 'The dandy,' according to Albert Camus, '… is always compelled to astonish. Singularity is his vocation, excess his way to perfection.' The dandy's whole attitude is a protest – it is often not clear against

---

18   d'Aurevilly, 1928, p 61.
19   d'Aurevilly, 1928, p 32.
20   d'Aurevilly, 1928, p 9.
21   Baudelaire, 1964, p 27.
22   The class-conscious presentation of Christian has no cinematic precedent, but Donald A Maxton claims that this 'well-worn theory' was firmly established in 19th-century *Bounty* literature (2008, p 217).

exactly what. 'The dandy is, by occupation, always in opposition. He can only exist by defiance'.[23] But will this turn out to be anything more than vanity? Camus maintained that 'the dandy can only play a part by setting himself up in opposition. He can only be sure of his own existence by finding it in the expression of others' faces'.[24] This opening encounter raises questions about what it will take to turn this dandy into a mutineer, to rouse him from his *ennui* and make him a rebel. The answer, of course, is Bligh; and, in the early stages of the film, two related sequences, one above and one below deck, anticipate the impending conflict between commander and officer.

Punishment, pedagogy and port

In his account of events aboard the *Bounty* in 1787, James Morrison alleged that, before the ship left England, William Bligh had purloined for his personal use two cheeses that were intended for the ship's supplies. As Caroline Alexander has said, this allegation is 'strikingly specific':[25] Bligh had supposedly ordered the ship's cooper to remove the cheeses, and then ordered another seaman to take them to Bligh's house. This unsupported allegation has entered *Bounty* legend, and even found its comic way into *The Caine Mutiny* as Captain Queeg's 'great triumph, the cheese investigation of 1937'. Nordhoff and Hall's *Mutiny on the Bounty* repeats Morrison's account, and both films exploit the incident to raise the dramatic conflict between Bligh and Christian.

In *1935*, after a crewmember has been wrongly punished for supposed theft of the cheeses, conversation at the captain's dinner table quickly gets into trouble. Bligh alone takes cheese: the other four at the table all refuse it, although Bligh offers it to them individually. Bligh demands an apology from Christian, and then dismisses him from the table. As the others also leave the table, the sequence ends with Bligh's exclamation: 'Before I've done with you, I'll make you eat grass.' In *1962*, this sequence is considerably expanded. The irascibility of Charles Laughton's Bligh is replaced by Trevor Howard's intransigence, here disguised as advice to his junior officers. Brando's Christian remains at the table, and his subtle responses to his commander are themselves a form of disguise.

---

23   Albert Camus, *The Rebel: An Essay on Man in Revolt*, Anthony Bower (trans), New York, Vintage, 1991 (1951), p 52.
24   Camus, 1991, p 51.
25   Alexander, 2003, p 336.

6. BRANDO ON THE *BOUNTY*

The conflict between Bligh and Christian in *1962* is less overt and less stark than in *1935*; but, as the patterns along which this conflict will develop become apparent, the sequence evokes some of Brando's most finely detailed acting.

After the shortfall of two cheeses from the ship's recorded supplies is reported, Christian, without a hat, handkerchief occasionally raised to his nose, casually accuses Gunner's Mate Mills (Richard Harris) of the theft, on the word of another man. Detached, smiling, Christian is none too concerned, but Bligh, at the gunwale, looks on with interest. He then intervenes with the order that the men's cheese ration be stopped while the shortfall is made up. Below deck, Mills reveals to the other sailors that Bligh ordered him to take the cheeses to his home 'as a favour'. In Mills' account, Bligh has appropriated the sailors' rations for his personal use.

Both Bligh and Christian overhear Mills' insistence that the captain is the thief. Bligh claims, with considerable satisfaction, that the Articles of War offer a remedy for just such an accusation. Christian, smiling no longer, but attempting to defuse the situation, says confidentially to Bligh that a few weeks without grog will teach Mills to hold his tongue. His suggestion is dismissed, and he is ordered to summon all hands to witness punishment. Looking back at the group of seamen, he follows Bligh out.

On deck, with all hands mustered to witness punishment, Bligh reads the relevant passage from the Articles of War. Christian passes his left hand over his head; his eyes are averted, his body restless. He is not detached from the situation now, and although he is clearly troubled, his thoughts are impossible to read. The 'Hats On!' order is given, to lend the punishment its due formality. During the lashing, Brown (the gardener) turns away, unable to watch. To turn away would be to disobey the captain's order, and so Christian cannot do this, but his eyes are occasionally averted, and close-ups suggest his problematic absorption in a troubling situation. All we know for certain is that he has disagreed with his captain about the appropriate punishment for Mills. Bligh watches Mills' lashing with grim approval, and then, after the company is dismissed, Christian follows Bligh from the deck. The Articles of War held behind Christian's back in his left hand suggest his ethically compromised situation.

In the subsequent dinner sequence, four men are seated at the captain's table: Bligh, Fryer (Eddie Byrne), Midshipman Ned Young (Tim Seely) and Christian. They are served by a steward (Gordon Jackson). Christian's back is to the camera, but the first cut shows him toying with his food, using his cutlery to keep it at a distance from him as much as to convey it to his mouth. He eats almost incidentally, without enthusiasm. There is no conversation, and the dinner is initially a drama of eyes and heads, with glances exchanged around the table as the men's heads bob to and from their plates. Young pleads that he is unwell, although Bligh orders him to eat. Christian shoots a glance at Bligh, to his right, then to Young, at his left, as if getting ready to enter the action, before putting down his cutlery. He then takes up his napkin, looks at it, wipes his mouth, opens the napkin, and flattens it against his chest before holding it away, then carefully folds and smooths it into a neat rectangular shape.

These gestures may be an elaborate expression of displaced distaste, but they also cover some confusion, and suggest both deliberation and evasion. The subsequent conversation concerning the punishment of Mills is superficially polite and, while Christian scrupulously observes the courtesies and conventions of rank when speaking to his captain, we cannot forget that he believes that Bligh is a thief and a liar. A plate of cheese is on the table between Christian and Bligh, usually close to the centre of the frame. Young, unable to stomach his food, leaves the table. Fryer and the attendant steward are virtually forgotten by the camera, which now concentrates on the drama between Christian and Bligh. Justifying the punishment of Mills, Bligh expounds his ideas about punishment, authority and command, which are predicated on a theory of cruelty as efficiency: 'This is a typical seaman: a half-witted, wife-beating, habitual drunkard. His whole life is spent evading and defying authority.' It is the professional sailor, not the accidental, dandified officer, who is the real snob here, holding his crew in contempt.

Christian listens earnestly, shifting occasionally in his chair. His right hand against the side of his face – Bligh is to his right – is more protective than supporting; he is not so much leaning on it as shielding it, covering his right eye, dropping first his eyes, then his little finger. It is a drama of body parts. When his hand moves to his chin, his little finger plays at his mouth, as if unsure how much to take in, or to reveal. Bligh, having finished his sermon, cuts the cheese and, at that instant, Brando's left hand, liberated from indecisiveness, makes for the decanter of port. He removes the stopper, fills his glass, replaces the stopper and returns the decanter to the table. Free to speak now, and apparently changing the subject, he says to Bligh, 'I'd be careful of that cheese if I were you, sir. It has a peculiar smell.

I think it's a bit tainted. But then of course it's a question of individual taste'. As the enormity of this subtle rebuke dawns on Bligh, Christian takes a thoughtful drink and then compliments 'a damn good port'.

This sequence is the first clue to Christian's developing inward identity. The more intriguing drama is of his own interiority rather than in the developing tension between commander and officer; and this internal drama finds expression in the insecure relationship between what Brando is doing, and what he is saying. His spoken language and his body language are in disharmony, and he masks the troubling severity of his opinion of Bligh by his remarks about the cheese and the port. Such rhetorical evasions express his indecisiveness about what to do with the suspicion that a major injustice has been perpetrated aboard the ship, and with the anxiety that his captain is a thief and a liar whose theory of command is predicated on cruelty.

Susan Mizruchi has identified the need to communicate '*beyond* language' as one of Brando's seminal principles of performance;[26] and Italian director Gillo Pontecorvo, who later directed Brando in *Burn!* (1969), has said, 'When things are psychological, we trust the face of Brando'.[27] Things are psychological enough in this sequence, where Brando's contempt for his commander provokes conflict with himself; both of these are suggested by his focused inscrutability, his actions and movements. But although dialogue may be subservient to attitude and gesture, it always exists in relation to those aspects of performance, supporting them, qualifying them or, occasionally, in counterpoint to them. In this sequence, Christian's politeness to his superior officer is scrupulous, but superficial. His concerned indecisiveness finds expression in his toying with the cutlery while, at the same time, it is masked by his elaborate play with the napkin. Objects, like the glass and the decanter, are used to arrange, organise and focus the displaced hostility that is covertly expressed in his insubordinate caveat about the cheese, which is itself then dispersed in his praise of the port. Throughout this sequence, dialogue, gesture and object are in increasingly dynamic interplay.

---

26   Mizruchi, 2014, p 150.
27   Mizruchi, 2014, p 150. Pontecorvo is quoted by Mizruchi (p 216). On 'the modern American concept of acting, which emphasizes behavior over the dialogue-based English tradition', see Scott Eyman, *John Wayne: The Life and Legend* (New York, Simon & Schuster, 2014, p 58).

A barrel of water

The cheese incident, the first major conflict between Fletcher Christian and William Bligh, establishes the pattern followed in the rest of the film, up to and including the mutiny itself. Bligh and Christian first disagree, then clash, with increasing personal animosity evident between them. Bligh's character is immovable and unchanging, as obdurate as John Milton's Satan, 'Like Teneriffe or Atlas unremoved';[28] whereas, in Christian, these confrontations provoke anxiety, driving him to go beneath his superficial persona to discover the unknown depths of his character. Bligh is the straight man around whom Christian must find himself, and the film allows Bligh nothing in terms of personal merit. In *1935*, Charles Laughton's Bligh was permitted dignity and humanity in his treatment of the sailors with him in the launch on the long haul to Timor and, while in command of the *Bounty* he never, unlike Trevor Howard's Bligh of *1962*, had anyone keelhauled. In *1962*, Bligh's decision to make for Timor is an executive order imposed on his men in the longboat, backed by the threat of the sword. After the mutiny, Christian gives Bligh his own personal sextant, 'so you can be sure it's a good one', so that even Bligh's remarkable feat of navigation in getting the 3,600 miles to Timor may depend on the indirect assistance of the man who cast him adrift.

Bligh's professional judgement is brought into most severe question by his decision to round Cape Horn in winter. This leads, literally, to a turning point on the *Bounty*'s voyage, and intensifies the ongoing confrontation between Christian and Bligh. As the wind and swell increase, with Bligh below deck, Christian orders the topgallants put away to save the straining masts. Bligh then emerges from the cockpit to order the topgallants wound out again, notwithstanding Christian's explanation of his own order. Bligh's order to release maximum sail has dangerous consequences for the crew; below deck, a barrel from the ship's cargo has come loose, and is careering unpredictably around. Christian takes charge, and heads a work party to make things safe by securing the rogue water barrel, which has evidently taken on a life of its own. Christian gives the order to let the ship run before the wind in order that the cargo can be stabilised by reducing the pitching movement of the ship as it heads into the fierce weather.

---

28   Milton, 1966, Book 4, line 987.

For the only time in the film, we see Christian here as a working sailor. Dressed in long, belted waterproof coat, boots, woollen beret and scarf, he is never less of a fop or dandy, but a capable and decisive officer leading his work party. In attempting to handle this crisis, Christian drops the dandy's pose of ironic detachment. Not only do we see him taking positive action, but we also see him working as part of a team – unthinkable within the dandy code of 'independence' and 'singularity'.[29] Although he is continually reassessing the situation, and giving the necessary orders, he is in as much danger as anyone and, at one point, is knocked off his feet. In this crisis of seamanship, Christian assumes his natural authority. For Charles Baudelaire, 'The distinguishing characteristic of the dandy's beauty consists above all in an air of coldness which comes from an unshakeable determination not to be moved; you might call it a latent fire which hints at itself, and which could, but chooses not to burst into flame'.[30] Here, for the first time in the film, the 'latent fire' of Christian's character breaks forth.

Bligh, who has been dozing in his cabin, then intervenes for the second time, with catastrophic consequences. Awakened by the changes in the movement of the ship, Bligh rushes on deck to countermand Christian's order again, refusing to hear any explanation of the necessity for it. As the ship again turns head to wind, the rolling motion loosens the barrel before it has been properly secured, and a seaman dies after being pinned beneath its weight. No one works harder than Christian to relieve or rescue the trapped man. Bligh here is at his most incompetent, and his most unfeeling. He has been negligent in making no attempt to discover why Christian gave the order that he did, and he is contemptuous of the man, Norman, for whose death he is responsible.

Christian now, for the first time, questions an order given by his captain by repeating it: '*Never mind Norman,* sir?' he asks incredulously. Throughout their subsequent conversation, although Christian takes exception to Bligh's attitude, he observes the courtesies and conventions of rank by continuing to address Bligh as 'sir'. But a new seriousness and intensity characterise his expression and tone. In his actions to try to save the sailor, and in challenging the captain when Bligh dismissively brushes aside the specific human cost of his own insane exercise of absolute authority, Christian has declared a value: the value of the individual life. Indeed, the

---

29   d'Aurevilly, 1928, pp 26–27, 70–71; Camus, 1991, p 52.
30   Baudelaire, 1964, p 29.

dandy figure has begun to be resignified, politically as a 'bloody traitor' (in Bligh's words), and ethically as the moral compass of the dramatic action. The class distinction between Bligh and Christian modulates into a conflict between opposing value systems, centred on the question of what it means to be a gentleman – or, in a phrase used later in a charged exchange between the two, an 'alleged gentleman'. While the title of 'gentleman' for Bligh means simply unearned privilege, for Christian it indicates allegiance to a standard of decency that he will ultimately defend at extraordinary personal cost to himself.

Neither Nordhoff and Hall's novel nor the earlier *Mutiny on the Bounty* film includes a sequence equivalent to that of the loose barrel. In each of these earlier narratives, the *Bounty*'s change of route to the Cape of Good Hope is purely a necessary change in direction, dictated by natural circumstance. In *1962*, we are plunged into a crisis of seamanship at the most hazardous point in the Southern Ocean. The cinematic precursor here is surely the typhoon sequence in *The Caine Mutiny* in which, as the ship pitches into crisis, Lt Maryk (Van Johnson) takes over command of the ship. He is on the bridge, as is Captain Queeg (Humphrey Bogart), and for the officers it becomes a matter of whose orders to obey. That, of course, is a key issue in *1962*, especially for Ship's Master John Fryer, when the mutiny on the *Bounty* does occur. In the Cape Horn sequence, the crisis of command represented by the pattern of countermanded orders prefigures the later situation aboard the *Bounty*, and thus foreshadows the mutiny to which the narrative is building. Meanwhile, the cannonading barrel is a metonym for the *Bounty*'s lack of appropriate authority.

The dandy is not a romantic hero

At the point of the *Bounty*'s turn-about off Cape Horn, mutiny is a cause without a rebel, and this situation continues throughout the remainder of the voyage to Tahiti. One important reason for this is this film's unique characterisation of Fletcher Christian as dandy rather than romantic hero. A series of scenes early in Part Two (after leaving Tahiti) establishes an important distinction between dandyism and romanticism. Upon learning from Brown, the gardener, that some of the breadfruit plants are dying from insufficient water, William Bligh orders the ladle from the crew's water cask to be placed at the top of the mast; any sailor who desires water must climb the mast to retrieve the ladle, and replace it after drinking. Sailors who lack the strength or agility to do this are in danger of dying from dehydration, from drinking seawater, or from the hazardous attempt to reach the ladle. The inhumanity of Bligh's behaviour is resented by all, including those who are themselves exempt from the water restrictions, such as Brown ('the most important man on the ship') and Midshipman Ned Young. Yet Christian remains silent on the point and, for a long time, complies with the order.

Four sequential scenes at this point in the film function to distinguish Christian from Bligh's more vocal critics on the ship. In the first of these scenes, Christian is on deck, wearing a mauve cravat and without his naval jacket. After polishing his sextant with a white lace handkerchief he turns to the gentlemanly activity of sketching. When a sailor who has gone aloft to fetch water falls from the rigging to his death, Christian reacts with a look of horror, but no words. One of the common sailors, however, rushes and strikes the captain, for which he is sentenced to the barbaric punishment of keelhauling the next day. In the following scene, Christian is in his cabin playing chess with himself. Ned remonstrates with him about the illegality of the punishment ordered by the captain, and demands that Christian respond to Bligh's cruelty. Christian refuses to be drawn; he even appears to make light of the situation, inviting Ned to stay and play chess with him, but Ned leaves in a temper. The next scene takes place on deck, where officers and crew are assembled to witness the sailor's punishment. As predicted in the previous scene by both Ned and Christian, the sailor does not survive the keelhauling. While the assembled men disperse, Christian appears lost in thought as he turns his officer's hat around and around in his hands; without speaking, he replaces it on his head as if thereby resuming his official naval persona. Obviously disturbed, he goes below deck to the officers' water cask where, still thoughtful, he bathes his eyes and takes a drink. Ned appears and refuses the water Christian offers him, saying 'I couldn't get it down'. In their subsequent exchange Ned comes across as emotional, warm-blooded and impetuous, while Christian is cold and aloof. Finally, Christian calls Ned 'a bore' for his emotional response, eliciting this judgement from his friend: 'You're exactly what you seem to be – a supercilious poseur without the slightest trace of humanity or compassion … One needn't look further for your character than the pomade in your hair.'

At this moment there is a vast emotional gulf between Christian and Ned, whose friendship we know to have preceded this voyage. Now, each is strangely aligned with their common enemy, Bligh. Ned articulates his condemnation of Christian in similar language to that previously used about Christian by Bligh. Christian meanwhile reproves Ned for his 'impertinence' and tells him to 'shut his arrogant mouth'. He now pulls rank: while addressing 'Midshipman Young', Christian taps the junior officer twice with his hat. This may be the film's most actorly moment, one of Marlon Brando's brilliant *coups de cinéma*. Brando reinforces Christian's words with a potent symbolic gesture, while simultaneously qualifying his character's gesture by using the hat to suggest the officer's insecurity; for, while Christian finds a use for his hat (which, after the keelhauling, he was unable to do), he stops short of putting it on, which alone would identify him absolutely with the power of constituted naval authority. The way in which he uses his hat to stress his words to Young silently suggests that Christian doesn't know how to wear it, and so his wielding of authority is also a withholding of authority. This action of tapping or prodding (the angle makes it impossible for the viewer to determine the exact nature of the gesture), forcefully intrusive as it is, bristles with uncertainties. Contact *per se* acknowledges connection. Christian's overt act of reproof may even cast a shadow of approval, his express rebuke covertly hinting at complicity, collusion, even sympathy. Brando's gesture is telling, in ways of which Christian is not consciously aware, as the physical punctuation of his verbal response to Young unintentionally expresses Christian's own repressed 'impertinence' to *his* superior officer. Although the sequence obviously dramatises a crisis in the relationship between the friends, its cross-currents gesture to the growing crisis in Christian's relationship with himself.

The sequence of these four scenes alternates between spaces above and below deck to show Christian's public and private responses to the increasing monstrosity of Bligh's rule. Interestingly, in the private, below-deck scenes, Christian aggressively refuses the role of romantic rebel offered (and modelled) to him by Ned, instead retreating into his dandy persona, but now emphasising the dandy's connection to privilege rather than dissent.

The character of Ned is important as it dramatises Brando's refusal of romanticism in his interpretation of Christian as a dandy. Part One of the film prepares the viewer for this. When Ned staggers down from the mast where he has spent the night as punishment for laughing at Bligh's walk (a misdemeanour in which Christian participated, but for which only the junior officer was disciplined), Christian asks lightly, 'Did you sleep well?' The younger man, full of outrage and self-pity, refuses to adopt this nonchalant tone as he describes his sufferings. Christian, *sotto voce*, encourages him to maintain his dignity by laughing off the incident, but Ned cannot disguise his feelings in such a manner. The scene is an attempt by Christian to teach his young friend the dandy's code: as Charles Baudelaire insisted, 'A dandy may be blasé, he may even suffer; but in this case, he will smile like the Spartan boy under the fox's tooth'.[31] Ned, however, subscribes to an opposite doctrine of emotional authenticity, as is shown in his naïve request to be married to his Tahitian sweetheart. Christian, by contrast, parts calmly from his lover, Maimiti. His farewell to her expresses little more feeling than his reaction to the parting gifts with which the Tahitians have just presented him ('Oh, isn't that jolly').

The contrast between Ned and Christian presents romanticism as dandyism's younger, less jaded and less self-disciplined cousin. As Jules Barbey d'Aurevilly wrote:

> Dandyism introduces antique calm into modern agitations; but the calm of the ancients came from the harmony of their faculties and the plenitude of a freely-developed existence, whereas the calm of Dandyism is the pose of a spirit which has already ranged among many ideas and is now too languid to be capable of animation.[32]

A dandy cannot be a romantic, because '[i]f one were passionate one would be too vital to be a Dandy'.[33] This seems to be exactly Christian's position in the scenes of conflict with Ned over the keelhauling and the water restrictions, as it is in a much earlier scene from Part One (before the landing in Tahiti), in which he absolutely declines to take part in or even react to an important meeting between Bligh and two of the men (later mutineers). Acting as a kind of shop steward for his mates, Gunner's Mate Mills, accompanied by the older sailor Smith (Hugh Griffith), goes to see the captain to point out that newly imposed food rationing is against 'the regulations'. Predictably, this attempt to persuade Bligh that 'right is right' fails, but what is most striking about the scene is Christian's presence as an unwilling observer of it. During the exchange between Mills and Bligh, Christian listens from his cabin where he sits in bed, dressed in a sumptuous red-lined dressing gown and a preposterous white nightcap, writing with a quill in a book while smoking an extraordinary long pipe more suited to opium than tobacco. This is the most outrageous

---

31 Baudelaire, 1964, p 28.
32 d'Aurevilly, 1928, p 17.
33 d'Aurevilly, 1928, p 23.

costume Christian has worn since the film's opening scene and, behaving at his most mannered and foppish, he looks and sounds so anomalous to the naval drama being enacted between master and men outside his cabin that he seems to inhabit a different world. Peering round the door, Christian acknowledges the others' presence, prompting an exasperated comment from Bligh that he has been given nothing to work with on this voyage but 'dirt … and empty silk caps'. This odd juxtaposition links Christian to the discontented and later mutinous men, but at this point he firmly disavows the connection: he closes the door on both his captain and his subordinates, sealing his cabin as a private haven of gentlemanly disengagement from their vulgar concerns.

According to the dandy code, as explicated by d'Aurevilly and later Baudelaire, such behaviour is not mere selfishness. Rather, it expresses a mode of dissent. Ironic detachment is the dandy's default mode when faced by the absurdities of a world governed by ambition masquerading as morality and power disguised as law. For Baudelaire, such detachment included aspects of 'the spiritual and stoical':

> In truth I was not altogether wrong to consider dandyism as a kind of religion. The strictest monastic rule … were no more despotic, and no more obeyed, than this doctrine of elegance and originality, which also imposes upon its humble and ambitious disciples – men often full of fire, passion, courage and restrained energy – the terrible formula: *Perinde ac cadaver!* [just as if a corpse].[34]

For Baudelaire, then, the dandy was distinguished not by lack of feeling, but by restraint of feeling. Interpreting Baudelaire's own practice of dandyism, Jean-Paul Sartre saw the dandy's voluntary submission to a set of arbitrary rules, punctiliously observed, as a form of discipline, which relieved the modern man from some of the terrible freedom to which he was condemned. Dandyism provided structure in a formless world. Around the same time, Albert Camus suggested that dandyism could be a source of 'coherence' in a post-religious age: 'The dandy rallies his forces and creates a unity for himself by the very violence of his refusal.'[35] Christian enacts such a gesture of refusal when he closes the door on Bligh, Mills and Smith. But he cannot refuse forever to engage.

---

34 Baudelaire, 1964, p 28.
35 Camus, 1991, p 51.

Mutiny

An important piece of information brought from the botanical experts at Kew by Brown, the gardener, at the beginning of the voyage, is that breadfruit trees have a 'dormant period' during which they cannot be transplanted. It is the desire to outrun the dormant period that sparks William Bligh's decision to travel around Cape Horn, and it is the necessity of waiting out the dormant period that keeps the *Bounty* at Tahiti for so long, giving the ordinary sailors a taste of a life far different from that endured under Bligh's command at sea. During preparations for departure from Tahiti, three men decide to make a run for it. They are headed off by Fletcher Christian and Ned Young, and returned to the ship. Bligh immediately adjudges them to be deserters, and has them confined in irons, preparatory to a court martial in Jamaica. Christian takes exception to the treatment and the punishment of these men, and he advances to confront his captain. Christian and Bligh face each other beneath a bulkhead. In this eyeballing situation, Christian drops the 'sir' in his address to Bligh and this indicates that *his* dormant period is over: overt defiance has replaced ironic, detached compliance. Echoing his earlier snobbery, Bligh wonders 'why an alleged gentleman should give his first loyalty to ordinary seamen'. 'Instead of to other *alleged* gentlemen?' Christian replies, enunciating each word carefully. His 'impertinence', Bligh declares 'shall be noted in the log', but, as Christian's further reply makes clear, the issue for him is not class, but cruelty: 'I have never met an officer who inflicted punishment upon men with such incredible relish.'

The mutiny itself is not premeditated. Christian acts spontaneously, and he acts alone. In specific disobedience of Bligh's order, he offers water to a sick man who will likely die without it. Bligh rushes towards the viewer, centre screen, and kicks the ladle from Christian's right hand. A full-force backhanded swipe from Christian's left hand sends Bligh staggering back across the deck, until he comes to rest on his hindquarters. Through his surprise and humiliation, Bligh realises immediately that he has won some sort of victory: 'Thank you – I've been puzzling for a way to take the strut out of you, you posturing snob.' He orders Fryer to take Christian below. Christian then strikes Fryer, takes a sabre from one of sailors and, back at the gunwale, announces that he is taking command of the ship. The mutiny has taken shape, but it's still a work in progress.

Christian's release of water from a cask to relieve a suffering seaman links the mutiny sequence to its precursor, the episode of the loose barrel at Cape Horn: as the film gathers momentum, water becomes a symbolic rhyme, tying together the crisis points in the relationship between Christian and Bligh. The historical importance of water aboard the *Bounty* cannot be overstressed. Joseph Banks, as mastermind of the expedition, stipulated that the ship 'must be supplied with as large a quantity as possible, so that the gardener may never be refused the quantity of water he may have occasion to demand'.[36] Bligh's control of the availability to the crew of drinking water is a provocative issue in *1935* as well as in *1962*, and also in Nordhoff and Hall, although there is no conclusive historical evidence that Bligh appropriated the men's drinking water for the plants.[37] But, as the conditions that give rise to the mutiny take shape, the adjectives used by Quintal ('sweet') and Christian ('fresh') lend the water a symbolic, elemental significance, that may also carry biblical resonance. When the wandering Israelites are desperate with thirst, the Lord instructs Moses to 'smite the rock' of Horeb, 'and there shall come water out of it, that the people may drink' (*Exodus* 17:6). Christian smites his captain, and his liberation of an elemental substance is a profoundly democratic action: now the people may indeed drink.

Although from this point Christian could not be more fully engaged in opposing Bligh's unjust rule, the film still resists the allure of romanticism. The most memorable glimpse of the historical Christian aboard the *Bounty* on the morning of the mutiny comes from the testimony of Thomas Ellison, one of the mutineers who would hang, at his court martial: 'My terror was more Increas'd, at the site of Mr Christian, he looked like a Madman is [sic] long hair was luse, his shirt Collair open'.[38] Ellison's testimony established the key elements of the Romantic iconography of the mutinous Christian as a kind of Byronic hero, and this was how Clark Gable played him in 1935, in swashbuckling mode, with his shirt open at the neck and his sleeves rolled between wrist and elbow. Marlon Brando's Christian is more composed. His defiance of a commander's orders by giving water to a suffering subordinate is calm and deliberate, and although the blow that initiates the mutiny seems an instinctive reaction to Bligh's violence, his actions throughout the scene express more a Lutheran '*ich kann nicht anders*' than a Byronic surrender to passionate

---

36   Cited in Patrick O'Brian, *Joseph Banks: A Life*, London, Collins Harvill, 1988 (1987), p 235.
37   Alexander, 2003, p 448.
38   Alexander, 2003, p 268.

feeling. It is significant, in the language of dress, that Brando's Christian is in full uniform when he strikes Bligh. Although his hat falls off in the ensuing melée and his hair becomes dishevelled in the fray (whereas Gable, strangely, has not a hair out of place), his collar and naval coat remain buttoned throughout. He looks more of a professional sailor in this scene than in many others. Indeed, although he now acknowledges the ethical impossibility of failing to oppose the tyranny embodied in Bligh, this Christian is no anarchist. 'I am taking command of this ship', he declares, and remains aloof from the carnivalesque indulgences of the other mutineers, who whoop with joy as they throw the breadfruit cargo overboard. Instead, Christian thoughtfully smooths his hair, restoring order to his appearance, as he would like to restore it to the voyage itself.

The historical record shows that, on his return to England, Bligh was honourably acquitted at his court martial at Spithead, where it was decreed that no blame attached to him for the loss of the *Bounty*. The cause of the mutiny was of no relevance to this legal procedure,[39] but, in *1962*, it becomes an important addendum to the legal verdict. Here the court martial takes place in the more imposing surrounds of Greenwich and, to its verdict of honourable acquittal, the court feels obliged to add comment in two parts. On the basis of evidentiary conclusion, the court laments, first, Bligh's 'excess of zeal'. While Bligh is not explicitly censured, the strong implication is that he must bear some responsibility for the mutiny. The court then goes on to say that, while no code can cover all contingencies and while justice cannot be put aboard ships in books, justice and decency are carried in the heart of the captain: 'It is for this reason that the Admiralty has always sought to appoint its officers from the ranks of gentlemen. The court regrets to note that the appointment of Captain William Bligh was, in that respect, a failure.'[40] Bligh's acquittal is thus doubly tainted, with indeterminate responsibility for the mutiny, and with the charged issue of 'gentility' that has driven his increasingly tense and antagonistic relationship with Christian. 'I am not leaving you, Mr Christian,' said Bligh as he left the *Bounty* for the last time, assuring the mutineer that he would always be behind him, rope in hand. But the

---

39 Alexander, 2003, p 172.
40 There may be some inconsistency in the script here. The first reference to Bligh in this sequence is to 'Lieutenant Bligh', which correctly identifies Bligh's rank aboard the *Bounty*. Later in the sequence, as we have seen, he is referred to as 'Captain'. Any such inconsistency is telling, for, as Caroline Alexander (2003, p 52) has said, the Admiralty's reluctance to accord Bligh the rank of captain surely contributed to any crisis of authority aboard the *Bounty*.

court martial addendum is a bitter defeat for Bligh, for now Christian will never leave him, moving through his mind by day, and a trouble to his dreams. Bligh, accorded no status by the Admiralty from which he has always craved validation, disappears from the film.

The existential dandy

Marlon Brando's performance contributes to the imaginative archive of *Bounty* representations a distinctly postwar interpretation of Fletcher Christian as an existential hero, placed in a moral world (constructed by William Bligh's command) that is both absurd and cruel, and forced to take responsibility for his existence through choices, decisions and actions that are defining and irrevocable. He is driven by a Sartrean imperative, unable finally to deny that responsibility falls upon the individual to choose how he or she will respond to the world in all its futility and injustice. In the minutes leading up to the mutiny, this imperative takes the form of a call to moral action, which Christian heeds. But, rather than lifting the existential burden, his actions merely intensify it. What next, after the grand gesture? How to continue, actively, to exist? How to deal with the continuing and terrible responsibility of exercising moral freedom?

Christian's post-mutiny traumas reflect the historical context of the film's production. In 19th-century literature, it was possible to imagine dandyism as an effective solvent of the troubles of the age. In Oscar Wilde's play *An Ideal Husband* (1895), Lord Goring, a 'flawless dandy',[41] not only uses his knowledge of human nature to resolve the plot but also reveals, beneath 'the delicate fopperies'[42] of his speech, manner and appearance, an emotional and ethical authenticity that allows him to claim the role indicated by the play's title. Like the character of Mirabel in Benjamin Disraeli's society novel *Henrietta Temple* (1837), Lord Goring is a '*dandy ex machina* responsible for a happy ending'.[43] The *Mutiny* of 1962, as befits its post–World War II context, offers no such easy certainty.

---

41   Oscar Wilde, *The Importance of Being Earnest and Other Plays*, Harmondsworth, Penguin, 2000, p 186.
42   Wilde, 2000, p 232.
43   Ellen Moers, *The Dandy: Brummell to Beerbohm*, London, Secker & Warburg, 1960, p 157.

In the first scene after the mutiny, we see Christian sitting alone in his cabin, his body uncharacteristically tense and graceless. Sounds of the sailors on deck celebrating the victory over Bligh emphasise his solitude and alienation from their communal joy. The cabin is strewn with richly coloured clothes, which are not part of Christian's naval uniform but represent the private wardrobe by which he has always signified his outsider status on the ship as well as his 'aristocratic' self-fashioning. His gorgeous scarlet cloak, cane, silvery suit and matching hat from the opening scene are all on display, seeming to frame – and mock – him in his despair. One could read the *mise en scène* as an allegorical tableau, the title of which would be 'vanity'. When Gunner's Mate Mills and the other main mutineers come below they are puzzled by Christian's depression: 'But we won, didn't we?', Smith exclaims naively. Christian wearily explains (after kicking away a piece of fine cloth that he has accidentally dropped) that they have only trapped themselves in a metaphysical prison, not locked in but locked out of a society they can never re-enter. He refuses the moral security offered by Smith, that he did 'what's right', although he finds some consolation in having shown allegiance to a higher authority than Bligh's: 'I believe I did what honour dictated and that belief sustains me.' This calls to mind Charles Baudelaire's comment on the dandy: 'If he committed a crime, it would perhaps not ruin him; but if his crime resulted from some trivial cause, his disgrace would be irreparable.'[44] In his own mind, Christian is not disgraced, but he is damned – self-exiled and trapped in a hell of his own making with no respite from the continuing existential necessity of making impossible choices for which he must always bear responsibility. As he pores over maps looking for a place of safety from the wrath of Bligh and the Admiralty, the consequences of his actions seem both inescapable and unfathomable. Fletcher Christian is now truly a Nowhere Man, for there is nowhere he can go, and nothing he can be. The contrast between the uniformed exile and Clark Gable's cheerful pirate, bare-chested and head-scarfed, could not be stronger.

In *An Ideal Husband*, Wilde showed 'the philosopher that underlies the dandy'[45] to be a kind of Japanese Buddhist, benevolent in his acceptance of the world's imperfections, his exquisite clothes expressing the arts of *iki* ('refined style') and *kire* ('the cut') as ways of signifying and responding to

---

44 Baudelaire, 1964, p 28.
45 Wilde, 2000, p 267.

the impermanence of all things.⁴⁶ Brando's Christian belongs to a different philosophical school, one created by the ideas of – amongst others – Jean-Paul Sartre and Albert Camus. In his analysis of the dandy-as-rebel, Camus quoted French romantic writer Petrus Borel: 'I was conscious of my power and I was conscious of my chains.' Camus commented: 'But these chains are valuable objects. Without them it would be necessary to prove, or to exercise, this power which, after all, one is not very sure of having.'⁴⁷ These words capture Christian's dilemma in the last part of the film. Without Bligh to position himself against, who will he be? To what use will he put the power unleashed when he cast off the chains that defined his dissent?

These questions are sharply posed for Christian by his Tahitian lover Maimiti when the *Bounty* returns to Tahiti after the mutiny. While the other mutineers rush ashore to renew their relationships with Tahitian women, Christian remains aboard ship, below deck, alone. When he fails to appear onshore, Maimiti goes to him, paddling a small outrigger canoe to where the *Bounty* rides at anchor. In this carefully composed shot, back-lit by the setting sun, Maimiti's silhouette converges on the larger shape of the ship. The visual imagery of this reversed beach-crossing establishes the poetics of contrast that determine the following sequence, in which Maimiti is the figure of agency, whereas Christian, once again, remains a mystery.

The next shot is a close-up of Maimiti's bare feet descending a ladder into Christian's quarters on the ship. On the rungs of the ladder are strewn various male fashion accessories – the *accoutrements* of Christian's dandyism, which in the first half of the film functioned as 'symbols of his aristocratic superiority of mind'.⁴⁸ Now, they are the detritus of his personal hell. As Maimiti's feet pick out a path between these now discarded items, the camera's movement traces a metonymy of contrasts, whereby the 'native' innocence and purity of her clean, naked feet offsets Christian's slovenly disregard for the luxurious appurtenances of an advanced civilisation. On the lowest rung of the ladder lies his naval hat, so carefully employed throughout the film to indicate Christian's fluctuating feelings about his professional identity, an identity that is now irrecoverable.

---

46   Graham Parkes, 'Japanese Aesthetics', in Edward N Zalta (ed), *The Stanford Encyclopedia of Philosophy*, 2011, plato.stanford.edu/archives/win2011/entries/japanese-aesthetics.
47   Camus, 1991, p 50.
48   Baudelaire, 1964, p 27.

The camera pulls back from Maimiti's feet to reveal the full panoply of disorder in Christian's cabin, an elaborately staged *mise en scène* that symbolises his inner turmoil and moral crisis. Dozing, dishevelled and slumped at his desk, Christian's appearance offers a striking contrast to the 'assurance in conduct'[49] he displayed in all his earlier encounters with Maimiti; on arrival in Tahiti, and in subsequent 'beach' scenes, he has carried himself with confident but casual dignity. Beside him, now, standing for the world he has lost, is a globe. In the gloom of the cabin, the crepuscular light picks out Christian's ruffled white shirt, its improbable brightness the last vestige of his dandyism. Christian's shirt is a discordant off-rhyme to Maimiti's simple, spotless white *pareu*, superbly enhanced by the frangipani behind her ear. This 'white noise' has a clear message: adrift between two worlds, neither of which he can now belong to, Christian does not know who he is, or even how to be, whereas Maimiti is immaculate in her native self-possession.

As she begins tidying the cluttered room, Maimiti's movements wake Christian, who initially affects indifference to her presence. Reporting what she has heard on the beach, in a compact Tahitian rendering of the mutiny narrative, she offers him yet another identity: 'Fletcher chief now.' Christian's rueful response fends off this identity but, courteously enough, humours her: 'A very small chief, Maimiti, running for his life.' Christian then gets to his feet and fiddles ineffectively with a chart. The emotional temperature rises as Maimiti's insistence that she will accompany him when he leaves Tahiti, and her refusal to engage with his statements that he 'cares for nothing in the world' and has 'nothing to share with anybody,', provoke him to explode into the first ungallant thing he has ever said to her: 'Are you deaf as well as ignorant?' This insult, born of frustration and impotence, is as revealing as it is shocking; utterly unbecoming for either an officer or a dandy, it declares decisively that Christian is now neither. It provokes a torrent of angry words from Maimiti, spoken in Tahitian, and not translated. Language goes into momentary limbo as the emotions repressed at their formal parting on the beach before the mutiny, having been compounded by subsequent events, are now unleashed. The scene ends with Maimiti returning to pidgin English to deliver a piece of proverbial Tahitian wisdom. 'Tahitian people say, you eat life, or life eat you.'

---

49   d'Aurevilly, 1928, p 17.

The values Maimiti expresses here are instinctive, and the reasoning of her island wisdom is simple: to survive, to live, is enough. Is it? By closing the scene with Maimiti's compelling utterance, the film grants it, and her, dramatic authority. Indeed, in line with a long tradition of European representations of Pacific Islanders, it places her in the overlapping roles of Bon Sauvage and Philosophe Nu, figures of beneficent otherness rhetorically constructed to voice criticisms of European civilisation or to present a philosophy contrasting – and implicitly interrogating – supposedly progressive concepts such as ambition and shame.[50] But, if this scene invites the viewer to see Maimiti and, by extension, any future Christian might have with her, through 'Rousseau-tinted spectacles',[51] the rest of the film dispels that thought. Christian's self-immolating attempt to save the *Bounty* from destruction by his fellow mutineers shows that he has not freed himself from the hope of one day reinstating himself in civilised society, and thus that he has not heeded Maimiti's 'traditional' wisdom.

The Tahitian proverb Maimiti quotes may be more resonant to the film's context than to the film itself, albeit in an ironic way. The injunction to eat life or be eaten by it is cruelly appropriate to the dog-eat-dog world of Realpolitik both in the United States and globally in the 1960s. When the film was released, in November 1962, President John F Kennedy had a year to live. His *Civil Rights Act*, stuck in Congress at the time of his assassination in 1963, was manoeuvred into law in 1964, thanks in large part to the political know-how of new President Lyndon B Johnson. Johnson's own *Voting Rights Act*, a pillar of his Great Society program, would become law in 1965. Such political changes failed to meet the social needs urgently expressed in Martin Luther King's march on Washington DC in August 1963; by race riots in Watts, Los Angeles, two years later; and by similar riots in cities throughout the United States in 1967. King was assassinated in April 1968, followed in June by Robert F Kennedy, the late president's brother, attorney-general and heir-apparent to his liberal legacy. Johnson, the last Roosevelt Democrat to hold presidential office, did not stand for his party's presidential nomination in 1968 and, in January 1969, Richard M Nixon, Dwight D Eisenhower's vice-president from 1952 to 1960, was sworn in as 37th president of the United States.

---

50   Neil Rennie, *Far-Fetched Facts: The Literature of Travel and the Idea of the South Seas*, Oxford, Clarendon Press, 1995, pp 7, 35; Rod Edmond, *Representing the South Pacific: Colonial Discourse from Cook to Gauguin*, Cambridge, Cambridge University Press, 1997, pp 226–27.
51   Edmond, 1997, p 228.

Plus ça change. Whatever fate may have befallen Fletcher Christian, Bligh was back. (William Bligh would, indeed, return, and he would face yet another rebellion, as governor of New South Wales, in 1808. He was effectively deposed from the governorship, as Nixon himself would in 1974 be deposed from the presidency.)

The triumph of authority over hope played out in US politics in the decade following the film's release was, in 1962, already an old story to the peoples of the Pacific. During the 1940s and 1950s, their visions of independence from colonial rule had been replaced with the reality of life under the postwar superpowers as an experience of crushing authoritarian abuse, supposedly justified by the aim of maintaining international security. In 1959 in Tahiti, a politically controversial trial consigned the charismatic independence leader Pouvana'a a Oopa to an eight-year jail term, followed by exile to France; he was alleged to have attempted to burn down the capital, Pape'ete, as part of a revolutionary conspiracy. Elsewhere in the Pacific, the use of the region as a testing ground for the world's most dangerous and destructive nuclear explosions revealed a merciless exercise of superpower over subordinate and largely voiceless communities. The most extreme environmental and human abuses in relation to Pacific nuclear testing occurred in Micronesia, where tests carried out by the United States at Bikini, Enewetak and Johnston atolls between 1946 and 1958 dwarfed in explosive force and radioactive fallout all other nuclear explosions before or since.[52] It is all the more shocking that the United States held these islands at the time in 'strategic trust' under UN authority, which committed the trustee nation to promote the entrusted islands' 'progressive development' while also respecting the Islanders' 'human rights and fundamental freedoms'.[53]

US bomb tests in the Marshall Islands ended in 1958. British nuclear testing at Malden and Christmas islands continued until 1962. France began testing nuclear weapons in its Pacific territories in 1966. While we do not suggest that there are any intentional references to the Pacific nuclear testing programs in the 1962 *Mutiny on the Bounty*, there are resonances between the film and this aspect of the historical context of its production. The brutal exercise of executive authority in defiance of human rights and natural justice connects the nuclear powers in the

---

52 Tilman A Ruff, 'The Humanitarian Impact and Implications of Nuclear Test Explosions in the Pacific Region,' *International Review of the Red Cross*, vol 97, 2015, pp 778, 780–81.
53 UN Charter, Article 76, quoted in Ruff (2015, p 793).

postwar era with Bligh's style of command as shown in the film. Like Bligh on board the *Bounty*, in their nuclear-testing programs the US, British and French governments disregarded the wellbeing of the subjects under their control and exhibited no remorse for the suffering they imposed on those subjects. With reference to the script of *1962*, we might call this the 'never mind Norman' syndrome. Examples from the era of Pacific nuclear testing include US Secretary of State Henry Kissinger's dismissal of the rights of the Marshallese with the comment 'There are only 90,000 of them out there. Who gives a damn?',[54] and a British military report prior to the 1957 Christmas Island bomb test, which justified exceeding internationally agreed levels of radiation because the resulting health hazards would arise 'only to primitive people'.[55]

The choice of test sites also resonates eerily with the later stages of the *Bounty* story. US naval officers tasked in October 1945 with finding suitable locations for future test explosions would recall, 'We just took out dozens of maps and started looking for remote sites'.[56] The mental image this statement conjures is an ideologically inverted copy of the scene, late in the film, where Brando searches his maps for a secret island where the mutineers can hide. The difference, of course, is that, whereas Christian and the mutineers became displaced persons as a consequence of their own actions, the inhabitants of Bikini and Enewetak atolls were exiled from their homes as a consequence of events controlled by the US military[57] – events initially cloaked in the costume of 'choice'. In 1946, Commodore Wyatt, the military governor of the Marshall Islands, made the Bikinians an offer they felt they couldn't refuse. Cynically exploiting the Christian values of the converted Islanders, he compared them to the children of Israel and offered them the chance to do God's will by temporarily giving up their homeland to atomic testing for 'the good of mankind and to end all world wars'.[58] Instead, the Bikinians and other Marshall Islanders found themselves trapped in a human, cultural and environmental nightmare, worsened by the knowledge that their accession to the American request had only contributed to the proliferation of the world's most lethal weapons. In 1954, the Marshallese

---

54   Quoted in Ruff (2015, p 777).
55   Quoted in Ruff (2015, p 779).
56   Quoted in Sasha Davis, *The Empires' Edge: Militarization, Resistance, and Transcending Hegemony in the Pacific* (Athens, GA, University of Georgia Press, 2015, p 61).
57   Stewart Firth, 'The Nuclear Issue in the Pacific Islands', *Journal of Pacific History*, vol 21, no 4, 1986, p 211.
58   Quoted in Davis (2015, p 63).

petitioned the United Nations to bring an end to weapons testing in their region,[59] but UN resolutions in 1954 and 1956 authorised the continuation of US nuclear tests, overruling the explicitly stated wishes of the Marshall Islanders.[60]

Conclusion: The end of freedom

The on-screen preamble to *1935* reads, in part:

> Neither ship nor breadfruit reached the West Indies. Mutiny prevented it – mutiny against the abuse of harsh eighteenth-century sea law. But this mutiny, famous in history and legend, helped bring about a new discipline, based upon mutual respect between officers and men, by which Britain's sea power is maintained as security for all who pass upon the seas.

Historically, this is nonsense: mutinies broke out in the British navy at Spithead and the Nore in 1797, years after the *Bounty* courts martial, and Cunard's *Lusitania* had been torpedoed and sunk in 1915; but the intention, presumably, was to offer reassurance to a world in social, economic and political unrest.

The Caine Mutiny also kicks off with a preamble:

> There has never been a mutiny in a ship of the United States navy. The truths of this film lie not in its incidents but in the way a few men meet the crisis of their lives.

Here, the film's focus is firmly on its individual characters, and any institutional or social implications are sidestepped. The on-screen afterword takes the form of a dedication, which the action of the drama, combined with its preamble, loads with cumbersome complexity: 'The dedication of this film is simple – to the United States navy.' The ethical difficulties raised by the mutiny depicted keep this dedication far from simple.[61]

---

59 Ruff, 2015, pp 795–96.
60 Ruff, 2015, p 793.
61 These complexities, which the film faithfully reproduces from the novel, are unpacked in Whyte (1957, pp 243–48).

On dry land, and just a year earlier than *The Caine Mutiny*, *The Wild One* (1953), in which Marlon Brando plays the iconically rebellious Johnny Strabler, is prefaced by a preamble that chimes with those quoted above.

> This is a shocking story. It could never take place in most American towns – but it did in this one. It is a public challenge not to let it happen again.

In this film, decent middle-American townsfolk rebel against the evidently impotent forces of law and order and, like the *Bounty* and *Caine* mutineers, take matters into their own hands. Johnny's rebellious behaviour is a bravura performance designed to cover his sensitivity, itself wonderfully realised in the exquisite smile of Brando to which the film builds. The film's truly 'shocking story' is the public challenge of social disorder wrought by law-abiding citizens.

All three films express terror of social disorder or institutional breakdown. The 1962 *Mutiny on the Bounty* shakes off the conservatism of its predecessors by showing no interest in such disorder, while also ensuring that anarchy does not follow from the mutiny, as Fletcher Christian takes command. But into what kind of brave new world does the *Bounty* sail? The mutineers may have rid themselves of William Bligh but, as Christian knows only too well and as he tells his newly appointed officers whom he addresses, with habituated if stilted formality, as 'gentlemen', they certainly haven't won. The burden of knowledge about this world falls on Christian, and its distinctive characteristic is the absence of God. 'May God help you' says Fryer to Christian on the *Bounty*'s deck, before joining Bligh in the longboat. Christian politely thanks him. One of his new officers, Smith, offers cosmic reassurance:

> When a man gives up as much as you did, just because he thinks it's right, the Good Lord would never let him down … Wherever we might go, you'll find a happy life, sir. It's God's will.

The telling word here is the plural 'we', which surely reminds Christian that his fate is tied to that of the other mutineers. And the valediction of Mills, who is truly responsible for Christian's death, also comes with a benediction, as he says to the dying Christian: 'May God have mercy on you.'

At this point Christian must be beyond God, for he has already been in hell for some time. We have seen him sitting, motionless and erect, in one of the 'brown studies' to which the gardener's voice-over refers, surrounded by the deconstructed costume in which he had boarded the ship; we have seen him kicking aside his furniture in frustration; and we have seen him hopelessly caught between the need to navigate and the desire to tear up his charts. There are no significant choices, and no meaningful direction, available to him. In the film's most interesting departure from the historical record of the mutiny, Christian does not repeat the words attributed to him by Bligh just after the mutiny: 'I am in hell – I am in hell'.[62] But hell is where he finds himself, either in his cabin or on Pitcairn, and there can be no more powerful image of hell than the hooded figure blundering through the flames on the burning *Bounty*'s lower deck in search of a sextant, to take him – where?

In the film's struggle between tyranny and freedom, tyranny is a given and freedom is the film's problematic – for Christian's dilemmas all involve the problem of freedom. Freedom from tyranny, to be sure, but liberation into what? The existential bleakness into which this film descends made it hard to end, and it falls to Ned Young to come up with an acceptably supple substitute for closure: 'We'll tell our story somehow, to someone.'

It's the most modern, most challenging of all *Bounty* stories.

---

62 Alexander, 2003, p 141.

7

Bounty Relics: Trading in the Legacy of Myth and Mutiny

Adrian Young
Denison University

Introduction: The thing with archives

A pressed rose fell gently from a brittle, ageing envelope onto the table in front of me. I was in the archives of the American Museum of Natural History in New York, working through the correspondence of ornithologist James Paul Chapin, who travelled to Pitcairn Island in 1935 as part of a museum expedition to study its flora, fauna and people. After leaving, the scientist maintained a correspondence with a local named Lucy Christian. It was an exchange between the small Pacific Island and New York that spanned three decades and more than 9,000 kilometres. The envelopes bore not only letters, but also trinkets, souvenirs and tokens of affection like the dried flower that fell from Chapin's long-archived envelope. Over the years, Chapin tucked American dollars into his letters, useful to the Islanders for trade with passing ships; Lucy Christian reciprocated with painted leaves, postcards and flower pressings. Together, three decades of such exchanges produced small piles of treasure on each side of the ocean, valuable not only for their material worth but also for the connections they represent.

Archives and institutional repositories the world over are littered with objects such as these, material things that, though scattered among the documents and folios that comprise most archival collections, fit uneasily between the flat pages of text into which they are so often found tucked. Pages of correspondence, of course, are physical objects, too – but material items like Lucy's flower comprise a super-textual archive of their own with unique stories to tell and novel perspectives to offer.[1] In our case, objects such as these constitute both the substance and the remnants of a Pacific island's engagement with the wider world, a two-century history of exchanges, entanglements, friendships and exploitations. In that sense, they can elucidate the way in which the Anglophone world built its relationship with and imagination of Pacific islands. At the same time, they are also the material things with which the English-speaking world so often built its memory of the *Bounty* itself; treasured souvenirs that linked their owners to an increasingly distant and mythologised past. The *Bounty* mutiny, and Pitcairn Island with it, retains an outsized place in the Anglophone imagination – as this volume attests. Relics like Chapin's play a significant part in maintaining it.

In this essay, I explore how the *Bounty* mythos has built and sustained its captivating power over visitors and readers around the world, using those objects gifted, traded and stolen from Pitcairn across the last two centuries both as my archive and as the principal protagonists of my narrative. At the same time, I want to chart the way that exchanges between Islanders and 'strangers' evolved over the course of two centuries.[2] From the moment of the outside world's rediscovery of Pitcairn Island in 1808, pieces of the *Bounty* wreck and objects crafted by the island's people changed hands, both as items of trade and tokens of affection. This chapter will follow the perambulations of these relics around the globe, locating in their paths and traces the connections from which the knowledge of a distant place was born and the memory of a mythologised moment was maintained.

---

1   For a rumination on the poetics of the archive, its allure, and the space between texts and things, see Helen Freshwater's 'The Allure of the Archive' (*Poetics Today*, vol 24, no 4, 21 Dec 2003, pp 729–58).
2   'Stranger' is not my term, but rather an autochthonous label translated loosely from a local word for *outsider*. The appellation used to identify Western visitors to Pacific communities is inevitably tangled in a fraught politics and poetics; Vanessa Smith, for instance, reminds us that 'friend' was, not unproblematically, among the most common terms deployed in histories of contact in her *Intimate Strangers: Friendship, Exchange and Pacific Encounters* (Cambridge, Cambridge University Press, 2010). Here, I use 'stranger', 'interlocutor', 'visitor' and 'tourist', and, where I can, I preserve the frame of reference from which the actors in my sources originate.

Through the history of those objects, it will also take some measure of the effect the exchange of material culture has had not only on the place of the Pacific in the Anglophone imaginary, but on Pitcairn's people, who not only traded in *Bounty* relics but were sometimes transformed by that trading into *Bounty* relics themselves.

Gifts, objects and material culture have long been a locus of scholarly interest, especially in the Pacific. Almost a century ago, Marcel Mauss famously wrote on the debts and obligations wrought by gifts and gift-giving.[3] In the years since, historians have documented the desire of sailors and scientists to collect from the Pacific islands they explored and colonised. Nicholas Thomas and scholars of his generation reminded us that the history of collection and gift exchange is inextricably linked to the politics and conditions of empire, and that the objects themselves, even if safely sealed in museum cases, retain their often violent colonial histories even now.[4] Today, there remains a continuing scholarly interest in material culture. Historians of Britain and historians of science alike have taken a 'practical turn', which has privileged the exchange and circulation of ethnographic and natural historical objects.[5] Moreover, an ever-growing number of authors in and beyond the history of science and exploration have treated objects as protagonists with their own varieties of agencies, histories and even subjectivities. In an early and influential essay, Arjun Appadurai perhaps put it best by arguing that 'commodities, like

---

3   Marcel Mauss, *The Gift: The Form and Reason for Exchange in Archaic Societies*, Ian Cunnison (trans), London, Cohen & West, 1966 (1924).
4   Nicholas Thomas, *Entangled Objects: Exchange, Material Culture, and Colonialism in the Pacific*, Cambridge, MA, Harvard University Press, 1991; CA Gregory, *Gifts and Commodities*, London, Academic Press, 1982; Annie Coombes, *Reinventing Africa: Museums, Material Culture, and Popular Imagination*, New Haven, Yale University Press, 1997.
5   Attention to objects in science studies was pioneered by Bruno Latour and proponents of 'Actor-Network Theory'; see, for example, Bruno Latour, *Science in Action: How to Follow Scientists and Engineers through Society* (Cambridge, MA, Harvard University Press, 1987); and Michel Callon, 'Some Elements of a Sociology of Translation: Domestication of the Scallops and the Fishermen of St Brieuc Bay', in John Law (ed), *Power, Action and Belief: A New Sociology of Knowledge?* (London, Routledge & Kegan Paul, 1986, pp 196–223). More recently, historians have become interested in the practical histories of scientific objects; see, for example, Jim Endersby, *Imperial Nature: Joseph Hooker and the Practices of Victorian Science* (Chicago, University of Chicago Press, 2010); Erika Rappaport, 'Imperial Possessions, Cultural Histories, and the Material Turn: Response' (*Victorian Studies*, vol 50, no 2, 2008, pp 289–96); Jennifer Sattaur, 'Thinking Objectively: An Overview of "Thing Theory" in Victorian Studies' (*Victorian Literature and Culture*, vol 40, no 1, 2012, pp 347–57); Lorraine Daston, *Biographies of Scientific Objects* (Chicago, University of Chicago Press, 2000); and Lorraine Daston, *Things That Talk: Object Lessons from Art and Science* (Cambridge, MA, Zone Books, 2007).

persons, have social lives'.[6] In the decades since, a range of authors both within and without a burgeoning school of 'thing theorists' have taken his edict to heart politically, analytically and narratively.[7]

This essay will build on that prolific scholarship by situating the story of intercultural exchange at a class of site that is still too often ignored in our historical narratives – a Pacific island that observers both past and present persistently deemed absolutely marginal to the main currents of empire, science and history.[8] The things assembled here will, however, prove theirs to have been an imperious oversight. An active attention to objects as agents in the history of cross-cultural encounter reveals that even post-mutiny Pitcairn Island, long described as perhaps the world's most isolated inhabited spot, was in fact connected to the wider world by an elaborate network of affectively charged trades and exchanges – as so many 'remote', 'marginal' and 'insular' spaces were. What's more, if we take up *Bounty* relics as our principal protagonists, we can not only learn something about how material things were used as a tool by people on the edges of empire and capitalism, but at the same time understand how their material culture aided in solidifying one of the most storied moments in Britain's history and culture.

---

6   Arjun Appadurai, 'Introduction: Commodities and the Politics of Value', in Arjun Appadurai (ed), *The Social Life of Things*, Cambridge, Cambridge University Press, 1986, p 3. For Appadurai, a commodity is literally 'any thing intended for exchange (1986, p 9).
7   See, for example, Jane Bennet's *Vibrant Matter: A Political Ecology of Things* (Durham, Duke University Press Books, 2010), which radically expanded Appadurai's attention to the politics of things; Bill Brown's famous essay 'Thing Theory' (*Critical Inquiry*, vol 28, no 1, 1 Oct 2001, pp 1–22); or even Neil MacGregor's popular *A History of the World in 100 Objects* (New York, Viking, 2011).
8   Some scholars have begun to write new histories of colonialism and intercultural exchange through objects and collections, including Maya Jasanoff's evocatively titled *Edge of Empire: Lives, Culture, and Conquest* (New York, Vintage Books, 2006). Nonetheless, both within and without the history of things colonial, sites beyond the categories of nation or empire are underserved in our historical narratives – as historians of the Pacific are uniquely aware. Greg Dening made a career out of evocative histories of so-called marginal islands and liminal beaches, see especially his *Islands and Beaches: Discourse on a Silent Land: Marquesas, 1774–1880* (Melbourne, Melbourne University Press, 1980). More recently, scholars building on the 'spatial turn', which was partially inaugurated by Dening himself, have written discursive histories of Pacific islands. See, for example, Beverley Haun, *Inventing 'Easter Island'* (Toronto, University of Toronto Press, 2008); Edward J Larson, *Evolution's Workshop: God and Science on the Galapagos Islands* (New York, Basic Books, 2002).

The *Bounty* chronometer as *Bounty* relic

All of the objects that will appear in this essay are, in one form or another, *Bounty* relics. I do not use the word 'relic' lightly. Indeed, it is not my term at all. In the catalogue of Britain's National Maritime Museum in Greenwich, several artefacts among its most prized possessions from the *Bounty* and Pitcairn Island are literally labelled 'RELIC'. Let us begin, then, by picking up and examining one such relic, while handling it with the cautious respect and deference owed to sacred artefacts. The object at hand is the *Bounty*'s chronometer, an antique timepiece small enough to fit in an open palm. It is roughly 10 centimetres across, a circle of polished brass framing a pearl-white face. Small black letters inscribe the name of its creator, Larcum Kendall, and its place of origin, London. Three dials grace its display; at one time they counted down seconds, minutes and hours, though the hands of all three lie motionless now. In those few years when sailors wound its spring and its hands still turned, however, it journeyed to and from the Pacific several times. It was through those movements and exchanges around the world and across the decades that its significance shifted – and a valuable navigational instrument transformed into a priceless relic.

The chronometer sits in leisurely retirement not far from the place it began its peripatetic life in 1771. Produced along the lines of clockmaker John Harrison's famous seawatch, the H4 (1761), it was among the first devices of its kind. Chronometers were a revolutionary technology in the 18th century; by keeping extraordinarily accurate time at sea, they solved the famous 'longitude problem'. Navigators had long used the stars to track ships' positions precisely as they sailed north and south, but tracking positions east to west was considerably more difficult (see Teriierooiterai, Chapter 1). An unvarying clock allowed a navigator to know the time at a given reference point that, when compared to the apparent local time, would indicate the longitudinal distance a ship had travelled. Most contemporary clocks were useless for that task because ships pitched and yawed with the waves, and the rolling sea interfered with a pendulum's swing. The chronometer eliminated this problem altogether by relying on a wheel and spring for regulation. Small enough to fit in a pocket and reliable even in the most raucous seas, the new instruments revolutionised maritime navigation.

Accordingly, early chronometers were extraordinarily rare and valuable instruments. Discounting the *Bounty* itself, Kendall's timepiece was by a wide margin the most expensive item entrusted to William Bligh when he set out for Tahiti in 1787. The Admiralty purchased Kendall's chronometer for a princely £200; for comparison, the *Bounty* itself cost £1,820. The timepiece had already guided James Cook's expedition to the Pacific and back and now it would guide the voyage of his former sailing master. Setting sail, it rounded the Cape, crossed the Indian Ocean, and lingered with the crew in Matavai Bay for five months. During the mutiny, though Bligh was given some navigation instruments to aid him and his loyal crew when they were abandoned on the ship's launch, the chronometer was too valuable and remained on board. Fletcher Christian used it to plot his path across the Pacific, and it remained in his hands through the mutineers' violent experiment in colonisation at Tubua'i.[9]

After abandoning that settlement, the chronometer aided Christian in his journey to Pitcairn – though it also caused the mutineers some consternation. During his exploration of the Pacific 20 years before, without the aid of chronometer, Philip Carteret rediscovered but inaccurately charted the longitude of Pitcairn Island. Christian chose Pitcairn as the mutineers' destination after reading Carteret's account, and he was despondent on finding only empty ocean at Carteret's coordinates. Chronometer in hand, he and his crew tacked eastward along Pitcairn's recorded latitude for another 300 kilometres until they at last saw a green-shrouded rock rise from the horizon.[10] After the mutineers landed on uninhabited Pitcairn, they set fire to the *Bounty* in the shallow waters of what would come to be called Bounty Bay – but not before taking from the ship what useful items they could, including its chronometer. The timepiece remained on Pitcairn for another three decades. Precisely who, if anyone, possessed it during that period remains uncertain. However, after a series of murders and reprisals left Christian,

---

9   There are dozens of accounts of the mutineers' journey but, for a meticulously empirical account, see Henry E Maude, 'In Search of a Home: From the Mutiny to Pitcairn Island (1789–1790)' (*Journal of the Polynesian Society*, vol 67, no 2, Jun 1958, pp 104–31). For more general accounts of the mutiny, see Sylvie Largeaud-Ortega's Introduction to this volume.
10   It is speculated that Carteret's erroneous record of Pitcairn's longitude and Christian's chronometrically informed rediscovery contributed to the mutineers' decision to settle the island, as it was thus less likely to be visited by other ships.

his co-conspirators and their male Tahitian captives dead, the timepiece eventually came into the possession of John Adams, the settlement's last surviving mutineer.[11]

The chronometer remained in Adams' hands until 1808, when Pitcairn Island's post-mutiny settlement was rediscovered by the American sealers of the *Topaz* and their captain, Mayhew Folger. Both the Pitcairn Islanders' first interaction with strangers and the chronometer's place in it are worth recounting in some detail, as their political and material parameters set the template for generations of exchanges to come. It was a fraught and dramatic moment, with both sides unsure of each other. Would these sailors take away the last surviving member of the *Bounty* crew to be judged and hanged? Would this lost community of law-breakers afford the Yankees a safe landing, or would they kill to keep their haven secret? On what terms would the outside world come to understand this insular place?

After some negotiation, the Pitcairners boarded the *Topaz* and the Americans in turn toured the island. In their narratives of the visit, the *Topaz*'s sailors described a peaceful community devoted to Adams, whom they recorded was a benevolent patriarch held in high esteem by the Islanders, most of whom were the children of Adams' crewmates and their Tahitian wives.[12] Adams answered the Americans' questions about the mutiny, by then already slipping into legend as one of the most famous episodes in naval history. Taken by the old mutineer's account and the island's now peaceful existence, Folger and his crew gave the Pitcairners what provisions they could spare. In return, Adams handed Folger the most valuable item he owned, the *Bounty*'s chronometer. In recognition of the extraordinary gift, Folger reciprocated with the more personal gift of a silk handkerchief. The timepiece, originally a valuable instrument of navigation, became instead an emotionally laden symbol of friendship. As such, it set the template for future interactions, in which the Pitcairners traded not only their stories of the mutiny but also their material supply of *Bounty* artefacts to earn their visitors' benevolence and benefaction.

---

11   For an account of Pitcairn's early history, see Trevor Lummis, *Pitcairn Island: Life and Death in Eden* (Brookfield, VT, Ashgate, 1997).
12   It is a frequently retold encounter but was first popularised in Amasa Delano, *Narrative of Voyages and Travels in the Northern and Southern Hemispheres: Comprising Three Voyages Round the World; Together with a Voyage of Survey and Discovery, in the Pacific Ocean and Oriental Islands* (Boston, EG House, 1817).

For Folger, the chronometer served not only as a sentimental souvenir but as a means to authenticate his discovery of the *Bounty*'s fate upon his return home. Folger's account of his encounter was incredible – the chronometer materially substantiated his credibility. In that sense, too, the chronometer set the mould for many *Bounty* relics to come; more than mere keepsakes, these souvenirs linked their owners to a distant place and served as material evidence of a story that so often seemed to occupy a more fictive register.

On Folger's return journey across the Pacific, both he and the timepiece were captured by the Spanish Navy, and the chronometer was confiscated by an enemy officer. Thus, the chronometer left his possession almost as quickly as it had entered it. During the following decades, its ownership and exchange are uncertain and unrecorded, though a British naval captain noted that it was sold in Valparaiso for three doubloons to a Spaniard named Castillo, whose family in turn sold it for 50 guineas to British naval captain Sir Thomas Herbert in 1840.[13] Herbert had the timepiece rated and it served, for the last time in its career, as a navigation aid during his voyage through the Pacific, ticking evenly alongside its more modern counterparts. At some point during that return voyage, its owner wound its spring for the last time. Once back in Britain in 1843, the chronometer joined a collection of *Bounty* and Pitcairn relics assembled by RA Newman of the *Sparrowhawk* for donation to the Royal United Services Institution (RUSI), where it went on display in a museum gallery.

But first, Newman inscribed the timepiece's peripatetic history into the metal on its obverse side:

> This timekeeper belonged to Captain James Cook RN and was taken by him to the Pacific in 1776. It was again taken to the Pacific by Captain Bligh in the *Bounty* in 1787. It was taken by the Mutineers to Pitcairn Island and was sold in 1808 by Adams to a citizen of the United States who sold it in Chile where it was purchased by Sir Thomas Herbert.

At this point, the chronometer's functionality as a navigational instrument was long superseded. Over the period of a century, the chronometer accrued successive sets of owners and significations; if it began its life as a valuable instrument of navigation and imperial ambition, it went on display half a century later as a souvenir of a distant place and as a relic

---

13   RA Newman, 'Note on the *Bounty* chronometer addressed to Sir John Barrow', *The Nautical Magazine*, 1840.

of imperial history, the antique vestige of a mutiny now safely returned to its rightful place at the imperial metropole, there carefully catalogued and contained in a glass display. The chronometer moved for the last time during the 1960s, when it and many of the RUSI's collections headed down the Thames to the National Maritime Museum. It remains prominently exhibited in the museum's 'Voyagers: Britons and the Sea gallery', silently taking measure of the distance between museum-goers and an ever more removed past.

Relics and reliquaries from a 'Victorian Eden'

The chronometer is not alone; nearby in Greenwich are other objects that speak to the evolution of Pitcairn Islanders' relationship with their visitors and to the outside world's image of the mutiny that produced their settlement. These objects are not always literally inscribed by their collectors, as the chronometer was, but they are nonetheless indelibly, if invisibly, marked by their service as signifiers of a distant time and place.[14] From these roving, representative objects, we can learn how their makers and collectors alike built historical memory of the *Bounty* and Pitcairn over time. Let us take, for example, Relic numbers 2 and 3 in the National Maritime Museum's catalogue, both of which sit on permanent display in the 'Voyagers' gallery alongside the *Bounty* chronometer. Relic number 2 (REL0002) is John Adams' gravestone.[15] REL0003 is a small, braided lock of Adams' hair mounted inside an ornate gold oval frame.[16] Why and how did these two objects, taken from the grave of a long-dead man on the other side of the world, become cherished relics in the imperial metropole?

To understand, we must read these material things themselves against both their Victorian context and the mutiny's shifting place in the Anglophone imagination. The resemblance of both objects to religious relics and their containers to reliquaries is not entirely incidental; both the lock of hair in its golden frame and the marker from Adams' tomb in its glass case testify to the religion-infused interest the Anglophone world

---

14   Walter Benjamin called the ineffable and original context of a work's production its 'aura', now a term of art in object studies: 'L'œuvre d'art à l'époque de sa reproduction méchanisée' (*Zeitschrift für Sozialforschung,* Jahrgang 5, 1936, pp 40–68).
15   Collections of the National Maritime Museum, Greenwich, United Kindom (NMM), REL0002.
16   'Pigtail', NMM/REL0003.

came to hold in Pitcairn. Though a number of Pitcairn Islander identities have come and gone, to the Victorians they were most commonly legible as the residents of a Protestant utopia, a 'veritable Eden' on Earth.[17] Early visitors to the island happily reported Adams' redemptive turn and credited the ageing ex-mutineer with the conversion of the settlement into what they described as a Christian paradise. 'They now form a happy and well-regulated society,' wrote British naval captain William Beechey after his 1825 visit in the *Blossom*, 'the merit of which in a great degree belongs to Adams, and tends to redeem the former errors of his life'.[18] The rehabilitated mutineer was, for his part, unsubtle in performing his religiosity before his guests. During Beechey's visit, he purportedly led a church service during which the same sermon was delivered three times 'lest any part of it should be forgotten or escape attention'.[19] The Islanders were orthodox in adhering to the practice of saying grace before every meal with their visitors, and proudly averred to all their guests that they never broke a vow.[20] Just as crucially, during trades with passing ships, the Islanders always asked for religious texts in addition to more practical supplies.

Beechey became the first of many visiting Royal Navy captains to promote the charitable donation of supplies to Pitcairn. In his expedition account, he made several notes of the island's lack of manufactured goods. When the Pitcairners came aboard his ship for the first time, the captain recorded their amazement at its size and provisions. The sailors were 'so rich', they told him.[21] Beechey solicited donations from his crew for the Islanders and subsequent ships' calls brought considerable charity. In 1841, for instance, the HMS *Curacoa* gave, among other sundries, 25 muskets, 25 bayonets, 20 swords, 150 fish hooks, adzes, spades, hammers, a small medicine chest, 59 religious tracts, a church prayer book, a mathematical textbook, a New Testament, a selection of hymns, publications of the American

---

17   I have lifted this particular phrase from the minor Rolf Boldrewood novel *A Modern Buccaneer* (London, MacMillan, 1894), in which the hero is seduced both by Norfolk Island and by one of its women. But the motif of Eden is rampant in the literature surrounding Pitcairn and Norfolk; Harry Shapiro was the first scholar to identify the island's 19th-century conception as a 'Victorian Eden' in a well-sourced chapter of *The Heritage of the Bounty: The Story of Pitcairn through Six Generations* (New York, Simon & Schuster, 1936).
18   Frederick W Beechey, *Narrative of a Voyage to the Pacific and Beering's Strait*, London, Colburn & Bentley, 1831, p 114.
19   Beechey, 1831, pp 121–22.
20   Beechey, 1831, p 102.
21   Beechey, 1831, p 97.

tract society, and a collection of sermons for the aged.[22] In return, naval visitors received not only stores of fresh fruit and vegetables but an array of historical relics. The shallowly submerged wreck of the *Bounty* served as a source of physical tokens of the island's famous past. Fragments of mouldering wood from the ship's hull, originally useless to the Islanders, now served as readymade curios.[23] Across the 19th century, an increasing number of sailors returned home with souvenirs from Pitcairn; like the chronometer, fragments of the *Bounty* and locks of John Adams' hair served as tangible reminders of personal contact with both the storied ship and the Islanders who survived as the mutiny's living legacy in the Pacific.

The same sailors penned accounts of life on Pitcairn, which circulated widely in the Anglophone world.[24] From them, readers received a narrative of the mutiny and settlement that was no longer framed as one of disobedience but rather of loyalty; not of violation, but of redemption. The settlement might have begun as a mutinous outpost but, thanks to its beloved patriarch, it now proudly flew the Union flag and held Anglican services. Sir John Barrow, a leading figure in the British Admiralty and a dominant force in Pacific colonisation, borrowed from the texts of his sailors and explorers, particularly those of Beechey, to pen his own history of the mutiny and Pitcairn. In it he wrote sympathetically of Adams:

> What is most of all extraordinary, the very man, from whom they have received their moral and religious instruction, is one who was among the first and foremost in the mutiny, and deeply implicated in all the deplorable consequences that were the results of it.[25]

Other authors in turn borrowed from Barrow's history to retell the patriarch's story in their own popular and religious tracts.[26] The image of a small, celebrated colony pursuing a morally and religiously exemplary

---

22 'August 18, 1841', Pitcairn Island Register, NMM/REC/61.
23 The *Bounty* hull was originally encased in copper plating, which was both sentimentally and materially valuable, but the Islanders sold most of it in 1831 to secure their passage back to Pitcairn after a failed resettlement attempt on Tahiti.
24 In addition to Beechey's, widely cited early accounts include: Delano (1817) and John A Shillibeer, *A Narrative of the Briton's Voyage, to Pitcairn's Island* (London, Law & Whittaker, 1817).
25 It was in fact Barrow who dispatched Beechey to the island; see John Barrow, *The Eventful History of the Mutiny and Piratical Seizure of HMS Bounty, Its Causes and Consequences* (London, J Murray, 1831, pp 169–70).
26 See, *The Converted Mutineer and His Bible Class: Or, John Adams and the Children of the Mutineers* (Boston, Massachusetts Sabbath School Society, 1855); TB Murray, *The Home of the Mutineers* (Philadelphia, American Sunday-school Union, 1854); *The Transformed Island: A Story of the South Seas* (Philadelphia, Presbyterian Board of Publication, 1854); translated into other languages for mission work, North India Tract Society, *Piṭkairn ṭāpū ke logoṇ ke bayān meṇ* (Mirzapore, 1866).

life served as a useful and bucolic counterpoint for ministers and moralisers anxious over an era of rapid industrialisation and a supposed 'crisis of faith'.[27] Nathan Welby Fiske, a minister and professor at Dartmouth, wrote a biography of Adams that was meant to serve as an object lesson to young readers; it even included an imagined dialogue between a mother and her children highlighting the more morally exemplary moments in Adams' life.[28] Some writers went so far as to transpose Adams' biography into an explicitly hagiographic register, positing his redemptive turn as the product of divine intervention. Anglican clergyman Thomas Boyles Murray, in his popular *Pitcairn: The Island, the People, and the Pastor* (1854), reported two of Adams' dreams as he underwent his conversion to Anglicanism. In one vision, a horrible being appeared and threatened to stab him with a dart. In another, he saw the future hellscape to which he, as a sinner, was surely doomed. Murray offered these two visions as the work of the Holy Spirit, 'whose merciful design it was to give [Adams] a better knowledge of himself, and a sense of the justice and goodness of God, and to bring him, an humble suppliant, to the throne of grace'.[29] It was a road-to-Damascus moment befitting a secular saint.

Adams died in 1829. The archive does not record who took a lock of his hair or precisely when – indeed, we must take it on faith that the hair is his at all. It was during a visit, however, which was partly promoted by Reverend Murray, that the lock left Pitcairn. Murray, alongside other Anglican clergy, naval officers and lay admirers, set up the Pitcairn Island Fund Committee, headquartered in London. They managed donations to the island, advertised its religious success and worked to ordain the island's then spiritual leader, George Nobbs, as an Anglican pastor. When Nobbs came to London in 1852 to receive his ordination, the Royal Navy deposited ship's chaplain WH Holman as his temporary replacement. Holman lived among the Islanders for a year and, before he left, the Islanders gave him the *Bounty*'s *Book of Common Prayer* and Adams' ponytail. The prayer book was a potent symbol of Pitcairn's morally

---

27   The extent to which a crisis of faith pervaded Victorian culture remains debated, but it was certainly a focus of period discourse; see Richard J Helmstadter & Bernard Lightment (eds), *Victorian Faith in Crisis: Essays on Continuity and Change in Nineteenth-Century Religious Belief* (Stanford, Stanford University Press, 1990); David Nash, 'Reassessing the "Crisis of Faith" in the Victorian Age: Eclecticism and the Spirit of Moral Inquiry' (*Journal of Victorian Culture*, vol 16, no 1, 1 April 2011, pp 65–82).
28   Nathan Welby Fiske, *Aleck: The Last of the Mutineers, or the History of Pitcairn's Island*, 3rd edn, Philadelphia, EC Biddle, 1845, pp 133–38.
29   Thomas Boyles Murray, *Pitcairn: The Island, the People, and the Pastor*, London, Society for Promoting Christian Knowledge, 1854, p 112.

infused history and religious identity and a powerful gift. As the personal relic of the island's most revered founder, the lock of hair, too, was an emotionally charged present. In Victorian society, hair was a celebrated mode of memorialisation and remembrance as a tangible connection with the departed. In the case of more famous figures, personal relics built on that tradition of personal memorialisation by positioning corporeal fragments like hair as didactically charged reminders of sanctified lives or sacred pasts.[30]

No archive records when, exactly, Adams' gravestone left Pitcairn, but it is likely that a sailor on the *Portland* took it during the same visit that either deposited or retrieved Holman.

After they arrived in London with chaplain Holman, Adams' relics went on display at the Royal United Services Institution, where they remained for a century. In their new context, Adams' artefacts made clear the *Bounty* mutineers' rehabilitation in the British national mythos. The *Bounty*'s *Book of Common Prayer* was reunited with the *Bounty* chronometer in a display of cherished national artefacts. Adams' ponytail, now ensconced in a gilded case, sat in the same museum as a lock of Lord Nelson's hair. Adams' gravestone sat in the same gallery as the *Victory*'s flag. The last mutineer's religious, corporeal and funerary relics were now the vital keepsakes of British national memory, artefacts of a celebrated moment in imperial history. Adams' Anglican turn rendered Pitcairn a site synonymous not only with treason but also, ironically, with loyalty. One 19th-century visitor, surveying the *Bounty* relics alongside the RUSI's other collections, wrote that the museum was 'well calculated to render the patriotic Briton proud of his country' – a remarkable achievement for the relics of a man whose co-conspirators were hanged for treason.[31] Today, the relics continue to serve a similar narrative purpose, housed alongside other patriotic relics in the heart of the National Maritime Museum.

---

30   Deborah Lutz, 'The Dead Still Among Us: Victorian Secular Relics, Hair Jewelry, and Death Culture', *Victorian Literature and Culture*, vol 39, no 1, Mar 2011, pp 127–42; Christiane Holm, 'Sentimental Cuts: Eighteenth-Century Mourning Jewelry with Hair', *Eighteenth-Century Studies*, vol 38, no 1, 2004, pp 139–43; Daisy Hay, 'Hair in the Disraeli Papers: A Victorian Harvest', *Journal of Victorian Culture*, vol 19, no 3, 3 July 2014, pp 332–45; Adriana Craciun, 'The Franklin Relics in the Arctic Archive', *Victorian Literature and Culture*, vol 42, no 1 Mar 2014, pp 1–31.
31   *The Collector*, vol 6, no 15, 1 June 1895, p 249; also published as 'Relics of the Past in London', *The Nation*, vol 60, no 1558, 9 May 1895, pp 357–58.

Adams' hair, prayer book and gravestone are only a small sample of the thousands of relics to travel the globe in the possession of sailors. Relics, like souvenirs, cut across geographic and temporal boundaries; though removed from their original sites and contexts, they nonetheless transcended time and space to connect their collectors and viewers with the places they remember or imagined.[32] As such, they served as distant ambassadors for Pitcairn, drawing the attentions of those who held them toward the distant island and the mutiny that founded it. That interest persisted multi-generationally. As heirlooms, *Bounty* relics were handed down through families and guarded as special treasures. In 1853, the HMS *Virago*'s surgeon obtained a small box supposedly made from the wood of John Adams' bed stand and metal from the *Bounty*. It stayed in his family for the rest of the century; in 1902, the surgeon's son could boast in London's *Daily Mail* that the family had preserved a relic given to them by that interesting island so long ago.[33] In 1837, a sailor aboard the HMS *Actæon* purchased the *Bounty*'s copy of William Buchan's *Domestic Medicine*. Fifty years later, his son placed the book in a gilded outer binding, along with a signed note from his father that testified that the 'book was in the possession of Fletcher Christian one of the mutineers until the time of his death'.[34] New meanings and inscriptions accreted on these objects as they changed hands and were passed down through generations, evolving from utilitarian things to affect-laden historical relics. But these objects also literally accrued new inscriptions and framings – a golden binding, a note of provenance, a list of owners and ancillary archives of their own.

Pitcairn's moral economy

What of the people who first produced and gifted Victorian *Bounty* relics, the Pitcairn Islanders themselves? Most textual accounts of the island's early history were written by strangers and are squarely written from an outsider's perspective. The archive of Pitcairn's earliest local texts is small;

---

32 The materiality of souvenirs is a growing locus of tourism research; see Nigel Morgan & Annette Pritchard, 'On Souvenirs and Metonymy Narratives of Memory, Metaphor and Materiality' (*Tourist Studies*, vol 5, no 1, 1 Apr 2005, pp 29–53); Michael Hitchcock & Ken Teague, *Souvenirs: The Material Culture of Tourism* (Aldershot, Ashgate, 2000); Kristen Swanson & Dallen J Timothy, 'Souvenirs: Icons of Meaning, Commercialization and Commoditization' (*Tourism Management*, vol 33, no 3, June 2012, pp 489–99).
33 Letter from William Ross, 4 Aug 1902, NMM/BGY/R/2/3.
34 William Buchan, *Domestic Medicine: Or, A Treatise on the Prevention and Cure of Diseases by Simple Medicines* (London, W Strahan & T Cadell, 1774), in the collection of the Caird Library, National Maritime Museum, 613.094 BUC.

one of the island's only early autochthonous records is its Register Book – a volume of births, deaths, marriages, weather and ships' visits. Like many of Pitcairn's early relics, the first register is no longer on the island. It left Pitcairn with its owner, Pastor Nobbs, during his journey to London in 1852, but was damaged by sea spray during a rough transfer by boat from the island to the *Portland*. Forced to start a new volume, Nobbs gave the old, saltwater-soaked book to Reverend Murray, who used it in writing his history of the island.[35]

Not only was the book a material gift, but its entries spoke to the motivations and concerns that framed Pitcairn's early exchanges with outsiders. The volume consisted mostly of notations of births, marriages and deaths. It also contained, however, a long record of ships and captains who visited Pitcairn, and many of those entries were signed by the visiting captains themselves, often with a flourish and a personal note. Each one was the record of an encounter between Pitcairn Island and an outside crew. From them, the Islanders could learn what mattered most to their guests; by the same token, we can learn from them something of the motivations that informed the island's exchanges. In 1852, Captain George Mathersby signed his name to the register and wrote:

> having spent two days ashore on this most interesting Island I cannot but express the pleasure it has afforded myself as well as all the officers of the *Daedelus* to have visited it. I have never before had the privilege of witnessing such an example of piety with every Christian virtue attached to it.[36]

The Islanders also recorded their own experiences in the Register and many listed the material goods that they received from passing vessels. The register's account of the 1852 visit by the *Portland*'s crew concludes, 'It is beyond our powers sufficiently to thank them. Among the many useful articles they left us, [*sic*] is a bull and a cow for which we have long wished'.[37] Describing the HMS *Sparrowhawk*'s 1839 visit, the Register records, 'In the afternoon the children of the school were examined and received the approbation of our respected visitors; Captain Stephens afterward divided a valuable present among the inhabitants'.[38]

---

35 That copy of the register is in the archives of the National Maritime Museum's Caird Library, where it is still accruing and building the interest of those who read it. 'July, 1854', Pitcairn Island Register, NMM/REC/61.
36 Captain Mathersby, 'Jan 29, 1852', Pitcairn Island Register, NMM/REC/61.
37 'August 11, 1852', Pitcairn Island Register, NMM/REC/61.
38 'November 8, 1839', Pitcairn Island Register, NMM/REC/61.

For Pitcairn, each exchange with outsiders was a profound opportunity; ships presented a magnificent and unrivalled bounty of material goods for the small island. But each visit was also a judgement. Had the Islanders lived up to their moral reputation? Were they as 'simple' and 'pious' as described?

Some visitors, aware of the dynamic at hand, fretted over the possibility of artifice in the Islanders' interactions with outsiders. In 1841, the medical officer on the *Curacoa* reported that the Pitcairners were 'anxious to conceal the facts' of their private disagreements: 'believing that it was only the character of their being a virtuous and innocent family which made the English Government, as well as the English people, take such an interest in their welfare and happenings'.[39] Holman certainly left the Islanders with that impression. A sailor on the *Portland* recorded one of his sermons to the Islanders: the chaplain reminded his congregants 'that the good conduct of the Islanders had made them respected' to the outside world.[40] The gifts of Adams' prayer book and ponytail served as material assurances that the island, far from tainted by its founding as a mutineer's hideaway, remained a redeemed, patriotic and Protestant utopia. Inside its gilded reliquary and locked in a glass museum display, they continued to do much the same in London a century later.

Pitcairn Islanders and their bodies as relics

Though many *Bounty* relics came from the wreck of the ship itself, original *Bounty* relics did not constitute an unlimited resource. In their place, it was not uncommon for the Islanders' bodies to produce the sentimental objects necessary for trade.[41] The Islanders were, after all, often conceived of by their visitors as the living relics of the mutiny. Pitcairners' hair was an especially common token of affection; Adams' ponytail was not the only lock from Pitcairn brought to Britain. In 1855,

---

39   William Gunn, Medical Journal of the HMS Curacoa (1841), The National Archives, London (NA), ADM/101/95/4A.
40   As quoted from personal correspondence in Diana Belcher's *The Mutineers of the Bounty and their Descendants in Pitcairn and Norfolk Islands* (New York, Harper Brothers, 1871, p 221). Belcher was a descendant of Beechey.
41   The metonymic power of capitalism to reify social relations and reduce people to objects or to allow objects to stand in for people was described early and famously by Karl Marx and later analysed in depth by Georg Lukács; see, Karl Marx, *Capital*, vol 1, especially 'Section 4: The Fetishism of Commodities and the Secret Thereof' (1867), and Georg Lukács, 'Reification and the Consciousness of the Proletariat', in *History and Class Consciousness* (1923).

George Nobbs wrote in his diary that 'the mania for making presents [is] still raging and the cutting off locks of hair is practiced on every head, to be woven in bracelets'.[42] Most of these went to visiting sailors. Captain James Wood, who called in 1849 on the *Pandora*, wrote that many of his crew 'contrived to establish flirtations, which, though short enough, brought long faces and wet eyes at parting, and many were the locks of hair, etc., which changed owners'.[43] Hair was, however, subject to fluid meanings and interpretations. George Inskip, a sailor on HMS *Comet* in 1831, asked the island's women if he could take cuttings of their hair. They sat down in a row and let the sailor work through their tresses with scissors. If the women thought this act was a token of romantic affection, they were not necessarily wrong, but were certainly only half right. Inskip kept the locks for decades afterward, remarking on how they 'show the contrast between the colour of the Tahitian and that of the mixed English breed'.[44] His was only the beginning of a long interest in the Islanders' bodies not only as historically or affectively laden symbols, but as signs of racial mixture and difference.

During the latter half of the 19th century, perceptions of the island and its uses as an exemplary space began to shift. Missionaries and sailors still penned glowing accounts of the island's pious morality, but another set of outsiders began to imagine Pitcairn and its people as a different kind of object lesson. Scientists and intellectuals, having read the morally infused literature on the island, came to regard its isolated population as ripe for anthropological and eugenic research. In 1856, the population of Pitcairn was removed to Norfolk Island, a former prison colony thousands of miles away. In the British parliament and in the press, the move was referred to as 'The Experiment'. Would the mutineers' descendants replicate their past success, they wondered, and turn another Pacific hell into a second pacific Eden? Though the terms of that experiment were originally framed as moral and religious, British intellectuals soon imbued it with scientific potential. Naturalist Alfred Russel Wallace wrote that the island remained 'of the highest social and political interest', as 'it is so rarely that social problems can be subjected to anything like a critical experiment'.[45] Much of Britain's scientific attention stemmed from the island's mixed Polynesian

---

42 George Nobbs, 'Tuesday, January 3rd', Register and Memorandum, Norfolk Island, 1861, transcription of microfilm copy held in the Mitchell Library, State Library of NSW, FM4/7365.
43 James Wood, 'Pitcairn Island in 1849', letter reproduced in Belcher, 1871, p 212.
44 George Hastings Inskip, 'Pitcairn's Island', NMM/MSS 76104.3, 87. Inskip's account, which in places plagiarised from that prepared by Thomas Boyles Murray, was written years after his visit.
45 Alfred Russell Wallace, 'The Mutineers of the *Bounty*, and their Descendants in Pitcairn and Norfolk Islands, by Lady Belcher', *The Academy*, 1 Feb 1871, p 108.

and British heritage and supposed isolation, which allowed them to serve as a 'natural laboratory' in anthropological debates about race mixture. Charles Darwin and members of the Ethnological Society of London, for instance, pointed to the Pitcairners' reproductive success in order to dispel the idea that mixed-race societies tended toward degeneration and infecundity, while at the same time a nascent eugenic school wondered over the Islanders' vitality and intelligence.[46]

Most discussions of Pitcairn in the scientific and popular press remained abstract theorisations built on the basis of travel accounts. Accordingly, on those rare occasions when Pitcairn Islanders visited Britain, they found themselves to be objects of fascination. When Russell McCoy visited London in 1881, his stay prompted considerable attention from the public and the press, a response that was due in no small part to the work of enterprising stage managers at the Royal Aquarium in Westminster who contrived to put him on display. The Aquarium was an all-purpose venue, home to stage plays, music and all manner of carnivalesque performances – including the exhibition of people from other parts of the world.[47] In the case of McCoy, visitors were invited, for a small fee, to meet this 'veritable Pitcairn Islander'. An English-speaking Christian, he proved a difficult figure to exoticise. Newspapers seemed to recognise the ironic disconnect between romantic Pacific image and quotidian embodied reality. 'There will be nothing but friendly welcome for this English South Seas Islander, who comes guarded by the not ineffective talisman of his wife's wedding ring,' declared one.[48] What did he think of London's modern wonders? 'His astonishment at beholding the steam-engines and railway carriages was very great,' reported another newspaper. 'He was very deeply impressed.'[49] McCoy spent an afternoon on display before a sympathetic Anglican clergyman rescued him from the ignominy and shuffled him offstage.[50]

---

46 John Crawfurd, 'On the Supposed Infecundity of Human Hybrids or Crosses', *Transactions of the Ethnological Society of London*, vol 3 1 Jan 1865, pp 356–62; Charles Darwin, *The Descent of Man and Sexual Selection in Relation to Sex*, 1871, p 154; FW Farrah, 'On Hybridity', *Journal of the Anthropological Society*, 5 April 1864, pp 222–27.
47 'Ethnographic' exhibitions of people were commonplace entertainments in *fin-de-siècle* Europe and America; see Sadiah Qureshi, *Peoples on Parade* (Chicago, University of Chicago Press, 2011); Roslyn Poignant, *Professional Savages: Captive Lives and Western Spectacle* (New Haven, Yale University Press, 2004).
48 'A Pitcairn in London', *Launceston Examiner*, 7 July 1881, p 3.
49 'Pitcairn Island', *Penny Illustrated Paper & Illustrated Times* (London), no 1034, 7 May 1881, p 300.
50 The story was retold in Rosalind Amelia Young, *Mutiny of the Bounty and Story of Pitcairn Island, 1790–1894* (Mountain View, California, Pacific Press, 1894, p 219).

In the hands of anthropological science, however, the reification of Pitcairn Islanders into objects of fascination was far more totalising.[51] Archaeologist Karen Routledge concluded her work on Rapa Nui/Easter Island in 1917 (see Molle & Hermann, Chapter 2) and, during her voyage home, she called on Pitcairn and collected two Islanders, the brothers Charles and Edwin Young, offering to take them to Britain.[52] Upon the expedition's arrival in Europe, Routledge deposited the Young brothers, along with the skeletal material she had excavated on Rapa Nui, at the Royal College of Surgeons' Hunterian Museum, an anatomical repository that remains the last resting place of thousands of human remains from around the world. There, they underwent an examination by Arthur Keith, the museum curator and one of the world's leading experts in physical anthropology and the science of race.[53] Keith recognised the rare opportunity presented by the arrival of the Youngs. These Islanders and their bodies were, to him, the relics not only of mutiny but of a century-old act of miscegenation, and thus scientifically valuable. Keith examined their bodies and skulls with calipers, taking over 30 measurements of each.

Their brains, Keith decided, were smaller than those of Europeans. The anatomist also carefully measured the hue of their skin and noted 'Polynesian' and 'European' qualities in each brother's morphology. These data were read against the skeletonised body of a Tahitian man who died in London in 1816, in order to determine the results of six generations of 'racial admixture'.[54] Keith pronounced that, while the brothers were physically healthy, they were, in racial terms, mentally deficient. Corporeal interest in the Islanders remade the Pitcairners' bodies into a new kind of *Bounty* relic. They had long served as markers of Englishness persisting unexpectedly in the remote Pacific. While earlier accounts emphasised their affinity with Britain, or at least a religious and romantic ideal of Britishness, later accounts emphasised, in racial and scientific terms, the Islanders' bodily differences. Rather than symbols of purity, the Islanders

---

51   Concomitant with the era's physical anthropology; see, Andrew Zimmerman, *Anthropology and Antihumanism in Imperial Germany* (Chicago, University of Chicago Press, 2001).
52   Katherine Pease Routledge, *The Mystery of Easter Island: The Story of an Expedition* (London, Hazell, Watson and Viney, 1919); see also her biography by JoAnne Van Tilburg, *Among Stone Giants: The Life of Katherine Routledge and Her Remarkable Expedition to Easter Island* (New York, Simon and Schuster, 2003). For more on archaeology, see Molle & Hermann, Chapter 2.
53   Katherine Routledge, letter to Arthur Keith, 29 Aug 1916, Keith Papers, Archives of the Royal College of Surgeons, MS0018/2/1/11/5.
54   Arthur Keith, 'The Physical Characteristics of Two Pitcairn Islanders', *Man*, vol 17, Aug 1917, p 121–31.

were now construed as anything but that, a hybrid people cast by a famous historical act not into paradise but rather into the interstices between racial categories. Routledge and Keith remade their skulls into relics of the *Bounty* crew's acts of 'racial admixture'.

Pitcairn Islanders remained the objects of scientific scrutiny for decades to come. The American anthropologist Harry Shapiro visited Norfolk Island in 1923 and Pitcairn Island in 1934 in order to take anthropometric measurements of the island's entire population.[55] His *Bounty* relics sit in the repository of the American Museum of Natural History, only a few shelves away from the pressed rose that fell from the envelope described in the opening pages of this essay. Shapiro's relics take the form of large, ruled sheets cataloguing every Islander's age, and eye and hair colour, alongside the width, length and height of their skulls. Most crucially, he recorded each Islander's genealogy, tracing each living Pitcairner's lineage back to the mutiny that begat their isolation and made them of scientific interest.[56] Shapiro also took hundreds of black-and-white photographs, a pair for nearly every Pitcairn Islander alive when he visited in 1934. In each set of portraits, a posed figure stares first straight ahead and then glances to the side in profile. These photographs were not mere keepsakes, but rather a scientific record meant to serve as a standardised archive of the Islanders' bodies. Shapiro's work among the Islanders was, in a mode consistent with the period's physical anthropology, in turns deeply intimate and detached. He spent hours touching and recording their bodies, only to convert them to quantifiable data. His field notes suggest an amicable but emotionally distant relationship between scientist and subject. Nonetheless, he left the island with a small, wooden shard of the *Bounty*'s rudder that he framed once back in New York.[57]

Ultimately, Shapiro used Pitcairner's bodies as evidence to intervene in the period's debates surrounding race and eugenics. He reported that anthropometry revealed them to be robust and healthy, overturning Keith's assessment and disproving the notions that either miscegenation

---

55   Harry L Shapiro, *Descendants of the Mutineers of the Bounty*, Memoirs of the Bernice P Bishop Museum, vol 1112, Honolulu, The Bishop Museum, 1929; and Harry L Shapiro, *The Heritage of the Bounty: The Story of Pitcairn through Six Generations*, New York, Simon & Schuster, 1936; Warwick Anderson, 'Hybridity, Race, and Science: The Voyage of the Zaca, 1934–1935', *Isis*, vol 103, no 2, 1 June 2012, pp 229–53.
56   Papers of Harry Lionel Shapiro, American Museum of Natural History, New York (AMNH), Boxes 33 & 35.
57   'Artifacts', Shapiro Papers, AMNH/Box F.

or Pitcairn's degree of inbreeding were biologically deleterious. His work became a key component of inter-war Anglophone race science and was cited in refutations of Nazi propaganda.[58] Shapiro, however, was not the last visitor to refashion the Islanders' bodies into objects of evidence. Indeed, the notion that the Islanders and their bodies are themselves *Bounty* relics persists to this day. Geneticists from the United States and Australia have done studies on Norfolk Island, taking samples of the Islanders' blood and collecting genealogies. Recent work has sought to identify markers of English and Polynesian ancestry in the mutineer descendants' blood, what one paper called 'the biometry of the *Bounty*'.[59] The material bodies of the mutineers' descendants remain, at least in the eyes of Australian and American biological science, invisibly but permanently marked by a historical act perpetrated by their forefathers.

Relics as souvenirs, souvenirs as relics

The transformation of perceptions of Pitcairn from moral paradise into eugenic dystopia in the first decades of the 20th century had severe effects on the livelihoods of the Islanders. As the 19th century gave way to the 20th, the Islanders found that their status and stories afforded them less and less benefaction from outsiders, not least the British Government.[60] Reports by visitors grew increasingly pessimistic and disillusioned. A colonial administrator who visited Norfolk Island in 1910 wrote, 'of course everybody coming here says "what grand people" … I called here one day passing in the steamer and I went to church. I said "what grand people". The next time I came here I found out what they were'. The Islanders, he claimed, had degenerated as a result of their heritage and only put on a moral act to appease their guests. Summarising the past half century since the 'experimental' transplantation of much of the population to Norfolk Island, he declared:

---

58   Elazar Barkan, *The Retreat of Scientific Racism*, Cambridge, Cambridge University Press, 1992, pp 143–48.
59   David A Mackey, Justin C Sherwin, Lisa S Kearns … Alex W Hewitt, 'The Norfolk Island Eye Study (NIES): Rationale, Methodology and Distribution of Ocular Biometry (Biometry of the *Bounty*)', *Twin Research and Human Genetics: The Official Journal of the International Society for Twin Studies*, vol 14, no 1, Feb 2011, pp 42–52.
60   The island's conversion to Seventh-Day Adventism also resulted in a diminution of support from their Anglican allies in Britain, though it conversely brought benefaction from co-religionists in the United States.

> I do not hesitate to say that no experiment has ever failed so dismally, and that the Norfolk Islanders of today, so far from being innocent and virtuous, are as debased, as idle, as immoral or – unmoral perhaps would be a more suitable epithet – a people as exists on the face of the earth.[61]

In response, however, another colonial office bureaucrat urged his colleagues to restrain their outrage. The Islanders on both Pitcairn and Norfolk, he argued, lived in the aftermath of history and were forced to adapt to their unique circumstances.

> We must take into consideration the fact that for a hundred years past the Community has lived on charity from passing vessels, and the Islanders have long ago learned that the romance surrounding their history, and their reputation for loyalty to the throne, as well as for simplicity and innocence and devout religious belief, have always been their assets; their stock-in-trade, in short, which leads to the good opinion of visitors and to consequent gifts ... Considering therefore, the whole history of these people, and their descent and conditions of life it is, perhaps, unjust to stigmatise as hypocrisy and deceit, the smooth face, the ingratiating manner, and the profession of religion which these poor people are, so to speak, compelled to put on in order to live.[62]

The Islanders, he said, were not the recipients of charity, the one-sided distribution of gifts from visitors to the objects of their benevolence. Rather, by adapting the roles into which outsiders cast them and building upon them, the Islanders participated in a reciprocal exchange.

If the 'romance surrounding their history' was the Islanders' 'stock-in-trade', then its value rose considerably and unexpectedly after the 1930s. Charles Nordhoff and James Hall penned a bestselling account of the mutiny and its aftermath in three novels that were read by millions and adapted into a series of films (see Largeaud-Ortega, Chapter 4; and Jolly

---

61   NA/CO 537/463. It was a moral appraisal that resonated with Pitcairn Island's infamous sexual abuse trials around the turn of the millenium. For a journalistic account of the trials, see Kathy Marks, *Lost Paradise: From Mutiny on the Bounty to a Modern-Day Legacy of Sexual Mayhem, the Dark Secrets of Pitcairn Island Revealed* (New York, Free Press, 2009). It is an unpopular book on Pitcairn. For a broader meditation on Pitcairn and Norfolk's persistence as objects of the outside world's moral imagination, see this author's dissertation, 'Mutiny's *Bounty*: Pitcairn Islanders and the Making of a Natural Laboratory at the Edge of Britain's South Seas Empire' (PhD dissertation, Princeton University, 2016).
62   NA/FO/687/15.

& Petch, Chapter 6).[63] In the years that followed, Harry Shapiro drew from his Pitcairn research to publish a popular book on the Islanders.[64] Magazines like *National Geographic* published positive, if heavily eroticised, accounts of island life.[65] This work was part of a general reestablishment of the South Pacific as a space of romanticised interest in American popular culture, a cultural shift that was concomitant with the American geopolitical ambitions in the Pacific.[66] Pitcairn Island, for the last decades derided by British administrators and intellectuals as an example of moral collapse and racial miscegenation, was exotic again. The inter-war period also saw Pitcairn Island reach its peak population of roughly 230. More materially, the opening of the Panama Canal in 1914 put Pitcairn Island roughly on the route between the West and New Zealand. Consequently, freight and passenger ships bound for Wellington and Auckland began to stop at Pitcairn in unprecedented numbers.[67]

Passenger liners and private yachts brought with them a new class of visitor: the tourist. Sailors had long left the island with *Bounty* relics and trinkets in hand, but steady visits by passenger ships created a souvenir market on a much larger scale, a trade that continues to this day. The tourists' most sought-after object was a genuine *Bounty* artefact, which even a century-and-a-half later could be found at affordable prices. Irving Johnson, an American who visited several times on a yacht, purchased a part of the *Bounty*'s rudder and several gudgeons in 1937. Eyeing the ship's antique vise, he offered the community a modern replacement and

---

63 Charles Nordhoff & James Norman Hall, *Mutiny on the Bounty*, New York, Boston & London, Back Bay Books, Little, Brown & Company, 1932; *Men against the Sea*, Boston & London, Back Bay Books, Little, Brown & Company, 1934; and *Pitcairn's Island*, New York, Boston & London, Back Bay Books, Little, Brown & Company, 1934.
64 Shapiro, 1936.
65 Irving Johnson & Electra Johnson, 'Westward Bound in the *Yankee*', *National Geographic*, vol 81, Jan 1942, pp 1–44; Irving Johnson & Electra Johnson, 'The *Yankee*'s Wander-world', *National Geographic*, vol 95, Jan 1949, pp 1–50; TC Roughley, '*Bounty* Descendants Live on Remote Norfolk Island', *National Geographic*, vol 118, Oct 1960, pp 558–84; Louis Marden, 'I Found the Bones of the *Bounty*', *National Geographic*, vol 112, Dec 1957, pp 725–89.
66 Julian Go, '"Racism" and Colonialism: Meanings of Difference and Ruling Practices in America's Pacific Empire', *Qualitative Sociology*, vol 27, no 1, Mar 2004, pp 35–58; Adria L Imada, *Aloha America: Hula Circuits Through the US Empire*, Durham, Duke University Press, 2012; Shelley Sang-Hee Lee & Rick Baldoz, '"A Fascinating Interracial Experiment Station": Remapping the Orient–Occident Divide in Hawai'i', *American Studies*, vol 49, no 3, 2008, pp 87–109; Robert W Rydell, *All the World's a Fair: Visions of Empire at American International Expositions, 1876–1916*, Chicago, University of Chicago Press, 2013.
67 For a comprehensive catalogue of every ship to visit Pitcairn, see Herbert Ford's *Pitcairn Port of Call* (Angwin, CA, Hawser Titles, 1996).

US$30.[68] After his return to the United States, he gave the items to the Mariners' Museum in Newport News, Virginia, where they remain to this day. Another gudgeon sold for US$20 and went to the Otago Museum in Dunedin, New Zealand.

The High Commission for the Western Pacific and the Colonial Office were deeply concerned about the flow of relics away from Pitcairn and into foreign or private collections and attempted to put a stop to their sale.[69] In correspondence with the prime minister's office, the high commissioner and the secretary of state for the colonies argued that 'the few existing relics of H.M.S. *Bounty* possess a unique historical interest … that the Islanders ought not to have allowed any of them to leave their custody' and 'that these relics should be preserved in the public interest'.[70] Johnson, for his part, hardly regarded the sale of *Bounty* relics as exploitative. In a letter to the Colonial Office, he defended his purchase in the context of the Islanders' long-running practices of gift exchange. His expedition, after all, had brought the Pitcairners clothes, dishes and kerosene, and he had taken them to Henderson Island to collect miro wood.[71]

Nonetheless, the affair marked the beginning of another shift in the valuation of *Bounty* artefacts. In the face of a changing market and a changing relationship with outsiders, both the British Government and the Islanders made efforts to retain what they had left. The Pitcairners set up a museum in Adamstown, where tourists today can still see *Bounty* relics alongside hundreds of ancient Polynesian stone adzes that the Islanders have collected over the years.[72] The economic incentives of the relic trade were difficult to stem, however, particularly in the face of the insatiable fascination with the *Bounty* story that the island's visitors so often effused. Even as late as 1973, a visitor to Pitcairn recorded that, as far as tourists were concerned, the museum merely served as 'a show window of historic merchandise that could be bought wholesale'.[73] Even administrators themselves could not be trusted; Norfolk Island governor Henry Evans Maude recorded that one of his predecessors had asked the inhabitants to 'hand over any material in their possession of historical

---

68 JS Neill, letter, 11 June 1937, NA/ADM 1/9687.
69 AB Acheson, letter, 15 Sep 1938, NA/ADM 1/9687.
70 Sir John Balfour, letter to Downing Street, 24 May 1938, NA/ADM 1/9687.
71 Irving Johnson, letter to Ronald Lindsay, 27 July 1938, TNA/ADM 1/9687.
72 These, too, were the subject of considerable trade with outsiders. Pitcairn Island resident Nelson Dyatt sold hundreds to the Otago Museum and other institutions across the 1930s and 1940s. See the 'Dyatt Collection' in the holdings of the Otago Museum which records holdings of 743 items from Pitcairn.
73 Ian M Ball, *Pitcairn: Children of Mutiny*, New York, Little, Brown, 1973, p 355.

value for safe keeping and presentation, but instead of depositing what he thus collected in the Mitchell or other library he took everything himself'. He dryly noted that 'the Islanders are therefore loath to show (and still more to lend) anything that still remains in their possession'.[74]

Because the supply of original *Bounty* pieces was hardly replenishable, while the tourist trade was inexhaustible, the mass production of new *Bounty* relics became all the more necessary. Pitcairn Islanders had long produced carvings, textiles and handicrafts for sale to passing ships but, during the 20th century, this expanded into a thriving home industry. The Otago Museum contains a representative set of common Pitcairn souvenirs, purchased by an archaeological expedition to the island in 1964. Locked away on a basement shelf are baskets woven from pandanus fronds and painted leaves, and miro wood carvings of sharks, turtles and the *Bounty*. Among the most striking items in the museum's collection is a model wheelbarrow that, like so many relics from Pitcairn, is inscribed by its maker. This one proclaims, in block letters, 'SOUVENIR FROM PITCARIN ISLAND MADE BY ELWYN CHRISTIAN'. The surname 'Christian' is often inscribed on carvings – tourists will pay a premium for an object made by a direct descendant of the famous mutineer. The inscription of a '*Bounty* name' fuses the material object with both the *Bounty* story and its maker's status as an authentic mutineer descendant – creating a hybridised and lucrative *Bounty* relic.

By the postwar period, the selling of Pitcairn became a well-rehearsed practice, one that continues to the present. The Islanders knew the schedule of calling ships well in advance and made radio contact with them as they approached. After a ship was sighted, the bell in the Adamstown town square was struck five times. Boxes of goods were loaded onto one or two of the island's launches before they motored through the pounding surf of Bounty Bay. At various points, there were prohibitions against women trading on the ships, but these encounters eventually became a community affair and men, women and children alike clambered out of the swaying launches and up rope ladders on the sides of visiting ships. Once on board, they set up a makeshift marketplace in no time. Douglas Thorsen described the well-ordered commotion in a 1982 account:

---

74   Henry Maude, 'Buffet's Diary', note in Pitcairn, Part I, A – Pitcairn Island, Box 1, Papers of Henry Evans Maude, Hocken Library, University of Adelaide.

> Every available table was spread with the miro-wood sharks, fish, birds, vases, walking sticks, turtles, miniature wheelbarrows, book-boxes, and basketware made from pandanus leaves. There were also hand-painted leaves, wall-pockets, fans, sun-bonnets, shell necklaces, coconut shell flower vases, and copies of the 'Guide to Pitcairn'. A selection of postcards and mounted sets of the postage stamps for which this island is famous. Each item had its set price and there was no bargaining; sales were brisk.[75]

From impromptu markets like these, souvenirs departed Pitcairn and wound their way across the globe, as they long had, but now in even greater numbers. These objects served not only as reminders of contemporary Pitcairn and its inhabitants, but of its mythologised past. Images of the *Bounty* and references to Fletcher Christian abound on objects manufactured by Islanders for Pitcairn's tourist trade.[76] In that way these items, however recently made, serve as *Bounty* relics, too.

Among the most prodigious and successful purveyors of *Bounty* relics is the Pitcairn Islands post office. Like many microstates, Pitcairn Island found that its unique heritage and well-known story were especially easily commoditised as ephemerae for stamp collectors. The island has been issuing stamps since 1940; by the 1970s, two-thirds of all government revenue were produced from stamp sales.[77] In an annual report on the island, a British administrator wrote that Pitcairn 'continues to remain solvent thanks to the philatelists of the world'.[78] Stamps were artificial *Bounty* relics par excellence. Like other *Bounty* relics, they left Pitcairn in the hands of tourists or visitors and circled the globe, capturing or stimulating the sympathetic imaginations of interested outsiders oceans away. Many were cherished by collectors who had no hope of visiting Pitcairn. It was a carefully constructed cultural diplomacy; Islanders and administrators worked hard to preserve the 'authenticity' of these postage-stamp relics and the images they evoked. Maude advised the government only to issue stamps on 'genuine' anniversaries and subjects, and to avoid 'fakes'.[79] Accordingly, most of their images work to remind the collector of the island's romanticised past. Pitcairn stamps range from images depicting the *Bounty* mutiny itself to scenes from the Hollywood films

---

75 Douglas Thorsen, 'Only on Pitcairn', unpublished manuscript, The National Library of New Zealand, MS-Papers-3926.
76 See, for example, the island's *Delectable Bounty* brand of honey.
77 D Harraway, letter to Harold Smedley, 24 Mar 1980, TNA/FCO 107/217.
78 'Pitcairn: Annual Review for 1976', TNA/FCO 32/1414.
79 Henry Evans Maude, letter to Thomson Reid Cowell, 8 April 1960, Part 1, A – Pitcairn Island, Box 1, folder Pitcairn Islands Commemorative Stamp Issues, Maude Papers.

it inspired. In my own small collection of *Bounty* relics is a set of postage stamps featuring *Bounty* relics: a set of four diamond-shaped stickers on which are illustrated the *Bounty*'s anchor, cannon, chronometer and a copper kettle. The images on the stamps are necessarily reproductions; only one of those four relics remains on the island today.[80]

Viewing relics from the beach

My collection also holds another relic that, while not a *Bounty* relic, is a distinctly Pitcairn one. It is a small polished black shard of obsidian that feels altogether too light to be entirely natural. I found it at a place called Rope, Pitcairn's only beach. Most of the island is ringed by intimidating and dangerous cliffs but, at Rope, a perilous climb will take the visitor to a secluded, rock-bound cove. There, a broad crescent of sand is littered with boulders and, on closer inspection, small pieces of washed-up detritus in every colour, most of them pounded smooth by years of waves and surf. The islands of the Pitcairn Group are covered in all manner of ocean-born litter. A 1994 expedition's survey conducted on nearby Ducie and Oeno islands found, on average, one piece of trash for every three square metres – what the study's authors tell us is 'a comparable amount of garbage to any beach in the industrialised Western world'.[81] They identified places of origin as diverse as Russia and Argentina. Most common were buoys and plastic fragments, but these ecologist-beachcombers also found plastic dolls' heads, bicycle pedals, asthma inhalers, an intact tinned meat pie and two plastic toy soldiers. I found much the same at Rope, where hermit crabs scuttle between washed-up sandals and bits of plastic pipe. Many centuries ago, the first Polynesian inhabitants of Pitcairn Island visited Rope to carve petroglyphs in its rock walls and to collect pieces of obsidian like the one I picked up from the rolling surf; today people who will never see its cliffs have marked it with an endless stream of rubbish.

Now, at the end of an essay on the material remnants of Pitcairn's post-*Bounty* encounters with the outside world, it seems an appropriate moment to make a summary accounting of the island's gifts and exchanges, of goods taken and received. Islanders and visitors alike have disseminated Pitcairn's relics around the globe. Much of the *Bounty* itself has long

---

80   www.stamps.gov.pn/BountyRelics.htm.
81   TG Benton, 'From Castaways to Throwaways: Marine Litter in the Pitcairn Islands', *Biological Journal of the Linnean Society*, vol 56, no 1–2, 1995, pp 415–22.

been broken up and sold as sentimental scrap, its instruments and stores commoditised as souvenirs or sanctified as relics. The island's residents have sold innumerable *Bounty* carvings and *Bounty* stamps. They have sent letters and pressed roses. Though now deposited in private and museum collections, these objects and their biographies reveal Pitcairn to have been, like so many Pacific Islands, part of a vast network of affect-laden exchanges. *Bounty* relics served as mediators, connecting contemporary Pitcairn to a mythologised past, and Islanders on the edge of empire to a narrative at the heart of Britain's imperial imagination. For Pitcairners, however, the trade in *Bounty* relics had its limits. The island gave up its *Bounty* relics, piece by piece. In exchange, Pitcairn has received, in turns, finished goods, tinned and frozen meats, fascinated interest, disinterested approbation, charitable benevolence, US and New Zealand dollars, and a never-ending stream of broken plastic.

Bibliography

A Hard Day's Night, Richard Lester (dir), Proscenium Films, 1964.

'A Pitcairn in London', *Launceston Examiner*, 7 July 1881, p 3.

Abott, H Porter, *The Cambridge Introduction to Narrative*, 2nd edn, Cambridge University Press, 2009.

Alexander, Caroline, *The Bounty: The True Story of the Mutiny on the Bounty*, London, Penguin Books, 2003.

Alvarez, Al (ed), *The New Poetry*, Harmondsworth, Penguin, 1962.

Anderson, Atholl, 'No Meat on that Beautiful Shore: The Prehistoric Abandonment of Subtropical Polynesian Islands', *International Journal of Osteoarchaeology*, vol 11, 2001, pp 14–23, doi.org/10.1002/oa.542

——, 'Faunal Collapse, Landscape Change and Settlement History in Remote Oceania', *World Archaeology*, vol 33, no 3, 2002, pp 375–90, doi.org/10.1080/00438240120107431

Anderson, Warwick, 'Hybridity, Race, and Science: The Voyage of the *Zaca*, 1934–1935', *Isis*, vol 103, no 2, 1 June 2012, pp 229–53, doi.org/10.1086/666354

Anell, Bengt, *Contribution to the History of Fishing in the Southern Seas*, Uppsala, Studia Ethnographica Upsaliensia, vol 9, 1955.

Appadurai, Arjun (ed), *The Social Life of Things*, Cambridge, UK, Cambridge University Press, 1986, doi.org/10.1017/CBO9780511819582

Armitage, David & Alison Bashford (eds), *Pacific Histories: Ocean, Land, People*, Basingstoke & New York, Palgrave Macmillan, 2014.

Ashcroft, Bill, Gareth Griffiths & Helen Tiffin (eds), *The Empire Writes Back: Theory and Practice in Post-Colonial Literature*, London, Routledge, 1989, doi.org/10.4324/9780203426081

Babadzan, Alain, *Mythes Tahitiens*, Paris, Gallimard, 1993.

Baert, Annie, *Le Paradis Terrestre, un mythe espagnol en Océanie, Les voyages de Mendaña et de Quirós 1567–1606*, Paris, L'Harmattan, 1999.

——, 'Alvaro de Mendaña (1542–1595), un explorateur du Pacifique sud au destin tragique', *Île en île*, June 2003 ile-en-ile.org/alvaro-de-mendana

Ball, Ian M, *Pitcairn: Children of Mutiny*, New York, Little, Brown, 1973.

Ballard, Chris, 'Oceanic Historicities', *The Contemporary Pacific*, vol 26, no 1, 2014, pp 95–154, doi.org/10.1353/cp.2014.0009

Banks, Joseph, *Banks's Journal: Daily Entries*, published by South Seas using the Web Academic Resource Publisher, 2004, southseas.nla.gov.au/journals/banks/bankindex.html

Banner, Stuart, *Possessing the Pacific: Land, Settlers, and Indigenous People from Australia to Alaska*, Cambridge, MA, Harvard University Press, 2007.

Baré, Jean-François, *Le Malentendu Pacifique. Des premières rencontres entre Polynésiens et Anglais et de ce qui s'ensuivit avec les Français jusqu'à nos jours*, Paris, Hachette, 1985.

Barkan, Elazar, *The Retreat of Scientific Racism*, Cambridge, UK, Cambridge University Press, 1992.

Barrais, Delphine, *La Dépêche*, Papeete, Tahiti, 26 October 2013, p 21.

Barrow, John, *The Eventful History of the Mutiny and Piratical Seizure of HMS Bounty, Its Causes and Consequences*, London, J Murray, 1831, pp 169–70.

——, *A Description of Pitcairn's Island and its Inhabitants*, New York, Harper & Brothers, 1854.

Barthel, Thomas S, *The Eighth Land: The Polynesian Discovery and Settlement of Easter Island*, Honolulu, University Press of Hawai'i, 1978.

Baudelaire, Charles, *The Painter of Modern Life and Other Essays*, Jonathan Mayne (trans & ed), London, Phaidon, 1964.

Beaglehole, JC (ed), *The Endeavour Journal of Sir Joseph Banks 1768–1771*, vol 2, Sydney, Angus & Robertson Ltd, 1963.

Beechey, Frederick W, *Narrative of a Voyage to the Pacific and Beering's Strait*, London, Colburn & Bentley, 1831.

Belcher, Diana, *The Mutineers of the Bounty and their Descendants in Pitcairn and Norfolk Islands*, New York, Harper Brothers, 1871.

Bellwood, Peter, *Man's Conquest of the Pacific: The Prehistory of Southeast Asia and Oceania*, Auckland, William Collins Publishers, 1978.

——, *The Polynesians: Prehistory of an Island People*, rev edn, London, Thames & Hudson, 1987.

Benjamin, Walter, 'L'œuvre d'art à l'époque de sa reproduction méchanisée', *Zeitschrift für Sozialforschung*, Jahrgang 5, 1936, pp 40–68.

Bennet, Jane, *Vibrant Matter: A Political Ecology of Things*, Durham, NC, Duke University Press Books, 2010.

Benton, TG, 'From Castaways to Throwaways: Marine Litter in the Pitcairn Islands', *Biological Journal of the Linnean Society*, vol 56, no 1–2, 1995, pp 415–22, doi.org/10.1111/j.1095-8312.1995.tb01101.x

Bernabé, Jean, *Éloge de la Créolité*, with Patrick Chamoiseau & Raphaël Confiant, bilingual edition, MB Taleb-Khyar (trans), Paris, Gallimard, 1989.

Bhabha, Homi K, *The Location of Culture*, London & New York, Routledge, 1994.

Birket, Dea, *Serpent in Paradise*, New York, Anchor Books, 1998.

Blanchard, M, 'Post-Bourgeois Tattoo: Reflections on Skin Writing in Late Capitalist Societies', in L Taylor (ed), *Visualising Theory: Selected Essays from the VAR 1990–1994*, New York & London, Routledge, 1994.

Bligh, William, *A Voyage to the South Seas, Undertaken by Command of His Majesty for the Purpose of Conveying the Breadfruit Tree to the West Indies in His Majesty's Ship the Bounty*, London, P Wogan, 1792.

——, *Mutiny on Board HMS Bounty*, London, Adlard Coles Nautical, 2014.

Bligh, William & Edward Christian, *The Bounty Mutiny*, New York, Penguin, 2001.

Boldrewood, Rolf, *A Modern Buccaneer*, London, MacMillan, 1894.

Bougainville, Louis-Antoine de, *Voyage autour du monde par la frégate du Roi, 'La Boudeuse' et la flûte 'l'Etoile'*, Paris, Gallimard, 1982.

——, *Voyage autour du Monde par la Frégate du Roi La Boudeuse et la Flûte l'Etoile (1767–68)*, Paris, La Découverte Poche, 1997 (1771).

Boyne, John, *Mutiny on the Bounty*, London, Black Swan, 2008.

Briand, Paul L, Jr, *In Search of Paradise: The Nordhoff–Hall Story*, Honolulu, Mutual Publishing Paperback Series, 1966.

Brodie, Walter, *Pitcairn's Island and the Islanders in 1850*, London, Whittaker & Co, 1851.

Brown, Bill, 'Thing Theory', *Critical Inquiry*, vol 28, no 1, 1 Oct 2001, pp 1–22, doi.org/10.1086/449030

Buchan, William, *Domestic Medicine: Or, A Treatise on the Prevention and Cure of Diseases by Simple Medicines*, London, W Strahan & T Cadell, 1774.

Buck, Peter H (Te Rangi Hiroa), *Vikings of the Pacific*, New York, FA Stokes Co, 1938.

Burrows, M, *Pitcairn's Island*, London, Society for Promoting Christian Knowledge, 1853.

Callon, Michel, 'Some Elements of a Sociology of Translation: Domestication of the Scallops and the Fishermen of St Brieuc Bay', in John Law (ed), *Power, Action and Belief: A New Sociology of Knowledge?*, London, Routledge & Kegan Paul, 1986, pp 196–223.

Camus, Albert, *The Rebel: An Essay on Man in Revolt*, Anthony Bower (trans), New York, Vintage, 1991 (1951).

Caplan, J (ed), *Written on the Body: The Tattoo in European and American History*, London, Reaktion Books, 2000.

Charleux, Michel, 'L'outillage lithique de l'île de Pâques. Considérations générales. Contribution à l'étude technologique et typologique de l'outillage pédonculé en obsidienne: les *mataʻa*', Masters thesis, Université Paris I Panthéon-Sorbonne, 1986.

Chiasson, Dan, 'Where's Brando?', *New York Review of Books*, vol 62, no 1, 8 Jan – 15 Feb 2015, pp 18–19.

Christian, Glynn, *Fragile Paradise: The Discovery of Fletcher Christian Bounty Mutineer*, Boston, Little, Brown, 1982.

Coetzee, JM, *The Lives of Animals*, London, Profile Books, 1999.

Collerson, Kenneth D & Marshall I Weisler, 'Stone Adze Compositions and the Extent of Ancient Polynesian Voyaging and Trade', *Science*, vol 317, 2007, pp 1907–11, doi.org/10.1126/science.1147013

Collins, Sara L & Marshall I Weisler, 'Human Dental and Skeletal Remains from Henderson Island, Southeast Polynesia', *People and Culture in Oceania*, vol 16, 2000, pp 67–85.

Conrad, Joseph, 'Youth', *Heart of Darkness and Other Tales*, Cedric Watts (ed), Oxford University Press, 1990.

Conte, Éric & Kenneth Dennison, *Te Tahata. Etude d'un marae de Tepoto (Nord), Archipel des Tuamotu, Polynésie française*, Puna'auia, Les Cahiers du CIRAP, vol 1, 2009.

Conte, Éric & Patrick Kirch (eds), *Archaeological Investigations in the Mangareva Islands (Gambier Archipelago), French Polynesia*. Archaeological Research Facility, no 62, Berkeley, University of California, 2004.

Conte, Éric & Guillaume Molle, 'Reinvestigating a Key-Site for Polynesian Prehistory: New Results from Hane Dune Site, Ua Huka, Marquesas', *Archaeology in Oceania*, vol 49, 2014, pp 121–36, doi.org/10.1126/science.1147013

Cook, James, *Cook's Endeavour Journal: Daily Entries*, published by South Seas using the Web Academic Resource Publisher, 2004, nla.gov.au/nla.cs-ss-jrnl-cook-about

Cook, James & James King, *A voyage to the Pacific Ocean: undertaken by command of His Majesty, for making discoveries in the Northern Hemisphere: performed under the direction of Captains Cook, Clerke, and Gore: in the years 1776, 1777, 1778, 1779, and 1780: being a copious, comprehensive, and satisfactory abridgement of the voyage*, 4 vols, London, W. & A. Strahan for G. Nicol & T. Cadell, 1784.

Coombes, Annie, *Reinventing Africa: Museums, Material Culture, and Popular Imagination*, Yale University Press, 1997.

Corney, BG, *The Quest and Occupation of Tahiti by Emissaries of Spain during the Years 1772–6*, 3 vols, London, Hakluyt Society, 1913–19.

Craciun, Adriana, 'The Franklin Relics in the Arctic Archive', *Victorian Literature and Culture*, vol 42, no 1 Mar 2014, pp 1–31, doi.org/10.1017/S1060150313000235

Crawfurd, John, 'On the Supposed Infecundity of Human Hybrids or Crosses', *Transactions of the Ethnological Society of London*, vol 3, 1 Jan 1865, pp 356–62, doi.org/10.2307/3014171

D'Arcy, Paul, *The People of the Sea: Environment, Identity, and History in Oceania*, Honolulu, University of Hawai'i Press, 2006.

Darwin, Charles, *The Descent of Man and Sexual Selection in Relation to Sex*, London, John Murray, 1871.

Daston, Lorraine, *Biographies of Scientific Objects*, Chicago, University of Chicago Press, 2000.

———, *Things That Talk: Object Lessons from Art and Science*, Cambridge, MA, Zone Books, 2007.

d'Aurevilly, Jules Barbey, *The Anatomy of Dandyism, With Some Observations on Beau Brummell*, DB Wyndham Lewis (trans), London, Peter Davies, 1928 (1845).

David, ACF, 'The Surveyors of the *Bounty*: A Preliminary Study of the Hydrographic Surveys of William Bligh, Thomas Hayward and Peter Heywood and the Charts Published from Them', Royal Navy Hydrographic Department, Ministry of Defence, Taunton, Somerset, 1982.

Davis, John, *The History of the Tahitian Mission 1799–1830*, CW Newbury (ed), Cambridge, UK, Hakluyt Society & Cambridge University Press, 1961.

Davis, Sasha, *The Empires' Edge: Militarization, Resistance, and Transcending Hegemony in the Pacific*, Athens, GA, University of Georgia Press, 2015.

Delano, Amasa, *Narrative of Voyages and Travels in the Northern and Southern Hemispheres: Comprising Three Voyages Round the World; Together with a Voyage of Survey and Discovery, in the Pacific Ocean and Oriental Islands*, Boston, EG House, 1817.

Delitte, Jean-Yves, *La Bounty. La Mutinerie des Maudits*, Grenoble, Glénat, 2014.

Dening, Greg, *Islands and Beaches: Discourse on a Silent Land, Marquesas 1774–1880*, Melbourne, Melbourne University Press, 1980.

———, *The Bounty: An Ethnographic History*, Melbourne University History Monograph no 1, History Department, University of Melbourne, 1988.

———, 'Ethnography on my Mind', in B Attwood, *Boundaries of the Past*, Melbourne, The History Institute, 1990, pp 14–21.

———, *Mr Bligh's Bad Language: Passion, Power and the Theatre on the Bounty*, Cambridge, UK, Cambridge University Press, 1992.

———, *Performances*, Melbourne, Melbourne University Press, 1996.

———, *Beach Crossings: Voyaging across Times, Cultures, and Self*, Melbourne, Melbourne University Publishing, 2004.

———, 'Writing, Rewriting the Beach: An Essay', in Alun Munslow & Robert A Rosenstone (eds), *Experiments in Rethinking History*, New York & London, Routledge, 2004, pp 30–55.

Diamond, Jared, 'Why Did the Polynesians Abandon their Mystery Islands?', *Nature*, vol 317, 1985, p 764, doi.org/10.1038/317764a0

Dodd, E, *Polynesian Seafaring*, Lymington, Hampshire, Nautical Publishing Company, 1972.

Douglas, B, '"Cureous Figures": European Voyagers and Tatau/Tattoo in Polynesia 1595–1800', in N Thomas, A Cole & B Douglas (eds), *Tattoo: Bodies, Art and Exchange in the Pacific and the West*, London, Reaktion Books, 2005, pp 33–53.

Douglas, Oliver L, *The Pacific Islands*, Honolulu, University of Hawai'i Press, 1989.

Driessen, HAH, 'Outriggerless Canoes and Glorious Beings: Pre-Contact Prophecies in the Society Islands', *Journal of Pacific History*, vol 17, no 1, 1982, pp 3–28, doi.org/10.1080/00223348208572431

Duff, Alan, *Once Were Warriors*, Auckland, Tandem Press, 1990.

Duff, Roger S, *The Moa-Hunter Period of Maori Culture*, 3rd edn, Wellington, Government Printer, 1977.

Dumont d'Urville SC, Jules, *Voyage pittoresque autour du monde*, Papeete, Haere Po No Tahiti, 1988.

Duperrey, Louis Isidore, *Voyage autour du monde : exécuté par ordre du roi, sur la corvette de Sa Majesté, la Coquille, pendant les années 1822, 1823, 1824 et 1825*, Paris, Arthus Bertrand Libraire Editeur, 1826.

Du Rietz, Rolf, *Peter Heywood's Tahitian Vocabulary and the Narrative by James Morrison: Some Notes on their Origin and History*, Banksia 3, Uppsala, Sweden, Dahlia Books, 1986.

Dye, Ira, 'Tattoos of Early American Seafarers, 1796–1818', *Proceedings of the American Philosophical Society*, vol 133, no 4, 1989, pp 520–54.

Eddowes, Mark, 'Etude archéologique de l'île de Rimatara (Archipel des Australes)', *Dossiers d'Archéologie Polynésienne*, Puna'auia, Ministère de la Culture de Polynésie française, 2004.

Edmond, Rod, *Representing the South Pacific: Colonial Discourse from Cook to Gauguin*, Cambridge, UK, Cambridge University Press, 1997, doi.org/10.1017/CBO9780511581854

Ellis, William, *Polynesian Researches, During a Residence of Nearly Eight Years in the South Seas Islands*, Newgate, Fisher, Son & Jackson, 1928.

Emory, Kenneth P, 'Stone Implements of Pitcairn Island', *Journal of the Polynesian Society*, vol 37, 1928, pp 125–35.

——, 'East Polynesian Relationships as Revealed through Adzes', in I Yawata & Y Sinoto (eds), *Prehistoric Culture in Oceania, A Symposium*, New Plymouth, NZ, Bishop Museum Press, 1968, pp 151–70.

Endersby, Jim, *Imperial Nature: Joseph Hooker and the Practices of Victorian Science*, Chicago, University of Chicago Press, 2010.

Erskine, Nicholas, 'Reclaiming the *Bounty*', *Archaeology*, vol 52, no 3, 1999a, pp 34–43.

——, 'The Pitcairn Project: A Preliminary Report of the First Integrated Archaeological Investigation of the Mutineer Settlement of Pitcairn Island', *Bulletin of the Australian Institute for Maritime Archaeology*, vol 23, 1999b, pp 3–9.

——, 'The Historical Archaeology of Settlement at Pitcairn Island, 1790–1856', PhD thesis, James Cook University, 2004.

Eyman, Scott, *John Wayne: The Life and Legend*, New York, Simon & Schuster, 2014.

Farrah, FW, 'On Hybridity', *Journal of the Anthropological Society*, 5 Apr 1864, pp 222–27.

Figueroa, Gonzalo & Eduardo Sanchez, 'Adzes from Certain Islands in Eastern Polynesia', in Thor Heyerdahl & Edwin N Ferdon (eds), *Reports of the Norwegian Archaeological Expedition to Easter Island and the East Pacific*, vol 2, *Miscellaneous Papers*, Stockholm, Monographs of the School of American Research and the Kon-Tiki Museum, no 24, part 2, 1965, pp 169–254.

Findlay, Alexander George, *A Directory for the Navigation of the South Pacific Ocean*, 5th edn, London, Richard Holmes Laurie, 1884 (1851).

Finney, Ben (ed), *Pacific Navigation and Voyaging*, Wellington, Polynesian Society Memoir, vol 39, 1976.

Firth, Stewart, 'The Nuclear Issue in the Pacific Islands', *Journal of Pacific History*, vol 21, no 4, 1986, pp 202–16, doi.org/10.1080/00223348608572543

Fischer, Steven R, 'Mangarevan Doublets: Preliminary Evidence for Proto-Southeastern Polynesian', *Oceanic Linguistics*, vol 40, no 1, 2001, pp 112–24, doi.org/10.1353/ol.2001.0005

Fiske, Nathan Welby, *Aleck: The Last of the Mutineers, or the History of Pitcairn's Island*, 3rd edn, Philadelphia, EC Biddle, 1845, pp 133–38.

Fitzpatrick, Scott M & Atholl Anderson, 'Islands of Isolation: Archaeology and the Power of Aquatic Perimeters', *Journal of Island and Coastal Archaeology*, vol 3, no 1, 2008, pp 4–16, doi.org/10.1080/15564890801983941

Ford, Herbert, *Pitcairn Port of Call*, Angwin, CA, Hawser Titles, 1996.

Forster, Johann Reinhold, *Observations Made during a Voyage Round the World*, Honolulu, University of Hawai'i, 1996 (1778).

Freshwater, Helen, 'The Allure of the Archive', *Poetics Today*, vol 24, no 4, 21 Dec 2003, pp 729–58, doi.org/10.1215/03335372-24-4-729

Gathercole, Peter, *Preliminary Report on Archaeological Fieldwork on Pitcairn Island*, University of Otago, Department of Anthropology, Jan–Mar 1964.

Gell, Alfred, *Wrapping in Images: Tattooing in Polynesia*, Oxford, Clarendon Press, 1993.

Genette, Gérard, *Figure III*, Paris, Seuil, 1972.

——, *Palimpsestes, La Littérature au Second Degré*, Paris, Seuil, 1982.

Go, Julian, '"Racism" and Colonialism: Meanings of Difference and Ruling Practices in America's Pacific Empire', *Qualitative Sociology*, vol 27, no 1, Mar 2004, pp 35–58, doi.org/10.1023/B:QUAS.0000015543.66075.b4

Goldman, Irving, 'Status Rivalry and Cultural Evolution in Polynesia', *American Anthropologist*, vol 57, no 4, 1955, pp 680–97, doi.org/10.1525/aa.1955.57.4.02a00030

Grace, Patricia, *Potiki*, Auckland and Harmondsworth, Penguin, 1986.

Green, Roger C, 'Pitcairn Island Fishhooks in Stone', *Journal of the Polynesian Society*, vol 68, no 1, 1959, pp 21–23.

——, 'Linguistic Subgrouping within Polynesia: The Implications for Prehistoric Settlement', *Journal of the Polynesian Society*, vol 75, 1966, pp 6–38, doi.org/10.1353/ol.2011.0014

——, 'Rapanui Origins Prior to European Contact: The View from Eastern Polynesia', in Patricia Vargas Casanova (ed), *Easter Island and East Polynesian Prehistory*, Santiago, Universidad de Chile, 1998, pp 87–110.

Green, Roger C & MI Weisler, 'The Mangarevan Sequence and Dating of the Geographic Expansion into Southeast Polynesia', *Asian Perspectives*, vols 41–42, 2002, pp 213–41.

Greenhill, SJ & R Clark, 'POLLEX-Online: The Polynesian Lexicon Project Online', *Oceanic Linguistics*, vol 50, no 2, 2011, pp 551–59, pollex.org.nz

Gregory, CA, *Gifts and Commodities*, London, Academic Press, 1982.

Guerout, Max, 'Les vestiges d'Amanu', *Bulletin de la Société des Etudes Océaniennes*, no 292/293, 2002, pp 12–23.

Gunson, Neil, *Messengers of Grace: Evangelical Missionaries in the South Seas 1797–1860*, Melbourne, Oxford University Press, 1978.

Haddon, A & J Hornell, *Canoes of Oceania*, Honolulu, Bishop Museum Press, 1975.

Harriot, Thomas, *A Briefe and True Report of the New Found Land of Virginia*, ReInk Books, 2018.

Hau'ofa, Epeli, 'The Ocean in Us', *The Contemporary Pacific*, vol 10, no 2, 1998, pp 391–410.

——, 'Our Sea of Islands', *We Are the Ocean: Selected Works*, Honolulu, University of Hawai'i Press, 2008, pp 27–40.

——, 'Past to Remember', *We Are the Ocean: Selected Works*, Honolulu, University of Hawai'i Press, 2008, pp 60–79.

Haun, Beverley, *Inventing 'Easter Island'*, Toronto, University of Toronto Press, 2008, doi.org/10.3138/9781442688414

Hawkesworth, John, *An Account of the Voyages Undertaken by Order of Her Present Majesty for Making Discoveries in the Southern Hemisphere and Successively Performed by Commodore Byron, Captain Wallis, Captain Carteret and Captain Cook, in the Dolphin …, Drawn up from the Journals …*, London, W Stratham, 1773.

Hay, Daisy, 'Hair in the Disraeli Papers: A Victorian Harvest', *Journal of Victorian Culture*, vol 19, no 3, 3 July 2014, pp 332–45, doi.org/10.1080/13555502.2014.947180

Hay, Douglas, Peter Linebaugh, John G Rule, EP Thompson & Cal Winslow (eds), *Albion's Fatal Tree: Crime and Society in Eighteenth-Century England*, London, Allen Lane, 1975.

Helmstadter, Richard J & Bernard Lightment (eds), *Victorian Faith in Crisis: Essays on Continuity and Change in Nineteenth-Century Religious Belief*, Stanford, Stanford University Press, 1990.

Henry, Teuira, *Ancient Tahiti*, Honolulu, BP Bishop Museum, 1928.

——, *Tahiti aux Temps Anciens*, Société des océanistes, no 1, Paris, Musée de l'Homme, 1968.

——, *Tahiti aux Temps Anciens*, Paris, Musée de l'Homme, Publication de la Société des Océanistes, no 1, 2000.

Hermann, Aymeric, 'Les industries lithiques pré-européennes de Polynésie centrale: savoir-faire et dynamiques techno-économiques', PhD thesis, University of French Polynesia, 2013.

——, 'Production et échange des lames d'herminette en pierre en Polynésie centrale', in F Valentin & G Molle (eds), *La pratique de l'espace en Océanie: Découverte, appropriation et émergence des systèmes sociaux traditionnels*, Paris, Séances de la Société Préhistorique Française, no 7, 2016, pp 205–21.

Heyerdahl, Thor, *Aku-Aku: The Secret of Easter Island*, Chicago, Rand McNally, 1958.

Heyerdahl, Thor & Arne Skjölsvold, 'Notes on the Archaeology of Pitcairn Island', in Thor Heyerdahl & Edwin N Ferdon (eds), *Reports of the Norwegian Archaeological Expedition to Easter Island and the East Pacific*, vol 2, *Miscellaneous Papers*, Stockholm, Monographs of the School of American Research and the Kon-Tiki Museum, no 24, part 2, 1965a, pp 3–7.

Heyerdahl, Thor & Arne Skjölsvold, 'Artifacts Collected on Certain Islands in Eastern Polynesia', in Thor Heyerdahl & Edwin N Ferdon (eds), *Reports of the Norwegian Archaeological Expedition to Easter Island and the East Pacific*, vol 2, *Miscellaneous Papers*, Stockholm, Monographs of the School of American Research and the Kon-Tiki Museum, no 24, part 2, 1965b, pp 155–68.

Hitchcock, Michael & Ken Teague, *Souvenirs: The Material Culture of Tourism*, Aldershot, Ashgate, 2000.

Holm, Christiane, 'Sentimental Cuts: Eighteenth-Century Mourning Jewelry with Hair', *Eighteenth-Century Studies*, vol 38, no 1, 2004, pp 139–43, doi.org/10.1353/ecs.2004.0059

Hooper, S, *Pacific Encounters: Art and Divinity in Polynesia 1760–1860*, London, British Museum Press, 2006.

Horrocks, Mark & Marshall I Weisler, 'Analysis of Plant Microfossils in Archaeological Deposits from Two Remote Archipelagos: The Marshall Islands, Eastern Micronesia, and the Pitcairn Group, Southeast Polynesia', *Pacific Science*, vol 60, no 2, 2006, pp 261–80, doi.org/10.1353/psc.2006.0004

Howe, KR, *Where the Waves Fall: A New South Sea Islands History from First Settlement to Colonial Rule*, Honolulu, University of Hawai'i Press, 1988.

Hulme, Keri, *The Bone People*, London, Hodder & Stoughton, 1984.

Hunt, Terry L & Carl P Lipo, 'Evidence for a Shorter Chronology on Rapa Nui (Easter Island)', *Journal of Island and Coastal Archaeology*, vol 3, no 1, 2008, pp 140–48, doi.org/10.1080/15564890801990797

Igler, David, *The Great Ocean: Pacific Worlds from Captain Cook to the Gold Rush*, Oxford University Press, 2013.

Imada, Adria L, *Aloha America: Hula Circuits Through the US Empire*, Durham, Duke University Press, 2012, doi.org/10.1215/9780822395164

Irwin, Geoffrey, *The Prehistoric Exploration and Colonization of the Pacific*, Cambridge University Press, 1992, doi.org/10.1017/CBO9780511518225

Jasanoff, Maya, *Edge of Empire: Lives, Culture, and Conquest*, New York, Vintage Books, 2006.

Johnson, Irving & Electra Johnson, 'Westward Bound in the *Yankee*', *National Geographic*, vol 81, Jan 1942, pp 1–44.

——, 'The *Yankee*'s Wander-world', *National Geographic*, vol 95, Jan 1949, pp 1–50.

Johnson, Sarah, 'Defining the Genre: What are the Rules for Historical Fiction?', Associated Writing Programs annual conference, New Orleans, Mar 2002.

Jolly, Roslyn (ed), 'Introduction', in *South Sea Tales*, Oxford, Oxford World's Classics, 1996.

——, *Robert Louis Stevenson in the Pacific: Travel, Empire, and the Author's Profession*, Farnham, Ashgate, 2009.

Jones, CP, '*Stigma*: Tattooing and Branding in Graeco-Roman Antiquity', *Journal of Roman Studies*, vol 77, 1987, pp 139–55, doi.org/10.2307/300578

Kahn, Jennifer G, 'Coastal Occupation at the GS-1 Site, Cook's Bay, Moʻorea, Society Islands', *Journal of Pacific Archaeology*, vol 3, no 2, 2012, pp 52–61.

Keith, Arthur, 'The Physical Characteristics of Two Pitcairn Islanders', *Man*, vol 17, Aug 1917, p 121–31, doi.org/10.2307/2788792

Kershaw, Alex, *Jack London: A Life*, London, Harper Collins, 1997.

Kirch, Patrick V, 'Polynesia's Mystery Islands', *Archaeology*, vol 3, no 41, 1988, pp 26–31.

——, 'Rethinking East Polynesian Prehistory', *Journal of Polynesian Society*, vol 95, no 1, 1986, pp 9–40.

——, *On the Road of the Winds. An Archaeological History of the Pacific Islands before European Contact*, Berkeley & Los Angeles, University of California Press, 2000.

—— (ed), *Tangatatau Rockshelter (Mangaia, Cook Islands): The Evolution of an Eastern Polynesian Socio-Ecosystem*, Los Angeles, Cotsen Institute of Archaeology Press, Monumental Archaeologica series, 2017.

Kirch, Patrick V & Éric Conte, 'Mangareva and Eastern Polynesian Prehistory', in Éric Conte & Patrick V Kirch (eds), *Archaeological Investigations in the Mangareva Islands (Gambier Archipelago), French Polynesia*, Archaeological Research Facility, no 62, Berkeley, University of California, 2004, pp 1–15, doi.org/10.1002/j.1834-4453.2010.tb00081.x

Kirch, Patrick V, Éric Conte, Warren Sharp & Cordelia Nickelsen, 'The Onemea Site (Taravai Island, Mangareva) and the Human Colonization of Southeastern Polynesia', *Archaeology in Oceania*, 45, 2010, pp 66–79.

Kirch, Patrick V, Guillaume Molle, Cordelia Nickelsen, Peter Mills, Emilie Dotte-Sarout, Jillian Swift, Allison Wolfe & Mark Horrocks, 'Human Ecodynamics in the Mangareva Islands: A Stratified Sequence from Nenegaiti Rock Shelter (Site AGA-3, Agakauitai Island)', *Archaeology in Oceania*, vol 50, no 1, 2015, pp 23–42, doi.org/10.1002/arco.5050

Kirk, Robert W, *Paradise Past: The Transformation of the South Pacific, 1520–1920*, Jefferson, North Carolina, McFarland, 2012.

Koenig, Robert, 'Les navires européens de la carte de Tupaia. Une tentative d'identification', *Bulletin de la Société des études océaniennes*, no 217, 1981, pp 985–91.

Kuwahara, M, *Tattoo: An Anthropology*, Oxford, Berg, 2005.

Labor, Earle, Robert C Leitz & Milo Shepard (eds), *The Letters of Jack London*, Stanford University Press, 1988.

Lamb, Jonathan, Vanessa Smith & Nicholas Thomas (eds), *Exploration and Exchange: A South Seas Anthology, 1680–1900*, University of Chicago Press, 2000.

Land, Isaac, *War, Nationalism, and the British Sailor, 1750–1850*, Basingstoke & New York, Palgrave Macmillan, 2009.

Langdon, Robert, *The Lost Caravel*, Sydney, Pacific Publications, 1978.

Largeaud-Ortega, Sylvie, *Ainsi Soit-Île. Littérature et anthropologie dans les Contes des Mers du Sud de RL Stevenson*, Paris, Honoré Champion, 2012.

——, 'Stevenson's *The Ebb-Tide*, or Virgil's *Aeneid* Revisited: How Literature May Make or Mar Empires', *Victorian Literature and Culture*, vol 41, 2013, pp 561–93, doi.org/10.1017/S1060150313000107

Laroche, Marie-Charlotte, 'Circonstances et vicissitudes du voyage de découverte dans le Pacifique Sud de l'exploration Roggeveen 1721–1722', *Journal de la Société des Océanistes*, vol 38, no 74–75, 1982, pp 19–23, doi.org/10.3406/jso.1982.2493

Larson, Edward J, *Evolution's Workshop: God and Science on the Galapagos Islands*, New York, Basic Books, 2002.

Latour, Bruno, *Science in Action: How to Follow Scientists and Engineers through Society*, Cambridge, MA, Harvard University Press, 1987.

Lareau, Paul J, *HMS Bounty Genealogies*, Little Canada, MN, PJ Lareau, 1994.

Lavachery, Henry, 'Contribution à l'étude de l'archéologie de l'île de Pitcairn', *Bulletin de la Société des Américanistes de Belgique*, vol 19, 1936, pp 3–42.

Laval, Honoré, *Mangareva, l'Histoire ancienne d'un peuple polynésien*, Papeʻete, Haere Pō, 2013 (1938).

Lebot, Vincent, 'La domestication des plantes en Océanie et les contraintes de la voie asexuée', *Journal de la Société des Océanistes*, 2002, pp 114–15, doi.org/10.4000/jso.1382

Lee, Shelley Sang-Hee & Rick Baldoz, '"A Fascinating Interracial Experiment Station": Remapping the Orient–Occident Divide in Hawaiʻi', *American Studies*, vol 49, no 3, 2008, pp 87–109.

Lesson, RP, *Voyage autour du monde entrepris par ordre du Gouvernement sur la Corvette. La Coquille*, Paris, Pourrat Frères, 1839, doi.org/10.5962/bhl.title.119917

Lewis, David, *We, the Navigators: The Ancient Art of Landfinding in the Pacific*, Honolulu, University of Hawaiʻi Press, 1972.

——, *We, the Navigators: The Ancient Art of Landfinding in the Pacific*, 2nd edn, Honolulu, University of Hawaiʻi Press, 1994.

London, Jack, *Tales of the Pacific*, Harmondsworth, Penguin Twentieth-Century Classics, 1989.

——, *Complete Short Stories*, Earle Labor, Robert C Leitz & Milo Shepard (eds), Stanford, Stanford University Press, 1993.

Loti, Pierre, *Le Mariage de Loti*, Paris, Flammarion, 1991 (1879).

Lovejoy, AO & G Boas, 'Islands of the Blest', in *Primitivism and Related Ideas in Antiquity*, New York, Octagon Books, 1980.

Lovett, Richard, *The History of the London Missionary Society 1795–1895*, London, Henri Froude, 1899.

Lukács, Georg, *History and Class Consciousness: Studies in Marxist Dialectics*, Rodney Livingstone (trans), Cambridge, MA, MIT Press, 1999.

Lummis, Trevor, *Pitcairn Island: Life and Death in Eden*, Brookfield, VT, Ashgate, 1997.

Lutz, Deborah, 'The Dead Still Among Us: Victorian Secular Relics, Hair Jewelry, and Death Culture', *Victorian Literature and Culture*, vol 39, no 1, Mar 2011, pp 127–42, doi.org/10.1017/S1060150310000306

MacGregor, Neil, *A History of the World in 100 Objects*, New York, Viking, 2011.

Mackey, David A, Justin C Sherwin, Lisa S Kearns … Alex W Hewitt, 'The Norfolk Island Eye Study (NIES): Rationale, Methodology and Distribution of Ocular Biometry (Biometry of the *Bounty*)', *Twin Research and Human Genetics: The Official Journal of the International Society for Twin Studies*, vol 14, no 1, Feb 2011, pp 42–52, doi.org/10.1375/twin.14.1.42

Makemson, Maud, *The Morning Star Rises, An Account of Polynesian Astronomy*, New Haven, Yale University Press, 1941.

Malinvoski, Bronislaw, *Les Argonautes du Pacifique Occidental*, Paris, Gallimard, 1922.

Marden, Louis, 'I Found the Bones of the *Bounty*', *National Geographic*, vol 112, Dec 1957, pp 725–89.

Marks, Kathy, *Lost Paradise: From Mutiny on the Bounty to a Modern-Day Legacy of Sexual Mayhem, the Dark Secrets of Pitcairn Island Revealed*, New York, Free Press, 2009.

Marx, Karl, *Capital: A Critique of Political Economy*, vol 1, London, Penguin, 1990.

Matsuda, Matt K, *Pacific Worlds: A History of Seas, Peoples and Cultures*, Cambridge, UK, Cambridge University Press, 2011.

Maude, Henry E, 'In Search of a Home: From the Mutiny to Pitcairn Island (1789–1790)', *Journal of the Polynesian Society*, vol 67, no 2, June 1958, pp 104–31.

——, *Of Islands and Men: Studies in Pacific History*, Melbourne, Oxford University Press, 1968.

——, 'Tahitian Interlude. The Migration of Pitcairn Islanders to the Motherland in 1831', *Journal of Polynesian Society*, vol 68, no 2, 1959, pp 115–40.

——, 'The History of Pitcairn Island', in ASC Ross & AW Moverley (eds), *The Pitcairnese Language*, London, André Deutch, 1964.

Mauss, Marcel, *The Gift: The Form and Reason for Exchange in Archaic Societies*, Ian Cunnison (trans), London, Cohen & West, 1966 (1924).

Maxton, Donald A, *The Mutiny on H.M.S. Bounty: A Guide to Nonfiction, Fiction, Poetry, Films, Articles and Music*, Jefferson, NC, McFarland, 2008.

Maxton, Donald A & Rolf E Du Rietz (eds), *Innocent on the Bounty: The Court-Martial and Pardon of Midshipman Peter Heywood, in Letters by Peter Heywood and Nessy Heywood*, Jefferson, NC, McFarland, 2013.

Maxwell Stuart, H & J Bradley, '"Behold the Man": Power, Observation and the Tattooed Convict', *Australian Studies*, vol 12, no 1, 1997, pp 71–97.

Mazellier, Philippe, Eric Monod, Bengt Danielsson & Marie-Thérèse Danielsson (eds), *Le Mémorial Polynésien*, vol 1, *1521–1833*, Papeete, Éditions Hibiscus, 1978.

McAlister, Andrew, Peter J Sheppard & Melinda S Allen, 'The Identification of a Marquesan Adze in the Cook Islands', *Journal of the Polynesian Society*, vol 122, no 3, 2014, pp 257–74, doi.org/10.15286/jps.122.3.257-274

Mead, Margaret, *Coming of Age in Samoa*, New York, Morrow, 1928.

Mehew, Ernest (ed), *Selected Letters of Robert Louis Stevenson*, New Haven & London, Yale University Press, 1997.

Melville, Herman, *Benito Cereno*, in *The Piazza Tales*, New York, The Library of America, 1984.

——, *Typee*, Oxford, Oxford University Press, 1996 (1846).

Mérimée, Prosper, *Tamango*, 1829, Paris, Magnard, 2001.

Métraux, Alfred, 'Ethnology of Easter Island', *Bernice P Bishop Museum Bulletin*, no 160, 1940, p 33.

Millerstrom, Sidsel, *Gravures rupestres et archéologie de l'habitat de Hatiheu à Nuku Hiva (Iles Marquises, Polynesie française)*, Puna'auia, Collection les Cahiers du Patrimoine – Archéologie, 2003.

Milton, John, *Paradise Lost, Milton: Poetical Works*, Douglas Bush (ed), 2nd edn, London, Oxford University Press, 1966 (1674).

Mizruchi, Susan L, *Brando's Smile: His Life, Thought, and Work*, New York, WW Norton, 2014.

Moerenhout, Jacques-Antoine, *Voyage aux îles du Grand Océan*, 2 vols, Paris, Adrien Maisonneuve, 1837.

Moers, Ellen, *The Dandy: Brummell to Beerbohm*, London, Secker & Warburg, 1960.

Molle, Guillaume, *Ancêtres-Dieux et Temples de corail: Approche ethnoarchéologique du complexe* marae *dans l'archipel des Tuamotu*, Tahiti, Collection Cahiers du CIRAP, vol 3, 2015.

——, 'Exploring Religious Practices on Polynesian Atolls: A Comprehensive Architectural Approach towards the *Marae* Complex in the Tuamotu Islands', *Journal of the Polynesian Society*, vol 125, no 3, 2016, pp 263–88.

Molle, Guillaume & Pascal Murail, *Recherches archéologiques et anthropologiques sur l'atoll de Temoe, archipel des Gambier. Rapport de la campagne 2010*, Punaauia, Université de la Polynésie française-CIRAP, 2012.

Molle, Guillaume, Pascal Murail & Aymeric Hermann, *Recherches archéologiques et anthropologiques sur l'atoll de Temoe, archipel des Gambier. Rapport de la campagne 2013*, Punaauia, Université de la Polynésie française-CIRAP, 2014.

Morgan, G & P Rushton, 'Visible Bodies: Power, Subordination and Identity in the Eighteenth-Century Atlantic World', *Journal of Social History*, vol 39, no 1, 2005, doi.org/10.1353/jsh.2005.0115

Morgan, Nigel & Annette Pritchard, 'On Souvenirs and Metonymy Narratives of Memory, Metaphor and Materiality', *Tourist Studies*, vol 5, no 1, 1 Apr 2005, pp 29–53, doi.org/10.1177/1468797605062714

Morris, Rosalind C (ed), *Reflections on the History of an Idea. Can the Subaltern Speak?* New York, Columbia University Press, 2010.

Morrison, James, *The Journal of James Morrison*, London, Golden Cockerel Press, 1935.

——, *Journal de James Morrison*, Papeete, Société des Etudes Océaniennes, 1981.

Mulloy, William, 'The Ceremonial Center of Vinapu', in Thor Heyerdahl & Edwin N Ferdon (eds), *Reports of the Norwegian Archaeological Expedition to Easter Island and the East Pacific*, vol 2, *Miscellaneous Papers*, Stockholm, Monographs of the School of American Research and the Kon-Tiki Museum, no 24, part 2, 1965, pp 93–180.

Murail Pascal & Éric Conte, 'Les sépultures de l'atoll de Temoe (archipel des Gambier)', *Les Dossiers d'Archéologie Polynésienne*, no 4, 2005, pp 164–72.

Murray, Rev Thomas Boyles, *The Home of the Mutineers*, Philadelphia, American Sunday-school Union, 1854.

——, *Pitcairn: The Island, the People and the Pastor*, London, Society for Promoting Christian Knowledge, 1853.

Mutiny on the Bounty, Frank Lloyd (dir), MGM, 1935.

Mutiny on the Bounty, Lewis Milestone (dir), MGM, 1962.

Nash, David, 'Reassessing the "Crisis of Faith" in the Victorian Age: Eclecticism and the Spirit of Moral Inquiry', *Journal of Victorian Culture*, vol 16, no 1, 1 Apr 2011, pp 65–82, doi.org/10.1080/13555502.2011.554676

Naugrette, Jean-Pierre, 'A la recherche de La Pérouse: Dumont d'Urville et le voyage second', in *Les Français et l'Australie. Voyages de découvertes et missions scientifiques de 1756 à nos jours*, Nanterre, Université Paris X-Nanterre, 1989, pp 79–88.

——, 'La lèpre comme métaphore. Questions de diagnostic et détection traumatique dans des nouvelles de Rudyard Kipling, Jack London et Sir Arthur Conan Doyle', in Caroline Bertonèche (ed), *Bacilles, Phobies et Contagions. Les métaphores de la pathologie*, Paris, Michel Houdiard, 2012, pp 17–40.

—— (ed & trans), Introduction to *Le Creux de la Vague*, Paris, GF-Flammarion, 1993, pp 21–33.

Newell, J, 'Exotic Possessions: Polynesians and their Eighteenth-Century Collecting', *Journal of Museum Ethnography*, vol 17, 2005, pp 77–88.

Newman, RA, 'Note on the *Bounty* chronometer addressed to Sir John Barrow', *The Nautical Magazine*, 1840.

Newman, SP, 'Reading the Bodies of Early American Seafarers', *The William and Mary Quarterly*, 3rd series, vol 55, no 1, 1998, pp 59–82.

Neyret, J, *Les Pirogues Océaniennes*, Association des amis des musées de la Marine, Paris, 1974.

Nobbs, George, 'Tuesday, January 3rd', Register and Memorandum, Norfolk Island, 1861, transcription of microfilm copy held in the Mitchell Library, State Library of NSW, FM4/7365.

Nordhoff, Charles & James Norman Hall, *Mutiny on the Bounty*, New York, Boston & London, Back Bay Books, Little, Brown & Company, 1932.

——, *Men against the Sea*, New York, Boston & London, Back Bay Books, Little, Brown & Company, 1934.

——, *Pitcairn's Island*, New York, Boston & London, Back Bay Books, Little, Brown & Company, 1934.

——, *The Bounty Trilogy*, Boston, New York & London, Little, Brown & Company, 2003 (1936).

North India Tract Society, *Piṭkairn ṭāpū ke logon ke bayān men*, Mirzapore, North India Tract Society, 1866.

Obeyesekere, Gananath, *The Apotheosis of Captain Cook. European Mythmaking in the Pacific*, Honolulu, University of Hawai'i Press, 1992.

——, *Cannibal Talk: The Man-Eating Myth and Human Sacrifice in the South Seas*, Berkeley, University of California Press, 2005.

O'Brian, Patrick, *Joseph Banks: A Life*, London, Collins Harvill, 1988 (1987).

Ohnuki-Tierny, Emiko, 'Introduction: The Historicization of Anthropology', in *Culture through Time: Anthropological Approaches*, Emiko Ohnuki-Tierny (ed), Stanford University Press, 1990, pp 1–5.

Old Sailor & G Cruikshank, *Greenwich Hospital: A Series of Naval Sketches Descriptive of the Life of a Man-of-War's Man*, London, J Robins & Co, 1826.

Oliver, Douglas L, *Ancient Tahitian Society*, Honolulu, University of Hawai'i Press, 1974.

Oliver, D (ed), *Justice, Legality and the Rule of Law: Lessons from the Pitcairn Prosecution*, Oxford University Press, 2009, doi.org/10.1093/acprof:oso/9780199568666.001.0001

One-Eyed Jacks, Marlon Brando (dir), Paramount, 1961.

Parkes, Graham, 'Japanese Aesthetics', in Edward N Zalta (ed), *The Stanford Encyclopedia of Philosophy*, 2011, plato.stanford.edu/archives/win2011/entries/japanese-aesthetics

Parkinson, Sydney, *A Journal of a Voyage to the South Seas, in His Majesty's Ship, the Endeavour*, London, 1773, southseas.nla.gov.au/journals/parkinson/001.html

Pâris, E, *Essai sur la construction navale des peuples extra-européens ou collection des navires et pirogues construits par les habitants de l'Asie, de la Malaisie, du Grand océan et de l'Amérique dessinés et mesurés pendant les voyages autour du monde de l'Astrolabe, La Favorite et l'Artémise*, Paris, Arthus Bertrand, 1841.

Pérez, Michel, 'Pitcairn. Au bout du monde, au bout des rêves', in Serge Dunis (ed), *D'Île en Île Pacifique*, Paris, Klincksieck, 1999, pp 235–77.

Petch, Simon & Roslyn Jolly, 'Brando in the Sixties', *Heat*, new series, vol 10, 2005, pp 157–72.

'Pitcairn Island', *Penny Illustrated Paper & Illustrated Times* (London), no 1034, 7 May 1881, p 300.

Poignant, Roslyn, *Professional Savages: Captive Lives and Western Spectacle*, New Haven, CT, Yale University Press, 2004.

Pratt, ML, *Imperial Eyes: Travel Writing and Transculturation*, London, Routledge, 1992.

Quanchi, Max & Ron Adams (eds), *Culture Contact in the Pacific: Essays on Contact, Encounter and Response*, Cambridge, Cambridge University Press, 1993.

Quirós, Pedro Fernandez, *Histoire de la découverte des régions Australes, Iles Salomon, Marquises, Santa Cruz, Tuamotu, Cook du Nord et Vanuatu*, Traduction et notes de Annie Berat, préface de Paul de Deckker, Paris, L'Harmattan, 2001.

Qureshi, Sadiah, *Peoples on Parade*, Chicago, University of Chicago Press, 2011, doi.org/10.7208/chicago/9780226700984.001.0001

Rappaport, Erika, 'Imperial Possessions, Cultural Histories, and the Material Turn: Response', *Victorian Studies*, vol 50, no 2, 2008, pp 289–96, doi.org/10.2979/VIC.2008.50.2.289

Rediker, M, *Between the Devil and the Deep Blue Sea. Merchant Seamen, Pirates, and the Anglo American Maritime World, 1700–1750*, Cambridge, UK, Cambridge University Press, 1987.

'Relics of the Past in London', *The Nation*, vol 60, no 1558, 9 May 1895, pp 357–58.

Rennie, Neil, *Far-Fetched Facts: The Literature of Travel and the Idea of the South Seas*, Oxford, Clarendon Press, 1995.

Rensch, KH, *The Language of the Noble Savage, the Linguistic Fieldwork of Reinhold and George Forster in Polynesia on Cook's Second Voyage to the Pacific 1772–1775*, Canberra, Archipelago Press, 2000.

Reynolds, Pauline, 'The Forgotten Women of the *Bounty* and their Material Heritage', paper presented at the Māori and Pacific Textile Symposium, 10–11th June 2011, Museum of New Zealand Te Papa Tongarewa, 2010, www.academia.edu/5830921/The_Forgotten_Women_of_the_Bounty_and_their_Material_Heritage

Robertson, George, *An Account of the Discovery of Tahiti. From the Journal of George Robertson, Master of HMS Dolphin*, London, Folio Society, 1955.

Roderick, Colin, 'Sir Joseph Banks, Queen Oberea and the Satirists', in Veit Walter (ed), *Captain James Cook: Image and Impact. South Sea Discoveries and the World of Letters*, Melbourne, Hawthorne Press, 1972, pp 67–89.

Rodriguez, M, *Les Espagnols à Tahiti (1772–1776)*, Paris, Société des Océanistes, 1995, doi.org/10.4000/books.sdo.476

Rolett, Barry V, 'Hanamiai: Prehistoric Colonization and Cultural Change in the Marquesas Islands (East Polynesia)', *Publications in Anthropology*, no 81, 1998.

——, 'Voyaging and Interaction in Ancient East Polynesia', *Asian Perspectives*, vol 41, no 2, 2002, pp 182–94, doi.org/10.1353/asi.2003.0009

Rolett, Barry V, Eric W West, John M Sinton & Radu Lovita, 'Ancient East Polynesian Voyaging Spheres: New Evidence from the Vitaria Adze Quarry (Rurutu, Austral Islands)', *Journal of Archaeological Science*, vol 53, 2015, pp 459–71, doi.org/10.1016/j.jas.2014.10.018

Ross, ASC & AW Moverley, *The Pitcairnese Language*, London, André Deutsch, 1964.

Roughley, TC, '*Bounty* Descendants Live on Remote Norfolk Island', *National Geographic*, vol 118, Oct 1960, pp 558–84.

Routledge, Katherine Pease, *The Mystery of Easter Island: The Story of an Expedition*, London, Hazell, Watson & Viney, 1919.

Ruff, Tilman A, 'The Humanitarian Impact and Implications of Nuclear Test Explosions in the Pacific Region', *International Review of the Red Cross*, vol 97, 2015, pp 775–813, doi.org/10.1017/S1816383116000163

Rutter, Owen (ed), *The Log of the Bounty: Being Lieutenant William Bligh's Log of the Proceedings of His Majesty's Armed Vessel Bounty in a Voyage to the South Seas, to Take the Breadfruit from the Society Islands to the West Indies*, London, Golden Gockerel Press, 1937.

——, *The Voyage of the Bounty's Launch as related in William Bligh's Despatch to the Admiralty and the Journal of John Fryer*, London, Golden Cockerel Press, 1934.

——, *The Court Martial of the 'Bounty' Mutineers*, Edinburgh & London, William Hodge, 1931.

Rydell, Robert W, *All the World's a Fair: Visions of Empire at American International Expositions, 1876–1916*, Chicago, University of Chicago Press, 2013.

Sahlins, Marshall, *Islands of History*, Chicago & London, University of Chicago Press, 1985.

Said, Edward, *Orientalism*, London, Penguin, 1985.

——, Afterword, *Orientalism*, New York, Vintage Books, 1994 (1978).

Salmond, Anne, *Two Worlds*, Auckland, Penguin Books/Viking Press, 1991.

——, *Aphrodite's Island: The European Discovery of Tahiti*, Berkeley & Los Angeles, University of California Press, 2009.

——, *Bligh: William Bligh in the South Seas*, Auckland, Penguin Viking, 2011.

Sartre, Jean-Paul, *Baudelaire*, Martin Turnell (trans), Norfolk, CT, New Directions, 1950.

Sattaur, Jennifer, 'Thinking Objectively: An Overview of "Thing Theory" in Victorian Studies', *Victorian Literature and Culture*, vol 40, no 1, 2012, pp 347–57, doi.org/10.1017/S1060150311000428

Saura, Bruno, *Histoire et Mémoire des Temps Coloniaux en Polynésie Française*, Pirae, Au Vent des Îles, 2015.

Schouten, Willem C, *The Relation of a Wonderfull Voiage made by Willem Cornelison Schouten of Horne. Shewing how South from the Straights of Magelan in Terra Delfuego: He Found and Discovered a Newe Passage through the Great South Seaes, and That Way Sayled Round about the World*, London, Nathanaell Newbery, 1619.

Schubel, Susan E & David W Steadman, 'More Bird Bones from Archaeological sites on Henderson Island, Pitcairn Group, South Pacific', *Atoll Research Bulletin*, vol 325, 1985, pp 1–13.

Serres, Michel, *Jouvences sur Jules Verne*, Paris, Ed de Minuit, 1974.

Seurat, Léon G, 'Sur les anciens habitants de l'île Pitcairn', *L'Anthropologie*, vol 15, 1904, pp 369–72.

Shakespeare, William, *Romeo and Juliet*, London, Penguin Popular Classics, 2017 (1594).

Shapiro, Harry L, *Descendants of the Mutineers of the Bounty*, Memoirs of the Bernice P Bishop Museum, vol 1112, Honolulu, The Bishop Museum, 1929.

——, *The Heritage of the Bounty: The Story of Pitcairn through Six Generations*, New York, Simon & Schuster, 1936.

Sharp, Andrew, *Ancient Voyagers in Polynesia*, Auckland, Paul Longman, 1963.

—— (ed), *The Journal of Jacob Roggeveen*, Oxford, Clarendon Press, 1970.

Shillibeer, John A, *A Narrative of the Briton's Voyage, to Pitcairn's Island*, London, Law & Whittaker, 1817.

Simmonds, Alecia, 'Friendly Fire: Forced Friendship and Violent Embraces in British–Tahitian First Contact', *Melbourne Historical Journal*, vol 37, 2009, pp 115–36.

Sinclair, Andrew, *Jack: A Biography of Jack London*, London, Weidenfeld & Nicolson, 1978.

——, 'Introduction to Jack London', in *Tales of the Pacific*, Harmondsworth, Penguin Twentieth-Century Classics, 1989.

Sinoto, Yosihiko, 'A Tentative Prehistoric Cultural Sequence in the Northern Marquesas Islands, French Polynesia', *Journal of the Polynesian Society*, vol 75, no 3, 1966, pp 286–303.

——, 'An Archaeologically Based Assessment of the Marquesas as a Dispersal Center in East Polynesia', in Roger C Green & Marion Kelly (eds), *Studies in Oceanic Culture History*, Pacific Anthropological Records, vol 11, 1970, pp 105–32.

——, 'Polynesian Occupations on Pitcairn and Henderson Islands, Southeast Pacific', paper, 38th Annual Meeting, *Society for American Archaeology*, May, San Francisco, 1973.

——, 'An Analysis of Polynesian Migrations Based on Archaeological Assessments', *Journal de la Société des Océanistes*, vol 76, 1983, pp 57–67.

Skinner, Henry D, 'A Classification of the Fishhooks of Murihiku, with Notes on Allied Forms from Other Parts of Polynesia', *Journal of the Polynesian Society*, vol 51, 1942, pp 208–21, 256–86.

Sloan, K, *A New World: England's First View of America*, London, British Museum Press, 2007.

Smith, Vanessa, 'Pitcairn's "Guilty Stock": The Island as Breeding Ground', in Rod Edmond & Vanessa Smith (eds), *Islands in History and Representation*, London, Routledge, 2003.

——, *Intimate Strangers: Friendship, Exchange and Pacific Encounters*, Cambridge, UK, Cambridge University Press, 2010.

Smith, Vanessa & Nicholas Thomas (eds), *Mutiny and Aftermath: James Morrison's Account of the Mutiny on the Bounty and the Island of Tahiti*, Honolulu, University of Hawai'i Press, 2013.

Smyth, WH, 'A Sketch of the Career of the later Capt. Peter Heywood, RN', *United Service Journal and Naval and Military Magazine*, vol 1, 1831a, pp 468–81.

——, 'The *Bounty* Again!', *United Service Journal and Naval Military Magazine*, vol 3, 1831b, p 305.

Sollewijn Gelpke, JHF, *On the Origin of the Name Papua*, Leiden, KITLV, 1993.

Spate, OHK, *Paradise Found and Lost*, London, Routledge, 1988.

Spivak, Gayatri Chakravorty, 'Can the Subaltern Speak?' in Patrick William & Laura Chrisman (eds), *Colonial Discourse and Post-Colonial Theory: A Reader*, Hennel Hempstead, Harvester Wheatsheaf, 1993.

Spriggs, Matthew, 'Les éclats du triangle polynésien', in Serge Dunis (ed), *D'île en île Pacifique*, Paris, Klincksieck, 1999.

Stefan, Vincent H, Sara L Collins & Marshall I Weisler, 'Henderson Island Crania and their Implication for Southeast Polynesia Prehistory', *Journal of the Polynesian Society*, vol 111, no 4, 2002, pp 371–83.

Stevenson, Robert Louis, *The Master of Ballantrae*, London, Macmillan, Tusitala Edition, vol 10, 1924a.

——, *In the South Seas*. London, Macmillan, Tusitala Edition, vol 20, 1924b.

——, 'A Gossip on Romance', in *Memories and Portraits*, London, Macmillan, Tusitala Edition, vol 29, 1924c.

——, *In der Südsee. Erzählungen und Erlebnisse, Mit Illustrationen von Wolfgang Würfel*, Berlin, Verlag Neues Leben, 1972.

——, *The Ebb-Tide: A Trio and a Quartette*, in collaboration with Lloyd Osbourne, Edinburgh University Press, 1995 (1894).

——, *A Footnote to History*, Auckland, Pasifika Press, 1996a (1893).

——, *South Sea Tales*, Roslyn Jolly (ed), Oxford World's Classics, 1996b.

——, *In the South Seas*, London, Penguin, 1998a (1896).

——, *Treasure Island*, Oxford University Press, 1998b.

——, *The Ebb-Tide*, in *South Sea Tales*, Oxford University Press, 2008.

Stokes, John FG, 'Stone Implements', in Robert T Aitken (ed), *Ethnology of Tubuai*, Honolulu, BP Bishop Museum Bulletin, vol 70, 1930, pp 139–40.

Swanson, Kristen & Dallen J Timothy, 'Souvenirs: Icons of Meaning, Commercialization and Commoditization', *Tourism Management*, vol 33, no 3, June 2012, pp 489–99, doi.org/10.1016/j.tourman.2011.10.007

Tagart, E, *A Memoir of Captain Peter Heywood, R.N., with Extracts from his Diaries and Correspondence*, London, E Wilson, 1832.

Tcherkézoff, Serge, *Tahiti – 1768. Jeunes Filles en Pleurs. La face cachée des premiers contacts et la naissance du mythe occidental*, Pirae, Au Vent des Îles, 2004.

Teehuteatuaonoa (Jenny), [Narrative I], *Sydney Gazette*, 17 July 1819.

——, [Narrative II], *United States Service Journal*, 1829, pp 589–93.

Teriierooiterai, Jean-Claude, 'Mythes, astronomie, découpage du temps et navigation traditionnelle : l'héritage océanien contenu dans les mots de la langue tahitienne', PhD thesis, Université de Polynésie française, 2013.

The Bounty, Roger Donaldson (dir), Dino de Laurentiis Company, 1984.

The Collector, vol 6, no 15, 1 June 1895, p 249.

The Converted Mutineer and His Bible Class: Or, John Adams and the Children of the Mutineers, Boston, Massachusetts Sabbath School Society, 1855.

The Caine Mutiny, Edward Dmytryk (dir), Columbia Pictures, 1954.

The Servant, Joseph Losey (dir), Elstree, 1963.

The Transformed Island: a Story of the South Seas, Philadelphia, Presbyterian Board of Publication, 1854.

The Wild One, Laslo Benedek (dir), Stanley Kramer Productions, 1953.

Thomas, Nicholas, *Islanders: The Pacific in the Age of Empire*, Boston, Yale University Press, 2010.

——, *Entangled Objects: Exchange, Material Culture, and Colonialism in the Pacific*, Cambridge, MA, Harvard University Press, 1991.

Thomas, Nicholas, A Cole & B Douglas (eds), *Tattoo: Bodies Art and Exchange in the Pacific and the West*, London, Reaktion Books, 2005.

Thompson, David, *'Have You Seen …?': A Personal Introduction to 1,000 Films*, New York, Knopf, 2008.

Torrente, Frédéric, *Buveurs de Mers Mangeurs de Terres*, Papeete, Te Pito O Te Fenua, 2012.

Van Tilburg, JoAnne, *Among Stone Giants: The Life of Katherine Routledge and Her Remarkable Expedition to Easter Island*, New York, Simon & Schuster, 2003.

Veccella, Robert, 'Le phare de la pointe Vénus à Tahiti (1767–1868); 100 ans d'histoire de la baie de Matavai', Masters thesis, Université Bretagne Sud, 2016.

Wahlroos, Sven, *Mutiny and Romance in the South Seas: A Companion to the Bounty Adventure*, Massachusetts, Salem House Publishers, 1989.

Wallace, Alfred Russell, 'The Mutineers of the *Bounty*, and their Descendants in Pitcairn and Norfolk Islands, by Lady Belcher', *The Academy*, 1 Feb 1871.

Wallin, Paul & Helene Martinsson-Wallin, 'When Migration Failed. On Christmas Island and Other "Mystery Islands" in the Pacific', in Paul Wallin (ed), *Migrations and Exchange in a Historical Perspective*, Kon-Tiki Museum, No Barriers Seminar Papers, no 3, 2000, pp 10–13.

Walter, Annie, 'Notes sur les cultivars d'arbre à pain dans le Nord de Vanuatu', *Journal de la Société des Océanistes*, vol 88, no 1, 1989, pp 3–18, doi.org/10.3406/jso.1989.2850

Walter, Richard K, 'The Southern Cook Islands in Eastern Polynesian Prehistory', PhD thesis, University of Auckland, 1990.

Walworth, Mary, 'Eastern Polynesian: The Linguistic Evidence Revisited', *Oceanic Linguistics*, vol 53, no 2, 2014, pp 256–72, doi.org/10.1353/ol.2014.0021

Watt, Ian, *Conrad in the Nineteenth Century*, London, Chatto & Windus, 1980.

Weisler, Marshall I, 'The Settlement of Marginal Polynesia: New Evidence from Henderson Island', *Journal of Field Archaeology*, vol 21, 1994, pp 83–102.

——, 'Henderson Island Prehistory. Colonization and Extinction on a Remote Polynesian Island', in TG Benton & T Spence (eds), *The Pitcairn Islands: Biogeography, Ecology and Prehistory, Biological Journal of the Linnean Society*, vol 56, nos 1–2, 1995, pp 377–404.

——, 'Taking the Mystery out of the Polynesian "Mystery Islands": A Case Study from Mangareva and the Pitcairn Group', in Janet Davidson & Geoffrey Irwin (eds), *Oceanic Culture History: Essays in Honour of R Green*, New Zealand Journal of Archaeology Special Publication, 1996, pp 615–29.

——, *Prehistoric Long-Distance Interaction in Oceania: An Interdisciplinary Approach*, New Zealand Archaeological Association Monograph 21, 1997.

——, 'Hard Evidence for Prehistoric Interaction in Polynesia', *Current Anthropology*, vol 39, 1998a, pp 531–32.

——, 'Issues in the Colonization and Settlement of Polynesian Islands', in Patricia Vargas Casanova (ed), *Easter Island and East Polynesian Prehistory*, Santiago, Universidad de Chile, 1998b, pp 76–86.

——, 'Centrality and the Collapse of Long-Distance Voyaging in East Polynesia', in Michael D Glascock (ed), *Geochemical Evidence for Long-Distance Exchange*, Westport, Bergin & Garvey, 2002, pp 257–73.

Weisler, Marshall I & Patrick V Kirch, 'Interisland and Interarchipelago Transport of Stone Tools in Prehistoric Polynesia', *Proceedings of the National Academy of Sciences*, vol 93, 1996, pp 1381–85, doi.org/10.1073/pnas.93.4.1381

Weisler, Marshall I & Jon D Woodhead, 'Basalt Pb Isotope Analysis and the Prehistoric Settlement of Polynesia', *Proceedings of the National Academy of Sciences*, vol 92, 1995, pp 1881–85, doi.org/10.1073/pnas.92.6.1881

Wendt, Albert, *The Mango's Kiss*, Honolulu, University of Hawai'i Press, 2003.

Whistler, Arthur W, *Plants of the Canoe People*, Lawai, Kaua'i, Hawai'i, National Tropical Botanical Garden, 2009.

White, J, 'Marks of Transgression: The Tattooing of Europeans in the Pacific Islands', in N Thomas, A Cole, B Douglas (eds), *Tattoo: Bodies Art and Exchange in the Pacific and the West*, London, Reaktion Books, 2005, pp 72–90.

Whyte, William H, *The Organization Man*, London, Jonathan Cape, 1957.

Wilde, Oscar, *The Importance of Being Earnest and Other Plays*, Harmondsworth, Penguin, 2000.

Williams, D, *Mutiny on the Bounty & Pandora's Box*, Lulu.com, 2015.

Williams Milcairns, S, *Native Strangers; Beachcombers, Renegades and Castaways in the South Seas*, Auckland, Penguin Books, 2006.

Wilmshurst, Janet M, Terry L Hunt, Carl P Lipo & Atholl J Anderson, 'High-Precision Radiocarbon Dating Shows Recent and Rapid Initial Human Colonization of East Polynesia', *Proceedings of the National Academy of Sciences*, vol 108, 2011, pp 1815–20, doi.org/10.1073/pnas.1015876108

Wolf, Eric, *Europe and the People without History*, Berkeley, University of California Press, 1982.

Wragg, Graham M & Marshall I Weisler, 'Extinctions and New Records of Birds from Henderson Island, Pitcairn Group, South Pacific Ocean', *Notornis*, vol 41, 2004, pp 61–70.

Young, Adrian, 'Mutiny's *Bounty*: Pitcairn Islanders and the Making of a Natural Laboratory at the Edge of Britain's South Seas Empire', PhD dissertation, Princeton University, 2016.

Young, Rosalind Amelia, *Mutiny of the Bounty and Story of Pitcairn Island, 1790–1894*, Mountain View, CA, Pacific Press, 1894.

Zimmerman, Andrew, *Anthropology and Antihumanism in Imperial Germany*, Chicago, University of Chicago Press, 2001, doi.org/10.7208/chicago/9780226983462.001.0001

www.ingramcontent.com/pod-product-compliance
Lightning Source LLC
Chambersburg PA
CBHW061246230426
43662CB00021B/2442